Britain since 1945

by P. J. Madgwick

Introduction to British Politics
Conflict and Community: Europe since 1750
    (with J. D. Chambers)
American City Politics
The Politics of Rural Wales: a study of
    Cardiganshire (with N. Griffiths and V. Walker)

by L. J. Williams

History of the South Wales Coal Industry
Britain and the World Economy 1920–1970
Are the British Bad at Manufacturing?

by D. Steeds

China, Japan and 19th Century Britain
    (with I. Nish)

Britain
since 1945

P. J. Madgwick
Head of Department of Law, Politics and Economics
Oxford Polytechnic

D. Steeds
Senior Lecturer in International Politics
University College of Wales, Aberystwyth

L. J. Williams
Senior Lecturer in Economics
University College of Wales, Aberystwyth

Hutchinson
London Melbourne Sydney Auckland Johannesburg

Hutchinson & Co. (Publishers) Ltd
An imprint of the Hutchinson Publishing Group
17–21 Conway Street, London W1P 6JD

Hutchinson Group (Australia) Pty Ltd
30–32 Cremorne Street, Richmond South, Victoria 3121
PO Box 151, Broadway, New South Wales 2007

Hutchinson Group (NZ) Ltd
32–34 View Road, PO Box 40-086, Glenfield, Auckland 10

Hutchinson Group (SA) (Pty) Ltd
PO Box 337, Bergvlei 2012, South Africa

First published 1982
Reprinted 1983

Printed in Great Britain by The Anchor Press Ltd
and bound by Wm Brendon & Son Ltd
both of Tiptree, Essex

British Library Cataloguing in Publication Data
Madgwick, P. J.
    Britain since 1945.
1. Great Britain – History – George VI, 1936–1952
2. Great Britain – History – Elizabeth II, 1952–
I. Title
941.085   DA592

ISBN 0 09 147371 3

Contents

Foreword

This book differs in significant ways from most history textbooks. The structure is not determined by chronology alone. The book does not begin in 1945 and move forward on a broad front to 1980. Instead, it takes three themes – economic policy, government and politics, and foreign policy – and traces and analyses each for the period of 1945–80. In the two chapters on economic and foreign policy the approach is mainly chronological. In the two chapters on government and politics the approach is necessarily more synoptic. These three major themes are each dealt with by a specialist in that field. However, history is about change over time, and an opening chapter sets up a chronological framework, to which the rest of the book may be related. The book may thus serve both as an account of history and as an introduction to the more specialist treatment of history by historians working respectively in the fields of economics, politics and international politics. There are places where the book challenges the reader to enter into more specialized analysis. This is deliberate and, we believe, justified: the historian cannot remain a layman in these fields. But the assistance of a teacher will sometimes – of course – be helpful.

Inevitably, a great deal is left out of a book as broad in its scope as this. The focus is on politics but the role of Prime Ministers is not overemphasized. This is we believe a useful corrective to interpretations which stress heroes and villains. The book is about policy; hence both the economy and the international scene are examined mainly from the perspective of government and government action. Social history and social policy are dealt with briefly in chapter 1: they deserve a book to themselves. A final chapter includes six selected topics which present some major aspects of the period for special study. These are written to combine an outline with some detailed illustration and analysis.

While the book differs as a history book, it also differs as a textbook. It is rather a teaching or study book, using 'documents' and exercises to encourage the student to reflect carefully on the material set before him. In this the book follows the model of P. J. Madgwick's *Introduction to British Politics* (Hutchinson, second edition 1976, reprinted 1981), which has proved acceptable to students in schools and colleges.

1 British history since 1945: an outline

1 Britain 1945–80

The period 1945–80 in British history cannot easily be divided into distinct periods of time. The year 1945 marking the transition from war to peace is clearly a good starting point. Though there were substantial continuities between wartime and peacetime, it really was important that killing and destruction ended in May in Europe and in August (1945) in the Far East. The year is also marked out in history by the election of the first Labour government with a parliamentary majority. Thereafter changes in government mark out some apparently significant divisions of time – Labour government to 1951; Conservative to 1964; then alternating in 1970, 1974 and 1979.

However, many crucial events, developments and themes in British history were not closely related to these dates: in economic affairs, the early 1960s (the shift towards planning); 1973 (the beginning of massive rises in the price of oil); 1976 (the intervention of the International Monetary Fund); in international affairs, 1956 (Suez) and 1973 (accession to the EEC). Few developments can be tied to one specific date. In governmental affairs, the long drawn-out attempt to reform British government began in the early 1960s, was pushed forward by the establishment of the Fulton Committee on the Civil Service in 1965, and petered out with the abandonment of devolution in 1979. In politics the weakening of the party system began in 1966 with the election of a Welsh Nationalist in the Carmarthen by-election, and may have ended with the return of two-party majority government in 1979. There seems to be emerging a case for regarding 1979 as one turning point.

Thus political history could broadly be organized around three periods:

1945–51 the Labour government;
1951–64 Conservative dominance;
1964–79 the weakening of parties.

Within these periods there were at least two other significant dates:

1956 Suez with its implications for British foreign policy;

1973 the beginning of the rise in oil prices, and of serious problems for the Western economies.

Dates of this kind are chosen not just for what happened but for what they symbolize. In the realms of symbolism, there is a case for picking out one other moment in Britain's history, a moment when 'post-war' ended and a time of uncertainties began – the funeral of Winston Churchill in 1965. This was an extraordinary occasion. Bernard Levin captured some of its quality in the following passage.

> Never before, not even for the funeral of President Kennedy, had so many kings, queens, presidents, prime ministers, generals, high commissioners assembled to do honour to one dead man. Never before had so many unprecedented honours been paid to one man, typified by the order from the President of the United States that the Stars and Stripes, wherever it flew throughout the world, should fly at half-mast from Churchill's death until his funeral, something never done for a foreign commoner since the founding of the Republic . . .

> It was as if, for a moment, the whole world, midway through a decade that everywhere was full of stresses of new worlds contending with old for mastery, had paused to remember the days when there was an old world, and the new one was gestating out of sight. It was the correct response for the death of a man who had taken part in a cavalry charge and lived to make, in what was almost his last speech as Prime Minister, the announcement that Britain was to manufacture hydrogen bombs . . .

> Over half the population of Britain, twenty-five million people, watched the ceremony, and the direct transmission to other countries, it was subsequently estimated, produced a total audience of something like 350,000.000, or more than ten per cent of the entire population of the world. (Levin, 1972, pp. 403–5)

The funeral of Churchill marked the death of a hero, and a farewell to greatness. The Age of Heroism had ended in 1945; the Age of Nostalgia lasted another twenty years.

2 1945–51

The end of the war

The war ended in the summer of 1945. It had lasted for six years for Western Europe (five of serious fighting, bombing, occupation and blockade); and for four years for Russia and the USA. In that time, some 40 million or more people had lost their lives, millions of others had been rendered homeless and vast areas had been destroyed. Britain, besides losing 400,000 lives, had suffered economically, and ended the war heavily in debt, her industry overstrained and distorted by war, and with obligations abroad far beyond her capacity to sustain.

The final act of war, the use of atomic bombs on two Japanese cities, was a frightening signal of the horrors of modern weapons. But the implications were little understood. Germany had suffered rather more than Japan by what came to be called 'conventional' bombing. Distrust of Russia was not widespread. After all, Russia had contributed massively to the winning of the war, and most people involved in the war, directly or indirectly, were naturally relieved to be freed from the elementary fears of battle, bombing and separation.

The destruction of lives and wealth ended in August 1945, but in other ways the conditions of war continued. The demobilization of the armed forces was necessarily slow; shortages of many kinds, including the rationing of food, clothes and fuel, continued; food rationing was not finally abandoned until 1954. In that year house building reached its post-war peak of 300,000. The condition of post-war Britain slowly improved, but the role of government in the lives of the people would never resort to the comparative disengagement of pre-war. By the end of the war 'the Government had . . . assumed and developed a measure of direct concern for the health and well-being of the population which, by contrast with the role of Government in the nineteen-thirties, was little short of remarkable' (Titmuss, 1950, p. 506). In the 1940s, life and history had three dimensions, war, pre-war and post-war. It was more than a decade before 1945 ceased to dominate political thinking.

The election of 1945

Wartime politics ended as dramatically as the war – but also with a long aftermath. In the early summer Churchill dissolved the coalition under which Britain had been governed since May 1940, and prepared for an election in July. The pressures for an election came mainly from the Labour party. The Parliament which was dissolved in 1945 had been elected ten years previously with a massive Conservative majority (429 altogether of 615 seats). Normal political opposition had been in abeyance during the war but there had been some political activity in the Labour party and associated groups, and plans for 'reconstruction', notably the Beveridge Report on Social Insurance, had been seized on as the basis of future policy. The end of the war against Germany in May 1945 was seen as the achievement of the major objective; and Churchill's status as Britain's 'war leader' seemed less necessary. Indeed, his leadership had been criticized, and it was in any case increasingly overshadowed by the massive dominance of the USA and USSR in the Allied war effort, and of the USA in the planning of the war on the Western side. For his part Churchill would have been happy to continue as Prime Minister in a coalition until the war in Japan was ended – another two years it was thought.

The result of the 1945 election shattered Churchill's hopes, and created a new pattern of politics in Britain. The confused three-party and 'national' politics of the 1920s and 30s were replaced by a new two-party system, in which a powerful Labour party was finally – forty-five years after its birth – established in power with a substantial majority. By the standards of the British system, this was a landslide election to match that of 1906. The votes and seats are indicated in Table 1.1. The Conservative party in Parliament had been almost halved; Labour rather more than doubled.

Table 1.1 General election results, 1945–79

Year Month Electorate	Total votes	% share vote	% share of electorate	No. of seats
1945 (July – 33.2m)				
Conservative	10.0	39.8	30.0	213
Labour	12.0	47.8	36.1	393
Liberal	2.2	9.0	6.8	12
Other	0.9	2.8	2.6	22
1950 (Feb. – 33.3m)				
Conservative	12.5	43.5	37.6	298
Labour	13.3	46.1	39.9	315
Liberal	2.6	9.1	7.9	9
Other	0.4	1.3	1.1	3
1951 (Oct. – 34.6m)				
Conservative	13.7	48.0	39.6	321
Labour	13.9	48.8	40.3	295
Liberal	0.7	2.5	2.1	6
Other	0.2	0.7	0.6	3
1955 (May – 34.9m)				
Conservative	13.3	49.7	38.1	344
Labour	12.4	46.4	35.6	277
Liberal	0.7	2.7	2.1	6
Other	0.3	1.2	1.0	3

| Year   Month | Total | % share | % share of | No. of |
Electorate	votes	vote	electorate	seats
1959 (Oct. – 35.4m)				
Conservative	13.8	49.4	38.8	365
Labour	12.2	43.8	34.5	258
Liberal	1.6	5.9	4.6	6
Nationalist	0.1	0.4	0.3	–
Other	0.04	0.2	0.1	1
1964 (Oct. – 35.9m)				
Conservative	12.0	43.4	33.4	304
Labour	12.2	44.1	34.0	317
Liberal	3.1	11.2	8.6	9
Nationalist	0.1	0.5	0.4	–
Other	0.2	0.8	0.7	–
1966 (March – 36.0m)				
Conservative	11.4	41.9	31.8	253
Labour	13.1	47.9	36.3	364
Liberal	2.3	8.5	6.5	12
Nationalist	0.2	0.4	0.5	–
Other	0.2	0.8	0.6	1
1970 (June – 39.3m)				
Conservative	13.1	46.4	33.4	330
Labour	12.2	43.0	31.0	287
Liberal	2.1	7.5	5.4	6
Nationalist	0.5	1.7	1.2	1
Other	0.4	1.5	1.1	6
1974 (Feb. – 39.8m)				
Conservative	11.9	37.9	29.8	297
Labour	11.6	37.1	29.2	301
Liberal	6.1	19.3	15.2	14
Nationalist	0.8	2.6	2.0	9
Other (GB)	0.2	0.8	0.6	2
Other (NI)	0.7	2.3	1.8	12

Year Month Electorate	Total votes	% share vote	% share of electorate	No. of seats
1974 (Oct. – 40.1m)				
Conservative	10.5	35.8	26.1	277
Labour	11.5	39.2	28.6	319
Liberal	5.3	18.3	13.3	13
Nationalist	1.0	3.5	2.5	14
Other (GB)	0.2	0.8	0.5	–
Other (NI)	0.7	2.4	1.8	12
1979 (May – 41.1m)				
Conservative	13.7	43.9	33.3	339
Labour	11.5	36.9	28.1	269
Liberal	4.3	13.8	10.5	11
Nationalist	0.6	2.0	1.5	4
Other (GB)	0.3	1.2	0.8	–
Other (NI)	0.7	2.2	0.7	12

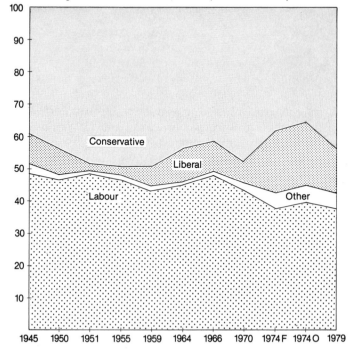

Percentage of total votes received, 1945-80 (based on table 1.1)

The plurality in popular votes, about 8 per cent, remains the highest since the war – Labour led by 6 per cent in 1966, the Conservatives by 7 per cent in 1979.

A political change of this order demands explanation; but there is very little sample survey evidence on which to base assessments of popular opinion. The following seem to be the main causes of Labour's triumph.

(i) Opinion in the war years had moved in a radical direction, seeing the 1930s as a disastrous decade (a not implausible though perhaps unfair view of unemployment and the 'appeasement' of Germany), and looking to a period of reform after the war. This shift in opinion seemed natural during the war. It was strengthened by the movements of wartime politics. In particular the Beveridge Report on Social Security, which was a massive best-seller, and was widely publicized in summary forms, appeared to answer the problems of the 1930s. Churchill avoided government commitment to its proposals, and personally intervened to stop its discussion in the armed forces. Labour, while officially observing the wartime political truce, informally adopted the Beveridge recommendations on comprehensive state insurance against misfortune, which filled out their own position. Thus Labour responded to the new radical currents of opinion. This might be presented as unfair tactics by the Labour party. But Labour was destined historically to inherit that radical shift of opinion.

(ii) Labour gained in credibility as a governing party by its participation in the coalition government. Clement Attlee served for five years as Deputy Prime Minister (a post specially created for the coalition), and had substantial responsibility for domestic policy. Four other leading Labour politicians held Cabinet posts.

(iii) The Conservative campaign emphasized Churchill's role as war leader. But the war was almost over; and Churchill regained some of his pre-war reputation as a somewhat unpredictable politician with little sympathy for the working classes.

(iv) A conscript army was inclined to vote against the officers, and for rapid demobilization.

The Labour government 1945–51

The period 1945–50 seems at first sight the clearest division of time in the whole of post-war history. A government new to power but supported by a large popular majority knew what it wanted to do and proceeded to do it. Labour had principles and a programme and applied both to the problems. This was not to happen again until the Conservative victories of 1970 and 1979.

In all three cases the interpretation is over simple. Certainly the Labour government enacted major legislation carrying into effect substantial parts of its programme.

nationalization – Bank of England, Coal Industry, Civil Aviation 1946; electricity 1947; railways, gas 1948, Iron and steel 1949.
social security – National Insurance Act 1946; establishment of the Health Service-National Health Service Act 1946; rent control acts 1946, 1949.

Family allowances had already been established by the wartime coalition, which had also reformed education in the Act of 1944. Indeed, in social legislation the general tendency of the Labour measures had been set under the coalition government. But Labour provided an impetus, direction and commitment which would have been different under the Conservatives.

Nevertheless the achievements of Attlee's government fell short of the socialist ideal. The nationalization programme was approached a little hesitantly by 'moderate' leaders like Morrison. Attlee himself held the classical socialist beliefs in public ownership and the abolition of classes, but rather as a belief in an after life – meanwhile here on earth our duty is to reform capitalism! The nationalization of steel was deferred and then lost when the government fell. The schemes of nationalization transferred ownership, but not control. The Bank of England in particular seemed to be undisturbed by what should have been a traumatic process of nationalization.

The new social security measures were based on the insurance principle (benefits related to contributions). This proved inadequate, at first for the elderly poor, later for the unemployed. The National Health Service was based on a compromise with the doctors over private practice and the independent status of doctors. A large area of domestic policy was covered by wartime regulations. These were maintained by Labour in face of immediate post war problems, shortages of industrial materials, housing and food.

In other ways, too, the Labour government of 1945 was swept along by events. This is evident in economic and foreign policy (see chapters 2 and 5). One bold stroke marked imperial policy – the 'granting' of independence to India, Pakistan, Burma and Ceylon in 1947. Given the nationalist pressures, this was not an act entirely of free will. But the Conservatives under Churchill would have resisted for longer, and Attlee could have drawn back from the civil war in India which followed British withdrawal. In the light of post-war, post-colonial history, Attlee's decisiveness looks right. For once a British government anticipated the course of history. In economics the crisis of 1947–8 stands out as the first of many post-war economic crises. Abroad the onset of 'cold war' (a new term) was marked dramatically by the Communist 'coup' in Czechoslovakia in 1948, and the

Berlin air lift, 1949. In 1950 'hot' war returned in Korea, and Britain plunged into a heavy rearmament programme (see chapters 2 and 5).

In political and social affairs five matters stand out:

(i) The heavy influence of the war on every aspect of British life. Government regulation had extended into every field of public activity and endeavour. According to A. J. P. Taylor, the system amounted to 'totalitarianism by consent.' Britain never recovered fully the 'freedoms' of the 1930s, nor wished to. Labour, never strong on the implementation of its socialist objectives, picked up a system of regulation ready-made.

(ii) Labour's socialism showed signs of slipping from the beginning. Morrison told the 1945 Labour Conference that the policy of nationalization must be argued out 'industry by industry on the merits of each case . . .' Morrison's lack of faith was justified in practice if not in theory by the practical deficiencies of Labour's commitment to nationalization. For example, there was no plan for the nationalization of coal; and the complexities of planning in a free society and an unpredictable economy were exposed in the winter crisis of 1946–7, when fuel ran out. True socialists rejected Morrison's approach, and scorned the difficulties. A delegate at the Conference of 1948 spoke for many through to the 1980s when he asserted: '. . . the large resources of production in this country ought to belong to the common people. When Churchill says, "You Labour people are doing it for doctrinaire reasons," I want him to be quite right. I want us to be doing it, from principle and doctrine . . . Ownership gives control . . .' By contrast, Morrison talked of 'sound reason' and 'the national interest'. Anthony Howard commented: 'The electoral triumph of 1945 was one of men over institutions; the victory of Parliament in the years that followed was one of institutions over men . . . the old bottles had won and the new wine had lost' (in Sissons and French, 1964, p. 33).

(iii) Aneurin Bevan's struggle with the medical profession to establish the National Health Service demonstrated the tenacity and effectiveness of a powerful profession, in defence of its interests. Some of this opposition had a slightly hysterical and partisan flavour. This was encouraged by Bevan's reputation as a socialist firebrand, and little discouraged by his actual behaviour as a negotiator ready to compromise. Faced with a serious threat by the doctors to refuse to co-operate in the health service, Bevan made concessions which were serious but not disastrous.

(iv) The Conservatives reacted constructively to the unexpected and traumatic defeat of 1945. The Research Department, led by R. A. Butler and including some future leaders (Maudling, Enoch Powell,

MacLeod), pressed the party towards an acceptance of what might be called 'the settlement of 1945' – the managed economy/welfare state as developed in the war years and taken over and extended by Labour. This conversion was set out in the Industrial Charter of 1947, which the Conference of 1947 accepted, albeit without joy. The Charter re-emphasized one part of the Conservative tradition, but a part which had not been dominant in government.

At the same time, the Conservatives modernized their organization and laid down rules which should have allowed the constituency parties to pay less attention to the wealth of their candidates.

(v) Labour fell in 1951 in a blaze of unpopularity which turned out to be a blaze largely kept alight by the Conservative press. One unfortunate phrase uttered by a government minister, 'We are the masters at the moment', was picked up, shortened to 'We are the masters now' and hurled back at the Government. (Such phrases echo down these years. Bevan called his opponents 'Vermin'. Macmillan said almost 'You have never had it so good,' and referred to a 'wind of change' in Africa. These phrases encapsulate but also distort history.)

Labour seemed in fact not to be entirely masters of their fate, and the press hammered away at their misfortune. One Conservative paper called on the King to 'send for Mr Churchill'. Some Labour ministers intrigued against Attlee. The House of Lords held up the Bill to nationalize steel, and non-co-operation by the industry prevented the implementation of the Act. The British steel industry became and remained a heavy political cross for all the governments of the whole post-war period – nationalized, denationalized, renationalized, and finally bankrupt.

For all the misfortune, Labour emerged from the 1950 election with an overall majority, and seventeen more seats than the Conservatives. Eighteen months later, apparently tired and dispirited, Attlee again and unnecessarily appealed to the electors. Labour won a slight majority of votes but a larger minority of seats. The Conservatives had returned but not to a triumph of 1945 proportions. It sufficed to give them thirteen years in power.

3 1951–64

Churchill and Eden, 1951–7

In their thirteen years in power the Conservative party had four leaders, the fastest turnover of leaders since the 1920s. Churchill was seventy-seven when he took up the office of Prime Minister for the second time, and already weakened by ill health. Two further strokes reduced him for a time to a state of incapacity which was carefully hidden from the public. Malcolm Muggeridge, editor of *Punch* at that time, claimed he received his largest 'collection of abusive communications' after publishing a cartoon suggesting that Churchill was unfit to go on as Prime Minister. This was, Muggeridge wrote, 'a proposition taken for granted in the conversation of most of his colleagues, as well as at most Conservative dinner-tables' (*New Statesman*, 6 Oct. 1964).

Churchill's second prime ministership scarcely matched the distinction of his first. His choice of rather elderly colleagues suggested he was trying to recapture the great days of his wartime cabinet. He struggled in vain to bring off a master diplomatic coup, building world peace by direct negotiation with Stalin. But Stalin fell ill and died, and world peace lay beyond the scope of simple summit diplomacy. The most striking legislative act was the establishment of commercial television. This was an early and well-documented example of influence and achievement by a pressure group in alliance with sections of a political party. The breaking of the BBC monopoly found little enthusiasm among some senior Conservatives, and Churchill himself was hardly interested.

Eden, the heir apparent for ten years or more, finally succeeded early in 1955, and shortly appealed to the electorate for confirmation in office. This the electorate did most generously – a majority of over sixty seats, and the highest proportion of the total vote in all the post-war years. A notable feature of the election was the budget which preceded it, plainly designed to win votes, and producing the first of many election year 'booms'. Only two Chancellors in the whole period (both Labour) resisted the temptation to buy votes in this way.

Eden's triumph was short-lived. By early 1956 both economic and foreign policy seemed to be faltering and the Conservative press harried the new Prime Minister. In particular, the *Daily Telegraph* called for the 'smack of firm government', a phrase which came to haunt every future Prime Minister. Eden, like his successors, was goaded into firmer action than could be sustained. The Suez intervention was in part a consequence of this personal crisis (see chapter 5). That operation collapsed in December 1956, and Eden, by then seriously ill, resigned in January 1957.

The Conservatives, both on the right and left of the party, had good reason to be troubled by these events, although only two junior ministers resigned and eight members pressed their strong disapproval of the intervention to abstention in a vote of confidence. In these circumstances Eden's departure proved not to be a disaster.

Macmillan, 1957–63

There followed the first of four sharply contested struggles in this period for the leadership of the Conservative Party. By contrast, the Labour party played out its ideological differences in bitter public contests, but settled the succession to the leadership by a vote of the parliamentary party. The Conservatives wisely adopted an election procedure in 1965 but employed it then and in 1974 to challenge and unseat the existing leadership. It would be mistaken to point much of a contrast between the two parties. In both, as serious political groups in contention for power, there was keen competition for the direction of the party; and in both simple loyalty sometimes yielded to ambition and high principle.

In 1957 R. A. Butler from the liberal wing of the party, was expected to become leader and Prime Minister. But the 'customary processes of consultation' (which went beyond the parliamentary party) picked out Macmillan. From the backbenches in the inter-war years Macmillan had propounded a radical Toryism, concerned with unemployment and poverty, and he remained a planner and reformer. As Prime Minister he spent a good deal of time on foreign and imperial policy, a choice which many Prime Ministers found seductive. But he also exercised his high political skills to restore the confidence of the party. In another premature election, in 1959, the Conservatives achieved their highest ever popular vote, 13.75m. and an overall majority of 100 seats. This was the first British election in which a significant part was played by television and opinion polls. The Conservatives, more deliberately and expensively than ever before, marketed their party through a massive advertising campaign. Labour responded in haste and desperation with some promises late in the campaign, which looked like crude bribes. Despite the crushing success of the Conservatives this was the last time in this period when a full-term government won re-election.

The 1959 election was the climax of the period of comparative prosperity known as 'affluence', and of comparative political quiet, an 'era of good feeling', associated with the label 'Butskellism' (after the Chancellor, R. A. Butler and former Chancellor, Gaitskell, the new Labour leader). 'Affluence' was both the fact and the feeling of prosperity, related to some significant improvements in the standard of living. Many of the old wartime controls, including food rationing, had been abandoned by the early 1950s, a process begun under Labour but pursued more enthusiastically and with more publicity by the Conservatives. They claimed they were 'setting the people free', thus skilfully associating the Labour party with the austerity of the post-war years, which was certainly in part unavoidable. Macmillan, as Churchill's Minister for Housing (and assisted by a junior minister with experience of the construction industry) responded to a call from the 1950 Party Conference and rapidly expanded the house-building programme. This passed the target of 300,000 houses a year set by the Conference in one year, 1954. The Conservative programme reversed Labour's emphasis on building council houses for rent, and inaugurated the property-owning boom. By the end of the 1950s the middle classes and more prosperous workers began to acquire not only houses but the 'consumer durables', cars, television sets, refrigerators, washing machines, which were the mark of comfort and 'affluence'. In the 1960s, telephones, holidays abroad and a child at university all added formerly middle-class amenities to the homes of many of the (former) common people. These were, as one historian wrote, 'the two happiest and most affluent decades yet in British history, when the rank and file of the nation really began to enter into its inheritance as a relatively wealthy, literate, liberal and property-owning democracy' (Proudfoot, 1974, p. 9).

In 1954 the Chancellor, R. A. Butler, declared that the British people might double their standard of living in the next 25 years. This was thought to be a daring forecast, but it proved to be true; though many other Western countries did much better. Butler's prediction was the call to arms of post-war politics, and signalled the new objective of government. Labour's former Chancellor, Gaitskell, did not of course dispute this objective. The Conservatives denationalized steel and road transport, but accepted the nationalization of coal and the railways (neither was capable of making a profit for private investors). The welfare state established by the Labour government was left intact. Full employment remained a common objective. Both parties could take credit that Britain in the 1950s was altogether a better country to live in than in the 1930s. In this suspension, temporary it turned out, of economic ills, the 'differences between the Parties had to be dreamt up by the politicians to keep the electorate interested. They did not, and could not, exist in the real world' (Proudfoot, 1974, p. 59). But the real world lay not far away.

The posters of 1959 had announced: 'Life is good under the Conservatives. Don't let Labour ruin it'. In fact ruin did not lie in the immediate future, and certainly not a ruin encompassed by the Labour party – but there were alarms and causes for alarm. Affluence was based on shaky economic foundations, and the economy faltered in 1956–7 and again in 1961–2 (see chapter 2). These crises disturbed the comfortable Conservative assumption that the British economy had solved the problems of the inter-war years, and had been troubled only by the immediate aftermath of war and an inexperienced and doctrinaire socialist government. The mood of the 1950s had also been based on a renewed international role. With the outbreak of the cold war and the war in Korea, Britain rediscovered her recent glory as a major partner of the Western Alliance. Western Europe would once more need defending (so the War Office thought at least). Defence expenditure rose to 12–13 per cent of national expenditure – good for employment though ultimately an intolerable burden on the exchequer. The Suez fiasco showed that the international status Britain rightly held at the end of the war was a mark of past achievement not of future potential. There were clear signs of the crumbling of empire, and no less than twelve colonies, mainly in Africa, became independent in the early 1960s. Britain was no longer a power of the first rank (now occupied by the new super powers, the USA and USSR); and even her position in the second rank was slipping.

It is impossible to say how deeply these events affected the British people. An American observer remarked shrewdly that Britain had lost an empire but not found a role – a statement which caused some dismay at the time among the political elites. The Conservative politician, Maudling, said the British had lost their pride but retained their conceit. It seems likely that older people, with experience of one or both world wars, and educated in the prevailing sentiments of patriotism and imperialism, were disturbed by the evidence of national decline. But a younger generation, reaching maturity in the 1960s, remembered little or nothing of the war, still less of the depression of the 1920s and 1930s and were probably less inclined to see national decline in this way.

The impact of this movement of generations on politics still lay in the future. For the moment – as the 1950s closed – Macmillan looked for a new direction. In economics his government took up planning with more vigour than ever before (see chapter 2). Abroad, Macmillan sought entry to the EEC, only to be rebuffed by de Gaulle in 1963; and negotiated a deal with the USA which, after one humiliating failure (the Skybolt missile), provided for a more or less independent British nuclear missile (Polaris). But the government appeared to be stumbling. In 1962 following a string of adverse by-elections and an apparent Liberal revival, Macmillan in an unprecedented move dismissed one-third of his Cabinet, thus seriously weakening his government by a device intended to strengthen it. The following year a scandal (the second in quick succession) broke. The War Minister, John Profumo, admitted after some prevarication to an adulterous relationship with a lady whose other connections linked her to the Soviet Embassy. Macmillan's honourable reluctance to pursue the erring Minister was cruelly exploited by the Labour opposition and the press, in an episode which provided some support to the British reputation for hypocrisy. The Report on the affair by Lord Justice Denning sold almost 150,000 copies, a tribute to the prurience rather than the thirst for knowledge of the British public. Perhaps clever politicians make their own luck. Macmillan's seemed to run out.

Douglas-Home, 1963–4

The last accident for Macmillan as Prime Minister occurred in the autumn of 1963. Macmillan fell ill and felt compelled to resign. This was quite unexpected, there was no obvious successor and no clear procedure for selecting one. Since the Party Conference was meeting at Blackpool, the competition to succeed took place in the full glare of publicity. There were three contenders: Lord Hailsham. who renounced his peerage under the

Act of 1963 inspired by Lord Stansgate (Tony Benn), Reginald Maudling and R. A. Butler. After due consultation Macmillan advised the Queen to send for the Foreign Secretary, Lord Home, who also renounced his peerage. Sir Alec Douglas-Home, as he became, was very little known, though he had substantial experience both of the House of Commons and of foreign affairs. It seems that Macmillan believed none of the other candidates had sufficient support, and once again he (and perhaps many Conservatives) wanted to keep out Butler. It must be conceded that the choice in these matters depends on a careful balancing of positive and negative feelings. But however hard the selection, the secret processes by which it was made were not acceptable to many Conservatives. Iain MacLeod (who with Enoch Powell refused to serve under the new Prime Minister) later published an article denouncing the 'magic circle' of power in the Conservative Party. A Conservative commentator in *The Sunday Times* thought that the Conservatives had ceased to be gentlemen.

Sir Alex's tenure of the office of Prime Minister was brief and, given the bare twelve months allowed him, undistinguished. In a bid for a modernizing theme, he backed one minister, Edward Heath, in legislation against Resale Price Maintenance (see chapter 4). But the new Labour leader, Harold Wilson, played a more plausible modernization card. In the election Labour scraped a victory by four seats and less than 1 per cent of the vote. Thus began a period of nearly fifteen years of which the Conservatives spent only four in office. But the long period of Conservative rule, 1951–64, which Labour called the Conservatives' 'thirteen wasted years' ended without a substantial vote of confidence in the Labour party.

The Labour party in the 1950s

The Bevanite split

The apparent lack of confidence in Labour was not surprising. The 1950s had been a traumatic decade for Labour. The party was from its origins a coalition of divergent interests and beliefs (see chapter 4). Under Attlee disagreements over nationalization and economic policy had been evident from the beginning, and differences over foreign policy emerged as Ernest Bevin on behalf of Britain took up a cold war stance. It was not easy to devise a consistent socialist foreign policy (Bevin did not try). A socialist might have preferred Russia to the USA, and an isolationist 'Little England' to the rewards and responsibilities of empire; and, given the streak of pacifism in the Labour tradition, the reduction of armaments to rearmament within NATO. But such simple principles did not fit the real world of international politics. The war against Germany and Japan had been a good socialist cause (at least after the German invasion of Russia in

1941); but as Stalin's Russia took over the countries of Eastern Europe, so all three elements in a socialist foreign policy looked unrealistic. Indeed, growing disillusionment with Russia changed fundamentally the outlook of British socialism in the post-war period – though without uniting the Labour party around some alternative view of socialism.

There were issues enough to disagree about, and simple loyalties were weakened by the loss of office in 1951 and by personal antipathies and rivalries centring on Aneurin Bevan. In 1951, after five years as Minister of Health and a few months as Minister of Labour and National Service, Bevan resigned, along with two junior colleagues, one of them, Harold Wilson. The occasion of these resignations was the proposal in Gaitskell's budget to make charges for spectacles and dentures supplied by the National Health Service. But Bevan and his colleagues also objected to the massive rearmament programme undertaken by the government in the face of the Korean War. Bevan argued that the programme, apart from distorting other expenditure programmes, was too large to be sustained. This view was shortly to be proved correct.

Bevan stayed on the back benches for five years and gathered around him a group of dissidents, the 'Bevanites', organized formally to influence, and often to oppose, official party policy; defying the Whips, and inciting the revival of Labour's procedures for parliamentary discipline. Disagreements spread to new issues, the rearmament of Germany, the development of nuclear weapons, and the Western obsession with defensive treaty organizations. In domestic affairs the Bevanites stood, vaguely enough, for socialism (see the extracts from Bevan's writing in chapter 4). Bevan's group captured a substantial number of seats on the Party's National Executive Committee but were opposed by the trade unions as well as the majority of the parliamentary party. Bevan himself came near to being expelled from the party. When Attlee finally, at the end of 1955, stepped down from the leadership (having stayed long enough to frustrate Morrison) Gaitskell easily defeated both Morrison and Bevan. Under the new leader Bevan accepted the post of spokesman on foreign affairs, and political, but not personal, reconciliation with Gaitskell followed. The following year at the Labour Conference in Brighton, Bevan broke with his group and denounced the policy of unilateral nuclear disarmament. In a famous phrase, quoted again in the 1980s, he faced the realities of international commitments and negotiations (and the unreality of conference resolutions). '. . . Everybody argued about the horror that the hydrogen bomb is in reality, but what this Conference ought not to do . . . is to decide upon the dismantling of the whole fabric of British international relationships without putting anything in its place, as a by-product of a resolution in which that was never stated at all . . . if you carry this resolution and follow out all its implications . . . you will send a Foreign Secretary, whoever he may be, naked into the conference chamber . . .'

One commentator described this as 'the greatest turning-point in the post-war history of the Labour Party' (Maclean in Cook and Ramsden, 1978 p. 55). It proved – if further proof were needed – that Bevan was a complex if erratic politician, a man of perceptive and powerful mind, sometimes seduced by his own rhetoric. On the major foreign policy issues of the time his judgement proved to be a sensible balance to the tendency of the USA, with the British government some way behind, to anti-communist hysteria.

Bevan's move failed to unite the party, which suffered three further blows. First in the election of 1959 the party suffered a third successive defeat, and this led to serious questioning of the party's capacity to win a majority. A widely publicized social survey – one of the first in British politics – posed the question, must Labour lose? The answer was, in effect, yes, if the party continues to appeal to a depressed working class; for it no longer exists (see p. 201). Second, taking a cue from this diagnosis, Gaitskell attempted to persuade the party to abandon Clause IV.4 in its constitution, which commits the party to nationalization 'of the means of production, distribution and exchange'. The party refused to be persuaded, and the matter was dropped. Third, the cause of unilateralist disarmament drew fresh vigour from the Campaign for Nuclear Disarmament, and massive support from the conversion of the leader of the TGWU. The union's block vote gave a majority for unilateralism in the 1960 conference, and led to Gaitskell's defiant 'fight and fight again' speech (see chapter 4).

Finally, as the Conservative government faltered, the Liberal party staged a remarkable revival. A string of good performances in by-elections in the early 1960s culminated in a massive turn-around of votes and the capture of Orpington, a normally safe London suburban constituency. 'Orpington Man' was born. The impetus ran down before the election of 1964, but the Liberals then took over 3 million votes. A characteristic pattern of subsequent politics showed up for the first time. The Labour party was no longer the natural alternative to an unpopular Conservative government. The diagnosis of 1959 together with persistent internal divisions, pointed to a bleak future for the Labour party.

The emergence of Harold Wilson, 1961–4

In this perspective, the achievement of Harold Wilson as party leader was impressive: the bleak future was to include eleven years in office; but, significantly, Labour had a working majority in only four of these years. Wilson succeeded in restoring a semblance of unity to the party. Bevan had died in 1960, Gaitskell in 1963. The leadership contest, in which Wilson defeated Brown and Callaghan, was competitive but not personally bitter. Wilson was a pragmatist in his own estimation, preferring practical and consensual solutions for existing problems to faith and ideology. He regarded the Clause IV dispute as a theological distraction, and gave little ideological emphasis to foreign policy. In the campaign Sir Alec hammered away at the British independent nuclear deterrent, an issue which he understood better than economics, but the voters were as usual much more interested in 'bread-and-butter' matters. Wilson presented a programme based on technology, economic growth and modernization; with some more specific appeals, tax reforms, the repeal of the Rent Act (1957), a new concern for the regions and Wales. The theme was vague in detail; it was a stance more than a programme. There was, too, much in the last years of the Conservative government to match Wilson's promises – a new approach to planning, and reports on education for example. The voters were not wholly convinced that the Labour party of the 1950s had been reborn. The Labour vote in 1964, which returned them to office, was almost the same, absolutely and proportionately as the vote in 1959 which seemed to condemn them to a permanent minority.

4   1964–70: The Labour governments

Harold Wilson was pre-eminent in the politics of these years. His 'presidential style' reflected his personal dominance among his colleagues; but it did not fit the constitutional basis of British government. The personal focus of his government enlarged his responsibility before the public, without providing him with the political power to match his responsibilities. In that way he suffered like all American Presidents from a power-gap. Hence it was not surprising that his reputation fell steeply from its high point in 1964 when he led the Labour party back to power.

His first days in office were marked by two developments characteristic of government in the 1960s and 70s. The number of ministers (the total of paid governmental posts), which was sixty in 1900, and about eighty in the 1950s, jumped to over a hundred. Thereafter the 'pay-roll' vote made up about one third of the government side of the House of Commons, and diminished the chances of parliamentary rebellion. Second, Wilson introduced a new fashion for the making (and unmaking) of ministries. In 1964 four new ministries were created – for Economic Affairs, Technology, Overseas Development and Wales. Later the Ministry of Labour was renamed the Department of Employment and Productivity. Of these only the Welsh Office survived beyond 1970.

The course of the Labour government fell into three periods. The first was concerned not with mere survival, but with the demonstration that Labour could govern effectively. The period ended with the general election of 1966 fought under the slogan, 'You know Labour government works'. Labour's majority shot up to one hundred seats, and their vote passed 13 million. This was a great personal triumph for Wilson, won over Edward Heath, his new opponent in the gladiatorial political contest he loved. Heath had replaced Sir Alex Douglas Home as leader of the Conservative party, following the first open elections for the leadership in 1965.

The second period was taken up with economic problems, in particular the fight against devaluation, which was finally lost at the end of 1967 (see chapter 2). In the last three years of the government, problems crowded in; persistent economic difficulties (see chapter 2); the attempt to regulate the power of the trade unions (see chapter 6); Rhodesia, which had declared unilateral independence in 1965; and Northern Ireland, which broke into civil war in 1969 (see chapter 6).

The unpopularity of the government, as indicated by the opinion polls in 1968–9, reached record depths, and Labour's vote in 1970 dropped to the levels of 1959–64.

The first of these periods was comparatively a time of hope. The last two periods were a time of crisis and despair. Crisis is a journalist's word and its meaning is imprecise. For the 1960s it conveyed emphatically enough a time of acute economic difficulties; something had to be done, but no one knew what. A certain frenzy replaced calm thought and deliberate action. The frenzy was encouraged by the media, which took up politics as another spectator sport. Altogether there was much talk of crisis. This led to an exaggeration of the balance of payments problem and generally encouraged a *sauve-qui-peut* attitude, particularly among workers concerned for their wages. At the same time, there was an excessive faith in institutions and expertise. This was the great age of the economists, but alas, the British economy seemed to decline in inverse proportion to the number of economic advisers employed in the government service.

A government locked into mortal combat with economic demons was further stressed and distracted by foreign problems – Vietnam, the British role east of Suez, accession to the EEC, Rhodesia (see chapter 5). The imminence of civil war in Northern Ireland really did present a crisis, and one which Wilson had to deal with amid at least two other emergencies.

Many events of the period 1966–70 set the agenda for at least the next fifteen years of domestic politics: two damaging dock strikes; the resignation of Frank Cousins, a senior trade union leader brought into government by Harold Wilson, over the issue of incomes policy; economic discipline enforced by the International Monetary Fund (mainly the reduction of government spending); abortive attempts to reform the trade unions and the House of Lords; an unsolved housing problem and a developing race problem; and the beginnings of nationalist discontent in Scotland and Wales.

A new political volatility reflected the scope and acuteness of these problems – though it was not fully explained by them. In Scotland and

Wales the Nationalist parties, for long negligible as electoral or political forces, began to make impressive gains in by-elections – beginning with Gwynfor Evans's victory at Carmarthen in July 1966, and Mrs Winifred Ewing's at Hamilton in November 1967, and in local elections. From the mid-1960s onwards by-elections tended to show large swings against the government. (Between 1945 and 1964 only 8 per cent of by-elections brought about a change in the seat; from 1964 to 1979 the proportion rose to 30 per cent). The standing of the parties in the opinion polls showed long periods of antipathy to the government, with some recovery at elections (recovery which proved inadequate for re-election except significantly for the minority or near-minority governments of 1964 and 1974).

Thus much of the movement of opinion evident in this volatility was hostile to government. This was evident in other ways. In both parties in parliament, but notably in the Labour party, discipline broke down, and 'backbench rebellion' became a frequent hazard for the government's parliamentary managers. Among the public, respect for politicians in general, and for the government in particular, diminished. New satirical television programmes in the 1960s prospered mainly on the denigration of politicians (some relief came in the 1970s when television comedy turned to the derision of other television programmes). Senior politicians wrote memoirs in a new style. In place of the bland and tedious literary monuments of an earlier generation, ministers (with the exception of Wilson, who was a traditionalist in these matters) wrote memoirs candidly revealing the inadequacies of their former colleagues. The wave of radicalism which swept the Western World in 1968 was a sharper youthful version of a more general loss of confidence in governments. Affluence, it seemed, led to higher expectations, which could not be fulfilled. Discontent was the companion of affluence.

As it wrestled with these problems the Labour government moved to the right, abandoning any residual socialist intentions and even, its critics said, the interests of the working class. The Conservative party, looking for a distinctive stance, and enjoying the ideological freedom of opposition, also moved to the right. At a conference in January 1970 at Selsdon, near Croydon, Heath and his senior colleagues laid out a programme intended to recover Conservative 'freedom' from the embrace of the socialist state. The new policies were in line with the Conservative tradition: the reduction of taxation; restraint of the trade unions; abandonment of prices and incomes policies; expansion of the police force; a positive role for Britain abroad. In education a noted liberal, Edward Boyle, was replaced by Margaret Thatcher, who thus attained her first front bench appointment. A decade later, as Prime Minister, she was to pursue a Selsdon programme, based on a more substantial commitment to monetarist economics and a more consistent personal determination.

Despite the apparent failures of the Labour government and the hostility of mid-term public opinion, Labour ran the Conservatives very close in the election in June 1970, taking over 12 million votes and 40 per cent of the poll for the last time in this period. It looks as if a substantial number of voters were uncertain of their voting intention; hence the comparative inaccuracy of the opinion polls, and the apparent significance of incidents during the campaign.

The events of 1970 were indeed a warning not only to pollsters but also to commentators on British politics. In the British system, government changes hands in response to quite small shifts in voting. In every election between 1950 and 1970, between 12 million and 13.7 million people voted Conservative; and between 12.2 million and 13.9 million voted Labour. Hence interpretations which imply massive shifts of opinion are misleading. In 1970 it was predicted reasonably enough, that the Liberals and the Nationalists would do well. This was not so. In August 1970 an editorial in *The Times* announced the end of the era of the welfare state and the start of an historical period characterized by the new anti-statist conservatism. That was not so. Then, during the 1970s the Liberals and Nationalists did very well indeed. But the two-party system survived the decade. In 1979 a new Conservative era began. . . .

The truth is, not that British politics is unpredictable, but that change is unlikely or slow, and still difficult to predict. There is no great interest in predicting that things will be much the same, but historians are wise to believe that this is likely to be the case.

5 1970–4: the prime ministership of Edward Heath

The Conservatives came to power with a precise and radical programme: the Selsdon programme, broadly a commitment to less government of better quality. But the government was soon embroiled in all of the problems of the 1960s, plus a few new ones. The consequences were severe: the modification or reversal of the new policies (known derisively as 'the U-turn'); the fall of the government (1974); and the subsequent ousting of Heath from the party leadership (1975). The course of events was quite as dramatic as this summary suggests. It was ironic that a government so determined to change the direction of British politics should have failed so radically.

In some respects Heath's government suffered from trying too hard. In economic policy the attempt to break out of the stop-go pattern of the 1960s led to a more dramatic repetition of the pattern (see chapter 2). In industrial relations, new legislation failed. In the light of Wilson's experience, that was perhaps predictable, though accident certainly played a part. But the more conciliatory approach towards the unions which Heath adopted also failed. Prolonged talks with the CBI and TUC in 1972 were broken by the TUC's insistence that wage restraint must be voluntary. An informal agreement with the miners' leader in 1974 seems to have collapsed because of misunderstanding (for relations with the trade unions see chapter 6).

The Heath government not only tried hard, it oversold its policies. This was certainly true of the reform of government which was intended as a central element in Heath's new style (see chapter 3). Few of the governmental reforms made much difference and some were by the end of the decade either rescinded (departmental changes), allowed to lapse (Programme Analysis and Review – PAR), or threatened with further change (local government and the health service). The much heralded joining of the EEC also brought few evident benefits, and some major disadvantages. This, too, was open to reversal by 1980. The commitment to begin the process of denationalization yielded only two comparative minnows, Thomas Cook and the Carlisle public houses.

It would be fair to add, however, that luck ran against Heath. The oil crisis was not alone responsible for economic difficulties, but it made them worse. The problems of Northern Ireland and Rhodesia constantly harassed the government. The policy of not supporting obsolescent and inefficient industry was first dramatized by a minister's unfortunate phrase about 'lame ducks' and then tested – to destruction – by the collapse of Rolls-Royce.

Finally, it must be said that the times were against successful government, as Heath's predecessor and successors discovered. The 'politics of confrontation' (intransigence, spoiling for a fight) with which Heath was associated reflected, rather more than his own alleged obstinacy, the new aggressive self-interest of occupational groups. Heath's government had to contend with the first national miners' strike for half a century, the first ever strike of civil servants, a series of public sector strikes, dustmen, power workers, postmen, which proved, except perhaps in the case of the postmen, that groups of workers were both able and willing to 'hold the country to ransom', as the cliché and over-dramatic phrase had it. To add to the government's anxieties, support for Nationalist and Liberal parties grew, and the prospect of political and constitutional disintegration darkened an already gloomy outlook.

The fall of the Conservative government in February 1974 was a direct though avoidable reaction to the miners' strike (see chapters 2 and 6). In a sense, therefore, the miners brought down the government; in another way, the government committed, so to say, involuntary suicide. Heath had spoken of a 'quiet revolution' in British government. His fall was, in its way, an unquiet revolution, one of the most disturbing episodes in post-war British history.

6 1974–9: the Labour governments of Wilson and Callaghan

The year 1974 continued to be a cataclysmic year in British politics. Once again it seemed that an age was coming to an end; but if politics were never to be quite the same again, some people could not tell the difference.

In the election of February 1974, the vote of both the major parties fell below 12 million; this had not happened to the Conservatives since 1966, and to Labour since 1945. By contrast the votes of the minor parties shot up: the Liberals to 6 million (their previous best result since 1945 was 3 million in 1964); the two Nationalist parties to 800,000. The Liberals took only fourteen seats with a vote equal to over half of the vote for the major parties. But the Nationalists did better, especially in Scotland. This pattern was repeated with minor variations in October 1974., The Liberal vote fell back slightly but SNP took eleven seats. Moreover, from 1974 the Ulster seats, formerly safely Unionist, hence Conservative, had now to be regarded as independent.

In the February Parliament, Labour had a majority of four over the Conservatives but were in a minority over all. Heath spent a weekend talking over a deal with the Liberals; but the arithmetic, the circumstances, and the Liberals' inclinations were against an arrangement. Wilson became Prime Minister, but once more in a fragile parliamentary situation. As in 1964–6, Wilson exploited the publicity advantages of being the government in office. When he appealed to the country in October, he won a clear victory (forty-two seats) over the Conservatives, but the minor parties held thirty-nine seats. By 1977, after by-election losses, Labour was once more a minority government.

Meanwhile, the Conservatives, demoralized by two electoral defeats, turned on their leader. The election procedure which elevated Heath in 1975, was now used against him. In a close and inevitably bitter campaign, he was replaced by Margaret Thatcher. The result was something of a surprise. Mrs Thatcher, who had served as Secretary of State for Education 1970–4, was comparatively little known. Her success was due to her own determination, and skilled organization, but also to the reluctance of some senior Conservatives to oppose Heath. Mrs Thatcher in effect led a backbench rebellion against an established but unpopular leader. She was not from the heart of the Conservative party, either socially or ideologically or in terms of experience and seniority – or of course as a woman. Mrs Thatcher was more of a political outsider than any of her predecessors since Bonar Law, or perhaps Disraeli.

Ructions in the Conservative party were not untypical of the times. The party system seemed to be going through a process of 'dealignment' (the weakening of party loyalties) which accompanied the general loss of confidence in government in the Western countries. The Kilbrandon Report, especially the Minority Report (1973), had diagnosed other related ills, 'powerlessness', a sense of remoteness from government, alienation. The referendums of 1979 (rejecting devolution to Scotland and Wales) and the election (which reduced Nationalist Members of Parliament from fourteen to four) checked and reversed the tendency, and raised doubts about its fundamental strength. The turnout in 1979 at 76 per cent was about the same as in 1966 and 1955; interest in the election and concern about the outcome were high. Moreover, though the major parties seemed in some respects to move apart, government continued, a little unsteadily it is true, to come from the centre. The period from 1974 until 1979 was perhaps, after all, an aberration, an uncharacteristic interlude. But no one could be sure that things would ever be quite the same again (see chapter 4).

Harold Wilson resigned as Prime Minister in March 1976. In the ensuing election for the leadership of the Labour party, James Callaghan defeated Michael Foot, the candidate of the left; but Callaghan immediately appointed him as Deputy Prime Minister. Callaghan's own position was near the centre of the party. As Chancellor of the Exchequer 1964–7 he had followed orthodoxy in resisting devaluation. His form of socialism was more labourism, a general concern for the interests of working people. Unlike most of his colleagues, he was not a university graduate, and his sympathies lay with the trade unions from whose ranks he had come.

The change of Prime Minister had little effect on the course of the government. The last substantial achievement of Harold Wilson was the referendum of June 1975 on the EEC. Continued British membership was confirmed by a popular majority of two to one. Thus, a major shift in policy which cut across British politics, and threatened to split the Labour party, had been accomplished, legitimized and, it was assumed, finally settled. But the promised benefits of the EEC seemed to wither, and by the end of the decade, the settlement seemed less sure. In the wake of the 1974 election, the unions were given their freedom. Inflation, beginning at 5 per cent rose to an annual rate of 26 per cent in the middle of 1975. British Leyland, the only large British-owned car manufacturer and the basis of a substantial part of the Midlands engineering industry, was hastily nationalized, to forestall bankruptcy. By the middle of 1976 the pound had fallen so low, and public expenditure risen so high, that the IMF had to be called in to support the economy (see chapter 2). The terms set by the IMF were thought to be tough – reduction in expenditure of £4 billion was required – and provoked a minor Cabinet crisis. Opponents of the IMF terms, led by Anthony Crosland, finally gave way, unconvinced but believing that continued argument would further weaken the pound.

This was hardly a turning point. The IMF compelled the Labour government along paths it had followed before. It was not a U-turn, because the government's previous signposted direction was less clear than Heath's. Nevertheless, the pattern stirred the memory. Sceptical observers might conclude that British governments spent the first two years in office trying in their different ways to sweep back the advancing tide with a broom.

Callaghan's government was buffeted by the IMF, the trade unions, Scotland and Wales, and Parliament. By the Lib–Lab Pact of mid-1977 he improved without fully securing his parliamentary position. The Liberals, under their new leader, David Steel, agreed to support the government on a confidence vote in return for consultation, and legislation for devolution and for European elections, with a free vote on proportional representation. The pact lasted for almost two years and gave Britain the nearest thing to a peacetime coalition government since 1931.

This was an interesting development since it was known that a substantial proportion of the electorate were usually ready to express approval of a coalition or a new centre party. But the classic argument still held; majority party government had advantages in clarity and responsibility, and was democratic in so far as the party represented popular opinion. The coalitionists claimed that this last condition was no longer true, and that a realignment of parties was necessary to the health of British democracy. But the pact was a long way from any fusion of parties and proved to be no more than a temporary holding device, helping Callaghan's government to survive for three years without a firm majority. Steel claimed that the pact had restrained Labour, and ensured a moderate government. But strictly that was the consequence of the minority Parliament. The Liberal party itself gained a taste of power, and wielded a modest influence. The weaker party in arrangements of this kind inevitably gets the worst of the bargain, securing little of substance, gaining no new friends, and losing old ones. In the event the Liberals seem to have suffered from the unpopularity of the Labour government, and alienated some of their more conservative voters. In the 1979 election the Liberal vote fell by about one fifth. However that was a normal fluctuation for the Liberals, where voters were mostly temporary fugitives from a major party. The causes of coalition, realignment and, the reform on which these must depend, proportional representation, were little if at all advanced by 1979.

The government pursued proposals for assemblies in Scotland and Wales, partly to secure the votes of the fourteen Nationalist MPs, partly from genuine conviction, partly in face of apparent discontent in Scotland and Wales. As with the EEC, the issue cut across party lines, and a majority in Parliament in favour of the government's proposals was even less certain. In the end, the two devolution Bills were passed only with the crucial concession that the Bills would have to be approved by referendums in Scotland and Wales, with 40 per cent of *the electorate* voting in favour. The government fought rather half-heartedly for the Acts in the referendum campaign, but was still humiliated by the failure of both to pass the 40 per cent mark. In Wales only 12 per cent of the electorate voted in favour

(20 per cent of the poll); in Scotland 33 per cent of the electorate, and 51.6 per cent of the voters.

For the moment at least, the government could turn its back on these peripheral problems. But their other parliamentary and economic problems were finally and fatally intensified by the trade unions (chapter 6). The fragile relations of Government and unions had been disturbed by changes among union leaders. They were still willing to talk with government, but not about wage restraint. In any case, the leaders could not control their members in the branches and on the shop floor. The fate of the government was finally settled by the 'winter of discontent', 1978–9, in which a rash of strikes showed up the government's impotence, and an unacceptable face of trade unionism, with which it was so closely associated.

The Parliament of 1974–9 had been remarkable for its capacity to challenge the government. The central rule of British politics, that the government dominates the House of Commons, was fitfully and then totally abrogated. This at least enhanced the interest of politics, reduced the quantity, and may have improved the quality, of government. Appropriately therefore, the government was finally overthrown by a vote of confidence in the House of Commons, the first time for over fifty years and only the fourth time in a hundred years.

The defeat was narrow, one vote, and could have been avoided by a more ruthless government. The margin of defeat in the ensuing election was larger. Ironically, the Scottish Nationalists who precipitated the vote (angry at the dereliction of the Scottish Assembly) fared badly in the election, and they were reduced from eleven to two seats. In 1974 (October) SNP had won 30 per cent of the vote in Scotland and were poised on the threshold of a massive breakthrough. In 1979 their vote fell back to 17 per cent. The threat of a disintegrating multi-party Britain had receded. Significantly the Conservative vote at 13.7 million returned to the level of the 1950s, though its share of the poll was lower, due to the higher Liberal vote. Labour did as well as in the 1974 elections, though worse than in any other post-war election. The Conservatives returned to Parliament with an overall majority of forty-three. Thus ended five years of apparent disintegration in British politics, and fifteen mainly unhappy years for the Conservative party. But Margaret Thatcher's arrival in office looked more like a change of dynasty than a Restoration.

7 1979: the Conservative government of Margaret Thatcher

Mrs Thatcher intended that her government should make a new departure; she could reasonably assume, in the tradition of British politics, that the electorate had given her a 'mandate' to do so. By early reputation, Mrs

Thatcher's rule was tough, even abrasive, in personal style; and ideological in content. There was some evidence for both these contentions, but also signs that the Prime Minister would not obstinately persist in a course she recognized as mistaken, and that ideology was in part, as with most governments, a rhetorical garnishing to more pragmatic policies. Even so, a sharp change of direction was apparent, and policies fitted well with traditional Conservative ideas.

In economic matters, the new government pressed monetarist ideas hard (see chapter 2). Public expenditure was sharply cut back. New restrictions were placed on the trade unions (see chapter 6). None of these moves represented a reversal of the Labour government's policies; the difference lay in extent, intensity and firmness of purpose. It seemed likely, too, that the Conservative government would reap the economic benefits of North Sea oil, which was flowing by the end of the 1970s in such volume as to constitute substantial wealth.

The scope for change in foreign policy was more limited, but the new government placed more emphasis on a strong foreign policy, pressing British interests in Europe, and renewing a cold war stance against Russia (see chapter 5). It seemed unlikely that this would make much difference, except to the costs of the defence budget.

The review of the history of the post-war period, particularly of the 1970s, indicates a tendency to superficial volatility within a deeper immobility. There is also a hint that governments experienced a crisis after about two years in office. These points might indicate a prognosis for the course of Margaret Thatcher's government. However, wise historians try not to predict the future, but to explain the past. This is difficult enough, especially for a period as complex as the thirty-five years following the end of the war.

8 Two major themes: the quest for leadership, the drive towards equality

Behind this account of the rise and fall of governments may be discerned two major themes, and several minor ones. The major themes were the quest for leadership and the drive towards equality.

The quest for leadership

Under the British constitutional system, the rise and fall of governments and Prime Ministers was the most apparent source of change in British politics. The Lib–Lab Pact of 1977 was the only variation in this pattern, a minor change in the party base of government without an election or a change of Prime Minister. Two kinds of question arise. First, how significant for political change were the major changes of government (1945, 1951, 1964, 1970, 1974, 1979)? This account of British political history shows many other elements of change not closely related to those changes of government. Second, what was the comparative significance of party and party leader in the changes of government? In particular, is it possible to write the history of the period around the story of Prime Ministers and political leadership?

It was widely assumed to be the case that Prime Ministers had a considerable influence on politics; they made a difference. Leadership was in fashion; but it had never really been out of fashion. The 'heroic' or 'great man' view of politics and history was normal (consider older school textbooks, the enduring taste for political biography, the naming of public buildings, the idea of public service, the honours system). The heroic view was strengthened by the experience of two wars and the kind of popular leadership exercised by Lloyd George and more obviously, Winston Churchill; and by the example of American Presidents, especially John Kennedy. Television enhanced the possibilities of this style of leadership, but earlier leaders had used radio, the press and the public meeting (including amplification equipment after about 1920) to the same end. Within the heroic view of politics, two words were much used in the post-war period, 'personality' and 'charisma'. Both were employed rather loosely. Sportsmen were often described as 'personalities', though endless media interviews showed so often that their main, if not their only, personal attribute, was high skill in their game. Politicians were assessed for 'charisma', literally grace, the gift of God; by development, a kind of personal magnetism attributed by the sociologist, Weber, to religious leaders. Charisma was more than the orator's crowd-pulling power, which Crossman attributed to George Brown and Quintin Hogg. After Churchill, only one politician could be regarded as possessing the magnetism implied in the term – Enoch Powell, who used his fine oratorical talents in fields peculiarly open to strong emotion, race relations and Northern Ireland. There is no doubt, too, that the monarchy, drawing on immense popular respect and affection, radiated a quality which came very near to the true meaning of charisma.

Plainly much of this discussion of leadership was not meaningful. It neglected the importance of success in sustaining leadership, and assumed too readily that some quality of leadership was a highly significant element in government. In the period 1945–80 no Prime Minister stood out as a leader in the heroic style. There were several reasons for this. Heroic leadership was more suited to international relations, especially in face of clear threats to national security and survival. The overriding concern of Prime Ministers for foreign affairs had weakened as Britain's role as a great power had diminished. It is estimated that in the years 1933–7, a period of foreign crisis and mass unemployment, the Cabinet discussed 1480 items of foreign business compared to forty-seven about unemployment. (Some part of this disparity is explained by the day-to-day nature of foreign policy compared with more stable, unchanging domestic problems.) A comparison for the 1960s or 1970s would almost certainly show a transformation in the use of Cabinet time, though even in the 1960s Cabinet proceedings began with reports on foreign affairs.

The retreat from foreign affairs was a reluctant one for all Prime Ministers, since the political possibilities, the chance to play a decisive and well-publicized role, were so great. Eden was described as 'the last British Prime Minister to believe that Britain was a Great Power and the first to confront a crisis which proved beyond doubt that she was not. Attlee and Churchill . . . shared that belief but matters never quite came to the test in their day' (Lord Blake in *The Sunday Times*, 16 January 1977). In fact the Great Power role continued to attract Prime Ministers. Labour governments clung on to their forces 'east of Suez' long after they had any influence; Wilson's unsuccesful attempts to solve the Rhodesian crisis were carefully stage-managed; the invasion of the tiny island of Anguilla received full television coverage. In foreign policy, political leaders had a theatre and a play in which they believed they had a fair part – better than the knock-about improvisations of domestic politics.

This became the major theatre, but the parts were comic not heroic – struggles against elusive enemies (economic decline); awkward allies (NATO and EEC); and their own people (loyal trade unionists and managers). Still some foreign issues, especially Rhodesia, took up time, but without profit: Crossman estimated that in December 1965 the Prime Minister spent half his time on the Rhodesia problem.

The domestic sphere bristled with difficulties. Decisions of great technical complexity fell to ministers. No one could tell the answers for certain. Hence, on a score of issues ministers either prudently postponed decisions (as on the Third London Airport and nuclear power), or jumped to the wrong answer (as with the development of the costly supersonic passenger aircraft, Concorde). Neither looked very heroic. Economic policy was a long record of failure. Success in the House of Commons, which was prized among politicians, did not much improve popular standing. Television was a powerful instrument for those with the skill to use it, but still a treacherous support. Politicians who prospered by television were also damaged by it. They were vulnerable in person and an easy target for the critic. Derision in a television comedy (and in the 1960s satire meant deriding politicians) could more than wipe out a brilliant parliamentary performance. People and parties became more difficult to manage. Sporadic scandals further lowered the standing of the profession. In these conditions it was hard to be a hero – yet the public seemed to crave for leadership of a heroic kind.

The gallery of post-war political leaders displays differing styles of personal leadership. Churchill and Attlee offered an obvious contrast between heroic, theatrical leadership and the laconic and humdrum. This was partly related to the difference between wartime and peacetime leadership; but there were sharp differences in character and style too. (See the contrasting accounts of 'the day I became Prime Minister' in Madgwick, 1976, pp. 59–60.) James Margach, a distinguished Lobby Correspondent, noted Attlee's complete disdain for public relations, rarely reading the newspapers, and coming alive at a press conference only when asked about a clue in that day's *Times* crossword (Margach, 1978, pp. 88–89). Macmillan by contrast 'was the first person to recognize that in the modern world of constant media exposure a Prime Minister has to be something of a showman . . . an actor-manager' (p. 115). Attlee's reputation for effectiveness and decisiveness has risen over the years, but not all of his colleagues admired him. Michael Foot, at the time a new young Member of Parliament, wrote, 'He gave no hint that he understood the need to sustain the allegiance of the nation; communication between him and the public was to be conducted by telepathy. He never seemed to realize that the engine of government must be refuelled with popular support and Party enthusiasm, or at least he regarded the work of stoker as too menial for himself to engage in . . . Never once did he summon his Ministers together for a free, uninhibited discussion of the grand strategy of his Government.' (Foot, 1973, p. 27).

Some leaders are skilled at securing consent by compromise; others display courage, 'grit', in sticking to the hard line and seeing things through. Gaitskell, leader of the Labour party 1955–63 and Mrs Thatcher, Prime Minister from 1979, were examples of the latter type. Gaitskell's confrontation with the party is reported in chapter 4. Mrs Thatcher quickly won a reputation for courage, abrasiveness, leading from the front – and rejoiced in a title bestowed by her Russian adversaries, 'the Iron Lady'. 'As Prime Minister,' she said, just before the 1979 election, 'I couldn't waste time having any internal arguments'; and she is reported to have told senior colleagues, 'Don't tell me *what*; tell me *how*. I know *what*.'

Such leaders may be admired at the time, but not loved until their uncomfortable firmness is a memory. Other leaders deliberately compromise, trim and 'fudge', papering over the cracks in order to hold the party or country together. They may soon acquire a reputation for lack of principle, deviousness, even dishonesty. This certainly happened to Wilson in his later years in office, and to some extent to Macmillan.

Wilson defended the leadership which concedes and compromises to achieve consent:

> To bridge a deep political chasm without splitting a party or provoking dramatic ministerial resignations is sometimes regarded as something approaching political chicanery. This is to subordinate the realities of 200

years of democratic politics to the demands of sensationalism. The highest aim of leadership is to secure policies adequate to deal with any situation, including the production of acceptable new solutions and policies, without major confrontations, splits and resignations . . .

In my view a constant effort to keep this party together, without sacrificing either principle or the essentials of basic strategy, is the very stuff of political leadership. Macmillan was canonised for it. (Wilson, 1979, pp. 121, 234).

The choice between these two kinds of leader is not easy. When Wilson succeeded Gaitskell as leader, Crossman commented, with relief, 'at last we have a leader who can lie'. Firm government sometimes seemed desirable. Eden, in 1956, attempted a firm foreign policy, and fell. Heath 'stood up to' the miners in 1974 – and fell. Callaghan tried to impose a 5 per cent limit on incomes in 1978–9, and fell. So firm leadership is difficult and dangerous. 'Deviousness' in the cause of consent may be the only way to have a policy at all.

Wilson pursued the politics of consensus and his one departure from this, the confrontation of 1969 with the trade unions, failed. Heath was by temperament more inclined to firm government, and found himself embroiled in the 'politics of confrontation'. He presented himself deliberately as an effective manager, bringing to government a new style of government. In a personal foreword to the 1970 manifesto he wrote:

During the last six years we have suffered not only from bad policies, but from a cheap and trivial style of government. Decisions have been dictated simply by the desire to catch tomorrow's headlines. The short-term gain has counted for everything; . . . Decisions lightly entered into have been as lightly abandoned . . . I am determined that a Conservative Government shall introduce a new style of government: that we shall re-establish our sound and honest British traditions in this field . . . decisions should be aimed at the long term . . . once a decision is made, once a policy is established, the Prime Minister and his colleagues should have the courage to stick to it . . .

In more rhetorical style, at the Party Conference in October 1970, which celebrated his election victory, Heath claimed: 'We were returned to office to change the course of history of this nation – nothing less . . . We are leaving behind the years of retreat.'

Heath's public personality suffused this challenging, radical, technocratic approach to government, with a certain coldness. He was 'not invariably tactful, and he can be brutal when in the mood'. By reputation he 'dislikes the long processes of collective decision-making' (James, 1972, pp. 116–17).

The contemptuous reference to Wilson's government in the manifesto was deliberate. A striking antipathy seemed to develop between these two men. 'Heath intensely disliked the gimmickry and flashiness which seemed to him to characterize Wilson's performance as Prime Minister; and his temper cannot have been improved by the frequent humiliation to which he was subjected on the floor of the House, at any rate in his early days as Leader of the Opposition, by Wilson's unparalleled dialectical skills. As time wore on, and Heath's contempt for Wilson deepened, he moved towards a posture of almost automatic opposition to anything Wilson said or did' (Stewart, 1978, p. 110). Prime ministerial leadership, in this and in other cases, was much affected by the gladiatorial contests of the House of Commons.

The politics of confrontation was not Heath's choice. He was caught up in the conflicts between unions and government that beset every government in the 1960s and 1970s. 'Confrontation' was a choice of the unions as much as the government, and the confrontations clearly raised more passion than almost any other event in the whole period. The accents of the Wilson government during the 1969 crises and the Heath government of 1974 all show up the stress and anger which distorted the judgements of rational men and skilled politicians. Even Sir William Armstrong, Heath's chief civil service adviser, involved himself in political matters to an unusual degree and seems to have influenced Heath to resist concessions ('the hawk of hawks' according to a colleague – S. Fay and H. Young, *The Sunday Times*, 29 February 1976) before he broke down and left the scene. Heath was in fact reluctant to call an election in January–February 1974, and rejected the deliberate staging of an election by candlelight (power being cut off), on the theme 'Who governs Britain?'. The delay possibly cost him the election: thus he was in the end trapped by his attempt to avoid confrontation.

Sir Stafford Cripps, who was Chancellor of the Exchequer 1947–50, illustrates another kind of strong leadership, based on profound moral conviction, and, it should be added, a lawyer's commitment to his brief. 'Cripp's confidence in the rightness of his own case made him an impossible subordinate and difficult colleague. It also made him an inspiring leader who was in fact able to appeal, as he hoped to the best of his listeners' (D. Marquand in Sissons and French, 1964, p. 184). Marquand argued that Cripps's style of leadership ('moral leadership') was inappropriate in a democracy but had a quality that would have made him a leader in a time of national emergency. In fact he was the most successful of all post-war Chancellors in his efforts to hold down wages and impose general austerity.

By the standards of these leaders of the 1945–76 period, James Callaghan falls between the full consensual style of a Wilson and a firmer Attlee; Margaret Thatcher appears to be a reversion to the Heath model, but with a style of her own. She is less of a party politician, more of a national leader than any of her predecessors except Churchill.

The element of individual personality is necessarily overstressed in this kind of analysis. In fact Prime Ministers are shaped as much by the political situations they inherit. Leadership styles varied according to personal character and predisposition, the considerations of senior colleagues, political conditions and the nature of the problems. Prime Ministers might have chosen (or have had the choice thrust upon them) to be concerned for a positive programme or for passive management of the status quo; to sustain and be sustained by one or two great themes, or to operate in detail over broad policy fields; to be more or less theatrical in style (bookies or bishops according to one distinction); to be more or less sensitive to party opinion.

The job of political leadership in post-war Britain was more demanding than ever before. Reputations for consistency and even integrity were constantly at risk. A reading of the massive diaries of ministers gives an impression of hurry and harassment, of tired men making hand-to-mouth decisions, in which choice was finally based on the undue weighting of party and 'presentational' factors. In historical perspective, two leaders, Macmillan and Wilson, showed skilful adaptation to the new limitations of their trade. The public still seemed to like its leaders in a grander mould, and Macmillan contrived that too. Leadership in the heroic style probably enhanced national morale and self-confidence. But in a democracy in decline the public had to make do with leaders with feet of clay. That was the great virtue of democracy – but life for the politicians was necessarily uncomfortable.

The drive towards economic equality

Equality as a political objective lay at the heart of the struggle between the parties (see chapter 4); and a good deal of economic and social policy was part of the struggle for or against equality. There were great problems in defining equality, so that being for or against it did not amount to a narrowly defined political position. Equality meant for the Conservative equality of opportunity (loosely defined) but not equality of condition or income. Socialists liked equality of income but this was an unpopular cause, not least among trade unionists fighting for differentials. Equality of esteem or regard was also desirable and even less practicable. The achievement of any kind of equality necessarily conflicted with individual freedom. Notwithstanding these difficulties, it was widely accepted even on the right that gross inequality should be diminished, and certainly on the left that equality was a condition of the just society.

It was a matter of common observation that Britain in the 1960s and 1970s was a more equal society than ever before. The gross indications of differences of class based on income had abated. Poverty had not been banished, especially for the old, but the mass poverty associated with pre-war unemployment had gone – and did not return when pre-war levels of unemployment returned in 1980. Affluence had spread more widely some of the amenities of the middle class by the late 1970s. Over half of the population owned cars and homes, and one-fifth deep freezers. Seven million people took a holiday abroad each year. Between 1965 and 1975 the consumption of wine more than doubled and spirits increased by 80 per cent. The number of telephones had more than quadrupled since 1950. Toilet paper, once little known in working-class houses, became a universal necessity. Dress, particularly among the young, was no longer clearly related to income, and the adoption of blue jeans annihilated differences both of class and income. Some widely distributed high technology products were wildly luxurious by the standards of a previous age – calculators and tape-recorders for example. A novel enthusiasm for antiques showed that simple material wants had been sated.

The impression of common observations was correct in some respects, misleading in others. Few miners in the 1930s owned cars and took their holidays on the Mediterranean. But the overall distribution of wealth had shifted very little. This is a difficult subject, but broadly research (especially by the Royal Commission on the Distribution of Income and Wealth, established by Labour and abolished by the Conservative government in 1979) showed the following (allowance must be made for some unavoidable inaccuracy in the statistics):

Wealth: the proportion of wealth owned by the top 1 per cent fell from 47 per cent in 1950 to 31 per cent in 1965, to 25 per cent in 1976. This meant that the top 1 per cent of the population still owned more of the country's wealth than the whole of the bottom 80 per cent. For the top 10 per cent the figures were 56 per cent in 1965 and 40 per cent in 1976.

Incomes: the top 1 per cent received as much as the bottom 20 per cent. The top 10 per cent took 33 per cent (27 per cent after tax) of all incomes in 1949; 26 per cent (22 per cent) in 1976. The redistribution mainly went to the benefit of the next highest groups, hence the share of income of the bottom 50 per cent, which was 23 per cent, did not change between 1949 and 1976. A typical managing director received about 36 per cent extra above his income in 'fringe benefits' or 'perks'.

Counting income and wealth together: the top 10 per cent were in the late 1960s nearly ten times better off than the poorest 10 per cent.

Taxation: though progressive, did comparatively little to change the distribution of income. Thus in 1976 the top 10 per cent received about a quarter of all income, which was reduced only by about 4 per cent by taxation. The bottom 10 per cent received about one-fortieth of all income and this was increased by less than half of 1 per cent by the payment of social benefits.

Poverty: the measurement of poverty depends entirely on definition. By the level of supplementary benefit of 1971 the number of poor fell from about one-fifth of population in 1953 to about one-fortieth in 1973. A government estimate of 1971 put the number of the poor at about 2 million people. Professor Townsend using more generous criteria later put it at between 5 million and 14 million. The poor were made up largely of the old, the unemployed and one-parent families.

Differences in income and occupation were associated with startling differences in *health and mortality*. Deprivation extended to life itself.

Nevertheless, Britain was just a little more equal than most other Western countries, but not so much as to suggest that Labour governments had been highly effective in the pursuit of equality.

In the light of all this, was Britain a class-divided society? In the sense of sharp differences in income, the answer appears to be, yes. But the term 'social class' implies feelings of solidarity, the awareness of boundaries, and conflict. In that sense, the answer is less clear.

To some extent class differences had softened and class conflict diminished. 'Affluence' had lifted up the whole social pyramid, the pyramid itself was marginally a flatter and more permeable structure. Social divisions grew more complex and a little less rigid. In particular, the middle class expanded, to include about 40 per cent of the people, and diversified. A new 'service class' of professional people developed, including the rapidly rising number of professional and technical workers especially in the public sector. These were not the old 'high' or gentlemanly professions, largely self-employed, barristers, surgeons, bankers, but the humbler trades of teacher, social worker, computer specialist, engineer, and so on. They were recruited from the newly-educated sons and daughters of the skilled working class and so provided a short ladder of mobility. They discovered that being middle class in post-war Britain was like owning a car – much less fun when almost everybody else had got that far.

The rise of this new class, and the comparative prosperity of the skilled working class, left at the bottom of the pyramid the lower or submerged class – the poor, the old, the unemployed, the parents of large families, and single parents. The achievement of post-war Britain – a modest liberation – was that this class, something like a tenth of the population, was a good deal smaller than its equivalent in the 1920s and 1930s.

This is the class structure seen by historians and sociologists. It was not a picture of society widely shared in post-war Britain. The middle classes, especially the upper sections, were most conscious of their status – they had more of it to feel threatened. Class behaviour showed up in voting (see chapter 4); in old-fashioned snobbery, much encouraged by the survival of the old aristocracy, and the use of titles; and in persistent complaints about the plight of the middle class. These were loudest in the 1940s and 1950s, and centred on the shortage of domestic servants and the cost of private schools, burdens which were said to be crippling the nation's backbone. A Conservative former minister complained in 1953 that 'senior Civil Servants are doing the washing-up and responsible business executives shining their own shoes'. Two Conservatives in a book on the English middle classes, published in 1949 and reprinted immediately, wrote: 'To attempt to make the hours of domestic service . . . conform to those of industry is unrealistic . . . From the point of view of the employer with children, a forty-eight hour week makes a resident domestic of so little use that it is probably worth while to resign oneself to daily help and thus save a bedroom and a maid's board . . .' (Lewis and Maude, 1949, p. 255).

Plainly such champions of the middle classes did not favour equality. But the working classes were not strongly egalitarian either. They fought for their differentials, regarded social security benefits for the poor with some hostility (compared with expenditure on education and health), and some of them according to a survey in the 1950s quite liked being governed by the old ruling class.

It seems, indeed, that class conflict was very far from intense in postwar Britain, though shadowy class differences and resentments were felt. Other divisions in society were probably more obvious – the great divide in housing; the division between the self-employed and the employee class; sharp differences between the young and the old; and a growing rift between the comparatively prosperous Southeast of England and the depressed North and West. Conflict across these divides was necessarily fragmented, and the great war of bourgeoisie and proletariat could not break out for lack of armies.

Social policy

Making Britain a more, or less, equal society was a function of economic and social policies. The promotion of full employment, and a comprehensive system of social security remedied the worst features of pre-war Britain. General prosperity at least lifted up the whole social pyramid, even though the bottom remained a long way from the top. Four major policy areas offered further opportunities for advancing the drive to equality – social security, housing, education and health. All four show that modest advances towards equality still left large gaps between rich and poor.

Social security

The Labour government enacted the principles of the Beveridge scheme for social insurance (National Insurance Act 1946). This ended four centuries of the Poor Law. Under the new legislation, it was intended that the citizen would be adequately safeguarded against old age, sickness and unemployment, by an insurance-based system without the much resented means tests of the 1930s. Poverty was not abolished, but there is no doubt that the number of people seriously lacking in food, clothing, shelter and warmth was very substantially reduced compared with the 1930s, (or indeed any previous period). In the 1960s and 1970s there occurred a massive growth of the social service professions, so that, for example, old people living alone (very common in Britain) might be visited by home helps, nurses, meals-on-wheels, and enjoy subsidized amenities like a telephone.

The new social security system had many faults. It was inevitably very costly. The insurance principle broke down and means testing was introduced for supplementary benefits. Administrative costs were high and the financial basis unnecessarily complicated. By the 1970s some people were being taxed and given benefits at the same time. There was some much exaggerated fraud, and a constant danger that there would be little incentive to take employment at low wages. Alarming stories circulated of Irish labourers with ten children enjoying life on 'the welfare'; of Pakistani families moving direct from London airport to comfortable hotels paid for by 'the welfare'. Social security was a favourite candidate for cuts, and an especial target for Conservative critics. Yet poverty and misfortune remained (what was an unemployed labourer to do?); and by the standards of Western Europe, Britain's welfare state was by no means generous.

Housing

In the mid-1930s well over 300,000 houses were completed each year, one fifth or so being local authority 'council' houses. In the best year of the 1945 Labour government, just over 200,000 houses were built (in difficult economic conditions), but the pre-war proportions had been reversed and four out of five were council houses. Aneurin Bevan, as Housing Minister, insisted on high-quality council housing and minimum standards were set, and remained, above those in private housing. In 1954 Macmillan reached his target of 300,000 houses, but now over one half were private. From the late 1950s private building ran ahead of council houses. Even so the high proportion of council tenants in Britain (over 30 per cent) was extraordinary in the Western countries. There were two other major elements in housing policy: tax relief on mortgage interest and regulation of rents in the private sector. The first was a substantial subsidy to the better-off, aiding them to invest in a rapidly appreciating form of wealth, especially in the early 1970s, and rising with interest rates in the late 1970s. The control of rents originated as a wartime measure to prevent excessive rent increases. It did this so effectively that the supply of accommodation for private rental diminished rapidly from 90 per cent of households in 1914 to 15 per cent or less by 1980.

The parties differed over housing policy, though less in practice than in rhetoric. The Conservatives encouraged private housing (a property-owning democracy) and attempted in their Rent Acts (notably in 1957 and 1972) to protect the interests of landlords. At the end of the period they deliberately encouraged the sale of council houses to sitting tenants. Labour encouraged the building of council houses and protected private tenants (notably in the Rent Acts of 1965 and 1974); but drew back from a restriction of the mortgagor's tax privileges. Labour made three attempts to capture for the state ('the community') the profits arising from the development of land, but measures short of nationalization of land simply closed down the market. This somewhat incoherent collection of housing policies was disturbed in the 1970s by the eagerness of the building societies to lend to mortgagors. This set off a massive inflation of house prices which effectively divided Britain into those who already owned houses, now much appreciated in value; and those who did not (and could now hardly afford the new high prices).

The product of housing policy by the 1970s may be summarized as follows:

(i)   a very high standard of housing, better than any other country except possibly the USA, and a gross surplus of houses (despite massive demolitions of old working-class housing);

(ii) the maldistribution of housing, so that many good houses were under-occupied, and some areas of the country had a disproportionate share of poor housing. There were still half-a-million occupied houses classified as 'unfit' in 1976–7;

(iii) substantial subsidies to two classes, mortgagors and council tenants. These subsidies were much increased by inflation and were somewhat higher for tenants than for owner-occupiers (though the difference was not as great as some owner-occupiers believed). By 1978 the subsidy equalled about 2 per cent of GDP, or £2.50 per household per week. If the subsidies had been returned by tax reductions, income tax could have been reduced by about one-fifth and more people would have gained than lost.

These subsidies distorted both investment (the British lived in good houses and worked in poor factories) and the housing market, encouraging over-occupation and immobility.

(iv) the sharp reduction of private rented accommodation; hence a severe housing problem for the old, for young single people and for one-parent families; a residue of unfit housing; and up to 50,000 adjudged homeless at the end of the 1970s.

These outcomes of housing were not intended, and they well illustrate the gap between rhetoric and policy on one hand; and the promulgation and implementation of policy on the other. Implementation failed to match intention. The Rent Act of 1957 was fiercely denounced as a landlord's charter, but made very little difference. Inflation changed policies, and governments refused to modify policies against the interests of the two great vested interests. The building societies (thoughtlessly) contributed to inflation. Altogether housing policy was not the deliberate invention of governments, but a messy outcome of steering and drifting.

Even so, the provision of housing was by the end of the period better and less unequal than before. The proportion of owner-occupiers had shot up from about one-quarter in 1947 to well over one-half in 1980. Council tenants, most of whom needed more help than the owner-occupiers (45 per cent in the late 1970s qualified for help with rent or rates), lived in houses of generally good quality; though many were unhappy in the 'high-rise' tower blocks which commemorated the planning and architectural enthusiasms of the 1960s.

The condition of housing reflected the general pattern of inequality in post-war Britain. The rich man still enjoyed his castle; most of the poor were not 'at the gate' but in pleasant little houses, subsidized by the government. This was not equality but nor was it gross inequality or inhumanity. However, there was still a submerged class of officially (as distinct from actually) homeless or badly housed people, many of them clustered in and near the centres of the old industrial cities.

Education

Education resembles housing in some respects. By 1980 there was more of it, badly distributed and accompanied by partisan disputation. The social strata which had the least housing tended also to get the least or the worst, education. But education differed from housing in two respects. Its clients (directly at least) were children, who did not count as much politically as the clients for housing; and its quality, and even its quantity, were less easily measured, and so open to dispute.

The increase in provision of education is clear from the statistics:

 (i) in 1938 only 38 per cent of 14-year-olds were in full-time education;
(ii) in 1947 the school-leaving age was raised to 15, thus raising the proportion to 100 per cent. In 1938 the proportion of 17- and 19 year-olds in full-time education was 4 per cent and 2 per cent respectively; in 1962, 15 per cent and 7 per cent; and, following the raising of the school-leaving age to 16 in 1973, the figures for 1975 were 28 per cent and 16 per cent.

By the 1970s, there were more schools, more teachers and smaller classes. Higher education expanded rapidly after the Robbins Report of 1963. A revolution in teaching methods and the lifting of the shadow of selection examinations transformed the primary schools.

The basis of the increased provision lay first in the Education Act of 1944, associated with R. A. Butler. That Act established a new settlement with the religious denominations, whose position had been the central concern of government in the previous century. The settlement was generous, both in finance and in religious matters; it included provision that the school day in all maintained schools must begin with an act of collective worship, and must include compulsory religious instruction (both were subject to a little used right of withdrawal on conscientious grounds). The Church of England, satisfied with these provisions (for which it had fought hard) and short of funds for new building, gradually gave up its denominational schools. The Catholics retained theirs, and gained new subventions for the extension of their system.

In the religious settlement, the Education Act was conservative. In other ways, it was forward-looking. The status of education and its support by central government were enhanced by the creation of a ministry. Education was to be provided free, and in effect in three kinds of school, grammar, technical and modern. Thus the 'secondary modern' replaced the old all-age elementary school, in which pupils who did not go to a grammar school stayed to the age of 14. For the first time all children were to receive some kind of 'secondary' education, and the school-leaving age was to be raised to 15 and then to 16. The scheme was based on intelligence testing at the age of 11 (the '11 plus') and the division of children into three types, corresponding to the three types of school, which should each enjoy 'parity of esteem'.

The Labour party – and many educationists – soon lost confidence in this system. There were serious doubts whether children could be divided in this neat way; and whether it was desirable to divide them. The grammar school had been the traditional path of mobility for the bright working-class child. But, it was claimed, this created a new 'meritocracy' little better than the old aristocracies of birth or money. The schools should concern themselves with the children, often from poorer homes, who seemed less able. In the right environment, children would acquire intelligence. This revolutionary idea was ultimately approved even by a Conservative Education Minister, Sir Edward Boyle. These ideas, stressing environment as the determinant of ability, led to the development of the comprehensive school, which recognized the potential of all children, and encouraged them to learn together in one community.

The Labour party adopted the comprehensive principle and applied it in 1965 and again in 1974 by calling for plans for reorganization. Their application was necessarily slow since new buildings were usually needed, and some Conservative local authorities exploited the scope for resistance. An Act of 1976 compelled local authorities to proceed to reorganization. (Whatever the merits of the education principle, it is clear that central government was not concerned with local choice.) By 1980 83 per cent of pupils in maintained schools were in schools reorganized on comprehensive lines. Research showed that their standards were good, though they could not match the concentrated academic achievement of the selective schools.

Conservative ministers of education were not inclined to approve plans for 'de-comprehensivization' of schools already reorganized. Much was made of parental choice, rather than the dreaded '11-plus', but it was not clear how parental choice could be reconciled with selection by academic criteria. The struggle over comprehensive schools was over, bar a good deal of shouting about their achievements. But the battle had moved to another field. The comprehensive school worked best as a neighbourhood school. But the private independent ('public') and semi-independent ('direct grant') schools had always attracted the children of the well-to-do and academically inclined children. They were part of a fundamental division in British society by which positions of wealth and influence were largely filled by people educated in the private schools and at Oxford and Cambridge universities (where the children from the private schools held a disproportionate number of places). The facts were fairly clear – whether one looked at bankers, bishops, brigadiers or cabinet ministers. But the social mechanism behind the facts were more obscure.

The children of top people (mainly, of course, the sons of top people) took the top jobs. Infiltration from below remained unusual. Social mobility was restricted and few people took more than one step in a generation up the social ladder. (For example, bank managers might have as father a bank clerk, but not an unskilled manual worker.) The education system was not a prime cause of social division; rather it was a consequence of existing divisions – but also a support of them. Socialists were right to be worried about the relationship between divided schools and a divided society. Doing something about the problem was plainly more difficult.

Once again it seemed that the drive towards equality achieved only a moderate inequality, the pyramid lifted up and flattened a little. Education had carried very high hopes in the post-war years. Some of these were disappointed. It looked as if education could not reverse the effects of even three or four years of poor environment. Nursery education and the education of fifteen–eighteen-year-olds lagged; some inner-city schools were patently failing to educate or even hold their pupils. Three major reports, Newsom, Plowden and Crowther, showed up problems which remained unsolved. The most fundamental inequalities were impossible to fight. The average child in the 1970s spent more time in front of a television set than in front of a class teacher. Parents who had themselves been poorly educated often placed too little value on education. Meanwhile educational administrators battled with the immediate practical problems of numbers, high in the 1960s and early 1970s, then falling rapidly with the birth rate.

All this is to review education from the point of view of social equality. But the mainspring of education in Britain had always been industrial efficiency and religious instruction. Neither had done well in the post-war world. Perhaps the lesson for those concerned with efficiency, and faith, as well as for the egalitarians, is that in education great expectations are likely to be disappointed.

Health

The establishment of the National Health Service by the Act of 1946 was one of the most substantial achievements of the post-war Labour government, and certainly the most enduringly popular. The Act nationalized the hospitals and brought general medical practitioners into a centrally financed, freely available public service. The Labour party had supported such a service since the 1930s, and Beveridge had assumed the provision of a national health service. The coalition government had approved an outline scheme in 1941, but Conservatives were uneasy about a thoroughgoing scheme, and the British Medical Association began to retreat from its earlier enthusiasm.

In the event the Conservatives opposed the Bill in detail but claimed to support the principle of a national health service. In fact, most of the principle lay in the detail. The doctors, through the BMA, mounted a major public revolt against the Act and attempted to boycott the operation of the new service. The doctors, like other groups of workers, have a right to defend their working practices. In this case, the BMA seems to have added political partisanship to narrow self-interest.

The Minister of Health, Aneurin Bevan, swung between provocation and diplomacy. On the eve of the inauguration of the service, he described the Conservatives, in a notorious phrase, as 'lower than vermin'. But he sought allies among the medical consultants and made substantial concessions to professional interests, notably in the structure (neither local government nor directly central government), the form of employment (a capitation fee, not a salaried service) and the provision of private treatment within the National Health Service. But Bevan never relaxed his determination to establish a free and comprehensive service. For him it was practical socialism – 'a triumphant example of the superiority of collective action and public initiative applied to a segment of society where commercial principles are seen at their worst' (quoted in Sissons and French, 1964, p. 244). In the end, the doctor's revolt collapsed when a third plebiscite showed that two out of three were willing to co-operate in the service.

With this victory the battle for the principle of a national health service had been won. Yet the principle was vulnerable to erosion if not direct attack. The new service proved costly, more costly even than education by the end of the period. In 1949 Bevan himself accepted the principle of charging for prescriptions; in 1951 Gaitskell imposed charges for spectacles and dentures – and Bevan resigned. Charges were subsequently raised but hardly extended. A more serious threat lay in the development of private medicine, and the double standards Bevan had always hated. In 1976 the Labour government legislated for the 'phasing out' of private beds in the public hospitals, on the reasonable ground that there was a substantial subsidy involved through the provision of support and technical services. The phasing out was ended by the new Conservative government in 1979. Therein lay a crucial difference between the parties – Bevan's ideal of an undifferentiated service for all, based on need, and a Conservative ideal (as in education) of a national minimum service topped by freedom to buy a superior service. Labour argued – for both education and health – that the private provision was morally repugnant and depressed the standards of the public service.

Another kind of inequality was prevalent in the health service – substantial disparities between regions. In particular the London area was generously provided with hospitals, compared with the North of England. Here London socialists were less enthusiastic to apply their principles, but governments in the 1970s moved slowly towards the modest redistribution of facilities. The problem of cost remained serious for the health service, especially as high technology medicine (much favoured by high technology doctors) grew ever more wonderful and ever more expensive.

The health service suffered other problems too. Its administrative structure was both heavy and relatively undemocratic. Reform in the early 1970s made little improvement, and further change was proposed in 1980. The hospitals were subject too to the unionization of public employees in the 1970s, and to major strikes in which union pickets controlled the admission of patients to some hospitals. At the same time, waiting lists for hospital treatment lengthened. The great ideals of 1946 seemed to be losing their force.

Yet the achievement of the health service was immense. Serious illness ceased to be a financial disaster. Poor people no longer chose their spectacles without eye testing at a counter in Woolworth's. Many serious diseases – diphtheria, tuberculosis, whooping cough, rickets – virtually disappeared. Infant mortality declined steeply. Some at least of this improvement was directly attributable to the provision of a public medical service. The health service, like education, was a service few people wished to cut.

Through these social policies and the management of the economy the Labour party stood for a progression towards equality, the Conservatives for a moderation of inequality. Labour responded to the emotion behind the famous 1945 cartoon by Zec, showing a returning soldier and his wife at the counter of the 'Tory Peace Stores'. Under the counter are hidden 'jobs', 'proper medical attention', 'good homes', 'decent schools', 'the fruits of victory'; but they are marked 'reserved for the rich and privileged'.

The soldier says angrily: 'What do you mean, you're out of stock? I've paid twice for these goods, once in 1914 and again in 1939.' The Conservatives listened more sympathetically to the cries of pain from the middle class, and tried often in vain to reverse the relentless trend towards public subsidy. This turned out to be a Canute-like gesture, sweeping the tide back with a broom.

Labour's problem was to make public provision serve its social ends. An editorial in *The Guardian*, following the election of 1979, questioned whether nationalization had been 'the liberating experience which the 1945 manifesto predicted. How many consumers today find it more liberating to do business with North Thames Gas than to shop at Sainsbury's or Marks and Spencer?' Again it seemed, that 'the power of the unions has become as greatly feared even among Labour voters as the power of the old-fashioned capitalist employer used to be' (*The Guardian*, 8 May 1979).

If Britain was a little more equal in 1980 than in 1945, the temper of British society was notably less egalitarian. Malcolm Muggeridge's comment in the early 1960s, allowing for some journalistic exaggeration, might apply to the whole of the period from the late 1950s to 1980: 'It has been a time of political, economic and moral free-wheeling, with the encouragement of every sort of soft indulgence, from betting and bingo to the Beatles . . . The records set up have been in road accidents, hire-purchase, juvenile delinquency and telly-viewing. It is the politics of the trough . . .' (*New Statesman*, 6 Oct. 1964, in Amis, 1977, p. 19).

Alongside competitive acquisitiveness there developed a competitive assertion of 'rights', the establishment of claims of advantage not equality, not only of the middle classes over the rest but of the employed over the unemployed, trade unionists over other workers, one form of house tenure over another and so on. Each group fought for state-guaranteed privilege against fellow citizens. In the optimistic idealism of 1945, the state would replace the self interest of the market and promote justice and equality. The next thirty years demonstrated that the state could be penetrated and colonized by the forces of competitive self-interest.

9 Some minor themes of the period

Decline

This book is full of evidence of the decline of Britain – international, economic, political. The idea of a golden age now past is a familiar one throughout history, and the meaning of, and evidence for decline needs to be carefully examined. Even so, there can be little doubt of the facts of the decline of economic and international power since the nineteenth century.

The timing and the degree of decline are more difficult to establish, and the justifiably high standing of Britain at the end of the war obscured the real weakness of the economy by then.

In international affairs the rise of the two superpowers left Britain plainly in the second rank, and the reluctant and patchy unification of Western Europe in the EEC could not compensate for this (though that was a substantial objective of the policy). The almost complete liquidation of the British empire meant more to British governments than to anyone else. Its major consequence lay in the new complexity and unpredictability of a much extended and fragmented international system. Domestic politics was marked by a sharp decline in confidence. The comfortable certainties of the old constitutional model either did not operate or were no longer thought to be valuable.

The loss of confidence worried British governments perhaps more than it worried the British people. They were diverted by comparatively trivial incidents, like the invasion of Anguilla (1967) or the raising of the Princes Gate siege (1980); deeply divided over Suez (though in the end with a majority in favour of intervention), and over Ulster, with a substantial minority favouring the withdrawal of troops. The decline of Britain as an old-fashioned Great Power was borne cheerfully by a people comforted for a while by national prosperity.

Liberation

Two fundamental social revolutions began in this period, the liberation of youth and the liberation of women. Young people were largely freed from the conventions of dress, coiffure, culture, and general subordination formerly imposed on them by the competition for jobs, and by military service. The first sign of the rebellion of youth was the Campaign for Nuclear Disarmament, in which young people mainly of the middle class provided the rank-and-file marchers. The revolution came in the 1960s with the sudden fame of the Liverpool singing group, the Beatles. Their style of dress, hair, music and speech appealed directly to youth. Thereafter the development of popular music, by precept and example, gave young people the signal to create new standards – by the mere sanction of numbers. The old disciplines could not be enforced in a liberal society against large and solidary groups. This was a key political lesson of the period, significant in Parliament and parties, in industry and in international relations. The liberation was profound but not total. The 'pop' music industry was itself engaged in massive exploitation of the young. Educational provision and employment opportunities lagged behind the cultural revolution. Crime committed by young people increased.

The liberation of women was similarly profound but even further from completion. Liberation depended on changes in sexual relations and economics. The development of new methods of contraception, and especially 'the pill', played a major part in effecting such gains as were made. By the late 1960s conception for many couples was a matter for deliberate choice. The Abortion Act of 1967 (a Private Member's Bill introduced by David Steel) further enlarged 'the woman's right to choose'. By the 1970s women had been freed, so it seemed, from the biological tyranny of their reproductive function, a remarkable victory against nature. This sexual revolution was accompanied by economic changes: smaller families, the spread of household machinery and the sharing by men in domestic chores lightened the traditional burden of women and enabled increasing numbers to go out to work. The revolution in woman's economic role and the independence it brought was helped forward by more impersonal economic forces, an expanding economy and the need for a larger work force. However, by the end of the period recession and mounting unemployment jeopardized these new freedoms as women found it harder to compete in a tightening job market.

The sexual and economic revolutions liberated women without giving them full equality with men. They made some gains in employment opportunities, marriage law, property rights and divorce. Still in 1980 there remained vast areas of discrimination related to the traditional division of labour and sex roles between men and women. Parliament, the civil service, almost any company office, gave evidence that women still lived in a man's world. The election of a woman, Mrs Thatcher, as leader of the Conservative party in 1975, and subsequently Prime Minister, was an accident, from this point of view, though one with substantial significance.

Again, liberation had its price. Alongside the liberation of women from reproduction, and clearly associated with it, there was a major revolution in sexual *mores*. It appeared that fear of pregnancy had been the main prop of sexual morality. Once the fear had been removed, sexual activity was liberated. There was a boom in contraceptive devices, abortion, pregnant brides, marriages and divorces, and 'single parents'. The Divorce Reform Act of 1969 was a landmark in this advance to freedom or license, or, as it came to be called, 'permissiveness'. The number of divorces increased rapidly. Whether this increased human happiness is not known, but it had much to do with the trebling of the number of one-parent families between 1963 and 1978. The burden of criminality was lifted from homosexuality (1967). 'Permissiveness' extended to literature and the arts. In a famous trial in 1960, D. H. Lawrence's novel, *Lady Chatterley's Lover*, was adjudged to be fit for publication without expurgation. By the 1970s there was very little which could not be written, displayed or performed. The liberal's faith in freedom was severely strained.

'Liberation' in other forms was patchy, and always ambivalent. What seemed liberation to one meant for another the abandonment of moral principle. This was a secular age, in which church attendance fell, and the number of people willing to deny any religious affiliation rose. Minimal religious belief did not decline proportionately. The Catholic Church grew, but adherence to its moral teaching weakened. It was an age of enlightenment, measured by technological advance and the expansion of higher education. The universities contributed to political life a growing number of politicians, some eminent advisers to government and some sporadic student militancy, notably in 1968 and 1972. The rapid development of the social sciences improved but complicated our understanding of society, and contributed a good deal of vacuous mystification. It was not clear that society or crime were the better for the criminal who could blame his troubles on 'the subculture in which I was socialized', rather than old-fashioned original sin. One of the few challenges to the value of free speech came, curiously, from university radicals, armed with Marcuse's notion of 'repressive tolerance' (which meant that tolerance should not allow mistaken theories to flourish).

·The state had been a necessary liberating force – liberating in the sense of relieving the common people from the burden of poverty, ill health, deficient education and so on. The state remained a great liberating force, certainly for the left. New calls arose for the state to intervene, especially in the environment. This was a vogue word of the 1960s and 1970s which in 1970 provided a pretentious new title for the old Ministry of Housing and Local Government. The state's liberating mission was extended to combat pollution and ugliness.

However, new liberating movements were directed against the state itself, especially in the fields of technology and the environment. The new radicals were concerned for example with the damage wrought by high spending but careless governments, building motorways across back gardens or dumping nuclear waste in the countryside. An Ecology party fielded fifty-three candidates in the 1979 election, campaigning for a retreat from economic growth based on technology. This 'green revolution' was a liberation still to come. By 1980 governments were more sensitive to environmental considerations; but the twentieth-century state was not about to retreat from the business of promoting economic and social well-being.

Law and order; lawlessness and disorder

There was a tension in this period between law and order and lawlessness and disorder. This was more evident in the 1960s and 1970s than in the comparatively calmer period immediately following the war. In historical perspective it looks as if this pattern did not differ markedly from earlier periods, in which there had been similar tensions and swings between submissiveness and protest.

In early 1970 the Conservative Shadow Home Secretary accused the

Prime Minister (Wilson) of presiding over the biggest crime wave in history. This was true according to the statistics, but it had little to do with the Labour government, and indeed the statistical trends continued under the Conservatives. In any case, criminal statistics are difficult to interpret because they reflect police action against crime, not crime itself. Some points were clear. The prison population doubled in the period (making prison overcrowding, hence prison discipline, a serious problem by 1980). The number of police also rose, but short of doubling. Some crimes, notably crimes committed by young people and crimes involving violence against the person, increased; so too did motoring offences. Despite some terrifying predictions, the crime of murder did not rise sharply after the abandonment of the death penalty in 1965. But criminals and policemen carried – and used – guns more frequently.

At the same time violence on the street associated with political or trade union causes increased; and was much magnified by television. Minor political battles occurred at Saltley in 1972 (miners' strike); in the streets outside the Grunwick photo-processing works in 1977 (trade union recognition dispute); and in Southall in 1979 (immigration). The latter was a massive clash between the National Front, the Anti-Nazi League and the police Special Patrol Group, in which one demonstrator was killed. The provocation of violence was undoubtedly an objective of many who took part.

The law was occasionally defied, by trade union pickets and by trade unions themselves, resisting the Industrial Relations Act of 1972. Councillors at Clay Cross, Derbyshire, rebelled against the Conservative Housing Finance Act of 1972, and were subsequently indemnified by the Labour government in 1975. This lawlessness seemed to some to go with, even to spring from, the social revolutions described above under the heading of liberation.

One other element completed a picture of a society in disarray, falling into indiscipline and violence – international terrorism. Britain had its own source of terrorism in Northern Ireland, and this intruded from time to time on the mainland. But other incidents of shooting, bombing and hostage taking had little to do with the British government. In the most dramatic of these in the spring of 1980 an operation by the Special Air Service to release hostages in the Iranian Embassy in Princes Gate, London, was seen live on television. At a time when American diplomats were held hostage in Iran, it seemed that Britain's long retreat was over.

This was not true of course. Both at home and abroad the power to discipline wrongdoers had declined. According to surveys, concern about 'law and order' had grown in the 1970s, and the Conservatives, under Mrs Thatcher, were ready to appeal to such sentiments. In practice, there was not much to be done, except give large pay increases to the police and the armed forces, and shower public congratulations on the anonymous heroes of the siege of Princes Gate. The death penalty remained a matter for a free vote in the House of Commons, which still had a majority opposed to it.

But there were counterflows in the tide of law and order. Libertarians questioned police procedures, and a Police Complaints Board was established. A House of Commons Committee concluded that the 'suspicion' or 'sus' law (allowing arrest on mere suspicion) must be amended, and determined to introduce a Bill themselves, if the government would not do so. Revelations of widespread corruption in the police force, especially in London, undermined the authority of the police. Interrogation and prison processes in Northern Ireland, and the Prevention of Terrorism Act 1974, worried some who believed that even a murderous civil war should be conducted with regard to individual liberties.

Behind the tug-of-war over law and order lay two profound differences of principle, on the propriety of violence on behalf of the state; and on the sinfulness of criminals. On the first issue, the liberal (and perhaps the realist) believed that counter violence rarely achieved its ends, it just relieved people's anger. On the latter issue, the fashionable liberal teaching of the 1960s and 1970s (the kind of idea that was dubbed 'wet' by 1980) was that crime should generally be attributed to social conditions, poverty and deprivation, not to old-fashioned wickedness on the part of the criminal. This was especially urged in exculpation of crime committed by young coloured people. This theory, obviously partly true, may not have been much consolation to the old lady who had suffered purse-snatching with violence, which was known by its American name of 'mugging'.

The search for identity

In a splendid passage at the close of his book on English history, 1914–45, the historian, A. J. P. Taylor, wrote:

> In the second World War the British people came of age. This was a people's war. Not only were their needs considered. They themselves wanted to win . . . No English soldier who rode with the tanks into liberated Belgium or saw the German murder camps at Dachau or Buchenwald could doubt that the war had been a noble crusade. The British people were the only people who went through both world wars from beginning to end. Yet they remained a peaceful and civilized people, tolerant, patient and generous. Traditional values lost much of their force. Other values took their place. Imperial greatness was on the way out; the welfare state was on the way in. The British empire declined; the condition of the people improved. Few now sang 'Land of Hope and Glory'. Few even sang 'England Arise'. England had risen all the same. (Taylor, 1965, p. 600).

In 1945 Britons knew who they were, and where they stood – and they did not then suffer A. J. P. Taylor's ambivalence about England and Britain. They were British, and part of a well-founded structure of empire, government and society – or so it might have seemed. In the 1960s and 1970s, confusion replaced these certainties. The splendid booming patriotism of the wartime cinema newsreels was replaced by neutral and niggling television reports of peacetime failures. The empire had collapsed, the church weakened. Britain was newly perceived to be multi-national as well as multi-racial. Citizens were diminished as consumers and members of occupational groups. Politicians were professionals and activists, rather than parliamentary representatives. The British polity fragmented, and in the old imperial sense there was no easy answer to the citizen who cried 'who am I?'. A Princes Gate siege, or, in the summer of 1980, a ferry boat running a fishermen's blockade into Cherbourg, stirred old imperial memories. So, if it had ever happened again after 1966, would have an English – or even a Scottish – victory in World Cup football.

One institution throughout the period survived fragmentation, erosion, decline and, for the most part, derision – the monarchy. It was above politics, yet through its charisma and symbolism, it had a powerful part in supporting, indeed enhancing, the traditional institutions of government. Through television the nation participated in the great royal occasions – the funeral of George VI, the coronation of Elizabeth II (1953) and her Jubilee celebrations (1977), the Investiture of the Prince of Wales (1969 – an effective counter to Welsh nationalism), the birthdays and the weddings. The monarchy survived a royal divorce with equanimity. A loyal public took pleasure in a television serial account of the abdication crisis of 1936, which was at the time widely regarded as the beginning of the end of the monarchy.

The monarchy survived and prospered and yet changed a good deal. It was still an essentially aristocratic institution, the armed services its preferred profession, horses its favourite sport, and great wealth its undoubted privilege. But members of the Royal Family had more direct, if carefully managed contact with the public. The BBC concerned itself less with trivial royal activities, though it still voiced the nation's reverence on special occasions. Skilled public relations replaced the automatic assumptions of regality. In that respect royalty kept up with the times. The last great and ancient institution was professionalized; and professionalism strengthened its capacity to add a flavour of hope and glory to an imperial nation in decline.

Holders of major political office since 1940

Date General Election (or other date of formation)	Party	Prime Minister	Chancellor of the Exchequer	Foreign Secretary	Leader of Opposition
(1940) 10.5	Coalition	W. Churchill; other: C. Attlee, Deputy Prime Minister, 1942–5	Sir K. Wood; 24.9.43 Sir J. Anderson	22.12.40 A. Eden	
(1945) 23.5	'Caretaker'	W. Churchill	Sir J. Anderson	A. Eden	C. Attlee
1945 26.7 and 1950	Labour	C. Attlee; other: H. Morrison, Deputy PM, 1945–51; A. Bevan, Min. of Health, 1945–51	H. Dalton; 13.11.47 Sir S. Cripps; 19.10.50 H. Gaitskell	E. Bevin; 9.3.51 H. Morrison	W. Churchill
1951 26.10	Conservative	Sir W. Churchill	R. Butler	Sir A. Eden	C. Attlee
1955 6.4	Conservative	Sir A. Eden	20.12.55 H. Macmillan	7.4.55 H. Macmillan; 20.12.55 S. Lloyd	H. Gaitskell; other: A. Bevan
(1957) 10.1	Conservative	H. Macmillan	P. Thorneycroft; 6.1.58 D. Heathcoat Amory; 13.7.62 R. Maudling	27.7.60 E. of Home	
(1963) 18.10	Conservative	Sir A. Douglas-Home	R. Maudling	20.10.63 R. Butler	H. Wilson
1964 16.10 and 1966	Labour	H. Wilson	J. Callaghan; 30.11.67 R. Jenkins	P. Gordon Walker; 22.1.65 M. Stewart; 11.8.66 G. Brown; 16.3.68 M. Stewart	Sir A. Douglas-Home; E. Heath (1965)
1970 19.6	Conservative	E. Heath	I. Macleod; 25.7.70 A. Barber	Sir A. Douglas-Home	H. Wilson
1974 4.3	Labour	H. Wilson	D. Healey	J. Callaghan	E. Heath; M. Thatcher (1975)
(1976) 5.4	Labour	J. Callaghan	D. Healey	A. Crosland; 21.2.77 D. Owen	M. Thatcher
1979 4.5	Conservative	M. Thatcher	Sir G. Howe	Ld. Carrington	J. Callaghan; M. Foot (1980)

A gallery of leading politicians

These are the major actors in British politics since 1945. See index for references in the text.

CHURCHILL, Winston (Sir).   *Leader of the opposition 1945–51, Prime Minister 1951–5*

Historians should use the word 'great' sparingly; but few would deny it to Churchill's prime ministership 1940–5. His leadership (and for once that word too is appropriate) in 1940 stands out as an inspiration to fortitude, boldness even, in time of adversity. With the entry of Russia and America into the war in 1941 Churchill's lead was vindicated: Britain could win the war after all (as Churchill himself remarked).

In peace-time his achievements did not match the distinction of wartime. During the 1945 election campaign he likened the Labour party (his colleagues until recently in the coalition) to the Nazi enemy just defeated. In opposition he allowed the party's research department to think afresh about the party's programme, though he did not welcome the results. As Prime Minister again (at the age of 77) he clung to office despite grave illness and incapacity, hoping in vain that he could make a historic contribution to peace by 'summit' meetings with Stalin and the President of the USA. Nevertheless, these last years of decline could not tarnish his deservedly splendid reputation.

ATTLEE, Clement (Earl).   *Deputy Prime Minister in the wartime coalition 1940–5, Labour Prime Minister 1945–51*

His reputation has grown, though in his later years he was intrigued against by his colleagues, and bitterly denounced by his opponents. His reputation rests on his wartime office and the undeniable achievements of the Labour government – the nationalization measures; the establishment of the modern welfare state; the liberation of India; and (more controversially) the development of a foreign policy suited to the cold war. He was more fortunate than his successors in that the Labour party had a programme, and he carried it out. Even so, the programme was by no means clear, and the economic problems of the immediate post-war period were severe. His virtue, looking back, lay in a certain straightforwardness, the lack of personal theatricality and the deliberate avoidance of contrived 'public relations'. His socialism was moderate and pragmatic. His weakness lay in his failure to inspire or motivate.

BEVIN, Ernest. *Minister of Labour and National Service 1940–5, Foreign Secretary 1945–51*

By 1945 Bevin had a long career behind him, as a trade union leader and as Minister of Labour in the wartime coalition. He had taken a leading part in the establishment of the trade union movement as an 'estate of the realm', consulted and deferred to by government. In wartime he mobilized the people to a degree well beyond that achieved in Germany. As Foreign Secretary under Attlee he supported the USA in the diplomatic transformation which marked the opening of the 'cold war'. This reflected his own anti-communist views, and Britain's last few years as a great power. For that reason he may be regarded as the last of the great Foreign Secretaries. He was also one of the few genuinely working-class figures in post-war British politics.

BEVAN, Aneurin. *Minister of Health 1945–51, Minister of Labour and National Service 1951*

As Minister of Health in the Attlee government, he was the ministerial architect of the National Health Service. Though plans for such a service had been developed during the war it seems unlikely that such a comprehensive scheme would have been established with out Bevan's political drive and skill. He made substantial but not disastrous concessions to the doctors. After his resignation in 1951 over the rearmament programme, Bevan led, or at least inspired, the dissident Bevanite movement in the Labour party, which was particularly opposed to the rearmament of Western Germany. But he returned to the Shadow Cabinet in 1957 and specifically defended Britain's possession of nuclear weapons. Bevan was, for Labour audiences at least, an inspiring speaker with a gift for socialist philosophizing. The actual content of this socialism was imprecise – as with many of his colleagues. Bevan drew his inspiration from the 1930s and was less sure of his philosophy when the enemies of the 1930s – the dictators and unemployment – disappeared. His fiery socialism was harmless enough, but he made enemies, and became a favourite target for the Conservative press – a red bogey. With Enoch Powell on the right, Bevan was one of the most interesting figures in post-war politics.

GAITSKELL, Hugh. *Chancellor of the Exchequer 1950–1, leader of the opposition 1955–63*

The only leader of the opposition since 1945 (so far) not to go on to be Prime Minister. His career is nevertheless of high interest for the struggles within the Labour party in the 1950s for power and programme. His position was challenged by Morrison, an ageing senior politician by the 1950s, and by Bevan. His personal relations with Bevan were tense, sometimes turbulent, though they co-operated formally after 1957. Their political differences were in fact complex. Gaitskell, like Attlee, but unlike Wilson and Callaghan, came from a solid middle-class background. But, again like Attlee, he committed himself to serve the interests of the working classes. His career is marked by impassioned public stands, against Munich in 1938, against communist infiltration in 1952, against unilateral nuclear disarmament in 1960. On the central question of nationalization he seems, despite his ill-judged campaign against the constitutional commitment (clause IV of the Labour party's constitution), to have been a socialist, even a doctrinaire one. Bevan differed from him in temperament and style more than in principle. Wilson differed from them both in regarding principles as 'theology', a ground for wasteful disputation.

EDEN, Anthony (Sir, Lord Avon).   *Foreign Secretary 1940–5, 1951–5, Prime Minister 1955–7*

Made his reputation by resigning in 1938 in disagreement with Chamberlain's foreign policy (there is room for doubt whether he was fundamentally opposed to 'appeasement' or uneasy about one episode in that policy). Returned as Foreign Secretary for the whole of the war and as Churchill's heir-apparent afterwards. His belated and brief tenure of the prime ministership ended in ill-health and disarray after the failure of the Suez intervention.

BUTLER, R. A.   *Chancellor of the Exchequer 1951–5, Home Secretary 1957–62, Foreign Secretary 1963–4*

From the Conservative Research Department he made a significant contribution to the rebuilding of the post-war Conservative party after the morale-shattering defeat of 1945. As Chancellor, in Churchill's government 1951–5, his record was no more distinguished than that of most Chancellors since 1945, but he seems to have invented the first pre-election boom. Though heir-apparent to Eden, he was not chosen as Prime Minister in 1957 or 1963 through the private consultations then used by the Conservative party. An enigmatic figure in post-war politics.

MACMILLAN, Harold (Sir).   *Foreign Secretary 1955, Chancellor of the Exchequer 1955–7, Prime Minister 1957–63*

A wealthy man, with aristocratic connections, but formed by service on the Western Front in the 1914–18 war, and as MP for a constituency in the depressed Northeast in the 1920s and 1930s. He advocated a middle-of-the-road, 'one nation' Toryism, paternalistic but compassionate. Coming comparatively late to high office, he led the Cabinet retreat from Suez, and succeeded Eden a few weeks later. He might be regarded as the last successful Prime Minister – rallying the party after Suez, exploiting the affluence of the 1950s ('You never had it so good' he almost said) and leading an imperialist party away from empire ('the wind of change' is blowing in Africa). In later years his luck ran out, as the weakness of the economy began to show up. His solution was for Britain to join the EEC. Discontents, scandals and illness led to his sudden resignation in 1963, leaving the party less than fully prepared to choose a successor. Macmillan has sometimes been compared with Harold Wilson – two 'actor-managers', true politicians in their concern for holding a divisive party together – for the presentation as much as the substance of policy, for a fascination with overseas policy, and with power itself.

HOME, Alec Douglas (Sir). *Foreign Secretary 1960–3, Prime Minister 1963–4, leader of the opposition 1964–5, Foreign Secretary 1970–4*

Sir Alex as Lord Dunglass was Parliamentary Private Secretary to Chamberlain at the time of Munich in 1938. His career was not distinguished, partly because he was in the House of Lords. But in 1963 he burst into history as the unlikely choice of the Conservative Party to succeed Macmillan as Prime Minister. Better-known candidates, Butler, Hailsham, Maudling, were passed over. Two senior Conservatives, Macleod and Enoch Powell, refused to serve under Home, and Macleod later denounced the influence of a Tory 'magic circle' in the choice of leader. Harold Wilson, the Labour leader, was able to exploit Home's aristocratic birth and ignorance of economics. Even so, Home lost the 1964 election by just five seats. The following year, the Conservatives established a system of election for the party leader, and Home was replaced by Heath. It is rare for the Conservative party to have been so evidently and publicly in disarray.

WILSON, Harold (Sir). *Labour Prime Minister for eight years between 1964 and 1976, the longest of any post-war holders of the office*

His reputation rose quickly in the 1960s as a skilful leader of the Labour party, and declined as quickly in the 1970s because it was said he was a party leader, a trimmer, a politician, rather than a statesman. The judgement of history is likely to emphasize the difficulties of the times in which he governed, and the tendency to fragmentation of the party which he led. If Eden was the first Prime Minister to face Britain's external weakness, Wilson was the first to face the consequences of Britain's economic decline. Eden fell, Wilson survived. Three points stand out in Wilson's career: his failure to solve the Rhodesian problem; his bruising clash with the unions in 1969 ('In place of strife'); his deep interest in the instruments and processes of government – hence a spate of inquiries and reforms and his own writings on the subject.

JENKINS, Roy. *Home Secretary 1965–7 and 1974–6, Chancellor of the Exchequer 1967–70, deputy leader of the Labour party 1970–2*

Held all the great offices of state except that of Prime Minister. Resigned as deputy leader of the Labour party in 1972 over the party's commitment to a referendum on the EEC (he was an enthusiast for British membership of the EEC). Left British politics in 1977 to become President of the EEC Commission and returned in 1981 as an emerging leader of a new Social Democratic party. Highly regarded (in liberal circles at least) as a liberal Home Secretary, actively pursuing greater legal freedom in matters of private morality, or of what liberals regard as private morality – abortion, homosexuality; also reforms in criminal justice, for example, majority jury verdicts and suspended sentences. A tough Chancellor of the Exchequer with an unusually good personal grasp of economics and finance. Jenkins was a highly literate man, author of acclaimed political biographies. A Welsh miner's son, his later style did not suit the Labour party; his taste for claret and croquet came to be treated as a kind of treason of the working classes. He suffered the frustrations of many able men in politics, especially those who aspire to lead the Labour party.

HEATH, Edward.   *Prime Minister 1970–4 and leader of the Conservative party 1965–75*

His arrival and departure both illustrated the ruthlessness which the Conservatives sometimes exercised in the pursuit of power. He began his term of office as a right winger (the Selsdon programme) but trimmed and turned in face of industrial disasters – the collapse of Rolls-Royce, strikes in major industries. He made fashionable the 'U-turn' in politics, unfortunately as a term of abuse. His government was brought down in the election of February 1974, precipitated by a miners' strike, and he was defeated in the leadership contest in the following year by Margaret Thatcher.

POWELL, J. Enoch.   *Financial Secretary to the Treasury 1957–8, Minister of Health 1960–3*

One of the most impressive of all in this gallery of political leaders, yet one who left his mark on the period without ever attaining an office above that of Minister of Health. He was a man of the highest intellectual calibre; his speeches are among the few by politicians of the period which repay sustained attention. He was also a man of principle, a devout parliamentarian and a British nationalist. His views on economics, defence and the health service were always challenging. In 1958 he resigned along with two colleagues, in disagreement over excessive government expenditure. But it was his position on immigration and the EEC which finally separated him from the Conservative party. In 1969 he was dismissed from the Shadow Cabinet, in February 1974 he declined to stand in support of the Conservative platform and urged the country to vote Labour. Subsequently he was himself elected for South Down in Northern Ireland, a seat which gave him an opportunity to develop his nationalist view of the United Kingdom.

He was best known for his opposition to immigration, and for the dramatic (some thought over-dramatic) speeches in which he saw Britain 'eroded and hollowed out from within by the implantation of a large unassimilated and unassimilable populations – what Lord Radcliffe once in a memorable phrase called "alien wedges" – in the heartland of the state' (speech, April 1976). But his opposition to British membership of the EEC was equally impassioned. In both these attitudes he reflected a substantial streak of popular (but less passionate and less intellectual) opinion.

CALLAGHAN James. *Chancellor of the Exchequer 1964–7, Home Secretary 1967–70, Foreign Secretary 1974–6, Prime Minister 1976–9*

Held all the major offices of state. As Chancellor, associated with the policy of avoiding devaluation, but finally carried it through. Originally a trade union official (and not a university graduate), he sided with the trade unions in the 'In place of strife' dispute in 1969. But he was not on the left of the party. As Prime Minister he presided over a right wing policy, combining control of the money supply, cuts in public expenditure and an incomes policy. His government was in a minority from 1977 and fell in 1979 after the 'winter of discontent' (militant trade union opposition to incomes restraint). His moderate, avuncular style did not suit the Labour party activists of the 1970s; but those who wanted government from the centre regarded the years 1977–9 as the best in the recent history of the government of Britain. In his later years, he was regarded as 'decent' rather than 'great', and more critically as a 'fudger' rather than a leader; these judgements implied that in difficult times, decency was the preferred quality, and even fudging might be preferable to sharp decision.

Supporting Players

There are many other figures with a claim to appear in this gallery. *Sir Stafford Cripps*, Chancellor of the Exchequer 1947–50, had the most successful incomes policy of all the post-war Chancellors. His style was austere and reflected his own profound religious convictions; and he was not without response in a people given to bouts of puritanism. *Herbert Morrison* had a long and distinguished career as leader of the old London County Council, and as a Cabinet minister from 1940 to 1951 (with one small break), and Deputy Prime Minister 1945–51. He appears in these pages as a moderate socialist, resisting proposals for nationalization. Like everyone mentioned here, he was not devoid of honourable ambition; and he was disappointed when Attlee clung on to the leadership of the Labour party long enough to secure the succession of the young Gaitskell. *Denis Healey* had a distinguished career in two difficult Cabinet posts, Defence (1964–70), Chancellor of the Exchequer (1974–9). His contribution to the sheer hard work of governing the country is probably as great as any other senior minister. In the more dramatic and glamorous politics of leadership he was (to 1981) less successful. As a Prime Minister *manqué* he is in good and numerous company here. *Mrs Margaret Thatcher* belongs in this gallery, and in history, as the first woman Prime Minister in Britain, and as the leader of the swing to the right after the 1979 election. But it is premature to go beyond that.

A statistical portrait of Britain in the period 1945–80

	Beginning[a] of period	*End of[a] period*	*Percentage change*	*Earlier Period for comparison*
Demographic				
Population[b] (millions)	50.6 (1951)	55.9 (1977)	11	41.5 (1901)[c]
Fertility[d]				
(children per mother)	2.14 (1951)	1.68 (1978)	−12	—
Age of marriage[d]				
Men	26.8 (1951)	25.1 (1977)	−6	26.9 (1901–5)
Women	24.4 (1951)	22.9 (1977)	−6	25.4 (1901–5)
Ageing of the population				
(% over 65)	10.9 (1951)	14.5 (1977)	33	5 (1901)
Life expectancy (at birth)				
Men	66 (1951)	69 (1974)	5	46 (1900–2)
Women	71 (1951)	76 (1974)	7	50 (1900–2)
Infant mortality (deaths in first year per 1000 births	50 (1945)	14.1 (1977)	−72	142 (1900)[c]
Divorces (total granted; thousands)	31 (1951)	136 (1976)	339	0.8 (1910)
Illegitimacy (% of live births)	5.0 (1950–2)	9.0 (1976)	80	4.3 (1900–2)
Deaths from certain causes[b]				
Tuberculosis	24,003 (1949)	1167 (1977)	−95	50,708 (1922)
Diphtheria	108 (1949)	0 (1977)	−100	4746 (1922)
Cancer	92,214 (1949)	142,874 (1977)	55	54,307 (1922)
Motor vehicle accident	4388 (1949)	7014 (1977)	60	—
Suicide	5074 (1949)	4468 (1977)	12	4209 (1922)
Economy				
Purchasing power of the pound[b] (1945 = £1.00)	£1.00 (1945)	14½p (1978)	−86	£2.92½ (1900)
Energy consumption[b] (metric tonnes coal equivalent)				
Total	221.0 (1950)	306.5 (1975)	39	—
Solid fuels	200.7 (1950)	116.7 (1975)	−58	—
Liquid fuels	80.1 (1950)	137.8 (1975)	72	—
Natural gas	0.1 (1960)	47.2 (1975)	471	—
Hydro and nuclear	0.2 (1950)	4.7 (1975)	23	—
Per capita (kilograms)	4358 (1950)	5464 (1975)	25	—
Passenger transport (1000 million passenger kilometres)				
Air	0.2 (1951)	2.1 (1977)	950	—

	Beginning[a] of period	End of[a] period	Percentage change	Earlier Period for comparison
Rail	39 (1951)	34 (1977)	–13	—
Road				
public	83 (1951)	53 (1977)	–36	—
private	57 (1951)	376 (1977)	560	—
bicycle	20.8 (1951)	4.0 (1977)	–81	—

Social welfare

	Beginning of period	End of period	Percentage change	Earlier Period for comparison
Public expenditure (selected services £ million)				
Social security	707 (1951)	15,441 (1978–9)	2084	—
NHS and welfare services	498 (1951)	8980 (1978–9)	1700	—
Education	398 (1951)	8702 (1978–9)	2086	—
The arts, libraries and museums	13 (1951)	387 (1978–9)	2877	—
Defence and external relations	1411 (1951)	9251 (1978–9)	556	—
Total	5830 (1951)	67,682 (1978–9)	1061	—
Public expenditure (selected services as % of total)				
Social security	12.1 (1951)	22.8 (1978–9)	88	—
NHS and welfare services	10.2 (1951)	13.3 (1978–9)	30	—
Education	6.8 (1951)	12.9 (1978–9)	90	—
Housing (%)				
Owner-occupied	26 (1947)	53 (1976)	104	—
Local authority	13 (1947)	32 (1976)	146	—
Rented privately	61 (1947)	15 (1976)	-75	—
Education (% receiving full-time education)				
10-year-olds	100 (1938)	100 (1975)	0	100 (1902)
14-year-olds	38 (1938)	100 (1975)	163	9 (1902)
17-year-olds	4 (1938)	28 (1975)	600	2 (1902)
19-year-olds	2 (1938)	16 (1975)	700	1 (1902)
Higher education (full-time students, thousands)				
University	82 (1945–5)	279 (1976–7)[b]	240	20 (1900–1)
Teacher training	28 (1954–5)	246 (1976–7)	515	45 (1900–1)
Further Education (advanced courses only)	12 (1954–5)			—

	Beginning[a] of period	*End of[a] period*	*Percentage change*	*Earlier Period for comparison*
Work and wealth				
Occupation (selected industries, thousands) Agriculture, forestry, fishing				
Men	1131 (1951)	283 (1976)	−75	1390 (1900)
Women	114 (1951)	99 (1976)	−13	67 (1900)
Total	1145 (1951)	382 (1976)	−67	1457 (1900)
Mining and Quarrying				
Men	675 (1951)	331 (1976)	−51	931 (1900)
Women	2 (1951)	15 (1976)	650	6 (1900)
Total	677 (1951)	346 (1976)	−49	937 (1900)
Textiles, clothing and textile goods				
Men	355 (1951)	352 (1976)	−1	980 (1900)
Women	887 (1951)	482 (1976)	−46	1587 (1900)
Total	1242 (1951)	834 (1976)	−33	2767 (1900)
Public sector employment (% of workforce)				
Total public sector	24.3 (1950)	29.7 (1977)	22	5.8 (1901)
Central government	4.8 (1950)	8.0 (1977)	66	1.0 (1901)
Armed forces	3.0 (1950)	1.2 (1977)	−60	2.5 (1901)
Local authorities	6.2 (1950)	12.0 (1977)	94	2.3 (1901)
Public corporations	10.3 (1950)	8.4 (1977)	−18	n.a.
Occupational structure (% of workforce) Employers and				
proprietors	5.0 (1951)	2.6 (1971)	−48	6.7 (1911)
White-collar workers	30.9 (1951)	42.7 (1971)	38	18.7 (1911)
Manual workers	64.2 (1951)	54.7 (1971)	−15	74.6 (1911)
Domestic servants (thousands)	499 (1951)	239 (1971)	−52	1390 (1921)
Married women in the labour force (as % of all married women)	21.7 (1951)	47.9 (1975)	121	9.6 (1911)
Real personal disposable income[b] (standardized with 1948 = 100)	100 (1948)	240 (1979)	140	—
Distribution of wealth (% of total wealth owned by top:)				
1%	42.0 (1951–6)[d]	24.3 (1976)[b]	−42	65.5 (1911–13)[d]
5%	56.7 (1951–6)[d]	48.8 (1976)[b]	−14	86.0 (1911–13)[d]
10%	76.8 (1951–6)[d]	65.3 (1976)[b]	−15	90.0 (1911–13)[d]

	Beginning[a] of period	End of[a] period	Percentage change	Earlier Period for comparison
Trade union membership (% of all employees				
Men	53 (1948)	61 (1976)	15	—
Women	26 (1948)	38 (1976)	46	—
Total	44.1 (1951)	49.6 (1974)	11	12.6 (1901)
White-collar unionism (% of all employees)				
White-collar	30.2 (1948)	39.1 (1974)	29	—
Manual	50.7 (1948)	57.9 (1974)	14	—
Leisure				
Holidays (millions)				
In Great Britain	25 (1951)	39 (1978)	56	—
Abroad	2 (1951)	9 (1978)	350	—
Total	27 (1951)	48 (1978)	78	— `
Paid holidays[b] (% of all full-time manual workers entitled to holiday with pay of:)				
2 weeks or less	97 (1960)	1 (1975)	−99	—
2 to 3 weeks	1 (1960)	1 (1975)	0	—
3 weeks	2 (1960)	17 (1975)	750	—
3 to 4 weeks	— (1960)	50 (1975)	infinite	—
4 weeks or more	— (1960)	30 (1975)	infinite	—
Motor vehicles in use (thousands)				
Cars	1770 (1946)	13,497 (1973)	663	8.5 (1904)
Total vehicles	3107 (1946)	17,014 (1973)	648	17.8 (1904)
TV licences millions)	1.5 (1951)	18.0 (1978)	1100	n.a.
Crime				
Serious offences[d] recorded by police, thousands)				
Burglary, robbery etc.	514 (1951)	2226 (1977)	333	—
Violence against persons	7 (1951)	82 (1977)	1071	—
Sexual offences	15 (1951)	21 (1977)	40	—
Criminal damage	5 (1951)	124 (1977)	2380	—
Other	6 (1951)	10 (1977)	67	—
Total	547 (1951)	2463 (1977)	350	—

Notes
[a] Actual dates appear in parenthesis. Tables refer to Great Britain unless indicated otherwise.
[b] United Kingdom
[c] Includes Southern Ireland
[d] England and Wales

Sources

Abrams, P., 1978. *Work Urbanisation and Inequality*, Weidenfeld and Nicolson

Annual Abstract of Statistics, HMSO

Annual Reports of the Registrar General for England and Wales, HMSO

Basic Road Statistics, 1971. British Road Federation

Butler, D. and Sloman, A., 1980. *British Political Facts 1900–1979*, Macmillan

Central Statistical Office, 1958- . *Economic Trends*, HMSO

   1970- . *Social Trends*, HMSO

   1974. *Facts in Focus*, Penguin

Employment, Dept of, 1971. *British Labour Statistics Historical Abstract 1886–1968*, HMSO

   1978. *British Labour Statistics Year Book 1976*, HMSO

Halsey, A. H., 1972. *Trends in British Society Since 1900*, Macmillan

Hansard, 9 May 1978. p. 487

Hey, J. D., 1979. *Britain in Context*, Blackwell

Marsh, D., 1965. *Changing Social Structure of England and Wales 1871–1951*, Routledge and Kegan Paul

OPCS, 1975- . *Population Trends*, HMSO

'Robbins Report': Committee of Higher Education, Cmnd 2154, HMSO, 1963

Silitoe, A. F., 1971. *Britain in Figures*, Pelican

United Nations, 1976. *World Energy Supplies*

2 The economy since 1945: trends and outline

1 Long-run trends

It is in the nature of short accounts of large and complex events that much is left out. It is certainly so in the following brief treatment of the British economy in the crowded first three decades or so after the Second World War. What is left out, however, necessarily colours the account: it is one among the many unavoidable sources of bias in historical writing. For this reason it seems worth specifying that the major criterion here used to decide what to include and what to omit was the relevance of particular people, events and policies to a small number of general trends. It is these trends, therefore, which are seen as the ultimate summaries of Britain's post-war economic experience.

Rising prices

What are these trends? There are four. Or, at least, four have been selected and will be listed with a few brief comments. The first is the general trend in the level of prices. This has been more or less continuously upwards since the war, so much so that to most people rising prices now seem an unavoidable, almost a natural, phenomenon. From such a perspective, indeed, the tendency of prices to rise hardly seems worthy of comment, much less worth singling out as a major economic characteristic of post-war Britain. It is of the utmost importance, however, to realize that such a long and persistent period of increasing prices (over four full decades) was a novel experience for modern, industrialized Britain. During the century and a half before 1940 there had, indeed, been periods in which prices rose: but these had never been so long and had always been followed by years in which prices fell. Measurement over such a lengthy period raises severe conceptual problems which are compounded by serious data deficiencies for the eighteenth and much of the nineteenth centuries: but if the overall trend of prices over these 150 years or so was upwards it was only to a modest degree. Thus for a period of at least four or five generations before the 1940s it was a reasonable expectation for people that, despite short-term fluctuations up and down, the long-run level of prices would be basically stable: the ending of such an era constitutes a major change. Perhaps more particular (and more pertinent) for assessing the significance of the rising trend since the 1940s is the need to realize that the overall direction of prices during the immediately preceding inter-war period was downwards. A whole generation – more than a whole generation – has now grown up without any experience of a falling price level. That is an important fact which requires explanation and which itself helps to explain other economic and social aspects of post-war Britain.

Unemployment

The inflationary trend seemed to become gradually more marked as time went on, and especially with the heavy price rises of the 1970s. The second trend, however, was one which although it ruled almost unabated until about 1970 thereafter became less decisive and, indeed, was widely challenged. Still, there was no doubting the fact that for at least a quarter century after the war Britain experienced exceptionally low levels of unemployment. Again, the significance of the post-war period as a period of low unemployment can only be grasped in relation to the experience of the past, and especially to the experience of the inter-war years. From 1923, when reasonably comprehensive figures first became available, until 1939 the annual percentage of insured workers who were unemployed never fell below ten and the average level for the whole period was 14.1 per cent. In contrast, from 1945 to 1970 the annual level of unemployment only once (in, as we shall see, the especially difficult circumstances of 1947) reached as high as 3 per cent, and the average for that quarter-century was only 1.9 per cent. Even in the 1970s, when unemployment re-emerged as a serious social problem, the highest annual figure was 6.2 (in 1977 and 1978) and the average level was 4.3 per cent. Associated with the high and stable level of post-war employment was an almost continuous annual increase in the total level of output until at least the early 1970s. This more or less persistent tendency for the real national income to rise from year to year represented, however, a much less sharp break with previous experience and hence hardly qualifies in itself as a distinctive trend in the post-1945 economy (See Feinstein, 1977, tables 6 and 8).

Government activity

For most people a more obvious and decisive trend was the tendency for government involvement in the economy to increase. In a broad sense there is little doubt that there was such a trend, at least to the end of the 1970s, but a few cautionary comments are also required. It is a process which it is impossible to measure with any precision and objectivity. Thus use has been made of a measure of total government expenditure as a proportion of gross national product to serve as an indicator of the part played by the government in the economy. But, apart from the considerable difficulties involved in making this measure, there is acute disagreement over what it means. Some (notably Bacon and Ellis, 1976) parade it as a horrifying illustration of the extent to which the government drains off most of the country's income; others argue that large parts of government expenditure merely represent transfer payments (like pensions and payments to service the national debt) which result in income passing from one group of private citizens to another group. It is argued that such transfers are only obliquely related to the part played by the government in the economy. Similar differences of definitions and interpretations surround other proxy measures, such as the number employed in the public sector as a proportion of the total numbers employed. On this basis, some suggest that the growth in the number of civil servants has sucked labour from 'productive' work, whilst others counter that, on this definition, many in the private sector are 'unproductive' whilst many government employees would be 'productive', even on this narrow definition of the term.

Moreover, there is one particular – but acute – problem in trying to demonstrate an upward trend in government activity during the post-war years: at the beginning of this period in 1945 there was already a very high level of government participation. This is not surprising: one of the few relative certainties in this field is the positive statistical connection between war and government activity. The long-run upward trend in government expenditure has taken the form of relatively steady or gently rising periods punctuated by big leaps forward, and the big upward leaps have mostly been associated with wars. Two of these wars – the major conflict of 1939–45 and the Korean War starting in 1950 – occurred before or near the start of our period in 1945 and had the effect of powerfully increasing government expenditure and activity. They were each followed by a period in which government involvement diminished. The scale and timing of these fluctuations add to the problems of measurement and make it impossible to discern any single, simple trend in the level of government activity in the post-war years.

The fact is that the reality of the process largely eludes precise measurement: it is to be found in the intangibles of time. No one comparing the inter-war years with those after 1945 could doubt that the government has come to take an altogether greater part in the economy and society, even if it were impossible to attach any exact measure to the increase. The whole range of activities had been widened in ways which are disguised when attention is directed just at the broad heads of government expenditure. It is not simply that more money is spent, but what is included under each of the broad heads of expenditure can be enormously altered over time. Thus regular government expenditure on education goes back to the first half of the nineteenth century but as late as 1900 it was still overwhelmingly restricted to primary (elementary) education. Apart from the expansion to secondary schools, most of the significant extensions into nursery and, especially, the wide variety of higher education (universities, polytechnics, further education colleges, and colleges of education and agriculture) has been a post-1945 development. In addition, the range of government activities has been even more significantly widened through the general expectation, which did not exist before 1939, that the government could and should exercise a general control over the economy. It was this acceptance, by governments and governed, that governments had a duty to intervene that represented the new trend which developed through the period and was not challenged until the last years.

The structure of the economy

The fourth and final characteristic which has been singled out for comment is the broad structural change in the economy. This is really a bundle of related tendencies which can be briefly indicated. First there are the changes in the actual industrial structure such as the sharp decline in the importance of industries like cotton and coal-mining and the rise in the relative importance of such industries as electrical engineering and motor vehicles. A second strand has been a shift in the relative importance of the broad sectors of employment. A very rough indication of the trend is conveyed by table 2.1

Table 2.1 Distribution of employment, 1949 and 1978

| | 1949 | | 1978 | |
	No. m.	*Per cent*	*No. m.*	*Per cent*
Primary	2.1	10	0.7	3
Secondary	10.1	47	8.9	40
Tertiary	9.6	44	13.1	58

Source: *Annual Abstracts of Statistics*

Thus the number engaged in so-called primary industries (mainly agriculture, fishing and mining) had declined both absolutely and relatively; the number engaged in secondary industries (roughly manufacturing, building, gas, electricity and water) has also declined in absolute and relative terms; but the number engaged in the tertiary service industries (distribution, insurance, banking, professional and scientific services, catering, local and national government) has risen both absolutely and relatively. The final structural tendency has been for the total workforce to grow only very slowly but for the proportion of women in the workforce to rise from 33 per cent to just over 40 per cent. In effect, the number of males in employment in the late 1970s was almost the same as it had been in the late 1940s: the only increase in the labour force had come from the additional number of women at work (there were 6.9 million women employees in mid-1948 and 9.4 million in mid-1978). Taken together, these three facets have meant that the years since 1945 have seen very substantial shifts in the overall structure of the British economy.

2 The economic effects of war

The story of the post-war economy will thus take as background the four major trends which have been outlined: rising prices; low unemployment at least into the 1970s; an extension of government activity; and shifts in the basic economic structure. In 1945 itself, however, the economy was more affected by the relatively short-term, but very severe, effects of war. Most of these were connected to, or derived from, one or other of two fundamental aspects: the extent to which resources within the economy were diverted towards war needs; and the extent to which Britain's external position (trade and investment overseas) was allowed to deteriorate during the war. It is generally agreed that the British economy was as completely transformed to a war footing as were the economies of any of the other belligerent nations, perhaps more so. This process, after a slow start during the period of the so-called 'phoney war' up to mid-1940, reached its peak in 1943. Thereafter as eventual victory seemed more and more likely there was, with the unenthusiastic concurrence of the Americans, some relaxation to allow the British economy to begin the readjustments necessary for peace.

Less obvious, but in many respects much more damaging, was the multiple erosion of Britain's external position. Exports fell but were not matched by comparable reductions in imports; overseas assets to the value of £1.2 billion were sold; gold resources were reduced; and in addition a large part of the expenditure of British troops abroad was simply met by piling up debts with countries like India, Burma and Egypt. Substantial grants (£5.4 billion) from the USA and Canada helped to ease the situation. Despite this generosity the simple inescapable fact was that the war had significantly eroded Britain's financial assets overseas whilst at the same time considerably increasing her external financial obligations. The implications of this have not perhaps been sufficiently noted and commented upon. But it is not too much to say that one of the corner-stones of the British economy in the nineteenth century – and, indeed, the first four decades of the twentieth – had been its position as a major international creditor: for a time after the war Britain was a net debtor. Such a sharp reversal of a position which had lasted for well over a century was bound to have important repercussions.

Before any attempt is made to trace these repercussions, however, it is necessary to provide a brief narrative of economic developments in Britain since 1945. The various trends and influences which have been identified operated in different ways and to different degrees depending on the particular historic context within which they operated: thus some chronological outline is essential to understanding.

3 1945–50: post-war problems and recovery

The ending of lend-lease and the US–Canadian loan

By 1945 the British war effort, in the sense of the extent of the nation's total resources which were devoted directly to war needs, had already passed its peak. From 1944 onwards ultimate military victory had become reasonably certain. The intention then was to shift the economy gradually towards a peacetime footing, to enable Britain to pay for her import needs by her own exports instead of relying on lend-lease aid from the USA. The lend-lease arrangements dated back to 1941 (before the official entry of the USA into the war) and essentially became a scheme which allowed Britain to secure supplies from America without having to pay for them in dollars or exports.

The transitional period during which lend-lease was to be reduced was expected to be lengthy, running from 1944 to the end of hostilities not just in Europe but in the Far East; and the war with Japan was expected to last for something like two years after victory in Europe. In the event, however, the use of the atomic bomb at Hiroshima ended the Japanese war only three months after the close of the European conflict. One of the unfortunate side-effects of this abrupt conclusion was the halting, almost literally over-night, of American aid to Britain. President Truman's decision to make an immediate cut in lend-lease threatened to undermine Britain's economic recovery since Britain was manifestly unable to pay for all the essential imported supplies.

Such disruption was almost beyond contemplation. Instead the government attempted to fill the gap by borrowing from the USA and Canada. The negotiation and parliamentary justification of these loans was the last great public service of the economist Lord Keynes. The American loan aroused much resentment in Britain where one Conservative rebel, Robert Boothby, described it as selling 'the British Empire for a packet of cigarettes'. It was not that the financial terms were harsh; the $3,750 million were to be repaid over fifty years at only 2 per cent interest and the first payment was delayed for five years. It was rather that many felt that a loan was inappropriate. Britain's plight had arisen from the greater degree, given the relative size of her economy, of her commitment to the common military cause, and from the unforeseen rapidity of the ending of lend-lease aid. Keynes exerted all his skill and charm to induce a more generous response from the Americans, but without success. Apart from their domestic political problems, the American negotiators seemed deeply suspicious that Britain wanted the funds simply to build up reserves and to restore the British empire as a rival economic power-bloc: it was not realized how totally the war had denuded Britain of external assets.

In any event the terms of the loan had included a major political condition: the immediate ratification by Britain of the Bretton Woods Agreement, which set out the methods and institutions for the future conduct of international trade and finance. These included the International Monetary Fund (IMF) which helped with balance of payments problems, but on strict conditions. At one level the formal ratification of the agreement raised no great problems since Britain, represented by Keynes, had played an important part in the negotiations at Bretton Woods in 1944 and favoured the basic principles of the agreement. At another, more practical, level, however, the exaction was alarming: the Americans insisted on the early implementation by Britain of the clauses calling for free currency convertibility (i.e. the unrestricted exchange of pounds sterling for dollars) and a rapid removal of restrictions on external trade. Britain had to put into effect the rules of the IMF not later than one year from the time – July 1946 – at which the agreement was ratified by Congress.

Document 2.1
The American loan of 1945: three comments

(a)   Viscount Simon, H L Deb., 17 Dec, 1945.

But whatever may be said as to the urgency of dollar provision, and however persuasively the noble Lord puts these documents before us, here is the plain fact: that I do not suppose there ever has been a very important international Agreement put before Parliament for acceptance in which it was found that the conditions attached to the Agreement aroused in this country such deep anxiety and such widespread distrust. I should doubt whether it has ever happened before. You may say of it, as Wordsworth said about the lovely village maiden, that it is a case where

. . . there are none to praise,
And very few to love . . .

Now we are told that some of our American friends are surprised at our disappointment.

(b)   Robert Boothby, HC Deb., 19 July 1946

I think we must realize on both sides of the House, whether we think it is a good idea to accept the Loan or not, that the obligation to accept full convertibility of sterling within one year from now, from which there is no escape, is bound to impose a heavy strain and burden upon us in this country. When we are all waving our hats in the air about American films and Virginian cigarettes, and that little bit of extra petrol, I think we ought constantly to bear in mind the situation which will confront us one year hence, when we take the first plunge into the icy sea of convertibility and free trade . . . In those circumstances, we shall be driven to increase the volume of our exports from this country not, as I see it, by 75 per cent above the 1938 level, but by at least 100 per cent if we are going to get through – and that under conditions of free currency convertibility, un-planned promiscuous trade, and cut throat competition . . .

(c) Lord Keynes, HL Deb., 18 Dec. 1945

I must, at this point, digress for a moment to explain the American response to our claim that for good reasons arising out of the past they owe us something more than they have yet paid, something in the nature of deferred lend lease for the time when we held the fort alone, for it was here that in expounding our case we had an early and severe disappoint-ment. It would be quite wrong to suppose that such considerations have played no part in the final results. They have played a vital part; we could never have obtained what we did obtain except against this background. Nevertheless, it was not very long before the British delegation dis-covered that a primary emphasis on past services and past sacrifice would not be fruitful. The American Congress and the American people have never accepted any literal principle of equal sacrifice, financial or otherwise, between all the allied participants. Indeed, have we our-selves? . . .

   . . . We soon discovered, therefore, that it was not our past performance or our present weakness but our future prospects of recovery and our intention to face the world boldly that we had to demonstrate. Our American friends were interested not in our wounds, though incurred in the common cause, but in our convalescence. They wanted to under-stand the size of our immediate financial difficulties, to be convinced that they were temporary and manageable and to be told that we intended to walk without bandages as soon as possible. In every circle in which I moved during my stay in Washington, it was when I was able to enlarge on the strength of our future competitive position, if only we were allowed a breather, that I won most sympathy. What the United States needs and desires is a strong Britain, endowed with renewed strength and facing the world on the equal or more than equal terms that we were wont to do. To help that forward interests them much more than to comfort a war victim.

The crisis of 1947

The attempt to meet the obligations imposed by the American loan led more or less directly to the major economic crisis of 1947, and also ensured that the benefit which the British economy derived from the loan was small and brief. The reason for this was that the pound could only reasonably be made convertible if a) Britain's overall balance of payments was not in deficit (and/or Britain held large reserves of gold or generally acceptable foreign exchange), and b) those countries trading with Britain were willing to hold sterling. Neither of these conditions prevailed. The overriding reality of the international economy in 1947, and for some years to come, was that for many of the goods needed for post-war restoration, the USA was the major source of supply and hence virtually all countries were desperately short of dollars. Making the pound convertible simply meant that any foreign holder, or earner, of sterling immediately converted these funds into dollars which Britain had to supply at the official rate (which itself overvalued sterling). Further, making sterling convertible was a unilateral act: the currencies of other countries were not convertible into dollars. Much of the American loan, therefore, was simply channelled via Britain to third countries. Under such conditions Britain's enforced 'dash for convertibility' in July 1947 could not last. It was, indeed, abandoned after five weeks but in the process many of the dollars needed for economic restoration had disappeared into the sand.

The crisis of 1947 was not, however, created only by convertibility. Imports from the USA exceeded exports and the dollar loan was used to plug the gap. Of course, this is what the loan had been intended for: but the size of the gap was much greater than expected so the loan was clearly not, as intended, going to cover Britain's trading deficits over a crucial three years. It was this fundamental imbalance in the external account which was the vital problem, but the position was also worsened at a critical time by the exceptionally severe winter of early 1947. It is not easy to recall the crushing impact of what was, up to then, the worst weather of the century upon an economy that was already acutely short of fuel. Street lamps were dowsed, transport largely halted, the domestic use of electricity was banned during the day (except for a couple of hours at midday). Above all many factories were closed because of lack of coal, thus causing substantial industrial disruption and – for the only time in the post-war period (until 1980) – driving unemployment, briefly, above 2 million in February.

The need for controls: the use of fiscal policy

The economic crisis of 1947 was significant for several reasons. It was the first of many such occasions. It set a pattern in that the immediate cause of the crisis was an acute balance of payments problem. It also set a pattern in that the response was to introduce an autumn budget – again the first of many – to curb the domestic level of activity. Above all, it induced the first glimmerings of realization that the nature of the long-run economic problem to be faced was not one of slump and deflation, but one of preventing an economy with a high level of activity from leading to an excessive demand for imports (thus causing balance of payments deficits) and inflationary pressures.

Something of this had already emerged. In a number of respects the strength of demand had meant that wartime restrictions, which were in general being cautiously eased, had to be not merely maintained but extended. In the spring of 1946 the weekly ration of butter, margarine and cooking-fat was reduced below its wartime level; in July bread rationing, avoided during the war, was introduced; in 1947 potato rationing, also avoided during the war, was accepted, as was the attempt to impose a peacetime direction of labour. It is against this background that judgement has to be made on the comment sometimes offered that Britain's trade gap in 1947 need not have been so large if the government had curbed home consumption earlier. To have done so would have been psychologically and politically difficult; as perhaps, for different reasons, would have the other main possibility of easement – cutting down on the costs of military expenditure overseas.

The extensive use of controls during these immediate postwar years reflected in part the unavoidable shortages arising from wartime dislocation. It also reflected in part the tendency for a Labour government to be less repelled by the use of direct controls. But it reflected, in addition, a realization of the necessity to deal with the problems of a tight economy, a realization which produced gradual shifts in economic policy. The clearest indicators that the economy was working with, in the phrase fashionable in the 1950s, a high pressure of steam in the boiler were the trends in prices and wages. Between 1945 and 1951 – roughly the period of the first post-war Labour government – manufacturing wage-rates rose by just under, and retail prices by just over, 35 per cent (*British Economy: Key Statistics, 1900–66*). The continuing successful commitment to full employment and a high level of activity in the economy made upward pressure on wages and prices more or less unavoidable. Low unemployment meant that labour was relatively scarce and hence tended to push up wages; high activity meant that the general level of demand was strong, and this tended to push up prices.

The main policy change used to contain these tendencies dated from 1947, and concerned fiscal policy. Very crudely this was the attempt by the government to use its budget to control the economy, and has become associated with Keynesianism. If the total level of demand in the economy was expected to be below that which was desired (say to maintain full employment) then the government would run a deficit on its budget: the expenditure by the government of greater sums than it received in revenue (taxes etc.) would increase the total level of demand and so raise employment. If the total level of demand was considered to be too high (simply pushing up prices rather than output) the government would run a budget surplus: the excess revenue would reduce the total level of demand. During the war the excessive demand upon resources had been so vast as to be well beyond budgetary control and was contained by a wide variety of direct measures (rationing, food subsidies, price controls etc.). The position changed gradually in 1945 and 1946, mostly by reductions in government expenditure, but the government only cautiously reduced the size of the (inflationary) budget deficits because there was still much expectation of a post-war slump (such as that which set in after the First World War from late 1920). The budget of April 1947 thus made relatively little change so that the crisis of the summer of 1947 was aggravated by a high level of demand. The switch in policy was signalled by the Chancellor, Hugh Dalton, in his emergency budget of November 1947 which instituted a betting tax, sharply raised purchase tax and increased the tax on distributed profits. All this led, as it was intended, to a large budget surplus. But Dalton has generally been given little credit for initiating the shift to a policy of restraining activity to meet the newly-emerging problem of inflation – largely because his November budget was also the occasion of his resignation over a minor leak of information.

Reliance upon the use of fiscal policy to control the economy was enthusiastically taken over by Sir Stafford Cripps who succeeded Dalton as Chancellor. He continued to aim at budget surpluses in order to keep down the level of internal demand. Cripps, moreoever, combined these fiscal impositions with fervent appeals for voluntary restraint, especially by unions seeking wage increases. These pleas were surprisingly successful – perhaps because Sir Stafford Cripps managed to make them sound like moral imperatives. At all events, despite a highly favourable labour market wages actually rose (5 per cent) more slowly than prices (8 per cent) between 1948 and the autumn of 1950. Despite all these limitations, however, and despite some strong additional favourable factors it was still not possible to avoid a crisis induced by the external weakness of the economy. Such a crisis occurred in 1949.

American aid and the 1949 devaluation

There were two additional favourable factors which were directly helpful for Britain's trading position at this time. The first was the provision of aid by the USA. In July 1947 the USA had obliged Britain to attempt an unrealizable currency convertibility, which seemed to suggest that America was absurdly optimistic about the pace of post-war recovery; but already in

June General George Marshall, as Secretary of State, had offered American aid to Europe on a scale that clearly indicated American recognition of the enormity of the problem of European economic recovery. There was naturally a warm response in Europe to Marshall's Harvard speech and Britain took the lead, with France, in initiating a conference to meet the main American condition – that the European nations should work out some co-operation amongst themselves. As a result, the Organization for European Economic Co-operation (OEEC) was formed in April 1948. Britain's positive role in its formation is worth noting since it contrasts strongly with British attitudes to the later formation of the Common Market of which the OEEC was one of the institutional fore-runners.

Aid under the Marshall Plan (formally the European Recovery Programme) transformed economic progress in Europe from sluggish, which was considered politically dangerous, to clearly perceptible, which raised new hope. From April 1948 to the end of 1951 some $11 billion was provided. Initially most of this took the form of grants of commodities (food, fuel, fertilizers) which were largely produced in the USA, but by 1951 over half the aid took the form of industrial raw materials, semi-processed goods and machinery. Britain was a major recipient (second only to France) until the end of 1950 when a surplus on her current balance of payments led Britain to cease to seek aid under the Plan. But from 1948 to 1950 Britain was fortunate that the trade gap was considerably eased by aid under the Marshall Plan. The second favourable feature was that, with the important exception of the USA, there was still generally a seller's market for exports. Moreover, even in the USA, British exports did not yet have to face much competition from the defeated powers of Germany and Japan.

None the less, despite these favourable factors, there was a major external crisis in 1949. The direct cause was a fall in the level of economic activity in the USA which cut American demand for imports from Britain and the Sterling Area. This was aggravated by speculation against the pound, which seems to have been given some encouragement by both US and IMF officials who wished to see some currency realignments, and also by some obstinacy and refusal to face facts by the government – perhaps made worse because Sir Stafford Cripps was ill. Faced with a large dollar deficiency and with British exports apparently unable to compete with American goods, it was decided in September 1949 to devalue the pound in relation to the dollar by just over 30 per cent. All the Sterling Area countries followed suit and so did most Western European countries although some of these – for example, West Germany, Italy and France – devalued to a much smaller degree. There is little doubt that some devaluation was necessary: the initial par values recorded with the IMF in 1946–7 had necessarily been fairly arbitrary and the strength and persistence of the dollar shortage emphasized the need for some revision.

However, there was at the time, and still is, disagreement as to whether the extent of the devaluation of the pound was excessive. The issue is important because the effect of devaluation is to raise the price of imports, so the larger the devaluation the greater the inflationary pressure from this source; whilst the reduction in the price of exports means that, whilst it is easier to sell, more has to be sold to earn the same amount of foreign currency.

At all events, the resolution of the devaluation crisis of 1949 marked the end of the post-war recovery phase for the economy. Given the magnitude and the novelty of many of the problems the transition had, in terms of basic economic performance, been effected with a large degree of success. There had, of course and especially in hindsight, been plenty of mistakes made by the government: such as the slowness with which it was accepted that there was an acute fuel shortage in early 1947 and a similar air of unreality characterized the government's approach to the convertibility crisis a few months later (just before the final deluge the Chancellor told the House that 'the additional burden . . . will be noticeably less than many people may suppose', HC Deb., 8 July 1947). But the government had shown considerable determination and courage in containing a boom which lasted much longer than had been expected. The steady pursuit over the long period from 1947 to 1950 of a policy of limiting consumer expenditure, despite the strong rise in output, was a substantial achievement. It was this which made room in the economy for the increases in exports and investment which were essential for future progress. It was this which also kept inflation and wage levels within reasonably narrow limits when the potential upward pressure had been very strong. Moreover, most of the restraint rested on the voluntary response of members of the community to the, admittedly formidable, moral suasion exerted by Sir Stafford Cripps.

Document 2.2
The devaluation of the pound, 1949

(a) From J. C. R. Dow, *The Management of the British Economy, 1945–60*, 1964, pp. 43–4

The extent of the devaluation was greater than expected, and it has been argued then and since to have been excessive. Sir Stafford Cripps's account of the reasons for going so far is of interest, not least for showing that the idea of floating rates, later to be so much in prominence, had powerful sponsors even at that date. 'Our first consideration' said the Chancellor 'was whether to adopt a fixed or, as it is called, a floating rate'. The latter had been rejected as being unsettling, and probably, destabliz-ing in the face of the speculative pressures to which sterling was subject.

The large devaluation of thirty per cent, to the new fixed rate of 2.80 dollars to the pound, had been decided for a number of reasons. To place British exporters 'in a fairly competitive position in the North American markets' it seemed necessary to go 'at very least as low as three dollars to the pound'. Some 'cheap sterling' transactions were already at below three dollars. 'Finally, it was necessary to make it absolutely plain that this was not a tentative first step but . . . that we had without doubt gone far enough'.

(b) From S. Pollard, *The Development of the British Economy, 1914–67*, 1969, pp. 361–2

The extent of the devaluation, 30.5 per cent, was far larger than seemed warranted by internal purchasing power or by international markets. Apart from the Sterling Area itself, few of the other countries followed Britain's devaluation to that extreme, Italy, for example, devaluing by 8%, Belgium by 13% and Germany by 20%.

Further, the decision to devalue at all was questionable, for in the existing conditions of import control little could be hoped for from reduced imports, while exports had still been held back, not so much by high costs as by sheer inability to produce. After the devaluation, more resources would have to be devoted to exports to buy the identical quantum of imports, and the under-valuation of the pound would inevitably lead to price rises at home, and was bound to breach the frail barriers against inflation built up over the years. The reason for the extent of the drop was probably 'psychological' to show the world the Government's determination to rectify the British balance of payments; but both the cause of the speculators' attack on sterling and its cure bore a disheartening resemblance to those of 1931.

(c) From *The Economist*, 22 Oct 1949

In and by itself, the devaluation of the pound sterling so artlessly announced by Sir Stafford Cripps on Sunday evening is no more than a confession of defeat by the Government. To the outside world, it has long seemed natural and proper that the pound should be adjusted to a level more in accordance with what the markets of the world are unconstrainedly prepared to offer for it. The majority of sober judges of affairs in this country have long felt that it was only a question of time before the decision to devalue was taken, and to many of them it had become apparent months ago that the time had come – indeed, was in danger of going by. But Ministers and the majority of their official advisers have been uncommonly stubborn in their refusal to face facts . . .

There can be no question of a 'ramp' either by bankers or by anyone else. It is the inexorable force of facts alone that has defeated the British

Government, the Treasury and the Bank of England and has made Sir Stafford Cripps eat so many of his past words. Of the two – the politicians and the experts – it is the inability of the experts to foresee what was coming that is the more disturbing. Once again, as in the convertibility crisis of 1947, they have been shown up as being too expert to have any common sense.

Exercise 1

The British economy since 1945

1.1 What have been the principal economic characteristics of post-1945 Britain?

1.2 It is often said that government intervention in the economy has progressively increased since 1945. How would you test this statement? What difficulties are there in 'measuring' government action?

1.3 Plot the rate of change of a) prices and b) wages between 1945 and 1980. Comment on your results.

Exercise 2

The Labour government's economic crises

2.1 Were the terms of the American loan harsh?

2.2 Was the economic crisis of 1947 the result of bad luck and bad weather?

4 The 1950s

The reduction of economic controls

It was, in some respects, the new decade rather than the change of government which signalled a different climate. The reduction of direct government controls, for example, was not a fresh departure introduced by the Conservative regime in 1951. Such controls had been abandoned on a significant scale from 1948 onwards. Harold Wilson – already displaying a flair for publicity – had from the Board of Trade initiated a bonfire of controls in 1948. Clothing, furniture, petrol and the so-called 'inessential' foods had ceased to be rationed by the end of 1950, by which date most consumer price controls had also been abolished. Some controls, especially over the industrial allocation of materials, were reimposed to deal with the problems arising from the Korean War; and it is likely that a Labour government might have retained some controls longer than did the Conservative administration. But well before the change of government there was no doubting that the general direction was strongly towards the dismantling of most direct government controls over the economy.

The area most resistant to the trend towards de-control was external trade where most imports were in 1950 still subject to government direction. Again, however, the most significant change – setting the pattern for the 1950s – was not associated with any domestic alteration in the party in government. It was provided, instead, by the setting up of the European Payments Union (EPU) in 1950. The essence of the scheme was that it greatly eased the conditions of trade between the member countries of OEEC. Instead of each country having to settle its trade payments more or less separately with each of the other countries on a bilateral basis, settlement was now made only on the net balance that each country had in its trade with all the other member countries put together. Moreover, arrangements were also made to provide credit facilities to ensure that trade was not stifled because of essentially short-term deficits by particular countries. The OEEC area was effectively converted into an area of multilateral trade. Moreover, the central part played by Europe in world trade made the EPU (and not the IMF) the key instrument for a cautious widening out of trade which led to the general resumption of currency convertibility in 1958 (more than a decade, be it noted, after Britain's enforced, expensive unilateral 'dash for convertibility' in 1947).

Another way in which an important characteristic of the British economy of the 1950s was determined before the change of government concerned the extent of government expenditure on defence. The immediate causal factor here was, of course, the outbreak of the Korean War in June 1950. The repercussions of this event were in some respects a reversion to the 1940s. It was partly responsible for the sharp rise in world commodity prices (although much of this would have happened anyway: even before Korea a very sharp rise in world industrial production, and a revival in American economic activity, was pressing prices sharply upwards). Inflation, which had been held in reasonable check in Britain for several years, was given a new impulse. The general shortages also led to a necessary reversion to controls and government allocation. And, of course, the sharp rise in import prices – by about two-thirds in the eighteen months from the end of 1949, a much greater rise than could be attributed to devaluation – led to yet another large external crisis. None the less, all these repercussions were more or less temporary. A longer-run effect was that the increased proportion of national income which was devoted to armaments as a result of the Korean rearmament programme was essentially sustained throughout the decade. The increased expenditure was, of course, introduced by the Labour government and then carried on by a succession of

Conservative governments, but such a bland statement overstates the degree of consensus. Two prominent members of the Labour government, Aneurin Bevan and Harold Wilson, resigned over the rearmament issue. The reasons they gave at the time were not always consistent or specific, but on the general thrust of the difficulty of accommodating a high level of defence expenditure in an economy as precarious as that of Britain in the 1950s they seem, in hindsight, to have had the better of the argument. In the short run the Korean rearmament requirements produced a disproportionate degree of disruption: they directly competed in materials and manpower with the needs of exports and the development of the newer areas of industry. In the longer run many would now see as one reason for Britain's relatively poor economic performance, the attempt to carry a greater defence burden than other European industrial nations, and a much greater burden than West Germany (or Japan).

Document 2.3
The resignation of Aneurin Bevan, 1951

(a) From J. C. R. Dow, *Management of the British Economy, 1945–60*, 1964, pp. 60–1

Mr Bevan chiefly attacked the scale of *American* rearmament, on the grounds that it would make such demands on 'the world's precious raw materials that the civilian economy of the Western world outside America will be undermined. We shall have mass unemployment . . . the foundations of political liberty and Parliamentary democracy will not be able to sustain the shock'. Because of shortages, the British rearmament programme was 'unrealisable'. Mr Bevan went on to attack the prospective rise in the cost of living – which it 'is clear from the Budget that the Chancellor of the Exchequer has abandoned any hope of restraining'. His objection to the health service charges was made as a subsidiary point. 'The Chancellor of the Exchequer . . . has taken £13 million out of the Budget total of £4,000 million', 'that is the arithmetic of Bedlam. He cannot say that his arithmetic is so precise that he must have the £13 million, when last year the Treasury were £247 million out.'

In his new position of 'comparative freedom', Mr Bevan went on to give this advice: 'Take economic planning away from the Treasury. They know nothing about it . . . they think they move men about when they move pieces of paper about . . . It has been perfectly obvious on several occasions that there are too many economists advising the Treasury, and now we have the added misfortune of having an economist in the Chancellor of the Exchequer himself.' (H. C. Deb. 23 April 1951, 34–43). Mr Wilson next day gave much the same grounds for his resignation. 'It is not a matter of teeth and spectacles.' He was 'strongly in support of an effective defence programme'.

But Mr Gaitskell's budget was based on estimates 'which included a re-armament programme which I do not believe to be physically practicable with the raw materials available to us' (H. C. Deb. 24 April 1951, 228–31).

(b) From *The Economist*, 28 April 1951

Mr Bevan does not argue that because the United States is rearming, as he thinks, too fast, Britain should contract out of rearmament altogether. His criticism of the defence programme is that it attempts too much because it is inconsistent with the maintenance of the standard of living and the social services. This is a disagreeable economic discovery that others have made besides Mr Bevan. If the proposed £1,300 million is the wrong figure, what is right – £1,200 million or £1,100 million? Could even Mr Bevan argue for less, or was the vigour with which he championed the present programme in the House of Commons less than three months ago just another manoeuvre?

The motives for the rush to pessimism are all too plain. When new charges were being put on the country for the expansion of the social services, no one was more willing than Mr Bevan to strain the economy to its limit to risk inflation, to decry caution, to put his faith in the expansion of production. What holds him back now is not a more realistic assessment of the expansive power of the economy but a difference of enthusiasm about the objective. Even if the reasons for pessimism about production were much stronger than they are, the most definitive conclusion to which they could lead would be that some of this year's £1,300 million for defence might not be spent until next year. Yet Mr Bevan is prepared solemnly to declare that the £4,700 million programme for the next three years 'is already dead'. This assertion has no meaning, unless it is an expression of Mr Bevan's wishes.

The revival of monetary policy

The most obvious way in which the return of a Conservative government affected economic policy was in the explicit acceptance that monetary measures could and would be used to supplement control of the economy through fiscal means. At this time, however, the emphasis in monetary policy was not placed on retaining control of the overall money supply but upon using shifts in the interest rate as an additional method of influencing the level of demand.

There was a real shift involved here. The maintenance of a low rate of interest as part of official policy had continued for so long that it had become something of a dogma. This policy of 'cheap money' had been introduced in 1932. It was made possible because Britain had, in the international financial crisis of 1931, left the gold standard and devalued the pound: high interest rates were no longer essential to attract foreign funds to maintain the reserves of gold and foreign currency. The initial objective of cheap money was to reduce the cost of servicing the National Debt and hence reduce the government's budgetary expenditure. A cheap money policy was then maintained throughout the 1930s because it was thought that low interest rates would encourage investment in industry and housing, thus helping to raise the general level of activity at a time of still-continuing high unemployment. The policy was retained during the war for quite different reasons. Cheap money was not now needed to stimulate investment and demand: on the contrary the problem now was to curtail demand. But instead of using dear money (high interest rates) as one means of controlling demand it was decided to keep demand down by other means (fiscal policy and direct controls) and keep money cheap to reduce the post-war cost of financing a much larger National Debt. This was a major decision and its wartime success created for a time a wide-spread consensus about the general virtues of cheap money, a view bolstered by the expectation that the post-war problem would in any event soon revert to that of the need to maintain and encourage demand. The initial broad attitude of acceptance needs to be borne in mind in assessing later attacks on Hugh Dalton for his strong efforts to sustain an active policy of cheap money from 1945 to 1947. After Dalton's departure a new balance was struck: no great effort was made to enforce cheap money but no direct use was made of monetary policy (higher interest rates) to control the level of demand. In a formal sense, therefore, Bank Rate (the equivalent of the present Minimum Lending Rate) was virtually unchanged at 2 per cent for the whole twenty years from 1932 to 1951.

From 1951 onwards Conservative governments pursued a more active monetary policy. It was an approach which fitted in more obviously with the rhetoric of Conservative economic philosophy since a change in interest rates limited government intervention to one specific act and then left individuals to make their own responses; whereas the Labour rhetoric was geared towards a greater use of direct actions determined by the government. In fact, however, the differences were more in the rhetorics than in the actual practices. It seems reasonably certain that if Labour administrations had continued into the 1950s they would have been edged towards making use of monetary measures, especially since recurrent balance of payments crises required means to attract overseas funds; and even for the Conservative governments monetary measures merely supplemented a continued reliance on fiscal action. Indeed, the first Conservative Chancellor to make a mild, but significant, attempt to revise priorities was dramatically unsuccessful. Peter Thorneycroft tried in 1957 to make a 'sound' currency take precedence over full employment as a policy objective, but his stand over this (on the badly-chosen issue of a marginal

Table 2.2 Indicators of economic activity, UK, 1945–80

	General index of retail prices (all items)		Manual workers[a] weekly wage rate index		Manual workers average weekly earnings[b]		Unemployment		Annual % change in GNP (at factor cost) constant prices	GDP per capita £ at 1975 prices	Gross fixed investment in manufacturing industry as % GNP at constant prices	Government expenditure as % of GDP	
	1975=100	annual % increase	31 July 1972=100	annual % increase	£	annual % increase	Number[c]	%[d]					
			Adult Male	Adult Male	Adult Male	Adult Male							
	(i)	(ii)	(iii)	(iv)	(v)	(vi)	(vii)	(viii)	(ix)	(x)	(xi)	(xii)	
1945					6.07		120,386	1.2					1945
1946					6.04	−0.4	391,939	2.5				28.3	1946
1947			26.4		6.40	6.1	281,161	3.1					1947
1948	23.1		27.8	5.3	6.90	7.7	307,823	1.8		922			1948
1949	23.8	3.0	28.5	2.6	7.13	3.5	291,146	1.6	+2.8	945			1949
1950	24.5	2.9	29.0	1.8	7.52	5.4	307,759	1.5	+3.9	971		19.5	1950
1951	26.7	9.0	31.4	8.2	8.30	10.4	214,524	1.2	+2.8	1006			1951
1952	29.2	9.4	34.0	8.2	8.73	8.4	489,623	2.1	−0.4	1004			1952
1953	30.1	3.1	35.5	4.4	9.33	6.8	334,520	1.8	+4.6	1047			1953
1954	30.6	1.7	37.0	4.4	9.90	6.2	269,057	1.5	+3.5	1081			1954
1955	32.0	4.6	39.6	6.9	10.85	9.5	242,920	1.2	+2.8	1109		19.7	1955
1956	33.6	5.0	43.0	8.7	11.75	8.4	250,376	1.3	+1.9	1125	4.3		1956
1957	34.8	3.6	45.2	5.0	12.15	3.3	297,099	1.6	+2.0	1141	4.5		1957
1958	35.9	3.2	46.2	2.3	12.68	4.4	472,920	2.2	−0.3	1132	4.2		1958
1959	36.1	0.6	47.6	3.0	13.15	3.2	449,468	2.3	+2.9	1165	3.9		1959
1960	36.5	1.1	48.8	2.5	14.09	7.1	334,683	1.7	+4.7	1209	4.4	17.5	1960
1961	37.5	2.7	50.8	4.2	14.99	6.4	299,392	1.6	+3.6	1243	5.0		1961

Year													Year
1962	39.3	4.8	52.5	3.3	15.59	4.0	431,883	2.1	+1.2	1243	4.6		1962
1963	40.1	2.0	54.4	3.7	16.13	3.5	516,135	2.6	+4.3	1286	3.8		1963
1964	41.4	3.2	57.1	4.8	17.51	8.6	354,214	1.7	+5.2	1343	4.1	17.0	1964
1965	43.4	4.8	59.3	4.0	18.83	7.5	305,334	1.5	+2.8	1371	4.4		1965
1966	45.1	3.9	62.2	4.8	20.17	7.1	291,674	1.5	+1.9	1394	4.5		1966
1967	46.2	2.4	63.6	2.4	20.55	1.9	539,149	2.3	+2.5	1422	4.3		1967
1968	48.4	4.8	68.2	7.2	22.15	7.8	552,760	2.5	+4.2	1480	4.4		1968
1969	51.0	5.4	71.9	5.4	24.83	7.4	533,816	2.4	+2.1	1501	4.6		1969
1970	54.2	6.4	78.8	9.6	28.05	13.0	578,751	2.6	+2.0	1528	4.8	21.3	1970
1971	59.3	9.4	89.1	13.0	30.93	10.3	762,144	3.5	+2.3	1569	4.4		1971
1972	63.6	7.1	99.6	11.7	35.82	15.8	813,657	3.8	+1.3	1589	3.8		1972
1973	69.4	9.2	115.0	15.5	40.92	14.2	582,225	2.7	+8.6	1710	3.5		1973
1974	80.5	16.1	134.8	17.2	48.63	18.8	549,379	2.6	−1.4	1687	3.9		1974
1975	100.0	24.2	178.9	32.7	59.58	22.5	880,063	4.2	−1.5	1678	3.7	24.2	1975
			209.8	17.3									
			All workers										
1976	116.5	16.5	215.3	18.6	66.97	12.4	1,271,826	5.7	+4.6	1741	3.4		1976
1977	135.0	15.8	227.4	5.6	72.89	8.8	1,341,691	6.2	−0.0	1763	3.7		1977
1978	146.2	8.3	263.5	15.9	83.50	14.6	1,386,810	6.1	+3.3	1814	3.8	23.4	1978
1979	165.8	13.4	296.2	11.3	96.94	16.1	1,299,282	5.8	+0.4	1824	3.8		1979
1st Q } 1980	184.6	19.1	346.9	19.1			1,509,200 }	6.3 }		451		24.6	1st Q } 1980
2nd Q	195.3	21.5											2nd Q

Sources: *The British Economy, Key Statistics 1900–66* (London and Cambridge Economic Service), *Economic Trends* (HMSO), *Annual Abstract of Statistics, Monthly Digest of Statistics* (HMSO), *National Income and Expenditure* (HMSO)

Notes

a All industries and services. Each June 1947, 1956–79. Monthly average 1948–55. May 1980.
b Figures in this series are not always strictly comparable due to change in classification or month of assessment but the general trend remains unaffected.
c At June 1945–8, July 1949–75, May 1976–80.
d Annual averages. Numbers unemployed as % employees. 1980 is a six months average.

excess of government expenditure) simply led in January 1958 to his resignation, and his two junior Treasury ministers – Nigel Birch and Enoch Powell – went with him. It is perhaps significant that it was this early monetarist martyr who – as Lord Thorneycroft and chairman of the Conservative party – was the architect of the party's victory in 1979, on a platform of monetarist policy.

'Butskellism'

The essential agreement of the most influential sectors of the two main political parties over the basis of economic policy were given a forceful, if somewhat ironic, verbal expression in the term 'Butskellism' (after the Conservative Chancellor, Butler, and his Labour predecessor, Gaitskell). It signified the extent to which the Conservatives made no serious attempt to reverse the major social and economic changes – the so-called Welfare State and the extension of public ownership of industry through national-ization – introduced by the first post-war Labour government; whilst Labour accepted that the bulk of industry would remain privately owned and capitalistic in nature. Both parties accepted that the basic objective of economic policy remained that of managing the level of demand in order to maintain full employment with minimum inflation. Perhaps even more fundamental was the general acceptance of the proposition that a major function of government *was* to control the economy.

The consensus rested on a widespread satisfaction at Britain's economic performance – or, at least, a general acquiescence in what was achieved. There was, indeed, a considerable basis for a favourable view, as Table 2.2 indicates. The level of unemployment remained extraordinarily low; output increased modestly but persistently; and prices moved only mildly upwards. These were the ingredients which allowed Harold Macmillan to ask for, and obtain, a further mandate for Tory government in 1959 on the basis of the appeal, 'You've never had it so good.' He was just in time. Although these basic indices of unemployment, output and prices con-tinued to behave in much the same way for another decade, Britain's economic performance increasingly came to be judged – by the electorate as well as the outside world – by its growth rate relative to that of other industrialized nations. On this basis there was widespread dissatisfaction.

In the 1950s, however, the shortcomings seemed mainly to concern the balance of payments. The external crises of 1947, 1949 and 1951 which it had been hoped could be attributed to the problems of post-war adjust-ment, were repeated in 1955 and 1957 when they could no longer be plausibly related to recovery. On the surface, however, they did not seem to occasion much alarm. The 1955 crisis came after a period from 1952 to 1955 in which economic policy had been generally expansionist in tone. There was a feeling that the need for the restrictions associated with war

Table 2.3 UK overseas trade, 1946–80

	Exports (f.o.b.)	Imports (f.o.b.)	Visible balance	Invisible balance	Current balance
1946	960	1,063	−103	−127	−230
1947	1,180	1,541	−361	−20	−381
1948	1,639	1,790	−151	+177	+26
1949	1,863	2,000	−137	+136	−1
1950	2,261	2,312	−51	+358	+307
1951	2,735	3,424	−689	+320	−369
1952	2,769	3,048	−279	+442	+163
1953	2,683	2,927	−244	+389	+145
1954	2,785	2,989	−204	+321	+117
1955	3,073	3,386	−313	+158	−155
1956	3,377	3,324	+53	+155	+208
1957	3,509	3,538	−29	+262	+233
1958	3,406	3,377	+29	+317	+346
1959	3,527	3,642	−115	+273	+158
1960	3,737	4,138	−401	+157	−244
1961	3,903	4,043	−140	+167	+27
1962	4,003	4,103	−100	+230	+130
1963	4,331	4,420	−89	+218	+129
1964	4,568	5,078	−510	+153	−357
1965	4,913	5,146	−233	+188	−45
1966	5,276	5,353	−77	+188	+111
1967	5,241	5,808	−567	+274	−293
1968	6,433	7,115	−682	+440	−242
1969	7,269	7,478	−209	+681	+472
1970	8,151	8,183	−32	+814	+782
1971	9,043	8,853	+190	+883	+1073
1972	9,423	10,184	−761	+923	+162
1973	11,937	14,523	−2586	+1498	−1088
1974	16,395	21,745	−5350	+1923	−3427
1975	19,330	22,663	−3333	+1601	−1732
1976	25,193	29,104	−3911	+2709	−1202
1977	31,734	33,973	−2239	+2015	−224
1978	35,071	36,564	−1493	+2257	+764
1979	40,689	44,001	−3312	+993	−2319
1980 1st Q	11,832	12,555	−723	+306	−417

Source: *Economic Trends* (CSO)

and post-war austerity were no longer appropriate, and that the 1949 devaluation had relieved the pressures of external trade. The Butler budgets of 1953 and 1954 were thus both expansionary, with tax cuts adding to the thrust already given to economic activity by Macmillan's energetic attempts to discharge Conservative election pledges to build 300,000 houses a year. But, in hindsight at least, it is clear that the 1955 budget went too far. Perhaps judgement was affected by the natural desire of the government to keep the economy buoyant during the run-up to the general election (the budget was in April, the election – at which the Conservatives increased their majority – in May). The reduction in income tax certainly increased the pressure in an already overheated economy (unemployment down to 1 per cent and imports rising). Already, by the summer, monetary restraints were imposed but these failed to prevent a balance of payments crisis which enforced a deflationary autumn budget. Still, it seemed both possible and plausible to explain the crisis as indicating nothing more serious than a piece of mis-timing, a slight error of economic management.

The 1957 crisis could be explained on similarly *ad hoc* grounds. The restraints imposed from the summer of 1955 were continued and reinforced in 1956 by a package of credit restrictions introduced in February and a mildly deflationary budget in April. Nor were they much relaxed by the 1957 budget. Thorneycroft, who became Chancellor in January 1957, seemed to be following the cautious path laid by his predecessor, Macmillan, who was Chancellor for just over a year from December 1955. None the less the autumn of 1957 saw a most serious currency crisis which was met by a further severe package of restrictions on credit and public expenditure and dramatized by raising the Bank Rate to the then extraordinary level of 7 per cent. The experience of such a large-scale external imbalance coming after a long period of internal restraint prompted some questions about the basic condition of the economy. But the force of the questioning was blunted because a more immediate explanation was to hand. It was widely argued that the economic crisis of 1957 was part of the legacy of the misguided Suez adventure (the British–French invasion of Egypt in November 1956). On this basis, the 1957 crisis could be shrugged off as an incidental misfortune or, as one leading economist put it, 'the most totally bogus' crisis since the war (Harrod, 1963, p. 145).

The reality was different, as will be seen. At the time, however, no significant shifts in economic policy were made or were generally thought necessary. It was this attitude which was perhaps symbolized by the resignations of Thorneycroft, Birch and Powell: they did think change was necessary but it was clearly a view which was not yet shared by Cabinet, party or nation. Instead the policies which had characterized the 1950s – economic management to sustain full employment with steady prices and healthy balance of payments – were continued to the end of the decade.

The 1958 budget gently relaxed the constraints whilst in the summer and autumn monetary policy became much easier. In 1959 there was a strongly expansionist budget with large reductions in both income tax and purchase tax; in October there was a general election and the Conservatives were again returned and again with an increased majority. It was another three months before it was necessary to begin imposing new restraints on the economy.

Exercise 3

The British economy in the 1950s

3.1 What was the economic significance of the rearmament decision of 1951?

3.2 How and why was monetary policy reintroduced in the 1950s?

3.3 What was Butskellism? Why did it seem an appropriate term for the 1950s?

3.4 How did the balance of payments come to seem the major restraint on the economy?

5 The 1960s

The euphoria of the election boom of 1959 rapidly gave way to the more sombre restraint of 1960. The experience, however, also seemed to drive home a more general lesson: that each attempt to expand economic activity in Britain seemed to lead directly towards balance of payments difficulties. There were two causes behind this association. First, the increased activity in Britain worsened the overall trading position because it led to greater imports and also, since selling at home was easier, reduced the incentive to export. Second, sterling was still a major international currency so any suspicion of its instability was liable to lead to strong speculation against the pound, reducing currency reserves and worsening the balance of payments.

In 1960 the problem was mostly one of a large trading deficit: in 1961 a substantial crisis occurred – despite an improving balance of payments – because of heavy speculation against sterling and in favour of the mark. In the latter case the comprehensive package of government measures (raised Bank Rate, increased taxes, credit squeeze, cuts in government expenditure, pay pause) in July 1961 pushed an already receding economy into sharp recession. The stop-go nature of economic management was now widely recognized and ritualized. From one point of view much of the 1960s experience can be seen as attempts to break out of this pattern.

Document 2.4
The 1960s – what had gone wrong?

(a) From R. E. Caves, *Britain's Economic Prospects,* 1968, pp. 42–3

Table 1–8 *Summary of Economic Performance, Indicators, and Policy Responses, United Kingdom, 1950–66*

Year	Growth	Unemployment	Balance of payments	Policy
1950	High	Low		
1951			Crisis	Stop
1952	Low	High	Improving	
1953			Improving	Go
1954	High		Good	
1955		Low	Crisis	Stop
1956			Crisis	
1957	Low		Crisis	
1958		High	Strong	Go
1959			Strong	Go
1960	High	Low	Weakening	Stop
1961			Improving	
1962	Low	High	Improving	Go
1963			Strong	Go
1964	High		Crisis	Stop
1965	Low	Low	Crisis	Stop
1966			Crisis	Stop

An overall view of economic change and policy responses is given in Table 1–8. A clearly defined pattern of stop-go emerges in relation to both policy and economic change. Although there is no objection to a sequence of expansionary and restrictive changes in policy if these changes secure a sustained performance of the economy, such success was not achieved. Rather, the effects of policy change themselves impose a stop-go pattern on the economy. To be sure, the stop actions were never so sharp as to result in unemployment which would be considered substantial by U.S. standards, but they did cause a sharply fluctuating growth rate and employment fluctuations which, by British standards at least, were undesirably large.

As Table 1–8 suggests, the key to the problem rests with the balance-of-payments position.

(b) From M. Stewart, *The Jekyll and Hyde Years: Politics and Economic Policy since 1964*, 1977, pp. 43–4

But blame was attached not so much to the fact that Britain's growth had been led by consumers' expenditure rather than by exports, as to the fact that this domestic consumer demand fluctuated so much from one year to another. Continuous government intervention, it was argued, expanding consumer demand when unemployment rose too high, and cutting it back when the balance of payments swung into deficit, made it impossible for businessmen to plan their future investment in any rational way. The sudden stops administered to the economy from time to time not only had the short-run effect of making businessmen postpone or abandon plans for new investment; over the years there was a cumulative effect, with Britain's capital stock becoming older and more obsolescent than that of competitor countries. And just as the suddenness of the stop phases had bad effects, so did the sharpness of the go phases: whenever the government expanded the economy it did so much too fast, with the result that British industry could not cope, and much of the rise in consumer and investment demand was satisfied by a surge of imports. This weakened the balance of payments further, while doing little to encourage a sustained rise in British investment.

(c) From P. D. Henderson (ed.), *Economic Growth in Britain*, 1968, pp. 17–19

In so far as any single factor can be held to account for the failures of the past, the balance of payments is the most widely accepted choice. There is a good deal of agreement that British balance of payments problems, and the periodic imposition of restrictive policies in order to deal with them, have been largely or partly responsible for holding back growth. In some formulations, this line of argument had led to a rather simple basic programme designed to improve British performance: governments should change the relative importance they have given to conflicting objectives, and should be ready to sacrifice external objectives – such as exchange stability – for higher growth; by doing so they would avoid the need to resort to 'stop-go' policies; and this in turn would ensure, either in itself or in conjunction with other measures, a much higher rate of growth . . .

In any economy in which the government tries to control the level of total demand, the need to restrain demand as well as to stimulate it may clearly arise. Further, if over a period the rate of growth of actual output considerably exceeds the growth of potential output, restraints will eventually be needed quite independently of the state of the balance of payments. To this extent, what can broadly be described as 'stop-go' policies are not in the least undesirable, but are indeed a necessary ingredient of economic policy. It is true that the restrictions imposed on each of three past phases of British economic expansion were affected, as to their timing, content and severity, by the state of the balance of payments. But it is also true that in each of these booms – in 1954–55, in 1959–60, and in 1963–64 – the rate of growth of output rose at a rate which could not have been sustained for long, even had balance of payments difficulties not arisen.

The dash for economic growth

The attempts were unsuccessful. In the aftermath of the 1961 crisis the government set up the National Economic Development Council (NEDC or 'Neddy') to bring together industry, the trade unions and the government to discuss economic strategies and policies. The intention of its proponents was that it would stress the need to increase the rate of economic growth and, indeed, in February 1963 it accepted as reasonable a 4 per cent growth target. In July 1962 the government had also established – although, and perhaps unwisely, without TUC support – the National Incomes Commission (NIC or 'Nicky') to attempt to secure some restraint on incomes during economic expansion. Thus armed, the government after a very cautious policy in 1962 (which partly led to Selwyn Lloyd's abrupt dismissal as Chancellor in July 1962), attempted to prevent the next boom from being cut off by balance of payments difficulties. Despite a mounting external deficit and rising speculation against sterling, Reginald Maudling continued his so-called,'race for growth'. In 1964 the economy was going and – it was argued – should not be stopped, or – in the then fashionable metaphor – the Chancellor should not shift his foot from the accelerator to the brake.

In one sense, this policy received very widespread support. There was a general belief that 'stop-go' was at the root of Britain's relative economic failure; NEDC had urged a commitment to accelerated growth; and the growth, if sustained, was expected to be the source of later exports which would meet the temporary external deficits. In this atmosphere the Chancellor was encouraged by a variety of professional and political opinion to drive straight through fluctuations in the balance of payments. In another sense the continuance of the boom right up to the October election, despite the size of the external deficit, was almost unavoidably partly influenced by political considerations.

In the event the political calculation almost came off – the Conservatives very nearly managed to win a fourth successive election – but the economic calculation did not. It had been intended to ride out the trade deficit which would arise because (mainly) of the – presumably temporary – extra imports being sucked in by the sustained growth. The deficit would be dealt with by other means than cutting down home demand – by extra foreign borrowing or by temporary import controls – until the greater productivity and competitiveness, which sustained rapid growth was supposed to bring, restored the situation 'naturally'. The trade deficit, however, was much greater than expected and the new, inexperienced and precarious (majority of three) Labour government was immediately faced with major external pressure on the economy. The situation was – not surprisingly – handled nervously and indecisively. The immediate package of measures – a largely neutral November budget, a raised Bank Rate, and the imposition of an import surcharge – amounted to neither a curb on the economy nor to a strategy for continuing the growth.

The devaluation of 1967

The result was a sort of creeping deflation. The 1965 budget was moderately restrictive, but failed to curb the level of activity or reverse the trade balance. The resultant renewed speculation against sterling prompted more restraints on investment and credit in July. There was then, for whatever reason, a lull in the external pressure during which time a general election was held (March 1966) which gave Labour a comfortable majority. The post-election budget in May was again mildly restraining. The major measure was the introduction of the Select Employment Tax aimed at inducing employers to release excess labour and also to switch the occupational distribution towards manufacturing and away from service industries. Any improvements to the economy that might have been hoped for from such time-consuming adjustments were, however, engulfed by renewed heavy speculation against sterling fed by continued trade deficits which had been exacerbated – but no more than that – by the long seamen's strike from mid-May to July. The government now reacted heavily. A Bank Rate increase was backed up by a package of restrictions announced on 20 July 1966. These were exceptionally severe and comprehensive – freezes on wages and prices, increased purchase tax, cuts in government expenditure, limits on foreign travel allowances, tighter hire purchase – but still only slowly eased the pressure on sterling.

Much more alarming was the full resurgence of an external crisis in the autumn of 1967. It is true that there had been a mildly expansionary budget in April and some relaxation of the credit restrictions in the summer; but neither of these was on a scale sufficient to produce an external crisis of the size that appeared in the autumn of 1967. Nor was it explicable in terms of other *ad hoc* events, such as the Six Day War between Israel and Egypt in June, the temporary embargo on Arab oil exports to Britain, the closing of the Suez Canal, the long dock strikes in London and Liverpool in September. All such events were important, of course, but they would not on their own have produced so drastic a run on the pound. On Saturday 18 November the pound was devalued by just over 14 per cent.

Document 2.5
The devaluation of 1967

(a) James Callaghan, Chancellor, HC Deb., 20 Nov. 1967

This change in the value of the £ will, of course, have the effect that the things we buy from abroad will cost us more and things we sell abroad will become cheaper for people overseas to buy.

This has both advantages and disadvantages. On the credit side, there will be substantial help to our balance of payments. On the other hand, because we shall need to pay higher prices for some of our imports we must expect in the coming months a small but noticeable rise in prices.

There will be no need for all prices to rise and the Government intend to maintain a careful check on the movement of prices in the coming months to ensure that there are no unnecessary increases. Because some rise in prices is inevitable, the Government will take, at the right time, the steps that may be necessary to protect the most vulnerable sections of the community from hardship . . .

The primary purpose of this change in the rate is to enable this country to secure lasting and substantial improvement in its balance of payments – of at least £500 million a year. Such a change round would have a profoundly beneficial effect on all aspects of our policy: on our foreign policy, our standing in the world, and our prospects for securing economic growth and full employment. But it would all be dissipated if the inevitable rise in prices were matched by a general increase in wage rates. This is what I meant in July when I said – I will read again what I said:

'those who advocate devaluation are calling for a reduction in the wage levels and the real wage standards of every member of the working class of this country.' – (Official Report, 24th July, 1967; Vol. 751, c. 99.) . . .

We are out for export-led growth. The purpose of this devaluation is to shift the emphasis of production towards exports. I emphasise that this is a shift in the use of our resources and that the reductions in public expenditure and private consumption are intended to make that shift possible and are not deflationary. They will not reduce total production. Indeed, as exports go on rising so total production will increase.

(b) From *The Economist*, 25 Nov. 1967

If Britain can achieve a £500 million a year basic improvement in its balance of payments, whole new vistas could be opened up. They will not just be such vistas as the possibility of removing the restrictions on overseas investment, important though such liberalisations are. Within Britain itself, it really should be possible to set about achieving the British economic miracle which the vast dormant resources of this country ought to permit, but which has constantly been prevented both by the over-hanging constraint of the balance of payments and by the impossibility of making any expansion an export-led one. But it will at once be obvious that this basic improvement of £500 million a year in the balance of payments can be achieved only on one condition. From now on, for every 1 per cent by which British wages per unit of output rise by more than competing countries' wages do, we must expect to lose up to 2 per cent of the needed rise in British exports. If a wage and cost inflation is allowed to creep forward in Britain, and if it adds to the initial cost inflation inevitably caused by devaluation itself, then the whole opportunity will have been thrown away.

The effect of devaluation was to make the price of British exports relatively cheaper for foreigners and to make foreign imports relatively dearer for British consumers. Whilst this would encourage exports and discourage imports there was no certainty that these movements would take place on a scale sufficient to close the balance of payments deficit, and every certainty that whatever improvements took place would be very gradual. The success of devaluation as a policy thus seemed to demand a continuing ability to borrow abroad to meet the short-term deficits, and that the economy would be able to provide the resources to supply the extra exports. Each of these requirements seemed to point to the need for restraint at home: the IMF would only lend if the government cut its expenditure and controlled the money supply; the exports could only be supplied if home demand was cut. The Labour government, to whom such deflationary trends were presumably especially distasteful, pursued these austere objectives with a remarkable tenacity. Not only was the by now familiar package of measures announced at the same time as the devalua-tion, and the IMF sent the formal Letter of Intent (to behave as the bankers wished) a few days later, but additional turns of the screw were applied in January and November 1968 as well as in the formal budgets of 1968 and 1969. Such a protracted onslaught involved a wide array of measures – tighter credit and hire purchase arrangements, cuts in expendi-ture, additional taxes – including such aspects as the postponement of raising the school-leaving age, cutting free milk in secondary schools and imposing charges in the health service. These were especially significant for the Labour party and its supporters.

The years of control were successful in their immediate objective: the current balance of payments which had been generally sharply unfavour-able in the 1960s was, in 1970 and 1971, transformed into a substantial surplus. In 1970, however, an ungrateful electorate dismissed the Labour party in favour of Mr Heath and the Conservatives. In fact, however, the election result probably had more to do with the government's abortive attempt in 1969 to place some restraint on the actions of trade unions. At all events the opening of the next decade coincided with a change of government.

The concern with economic growth

Broad shifts in such imponderables as the overall economic climate and the general level of people's expectations do not coincide neatly with a shift from one decade to another. None the less, the 1960s were noticeably different from the 1950s and, moreover, an awareness of the difference was quite early reflected in public discussion and newspaper comment. Such differences are, of course, not easy to define, and would be defined by different people in different ways – or, at least, with a different emphasis. These cautionary notes need to be borne in mind in considering what follows. Perhaps the most significant change was the shift in what people would accept as being a satisfactory economic performance. In the 1950s most of the adult working population had started their working lives during the inter-war period. So the persistent attainment of full employment was in itself a major achievement. And so was the accompanying growth in output, especially as – with the removal of wartime constraints – the extra output was rapidly reflected in extra consumption. Things were un-doubtedly improving and for a time that was enough.

Gradually, however, the point of perception changed. The general view ceased to be directed towards noting that the British economy was growing and that its rate of growth compared reasonably with Britain's past; instead it was directed more and more towards noting Britain's rate of growth relative to the growth rates of other countries. The result was disillusion-ing. The satisfaction of the 1950s gave way to sullen discontent as analysis after analysis around the turn of the decade revealed that Britain came at or near the bottom of the growth tables which became so fashionable. There is no doubt, moreover, that for many people Britain's relative economic decline was even more unpalatable because the most persistently successful economies were those of Germany and Japan, former enemies who had been defeated in the war.

At all events, the broad result was to shift expectations. Full employ-ment and modest growth were no longer enough: the *rate* of growth should also be comparable to that of other developed, industrial nations. The attempt to accommodate this desire had repercussions on the economy and economic policy. Only two of these effects will be directly dealt with here, but the two – planning, and the balance of payments – were especially wide-ranging in their impact.

Document 2.6
The concern with economic growth

(a) From R. E. Caves, *Britain's Economic Prospects*, 1968, p. 232

There is little doubt that the British people would have regarded the post-war record of their economy as highly satisfactory if the United Kingdom had been an isolated state. But, while British growth was above its earlier rates, growth rates of the other larger countries of Western Europe were much higher still. The rate of growth of Britain's total national income was, indeed, the lowest among all advanced countries. Comparisons with seven other Western European countries and the United States are shown in Table 6–1 for 1950–64 (which includes years when some continental countries were still emerging from severe wartime distortions) and for 1955–64. Not only did the United Kingdom stand last among these countries in growth of total national income; it also ranked last in growth of national income per person employed over the 1950–64 period as a whole and was above only the United States in 1955–64. It ranked next to last (above only the United States) in growth of national income per capita in both periods.

Table 6–1 *Growth Rates of Real National Income (Total, per Person Employed, and per Capita), 1950–64 and 1955–64* (Percentages)

Country	National income		National income per person employed		National income per capita	
	1950–64	1955–64	1950–64	1955–64	1950–64	1955–64
Germany	7.1	5.6	5.3	4.3	5.9	4.3
Italy	5.6	5.4	5.2	5.4	4.9	4.7
France	4.9	5.0	4.7	4.7	3.8	3.7
Netherlands	4.9	4.3	3.7	3.1	3.5	2.9
Norway	3.8	3.9	3.6	3.7	2.9	3.0
Denmark	3.6	4.8	2.7	3.5	2.9	4.1
United States	3.5	3.1	2.2	2.0	1.8	1.4
Belgium	3.4	3.5	2.8	3.0	2.8	2.9
United Kingdom	2.6	2.8	2.0	2.3	2.2	2.1

(b) From P. D. Henderson (ed.), *Economic Growth in Britain*, 1966, p. 9

Ten years ago the publication of a book on economic growth in Britain would have been a rather surprising event. Today this seems an obvious subject to choose, and there are a good many recent publications which deal with it. The explanation of this contrast is to be found in a gradual change of emphasis in economic thinking, and in the mental attitudes of those concerned with economic policy, a change which has been brought about by a number of related influences. A good illustration of it can be found in the changing content of economic textbooks. For example, in the first edition of Professor Samuelson's excellent and widely used introductory text, there was no section which was specifically devoted to economic growth, while in the current (sixth) edition there are three substantial chapters.

(c) From T. W. Hutchinson, *Economics and Economic Policy in Britain, 1944–66*, 1968, pp. 125–6

Very little or no *distinct and explicit* discussion of economic growth as an objective of policy is to be found in the various debates on British post-war economic policy until about the middle fifties. Of course, *implicitly* the growth objective was present. In the central Keynesian problem of a major rise in the level of activity and employment, raising output significantly in the short run is, of course, included; and the short-run problem of maintaining a high level of activity and output with regard to existing resources leads on logically to the problem of the growth of resources.

Interest in growth rates of GNP obviously depends considerably on regular and reliable statistics of GNP. Mr Colin Clark's great work, *The Conditions of Economic Progress* (1940), was one major landmark, and of course, the first National Income White Paper of 1941, was another. But it was not until the early or middle fifties that, with improving statistics, and after the recovery and readjustment from war to peace had been more or less completed, that international comparisons of current, or very recent, growth-rates began to become significant. Since other European countries had inevitably been slower than Britain in recovering immediately after the war, it was only as their recovery advanced in the middle fifties that invidious questions of comparative growth-rates began to emerge (under the stimulus, notably, of reports from ECE and OEEC).

Economic planning

The much greater stress given to the desire to increase the growth rate led more or less naturally towards a renewed concern with planning. Close definitions of 'economic management' and 'planning' are not easy and would lead far afield. But perhaps a looser, more pragmatic statement to indicate the sort of distinction which is intended here would be useful. Economic management, then, is meant to connote a system whereby the economy is maintained at a steady (and normally relatively high) level of activity. It emerged with Keynesian economics because Keynes provided both a theory (to justify) and an outline mechanism (to make practical) such action on the part of the state. Initially the intention was (it was certainly the intention of Keynes himself) that such interventions would be minimal: the state would give occasional nudges to an economy which would otherwise continue to run along private, capitalistic lines. For Keynes, economic management was a way of supplementing, strengthening and preserving the essential capitalistic values: it was not meant as a substitute or replacement for capitalism. Almost unavoidably over time the interventions in the economy increased (once governments accepted responsibility for the overall working of the economy they became expected to meet more specific requirements). Economic management thus became associated with the so-called 'fine-tuning' of the economy. But economic management is nonetheless a term best limited to a process of controlling a few broad parameters (aggregate demand, employment etc.) and leaving the rest of the economy to adjust. Planning is more positive and wideranging. It involves something like deciding at a particular point in time where it is desired (by the planners or the community or some group) that the economy should be at some future time. This target should be different from what would be expected to happen by simple projections of present trends, otherwise no significant planning is required. The planning consists of ensuring that the target is feasible with the resources available and indicating and implementing the policies necessary for its achievement.

There had been earlier public discussion of planning which had been significant (in volume, at least) in the 1940s. At that time it had been prompted by the hopes or fears of what was portended by the return, in 1945 for the first time, of a majority Labour government. No doubt some capitalistic blood was curdled by the publication, in 1944, of Hayek's *The Road to Serfdom* and, in 1948, Jewkes's *Ordeal by Planning*, and much rhetoric flowed across hypothetical barricades: but the actions of the government were difficult to reconcile with any notion that it was guided by any intention of undertaking a persistent pursuit of planning. Inheriting a large wartime apparatus of control, the government was clearly reluctant to put it to any positive planning use, and strove to reduce the controls. Having put through an extensive programme of nationalization a planning government would undoubtedly have used its control over the 'commanding heights' of industry (coal, fuel and power, transport) as a major lever to shape the economy to the desires of the administration. Instead the form (independent corporations) chosen by the government for the nationalized industries deliberately distanced these industries from direct government control. What did, mostly, guide the government was, firstly, the sheer necessity to cope with the appalling shortages and distortions inherited from the war; and, secondly, the intention to manage the economy as a way of avoiding what were generally considered the serious economic shortcomings of the inter-war years.

Some part of the impetus given to the discussions about planning in the early 1960s derived from the availability of what seemed to be a suitable model, namely the procedures which had evolved in France during the 1950s and which became known as 'indicative planning'. The essence of the system was that the government would indicate a rate of growth which was feasible and desirable, having regard to such constraints as the need to limit inflation, maintain employment, and protect the balance of payments. The implications of this are then discussed between government, businessmen and unions both at national level and in disaggregated sectoral terms. The aim is to create an atmosphere in which private decisions (especially about investment) will be taken which will be favourable to the general attainment of the plan. The method seemed appropriate to a mixed economy where the ownership of property, and thus the power of making decisions, was dispersed. It would, it was hoped, reduce the risks of decision-making by encouraging businessmen to share common assumptions about the medium-term progress of the economy, whilst at the same time leave those decisions to be made on a voluntary basis.

It was considerations such as these which induced the main employers' organization, the Federation of British Industries (FBI), not simply to accept the possibility of planning but to take a leading part in pressing for its adoption. It was the French style of planning, backed up by the growing awareness of France's better growth experience, which was favourably received at a special FBI conference on 'The Next Five Years' held at Brighton in November 1960. Since various other influential groups were attracted towards planning as a means of securing the generally desired 'leap forward' by the economy, and since the tighter methods of Soviet-style 'command' planning were both impractical and unattractive, there was an extraordinary convergence towards indicative planning as the favoured solution. Here the influence and example of France were important. The mood was fed by the French planning authorities who encouraged a great deal of to-ing and fro-ing across the Channel by British officials, economists and journalists. Some of the essential apparatus was created with the establishment of NEDC and NIC in 1961–2, and the movement received its first – and final – formal expression in the publication of the National Plan in September 1965.

By then the atmosphere of the early 1960s, heady with optimism, had already largely dissipated. The collapse of Maudling's 'race for growth' and the severity of the ensuing crisis had sapped the confidence that was essential if various groups were going to act on the basis of a belief in the projected rate of growth of 4 per cent a year for the period up to 1970. Above all, the government which had set to work to prepare the plan as soon as it came into office in 1964, and had established for the purpose a Department of Economic Affairs presided over by a senior minister, no longer had the will to carry it through. That, at least, seems a reasonable conclusion to draw from the increasing commitment of the government to the defence of the existing external value of the pound. Such a course was bound to demand internal restraint on the level of activity. A commitment to the plan demanded expansion and rested on a rate of growth of exports which was only conceivable – and even then not very likely – if British exports were made competitive by devaluing the pound.

The euphoria built up around indicative planning during the first half of the 1960s was always precariously based. The analogies between France and Britain were never as close as assumed. The French plans were never as neutrally indicative as was being suggested and the whole process in France drew, to a much greater degree than was being admitted, on a long tradition of direct and specific involvement by French governments in industry and the economy. The expectations of the scale, and still more of the speed, with which deep-seated attitudes within an economy could be shifted were always unrealistic. Above all, the extent to which 'planning for growth' would be compatible with the balance of payments needs was never sufficiently explored.

Document 2.7
Planning

(a) The Conservatives and planning
From 1964 general election: Conservative party manifesto

NEDC and planning
We have set up the National Economic Development Council, bringing together Government, management and unions in a co-operative venture to improve our economic performance. This has been followed by the establishment of Economic Development Committees for a number of individual industries.

NEDC gives reality to the democratic concept of planning by partnership. In contemporary politics the argument is not for or against planning. All human acitvity involves planning. The question is: how is the planning to be done? By consent or by compulsion?

The Labour Party's policy of extended State ownership and centralised control would be economically disastrous and incompatible with the opportunities and responsibilities of a free society. Conservatives believe that a democratic country as mature as ours must be self-disciplined and not State-controlled, law-abiding without being regulation-ridden, cooperative but not coerced.

(b) Labour's national plan
From 1964 general election: Labour party manifesto

1. A National plan
Labour will set up a Ministry of Economic Affairs with the duty of formulating, with both sides of industry, a national economic plan. This Ministry will frame the broad strategy for increasing investment, expanding exports and replacing inessential imports.

In the short term Labour will give priority to closing the trade gap.
(a) By using the tax system to encourage industries and firms to export more.
(b) By providing better terms of credit where the business justifies it.
(c) By improving facilities and help for small exporters, particularly on a group basis.
(d) By encouraging British industry to supply those manufactures which swell our import bill in time of expansion. With proper stimulus we can produce many of those things we are now forced to import from abroad.

But in the long run a satisfactory trade balance will depend upon carrying out Labour's overall plan to revitalise and modernise the whole economy. It will depend upon maintaining a steady and vigorous programme of long-term expansion.

Tax policies will contribute directly to the aims of the national plan. They will be used to encourage the right type of modern industry. Above all the general effect of our tax changes will be to stimulate enterprise, not to penalise it.

2. Plan for industry
Within the national plan each industry will know both what is expected of it and what help it can expect – in terms of exports, investment, production and employment. Farmers, too, will be given a new certainty with the establishment of Commodity Commissions to supervise and regulate the main imported foodstuffs and to balance imports with home production.

If production falls short of the plan in key sections of industry, as it has done recently in bricks and in construction generally, then it is up to the Government and the industry to take whatever measures are required.

Public Ownership The public sector will make a vital contribution to the national plan. We will have a co-ordinated policy for the major fuel industries. Major expansion programmes will be needed in the existing nationalised industries, and they will be encouraged, with the removal of the present restrictions placed upon them, to diversify and move into new fields: for example, the railways' workshops will be free to seek export markets, and the National Coal Board to manufacture the machinery and equipment it needs. Private monopoly in steel will be replaced by public ownership and control. The water supply industry, most of which is already owned by the community will be reorganized under full public ownership.

(c) From *The National Plan*, 1965, pp. 2–3

The nature and purpose of planning

10. Our economy, like most others in the modern world, is a mixed one. The Government element is important; public spending is a large part of total expenditure; for this reason the Government must raise large sums in taxation; a large part of the basic industry of the country is carried on by public corporations; the Government are able to exercise authority in many other fields. All this gives the Government great economic power and influence. They intend to use this to secure faster growth and national solvency.

11. Most manufacturing industry and commerce is, and will continue to be, largely governed by the market economy. But this does not necessarily, and without active Government influence, bring about the results which the nation needs – for example, sufficient exports to pay for our imports and other overseas expenditure. Also, the forces of competition often operate too slowly. Then again, where productive units are large and investment decisions have to be taken two to five years ahead, competing companies tend to bunch their investment, holding back and moving forward together, producing surplus or over-stretched resources. There is, too, little doubt that inadequacy of investment in British industry has resulted in increasing home demand being met by a greater flow of imports than the economy could afford.

12. Sometimes Government action may be required to strengthen the forces of competition, for example, by reinforcing the legislation against restrictive practices or providing for more disclosure in company accounts. In other cases, such as the regional distribution of industry, and transport, important social costs arise which are not expressed in market prices; and positive Government action is required to supplement market forces. Each case must be judged on its merits. The end product of both co-operative planning and the market economy is an internationally competitive industry; and in securing this aim they complement each other.

13. Both Government and industry have to plan several years ahead and it is desirable to co-ordinate the forward estimates of both. Public expenditure cannot be planned realistically without some idea of the rate at which the economy can be expected to grow and of the size of

other claims on resources, for example, for industrial investment. For this reason the assembly of the forecasts and plans of private industry is a great help in planning the public sector. Similarly, industrialists should benefit, both from the collection of the plans of other industries which are their customers, and from a knowledge of the intentions of Government – by far the largest buyer in the country.

The balance of payments and the 1967 devaluation

The last issue was fundamental because concern with the balance of payments was the other great obsession of the decade. The concern was well enough founded. For one thing there was a perceptible worsening of the current balance between the 1950s and the 1960s. In the former decade the balance of payments on current account was normally favourable (except for 1951 and 1955) and there was a positive balance for the decade of over £1000 million: in the latter decade the current balance was normally unfavourable (except for 1962, 1963, 1966 and 1969) and there was an overall debit for the decade of over £500 million. In the second place an unfavourable balance, especially with a fixed exchange rate, usually meant a run on sterling which led to measures (restrictions on home demand, higher interest rates) designed to attract back foreign lenders. Thus poor balance of payments performance seemed to be incompatible with the desire for faster growth which loomed so large in the 1960s.

The year-by-year effects of the balance of payments difficulties have already been indicated. A few words need to be added, however, on the related issues of devaluation and the role of sterling as an international currency. Sterling has been used as an international currency for a very long time. Before 1914, indeed, a large part of world trade – even when it did not directly involve a British buyer or seller – was conducted in sterling and the accounts settled in London. Despite the long decline in Britain's relative importance in world trade, sterling continued to play an important, though less dominant international role. Partly this was the continuance of a tradition. Partly it was because Britain was still a major trading nation. Partly it was because the City of London argued that its significance as a world financial centre would be weakened if sterling did not act as a key international currency. Partly it was because after 1945 the sterling balances held abroad were too large for Britain to have repaid in the short run. (Many of these debts accumulated initially during the war as part of Britain's military expenditure in countries like India and Egypt. They totalled £3500 million in 1945, and although their distribution and composition changed over time they were still high – averaging £2500 million – in the 1960s.) Foreigners were, however, willing to retain their sterling balances if they served as part of their international currency reserves – as long as they were sure that the value of such balances would be upheld.

It was here that there was a two-way link with the issue of devaluation. On the one hand, foreigners would be reluctant to hold sterling if they thought its external value was likely to be reduced; on the other hand, the nervousness of foreign holders made it more difficult to maintain that value. Thus sterling's role as an international currency made it more difficult to use devaluation as a policy measure, and at the same time made it more difficult to avoid using devaluation as a policy measure. It encouraged and magnified the periodic speculation against sterling: thus any deficit on Britain's current balance of payments would have a disproportionately adverse effect on Britain's reserves of gold and foreign currency. The position worsened in the 1960s both because the final return to full international currency convertibility in the late 1950s made such speculation difficult to counter, and because, as already indicated, the balance of payments worsened. Sterling's role as an international currency made recurrent crises more likely and necessitated internal economic policies more restrictive than would have been justifiable simply from Britain's actual trading position.

Too much should not, however, be made of the reasonableness of the doubts. The fact is that it emerged with increasing clarity in the 1960s that the pound was overvalued. A wide variety of people, for various reasons, still refused to accept the basic consequence: that devaluation was more or less unavoidable. In the City they refused to do so because they thought London's role as an international financial centre depended on a fixed value for the pound and because they rightly thought that the need to direct all economic policies to maintaining that external value would put curbs on the actions of governments, especially Labour governments. Many believed that the particular existing external value of the pound was associated with the honour and status of the nation. Other countries, and especially the Americans, were anxious to maintain the value of sterling because once sterling went the growing weakness of the dollar, increasing with the rising deficits because of war expenditure in Vietnam, would be exposed. The refusal to accept that the pound was overvalued does not mean that the overvaluation was not clear, or that it is only clear in hindsight. Many were well enough aware of it at the time. Indeed, in this respect the almost daily radio and television reports on the 'health' of the pound – a characteristic of the decade – are most revealing. On the one hand they illustrated how much the fixed value of the pound had been built into a matter of national importance: on the other, these reports only made sense if they really indicated a general awareness of the fundamental nature of the malaise of sterling. The reports were like the hushed communiqués issued about a dying monarch.

Above all, and most unfortunate, was the refusal of the new government in 1964 to recognize that the pound was overvalued. The reasons for this can only be guessed at: the initial advice that was given; the fear of devaluation being again (as in 1949 and – though incorrectly – in 1931) associated with a Labour administration; the desire to maintain a 'special relationship' with the Americans; and – as more moral capital became invested in denials of devaluation – eventually a degree of simple obstinacy. The consequences, however, were considerable. The alternative to devaluation was deflation: high interest rates to attract in foreign funds, curbing home demand to restrict imports. It was a reasonable alternative if the external pressure arose merely from a temporary imbalance in Britain's overseas trade. But if – as seemed more likely – it reflected a more fundamental lack of competitiveness then any attempt to relax the internal deflation would immediately create a new crisis. Thus the government, elected to effect a break-through into planned growth, condemned itself to a struggle to maintain a parity of $2.80 to the pound. And in vain. In November 1967 the pound was devalued by 14.3 per cent to a parity of $2.40.

It would be misleading to attach too much weight to a single aspect of the economy, still less to a single government decision on economic policy. None the less, the failure of the Labour government to devalue on coming to office in 1964 does, in retrospect, seem especially fateful. For the country it meant a deflection of economic effort towards a goal – the maintenance of the external parity of sterling – which was not attained and was probably unattainable. For the government it meant that the benefits of devaluation – the easing of external pressures on the economy – came too late to allow the pursuit of more positive domestic policies.

Document 2.8

Labour's fatal blunder? – the refusal to devalue

(a) From Harold Wilson, *The Labour Government, 1964–70: a personal record*, 1971, p. 6

There was comment, and this has been subsequently echoed, that we made an initial, even a fatal, blunder in our decision not to devalue within twenty-four hours of taking office, when we could have put all the responsibility on our Conservative predecessors. Politically, it might have been tempting and we were not unaware of the temptation. But I was convinced, and my colleagues agreed, that to devalue could have the most dangerous consequences.

The financial world at home and abroad was aware that the postwar decision to devalue in 1949 had been taken by a Labour Government. There would have been many who would conclude that a Labour Government facing difficulties always took the easy way out by devaluing the pound. Speculation would be aroused every time that Britain ran into even minor economic difficulties – or even without them. For we were to learn over the years that it was all too easy for those so minded to talk the pound down on the most frivolous of pretexts.

When, three years later, devaluation was forced upon us, the whole world recognized that there was no alternative – central banks and governments accepted the decision as necessary, recognizing the courage and determination we had shown in our fight to hold the parity. And for these reasons they backed us wholeheartedly, and only a few countries followed our example by devaluing their own currency. In 1964 there would have been no such acceptance: in 1964 the true facts of Britain's deficit were not known and politics, rather than economic necessity, would have been blamed.

But there were other considerations. We might well have started off an orgy of competitive beggar-my-neighbour currency devaluations – similar to those of the 1930s – which would have plunged the world into monetary anarchy, and left us no better off – even, perhaps, stimulating economic nationalism and blind protectionism abroad.

There were also strong reasons in terms of the domestic, economic and political scene. I had always argued – and continued to argue for the next three years – that devaluation was not an easy way out; that, by its very nature in cheapening exports and making imports dearer, it would require a severe and rapid transfer of resources from home consumption, public and private, to meet the needs of overseas markets. This would mean brutal restraints in both public and private expenditure over and above what was required by the domestic situation we had inherited.

(b) Life Begins at $2.40
From *The Economist*, 25 Nov. 1967

The devaluation of the pound sterling last weekend was not caused by any banker's ramp, or wickedness by speculators, or even any sudden upsurge in either the incompetence or the revived commonsense of the present British Government. It was the inexorable pressure of facts alone that caused Mr Wilson and Mr Callaghan to eat so many of their past words, and any dangers that now beset Britain or the international monetary system arise mainly from the fact that their meal has been so unconscionably long delayed.

It has been clear for some years that sterling has been overvalued in relation to the main trading currencies of continental Europe and Japan. In far too many goods, especially very modern goods, the attenuated gap between the British factory's selling price and the attainable retail selling price in foreign markets has meant that everybody concerned in the process of selling British exports – the manufacturer, the export merchant, the import agent abroad, the foreign wholesaler, the foreign retailer – has had to take a smaller profit, at the margin, than if he were dealing in competing foreign products. Not surprisingly, therefore, Britain's share of the world trade in manufacturing has diminished year by year; and there has never been any real chance of pushing it up again, even when Mr Callaghan squeezed men into unemployment until the voters in every by-election squeaked, so long as this state of overvaluation persisted.

Much of British industry and most of the City of London joined with the Government in its ostrich-like refusal to recognise what was happening. The City had been especially shrill in its opposition to devaluation, and thus especially culpable because everybody knows that in as arcane a matter as this a Labour Government has been terrified of its views. To a sound banker it should have been obvious that the only honest and maintainable exchange rate for sterling was the rate that the markets of the world were unconstrainedly willing to pay for it, without bribes through especially high interest rates or taking especially expensive hedging cover. For some time that equilibrium rate has not been $2.80. It is no good saying that Britain's long delaying fight against devaluation, fought with other people's money, has been obligatory in order to try to avoid default and dishonour. Once sterling had reached an obviously untenable position, every day's delay in devaluing has merely meant further losses to the reserves – and has also meant that the eventual devaluation would have to be bigger, and have to cause even more disturbance to the world monetary system.

(c) From W. Beckerman (ed.), *The Labour Government's Economic Record, 1964–70*, 1972, p. 61

The true story of why the Labour Government did not devalue earlier will probably never be known to the public, but there seems to be little doubt that the initial decision not to devalue when they took office in October 1964 was almost entirely political and was dictated by the narrowness of the majority. In such conditions the probability of being forced to an early election was considerable and the judgement of the Party leaders was that if the Labour Party were to go to the electorate after having devalued almost immediately it had taken office, and given that the previous devaluation of the pound was also carried out by a Labour Government (in 1949), it would certainly be defeated. Labour could not, so it was believed, survive being so clearly marked as the Party that always devalued the pound. Having made this decision, it was necessary to minimize the threat to the pound by increasingly categorical assertions that the pound would never be devalued, and even on the charitable assumption that these assertions were intended primarily for overseas consumption they had the effect of making the leaders of the Party feel publicly committed never to devalue the pound.

Of course, this political judgment is understandable during the period up to the Spring 1966 General Election. But the real mystery is why the pound was not devalued after Labour had won the Spring 1966 election with an overwhelming majority. To some extent it is likely that the sheer euphoria of a great electoral victory left the Government in no mood to come down to earth and face the most unpleasant problem of going back on a public commitment not to change the exchange rate. Also, it is likely that unwillingness to go back on this commitment once the election had been won led to sheer wishful thinking about the extent to which the balance of payments would solve itself anyway, though by early 1966 there was probably hardly an economist in the country who did not advocate devaluation. After the Labour Government won the election of Spring 1966 with a handsome majority and could look forward to five years of uninterrupted power as long as there was no catastrophe, there was no further excuse for not devaluing the pound.

Exercise 4

The British economy in the 1960s

4.1 Account for the concern, during the 1960s, with economic growth.

4.2 Explain the enthusiasm of a Conservative government and of many private enterprise businessmen for indicative planning.

4.3 What was meant by stop-go? Why was it considered harmful for the economy?

4.4 Was the 1967 devaluation three years too late?

4.5 What was the significance of sterling's role as an international currency?

6 The 1970s

The new decade opened with a new government. But although the Conservatives regained control in 1970, the economic turning point of the decade came a few years later and was signalled by quite different events. In particular, some of the major characteristics of the 1970s – mounting inflation and rising unemployment – came to be associated with the quadrupling of the world price of oil in 1973–4. But this did not mean that the economic difficulties of the Western nations were caused by the oil increases. Even less did it mean that the economic problems of Britain – soon to have oil supplies of its own – were so caused. Indeed, all the most worrying economic trends of the years after 1973 – the pace at which prices were rising, the growing unemployment, the rate of growth of imports, the accelerating size of wage demands – were all evident beforehand.

The second 'dash for growth'

Before tracing the emergence of these characteristics, however, a rapid outline of the economic events of the 1970s is necessary. At the beginning of the decade Britain had a massive surplus on its current balance of payments: a combination of the improved competitiveness of British goods after the 1967 devaluation and the cautious restraint imposed on the economy by Roy Jenkins, who succeeded Callaghan as Chancellor immediately afterwards, which made sure that potential exports were not deflected by a high level of home demand. The budgetary restraint was continued in 1970, a fact which some commentators felt lost the election for the Labour party. There is no doubt, however, that the economic inducements offered by the Conservatives had a positive attraction for the electorate. They included the reduction of government expenditure, cuts in the level of income tax, curbs in the power of trade unions and a greater reliance on the market. This was the Selsdon Programme, (so called because it had been put together at a pre-election conference of Conservative leaders at the Selsdon Park Hotel).

In practice the new philosophy seemed to be, or to become, incorporated into a fresh 'dash for growth' in what became known as the 'Barber boom'. Anthony Barber, the new Chancellor, introduced a series of expansionary measures. These started in the autumn of 1970, and continued through the 'normal' budget in March 1971, a reflationary package in July and another expansionary budget in March 1972. For a government committed to non-intervention the scale of the stimulus given to the economy was very substantial, especially in the second half of 1971 when bank credit was made much easier and, in a major reversal of policy, public expenditure was substantially increased. The government seems to have been largely motivated at this stage by a laudable desire to reverse the rising trend in unemployment and push up the rate of economic growth. It was in part misled because the available information on the state of the economy seriously underestimated the extent to which it was already expanding.

The results were well-nigh disastrous. Prices rose sharply, imports soared – but the rate of growth and the level of unemployment were slow to respond. The effects were substantially worsened because two other major related aspects of industrial policy had, over the same years, also gone awry. The first was the government's insistence that it would no longer come to the assistance of declining companies. This stance seemed to be central to the declared determination to allow the stern, salutary discipline of the market to have its full expression on the inefficient firms. Thus when the Upper Clyde Shipbuilders, a firm created and subsidized by the previous Labour government, went into liquidation in June 1971 the new government bravely averted its eyes from the death throes of this 'lame duck'. In the event, the workers refused quietly to disappear and embarked on a direct occupation of the yards. Eventually the government intervened by providing funds for a fresh firm called Govan Shipbuilders. It was unfortunate for the government that the other major test of its policy in this area concerned Rolls-Royce, a name resonant with British industrial pride and prestige. When this company collapsed in February 1971, the government – which had already extended financial aid in November 1970 – rapidly came to the view that the jobs, capital and technology embodied in the firm justified its continuance 'in the national interest'. Rolls-Royce was (mostly) nationalized and given a large sum (£130 million) of public money.

Document 2.9
Lame ducks and roosting chickens

From M. Stewart, *The Jekyll and Hyde Years: Politics and Economic Policy since 1964*, 1977, pp. 134–5

A key strand in the philosophy of the new Conservative Government was the insistence that the State must not go on propping up ailing industries. A more rigorous competitive climate must be created, in which the less efficient firms and industries would go under, releasing capital and labour to flow into the efficient, expanding firms and industries on which economic growth and competitiveness in world markets depended. The point was well summarized in a Commons debate on 4 November 1970 by Mr John Davies, the newly-appointed Secretary of State for Trade and Industry, who said that the country's essential need was 'to gear its policies to the great majority of people, who are not lame ducks, who do not need a hand, who are quite capable of looking after their own interests and only demand to be allowed to do so.' The vast majority, he added, in case anyone had missed the point, 'lives and thrives in a bracing climate, and not in a soft, sodden morass of subsidized incompetence'. This was all stirring stuff. But when the chips were down, would the Government really withhold help from a big company in trouble?

The matter was soon put to the test. The two most dramatic cases were shipbuilding, an industry with a past, and aero engines, an industry with, perhaps, a future. In 1949, nearly half the ships launched throughout the world were built in Britain; twenty years later, the figure had collapsed to 5 per cent. Nowhere were the problems associated with this decline more acute than on the upper Clyde. Late in 1967 the Labour Government had attempted to salvage the situation by amalgamating five firms into Upper Clyde Shipbuilders, and by the time it left office in June 1970 had poured in some £20 million of aid. This was precisely the kind of lame duck John Davies had in his sights, and in October he made a decision that was not so much a shot between the eyes as a blow below the belt: no further government credits would be provided to shipowners wanting ships built at UCS. These credits were in fact restored in February 1971, but in the meantime fatal damage had been done – admittedly to a patient already in a fairly critical condition – and in June the company went into liquidation. Unfortunately the workers did not quietly redeploy themselves into more efficient industries, as the Conservative script had demanded, but occupied the shipyards and refused to budge. Out of a confused situation came a new company – Govan Shipbuilders – backed by much larger sums of public money than had been injected into the industry by the Labour Government. And just visible in the distance, as the smoke of battle lifted, could be discerned the figure of Mr Davies in full, though well-dissembled, retreat.

A second aspect of the government's industrial strategy had been to insist on some changes in the law relating to trade unions, changes which would reduce the power wielded by trade union leaders. The Industrial Relations Act was by August 1971 duly pushed through Parliament against fierce Labour opposition (which many thought ill-accorded with the strenuous efforts of the previous Labour government itself to change the law in this area). The efforts to impose the law, however, encountered more or less continuous resistance from the trade union movement. The imprisonment in the summer of 1972 first of three dockers and, after their release had been engineered to save the government embarrassment, then of a further five, brought matters to a head. The law provoked opposition, but, beyond this, it was seen to be ineffective in obtaining the desired benefits and uncertain and unpredictable in its operation. The government abandoned its attempt to chasten the trade unions.

Earlier in 1972 the government had also had the first of its two bruising encounters with the National Union of Miners. The miners had a general reputation for militancy but so far as this was expressed in strike action it usually took the form of a large number of stoppages at individual pits or, at most, a stoppage in a particular district or coalfield. There had not been a national miners' strike since 1926. Several reasons contributed to the one which started in January 1972. In the 1960s a major obstacle preventing miners acting in unison had been removed with the negotiation of the National Power Loading Agreement of 1966. Effectively this aimed gradually (by 1971) to do away with differential rates of pay between the different coalfields, in favour of common standard rates. Previously most miners, especially in the more productive coalfields, saw their main interest over pay in the district negotiations over their piece rates; now they all had a common interest in the national day rates. The institutional basis for unified action had thus been provided. In addition, the industry had been contracting rapidly since the late 1950s. On the expectation of a permanent continuance of cheap oil, pits had been closed down and the number of miners continually reduced. In a declining industry, miners' wages had been falling relative to wages in other industries. By 1971 the miners were determined to reverse this trend. Moreover, in 1971 the miners' conference revised their rules governing the calling of national strikes: a national ballot was still required but a strike could be called on a majority of 55 per cent instead of the previous requirement of a two-thirds in favour. Thus both the motivation and the machinery for national action had been provided.

The government seemed to have little appreciation of these realities and even less awareness of the mood of the miners. The calculation was that miners would be curbed by the realization that disruption, in the face of government firmness, would only lead to many permanent closures. But, as a deterrent, this was a broken reed: the miners saw only that fifteen years of closures had left them relatively worse off. The government seemed to be on more solid ground in relying on the large stocks of coal. The situation was, however, transformed to the surprise of all – even the miners – by the astonishing success with which so-called, 'flying' pickets were used to neutralize these stocks, especially at the power stations. The government, so far from calmly sitting out an ineffective stoppage, was forced to declare a State of Emergency and a three-day week. The miners secured increases of 30 per cent (see chapter 6).

Oil and coal

In June 1970 the Conservatives had taken office with what they considered to be a weighty and measured economic strategy: by mid-1972 it was in ruins. And the oil crisis was still more than a year away. In the meantime, the government switched to an active incomes and prices policy to curb the very marked inflationary trends which had been released by the 'Barber boom'. In November 1972 a statutory standstill on pay, prices and dividends was instituted largely because the government could reach no voluntary agreement with a deeply-antagonized TUC. Stage Two of the new policy took the form of the setting up of a Pay Board and a Prices Commission (two bodies to replace the Prices and Incomes Board which the same government had, in its initial non-interventionist euphoria, killed off in March 1971), and the application of pay norms which favoured the lower-paid workers. The intention, however, remained until mid-1973 that of continuing to expand the economy and reducing the level of unemployment. Unfortunately this showed up less in the form of increased output than in the form of increased prices.

Everything now began to fall apart. Prices were rising rapidly. Their increase was further fuelled by a sharp rise in the price of imported commodities in reaction to the demand arising from the general boom in Western industrialized countries in 1972 and 1973. The situation was further worsened because the value of the pound – which since June 1972 had been allowed to float – was falling and so increased the cost of imports. And much of the demand generated by the boom had been, as usual, going in the form of extra demand for imports. The incomes policy was thus subjected to great strain when the government introduced its Third Stage in October allowing for wages increases to a maximum of 7 per cent and a limit of increases to £350 p.a. It was at this point that the Arab–Israeli War, which initiated the oil crisis, started on 6 October 1973. It is important to indicate the sequence in order to emphasize that, by the autumn of 1973, the British economy already faced acute difficulties. It is convenient for some and comforting for many to attribute the general economic failures of the 1970s simply to the dramatic rise in the price of oil: but it is misleading – especially if the already existing British situation of rising prices, faltering output and balance of payment strain is ignored.

None the less, the oil crisis was dramatic and its consequences were substantial. The Organization of Petroleum Exporting Countries (OPEC) had for a few years been gently nudging oil prices upwards and, at a meeting in Vienna in September 1973, had planned a more rigorous push. The Arab–Israeli War transformed all this. The Arab oil producers, who dominated OPEC, cut back on oil output to exert diplomatic pressure on the West. It worked: Europe (or, at least, the EEC of which Britain had just become a member) dutifully pressed conciliation upon the Israelis. The war was over in three weeks: but it had given OPEC a glimpse of its potential power which it exercised to force large and rapid price rises. In the last quarter of 1973 the price of oil almost quadrupled.

The world industrial boom of 1972–3 had already been flagging: the oil crisis hastened and deepened the recession. The four-fold increase in oil prices shifted international financial resources towards the OPEC countries. Several of the most important of these, however, were low population countries with a small demand for industrial products. There was therefore a drop in overall world demand – at least until the time when means could be devised for OPEC countries to recycle their foreign earnings back into the international economy. Britain was particularly hard hit by the general international recession because she had already been running substantial balance of payments deficits and experiencing rapid price rises.

The Heath government had already taken moves to apply some brakes to the economy by, in the summer of 1973, announcing curbs on future levels of government spending and raising the Minimum Lending Rate to 11½ per cent. They also launched – the announcement coincided with the war in the Middle East – Stage 3 of their incomes policy (allowing for wage increases of 7 per cent up to a maximum of £350 p.a.; together with provision for automatic monthly threshold payments after price increases exceeded 7 per cent of their level in October 1973, and the possibility of additional payments for working 'unsocial hours'). A December budget further tightened public expenditure plans and the availability of credit.

These reactions were, at the least, prudent even if the sharp switch in government policy from expansion to contraction was drearily familiar. In some respects, however, the government measures seemed more promising: the Stage 3 proposals embodied an incomes policy which was more fully-articulated, more coherent and flexible, than anything that had been tried before. Moreover, the government had a reasonably secure parliamentary position and over eighteen months of its possible term still to run. And yet within a few months Edward Heath's Conservative government was driven from office and replaced by a Labour government under Harold Wilson.

The explanation for this lay in Heath's second clash with the miners. In one sense this was most surprising because such care had been taken to avoid a clash: in the summer of 1973 the Prime Minister had had a secret meeting with the NUM President, Joe Gormley (and the head of the civil service, Sir William Armstrong) at which it was agreed that the miners would be offered and would settle for, an increase above the limits set by the government's income policy. In another sense the clash was not at all surprising: Heath failed to understand the miners. The arrangement went wrong at the outset. The NUM is an ultra-democratic body. If Gormley was to get his secret agreement accepted by his National Executive it was essential that the extra money for the miners should appear to have been extracted only after a long, hard fight from a government determined to maintain its incomes policy. But the National Coal Board offered the full amount at the beginning. The offer was refused. Perhaps Heath felt that an agreement made had been dishonourably broken. At all events, the government refused to increase the offer, although that was the only possible basis for a negotiated settlement. It even made economic sense since these events were unfolding against the mounting oil crisis (the NCB offer had been made four days after the start of the Arab-Israeli War), which seemed likely to raise the value of other fuels like coal. The lesson the government received from the Middle East conflict seemed solely concerned with the need to draw up battle lines. In December industry and commerce were reduced to five-day working, and this was to become three days from January 1974. The miners had already mobilized the power workers and the railwaymen to assist them in any campaign. In this atmosphere, hot with hostility, the wages issue drifted into a direct power struggle between the government and the miners. The zealots on both sides were content with this but many others were not. The most remarkable and determined attempt to reverse the drift came from the TUC alarmed at the crippling effects of the three-day week. On 9 January the offer, backed by the leaders of the major unions was made that if the government gave the miners an additional increase, the other unions would accept this as a special case and not use it as part of their own wage-bargaining. The offer was brusquely rejected by Barber for the government, and with it went the last real hope of a negotiated settlement. Heath was strongly pressed by many leading Conservatives to opt for an early election on the simple emotive issue of whether the government or the unions ruled the country. The miners, after an overwhelming ballot in favour, came out on strike on 9 February. The election was called for 28 February. In a close result, accurately reflecting the ambivalence of the electorate, Labour won a few more seats than the Conservatives (despite polling fewer votes), but had no overall majority. After a few days of uncertainty, while Heath vainly attempted to form a coalition with the Liberals, Harold Wilson became the new Prime Minister.

The mid-1970s: the economy out of control?

The initial course of the new government was largely set by its electoral stance. The miners were given increases averaging around 25 per cent; the Stage 3 incomes policy was abandoned; and the Pay Board abolished. The problems, however, remained and showed every sign of getting worse. The world recession and rising commodity prices (especially of oil) meant a worsening balance of payments. The exports to pay for these required two conditions: that the level of internal prices should not rise so fast as to make British exports uncompetitive, and that internal consumption (public and private) should be checked sufficiently to make available the resources for exports. The voluntary incomes policy favoured by the government seemed unlikely to produce these requirements, especially as it was embodied in a so-called 'social contract' between the government and the unions which seemed unduly one-sided. Prices, especially of food and rent, were to be constrained; income and wealth redistributed; the Industrial Relations Act repealed; but the voluntary wage restraint was expressed only in vague, unspecific terms.

The result was predictable. The government, anxious to establish its Labour identity, pursued policies which were progressive, if not socialistic; wage earners pressed for, and obtained, large increases. In the ominous conditions of 1974 the consequences were equally predictable – and un-palatable. There was an acceleration in prices (despite the food and rent subsidies of the March budget and the rate subsidies and reduction in VAT of the July budget), and a worsening of the balance of payments. These were time-bombs, however, and their clocks did not run out until the crisis of 1976. But their immediate effects were not disruptive, employment remained high and so did incomes, whilst the reformist measures of the government were widely welcomed. A new election in October improved the government's position; instead of being a minority administration the Labour party had an overall majority of three.

Although Denis Healey's November budget – his third in nine months – began to impose some constraints (a big increase in petrol prices and an intention to phase-out subsidies to nationalized industries) wage increases continued to run at levels over 20 per cent. It was the pace of wage inflation, indeed, which accounted for most of the vast increase from £2.7 billion to £6.3 billion in the public sector borrowing requirement (PSBR) revealed in the November budget, although the food and rent subsidies, the increase in the Regional Employment Premium and the reduction in VAT included in the earlier budgets had also contributed. At the centre of the November budget, therefore, was the Chancellor's warning that public expenditure would only be permitted to grow very slowly in real terms over the ensuing years. This was despite the fact that unemployment was increasing; yet since 1945 the normal government response to rising unemployment had been to step up the total level of activity in the economy by running a budget deficit (increasing public expenditure). This strategy had been brought more and more into question during the 1970s as the rate of inflation gradually replaced the level of unemployment as the most significant economic indicator. It was in 1974 that the switch in priorities was signalled. This was not surprising. By the time of the November budget even the sharp increase in the number of unemployed (from 2.3 per cent to 2.7 per cent: an increase of over 100,000 in the previous year) was overshadowed by the 17 per cent increase in retail prices and the 20 per cent increase in wage rates. Moreover, both wages and prices were perceptibly accelerating.

So was the PSBR. Public sector wage increases and the cost of subsidies (especially on housing) made the government deficit for 1974–5 greater than expected (at £7.6 billion), and pointed towards a still greater deficit in the coming year. The budget, despite stagnant output and rising unemployment, was deflationary in that it aimed to reduce this deficit. Mostly this was done by increasing government income through higher taxation, rather than by decreasing government expenditure which, it was claimed, could only be substantially constrained over a period of years. The immediate effects of this tighter government line were negligible – or, at least, did nothing to slow down, still less to reverse, a deteriorating economic situation. Industrial production through the spring and summer of 1975 was actually declining, but wage settlements were being made with increases of 25 per cent; the external value of sterling slumped (although the balance of trade improved); and prices soared. This last aspect was crucial. Although prices had been rising more or less continuously for a whole generation, the upward surge that set in around 1972 seemed a new, and increasingly dangerous, phenomenon. In the summer of 1975 it was realized that prices had risen by over 25 per cent in a single year and this bred an atmosphere of nervous instability where even hyper-inflation (the complete collapse of the value of money) seemed a serious possibility.

It is possible that the air of foreboding and vulnerability helped to produce the decisively affirmative result to the referendum held on 5 June to decide whether or not Britain should remain a member of the EEC: it is certain that it made it politically possible for the government to revert to an incomes policy. The policy laid down in August 1975 was that wage increases should be limited to a maximum of £6 a week over the next year. The policy was simple, easy to administer, would help curb inflation, and could be represented as voluntary since the TUC was now ready to lend its support to wage restraint. But it was still not enough; not even when in the following year the TUC accepted an even tighter control over wages, limiting increases for the next year to less than 5 per cent, which meant accepting a significant decline in the standard of living of most workers. The problem was lack of time, especially to solve the external trading deficit which, by 1976, had become the central economic difficulty.

The chickens of the post-1970 governments now came home to roost. The Barber boom had eroded, but not reversed, the vast balance of payments surplus built up by the ultra-caution of Roy Jenkins after the 1967 devaluation. But the generally high level of world trade disguised the effect of Britain's decline in competitiveness. From 1973 onwards, however, it seemed (later revisions showed that the trade figures were over-pessimistic) that a balance of payments deficit on a large scale had opened up. This derived from several sources – the general decline in world trade hit Britain especially hard as its rate of inflation was greater than that of most of its competitors, whilst the vastly-increased oil prices pressed up the total value of imports into Britain. Until mid-1975, however, there was a great deal of complacency on this issue: it was often argued that since much of the problem 'only' arose because of the oil crisis that it could be ignored. This extraordinary view was given some plausibility because it was possible, though hardly prudent, to ignore the mounting problem because foreigners, and especially oil producers, were willing to leave their money in Britain. The rumblings in mid-1975, drove the government and even the TUC to rethink attitudes about incomes policy, and exposed the fragility of this position. In 1976 it was totally smashed. Foreigners were reluctant to hold more sterling so the value of the pound fell sharply in the spring of 1976. The government hastily patched up arrangements for short-term loans, but there was not much prospect that confidence in sterling would have been restored by the time these ran out at the end of the year. At that stage some more permanent arrangement would have to be reached.

Restraint from outside: the IMF loan

The most obvious form for a more permanent arrangement was for the government to reach agreement by which the International Monetary Fund

(IMF) would provide additional loan facilities. There would, however, be a high price attached to any such agreement. The IMF would not, or would say it would it not, provide the financial support unless the British government agreed to follow economic policies which were acceptable to the IMF. The requirements of the IMF were likely to reflect the nature of the institution. In particular, it was a bankers' organization heavily dependent for its funds on the USA: and the kind of policies that bankers and the US government found most desirable were unlikely to coincide with the priorities of a socialist government in Britain.

Many in Britain were ready to press for acceptance of a loan from the IMF on whatever terms that institution dictated. Prominent amongst those holding this view were many influential people in the City and virtually all the financial press who positively welcomed the prospect of an external body imposing constraints upon a Labour government in Britain. In this they were joined, naturally, by the Conservatives and, what should have been rather less natural, by many in the Labour government who saw attractions in being able to appeal to unavoidable external necessity to justify the unpleasant internal policies which they were forced to pursue. At the time, indeed, it was easy enough to gain the impression that there was no conceivable alternative to accepting – as the government did in December – the heavily deflationary IMF package, involving accelerated and increased cuts in public expenditure and a tight control of money and credit. The government accepted that the measures would involve a cut in an already stagnant level of economic activity and an increase in the level of unemployment. As part of its own response the Labour government, committed to extending public ownership, planned to sell off £500 million of the government's share-holding in BP.

Essentially the IMF attempted to impose the conservative monetarist solution to inflation. There was little serious discussion of the most plausible alternative: to raise output and increase the level of activity in the economy (unemployment was already over 5½ per cent). The two main dangers of such an approach were that it would give additional impetus to inflation and that the higher domestic incomes would (because of Britain's high propensity to import) simply be spent overseas instead of acting as a source of demand for home manufacturers encouraging higher investment and reducing unit costs. The inflationary danger, it was argued, could be met by an intensified incomes policy: the balance of payments threat could be countered by the imposition of direct import controls. There were many problems with such an approach and it may not have been feasible. But the argument went by default: there was no serious examination of an alternative policy.

In the event, the pattern of government policy was set until the end of the decade, or, at least, until the end of the Labour government in May 1979: restraining public expenditure, controlling the money supply and sustaining an incomes policy. It is perhaps significant that it was the collapse of the incomes policy in the winter of 1978–9 which heralded both a new bout of rising inflation and the collapse of the Labour government. Three years of wage control had been associated with a fall in the rate of inflation. The government wished to continue the trend and laid down an even tighter guideline of 5 per cent for wage increases from August 1979. But three years of wage restraint had built up many frustrations and anomalies. The TUC warned the government that a 5 per cent norm would not allow enough flexibility. The Prime Minister stuck obstinately to his target and there was an explosion of worker unrest, the 'winter of discontent', especially amongst public service workers.

Document 2.10
The IMF loan, 1976

(a) From W. Keegan and R. Pennant – Rea, *Who Runs the Economy?*, 1979, pp. 145, 167–8

The IMF team, under former Bank of England official Alan Whittome, did not arrive in London until 1 November. October had been· a dark month during which Minimum Lending Rate was raised to a record 15 per cent, to the chagrin of the Prime Minister; the pound had fallen to $1.55½; and people wondered why it should not go on falling indefinitely. By this time even the hard-line Keynesians in the Treasury were resigned to some further public spending cuts: but their estimates of what needed to be done were nearer £2 billion than the £5 billion urged by some officials . . .

. . . British Government sources interpret the Fund's tactic that November as of putting its weight behind the Treasury minority view that large cuts had to be made in the PSBR. But whereas the PSBR case had been made largely in terms of the need to restore confidence – 'and how good for confidence is zero growth?' was the reply – the IMF tried to strengthen the intellectual case. Although Denis Healey was at first recalcitrant, he appears to have been more receptive to the IMF arguments than some of his senior advisers, and was finally won round. He then had to persuade the Cabinet. The cuts he and the Treasury finally agreed on amounted to £3 billion off the PSBR over two years, against the £4 billion wanted by the IMF team.

When Callaghan eventually realised, after a visit to Schmidt at the end of November, that there was no way in which the IMF terms could be softened beyond a certain point, he backed Healey: and after bitter in-fighting, the Cabinet went along with the package. The IMF loan was agreed and announced early in December; the safety net for the sterling balances followed in January 1977.

The autumn of 1976 has been portrayed essentially as a fight between the US Treasury and Britain. Although Callaghan felt let down by the

Germans at one point, the German Government itself believed it had quite an influence in making life easier for Britain in the end than Simon and Yeo wanted. The US National Security Council economist at the time, Bob Hormats, maintains: 'the point is that the Treasury is responsible to the President. Ford was not going to let Callaghan down in the end. And, in the end, for this reason, neither would the Treasury.'

(b) From *The Sunday Times*, 28 May 1978, Stephen Fay and Hugo Young

Who really won this year-long struggle of wills? 'Everybody won,' says Ed Yeo, 'until they read the small print.' But they did a bit better than that. As Yeo also remarks: 'In the approximate world of politics, everybody did win.'

Denis Healey, having stared national bankruptcy and personal ruin in the face, averted them. The IMF, having asked for a £4bn cut in the PSBR, was satisfied with £3bn. But most of the Cabinet originally wanted far less.

Jim Callaghan established himself as Labour's most authoritative leader since Attlee. He seized control of economic management and demonstrated an ascendancy over his colleagues which he has never lost. His original judgment of the Labour Party may have been luridly pessimistic; but holding it together was a victory of sorts.

Harold Lever's sense of triumph is less strong. He always thought the IMF's deflationary demands unnecessary, and believed that more foresight in 1974 might have avoided the 1976 crisis altogether. But what he won was significant: the conversion first of Callaghan then of Ford to the importance of the sterling balances.

The Left, equally, believe they won something. Without them, social security benefits might have been reduced. More obliquely, the Bennites take comfort from seeing their prophecies, as they believe, come true: rising unemployment, stagnant investment, higher imports, significant 'underspend' in the public sector.

The men from the American Treasury also think they won. Although Ed Yeo reminisces sentimentally about the exercise being a victory for the British people, he is in little doubt that he and Arthur Burns, by their defence of monetarist virtue and sound economic housekeeping, saved the pound.

If any one of these claims is truer than the others, it is the Americans'. For the resolution of the 1976 crisis was a success for the system of international financial diplomacy, in which they carry the heaviest guns. Although British Ministers will go to their graves denying it, the facts of this story suggest that without American and IMF pressure, the Cabinet would not have taken the measures which, with remarkable speed, stabilised the currency.

Having surrendered to this strategic pressure, Callaghan used consummate skill to make it work politically. But the assault on Keynesian principles and socialist aspirations was initiated by the monetarist housekeepers in Washington.

Industry, oil and the EEC

Within the broad strategy of exercising a stagnating restraint to slowly squeeze out excessive inflation, there were of course changes in the specific economic problems which emerged as well as in the broad context within which the strategy was exercised. In industry most government action was *ad hoc* in character. Rescue operations were undertaken for some important firms, such as British Leyland and Alfred Herbert, which were later taken into public ownership. A more dubious case, though it involved a lot of jobs, especially in Scotland, was the granting of £160 million to the American car firm of Chrysler in December 1975. Tony Benn, who presided over the Department of Industry till June 1975, aroused much antagonism by giving assistance to firms not considered to be so vital, and even assisting the setting-up of some forlorn workers' co-operatives like Scottish News Enterprises, Norton Villiers and Kirby Manufacturing. The National Enterprise Board (NEB) was supposed to have provided a more coherent form of protecting jobs and encouraging investment in manufacturing. The NEB was not, however, made operative for more than two years after Labour took office in 1974 and, even then, it was specifically to operate in an unplanned atmosphere and to avoid the exercise of any compulsion over private industry. All of this was, in the context of the economic crisis of 1976, plausibly described as 'realistic', but could hardly be said to provide a systematic scheme to encourage investment in manufacturing industry. However, the government did provide in its White Paper on Industrial Strategy in November 1975 for the setting-up of nearly forty Sector Working Parties aimed at improving the performance of manufacturing industries by seeking a voluntary consensus between owners, workers and government.

There were two major changes in the broad context within which British economic policy was pursued. The first was the steady growth in North Sea oil. The economy had gained from supplies of gas since the early 1970s, but the oil contribution only became significant from about 1976 onwards when oil production leapt from 1.6 million metric tonnes in 1975 to 12.1 million tonnes in 1976. By 1979 North Sea oil output (around 75 million tonnes) amounted to almost 80 per cent of British oil consumption, and the oil and natural gas together constituted about one-half of UK primary fuel consumption. Much might be said on this, but one simple and chilling point will suffice. In the energy-fraught 1970s it was a massive economic advantage suddenly to become a major oil producer. By 1979 it was estimated that (at 1978 prices) North Sea production added £3.8 billion to the gross national product and made a contribution to the balance of payments of a staggering £8 billion. Yet the economy was apparently stagnant (output in 1979 was only 10 per cent higher than in 1975), whilst the estimated balance of payments *deficit* on current account for 1979 was £2.5 billion (most of these figures are taken from CSO *Monthly Digest of Statistics*, February 1980).

The other main contextual change of the 1970s was more ambiguous but no more comforting. Britain became a member of the EEC. In 1972 Britain, under the Heath government, had completed negotiations for entry but, because of substantial opposition especially in the Labour party, the issue was not finally (as it then seemed) resolved until the referendum of June 1975 gave a two to one majority in favour. There had always been doubts and divisions over the economic benefits to Britain of EEC membership. In the event, however, it was clear that the challenge from Europe did not revitalize British industry – perhaps simply because Britain joined at a time when world trade growth had dwindled and with it much of the buoyancy of the Common Market. Even more clearly it emerged that the costs of membership to Britain, especially in terms of supporting the Common Agricultural Policy, were mounting and represented a substantial balance of payments leakage.

1970s trends: inflation, employment, wages, imports

At a still higher level of generality, a few broad remarks need to be made about the characteristic economic trends of the 1970s – rising prices, increasing unemployment, accelerating wage demands and a strong propensity to import – as well as noting briefly the ways in which those trends affected economic thinking.

Inflation has been a persistent feature of post-war Britain. Until about 1967, however, the problems which this raised did not seem insuperable. The only period at which prices rose at a threatening pace was 1950–2 when the rate of increase was about 9 per cent per annum. That was an understandable outburst, since these years witnessed the effect of the devaluation of 1949 (the lower external value of the pound necessarily raised the prices of imported food and raw materials), together with the higher cost of commodities because of the boom associated with the Korean War. From 1952 to 1967, however, the average annual rate of price increases in Britain was about 3 per cent. It was always recognized that the policies necessary to keep up the aggregate level of demand and employment would necessarily involve some inflationary pressure. This seemed a reasonable price to pay in the 1950s and 1960s when the rate of inflation seemed to be generally low and steady.

There were some ominous signs even before 1967. Thus the pace of inflation seemed more marked in the 1960s than it had been in the 1950s. The real change, however, came after 1967. In part this was simply the effect of the devaluation of that year which raised prices by making imported goods dearer. But that effect should, after a year or two, have worked itself out as seems to have happened after the 1949 devaluation. On this occasion, however, the increased upward trend continued. Even before the oil price rises in 1973, prices in Britain from 1967 to 1973 were increasing at an average rate of 7½ per cent. More ominous still was the tendency for the rate of inflation to increase as it did almost continuously from 1967 to 1975 when the rate was almost 25 per cent (see table 2.4). The rate of increase then fell between 1975 and 1978 when it was reduced to less than 10 per cent, but in 1979 – perhaps with the collapse of the policy of wage restraint – the rate again increased.

Table 2.4 Retail prices, unemployment and wage rates, 1967–79

	Prices[a] *% change on previous year*	*Unemployment*[b] *%*	*Wage rates (manual workers, all industries) % change on previous year*
1967	+2.5	2.2	+3.9
1968	+4.7	2.3	+6.5
1969	+5.4	2.3	+5.3
1970	+6.4	2.5	+10.0
1971	+9.4	3.3	+12.9
1972	+7.1	3.6	+13.8
1973	+9.2	2.6	+13.7
1974	+16.1	2.5	+19.8
1975	+24.2	3.9	+29.5
1976	+16.3	5.3	+19.3
1977	+15.9	5.7	+6.6
1978	+8.2	5.7	+14.1
1979	+13.2	5.4	+15.0

Notes
[a] All items: retail prices, average for year.
[b] UK excluding school leavers and adult students. Annual average.
Source: calculated from *Economic Trends* (CSO)

Similarly the unemployment experience sharply differentiated the 1970s from the preceding quarter century. In the 25 years before 1970 the annual average level of unemployment had only once, in the desperate crisis and crippling weather of 1947, touched 3 per cent and had averaged 1.9 per cent. In the 1970s the rate was normally over 3 per cent, reached nearly 6 per cent and averaged 4 per cent. The number registered as unemployed, considered high at half a million in 1970 was more than double this level at over 1½ million in 1979 and reached 2½ million by the end of 1980.

Over the same period wages showed a similarly accelerating trend. In the 1960s (until the last two years of the decade) wage rates were rising but the annual rate of increase was less than 5 per cent per annum. Purists complained that wage rates were increasing faster than gains in productivity and that this tended to push up prices. But since both price inflation and wage inflation seemed to be contained within fairly narrow limits, most people were prepared to accept that as constituting a reasonable approximation to stability. The upward drift of wages and prices certainly seemed preferable to the likely consequences – higher unemployment and lower growth – of any serious deflationary attempt to squeeze them out. The 1970s witnessed a dramatic change. Annual percentage wage rate increases were always in double figures and rose to nearly 30 per cent in the single year of 1975. And again, like the shift in the inflation rate, it is important to notice that the change preceded the oil crisis.

All this was disconcerting. It was disconcerting because economic indicators were behaving in ways they were not supposed to. In particular, it had long been accepted that unemployment and wage rates should move inversely, that is that when unemployment increased the rate of growth of wage rates should decrease. Indeed, more recently this relationship had been formally incorporated into the economists' tool-box as the 'Phillips curve' and seemed to survive substantial testing. But in the 1970s a *rise* in the level of unemployment was accompanied by an *increase* in the rate of growth of money wage rates. Observers were surprised, for a time at least, to see the coincidence of a decline in the rate of growth (or even the absolute level) of general economic activity and a continuation (or even an acceleration) of rising prices. This phenomenon of the 1970s came to be described as 'stagflation'.

Revisions in economic thinking

These changes surfaced in the 1970s, and they were exacerbated by such particular events as the increase in oil prices, but they were not the product of that decade. They had been a long time coming and one consequence was a major reappraisal of the relationship between the government and the economy. At an overall level this relationship had, ever since the war, been guided by the economic ideas of John Maynard Keynes.

In this context, the essence of the Keynesian system was the deliberate use of government fiscal (budgetary) policy to keep the economy at a high level of activity. If the level of activity fell (raising unemployment), then the government would budget for a deficit, and the resultant excess of government expenditure over revenue would pump extra income into the economy to stimulate renewed activity. And if the level of activity was too high (reducing unemployment) a government surplus would extract funds from the economy and reduce the general level of activity. In Keynes's formulation the objective of this governmental intervention in the economy was defensive: it was a necessary concession to keep intact the capitalistic system which Keynes considered to be essential to the maintenance of the fundamental liberal values which were his main concern. In the 1930s, when Keynes evolved his theories, all this had seemed to be endangered. Left to itself the capitalist system seemed to produce fluctuations of an intensity (especially in a downward direction) which were unacceptable and which stimulated political attacks from both the left and the right. Keynesian theories pointed to a use of government fiscal policy to moderate these fluctuations and tensions.

In the course of the application of this system in post-war Britain, both its philosophy and its mechanism were substantially adjusted. In the view of Keynes the management of the economy by the government would only require occasional interventions at an aggregate level to a system which would otherwise be mostly left to regulate itself: economic management would consist of 'nudges' to prevent the economy sliding too far in one direction or another. But, partly because the method seemed so successful in keeping employment very high without generating high and rising rates of inflation, more and more came to be demanded of economic management. Governments (whether Conservative or Labour) expected, and were expected, to respond much more immediately to economic changes; and many economists believed, or persuaded themselves, that this was possible. Economic management thus developed towards a process of 'fine tuning' the economy, which represented a substantial change in philosophy. The result was a more continuous response by governments to changes in the economy, and the shift was partly associated with a tendency for the public sector of the economy to become relatively more important.

At the same time, more was being asked in terms of results. At first the object was mostly to maintain a high level of employment, meeting the commitment to full employment embodied in the White Paper of 1944. On that criterion economic management could be said to have been spectacularly successful for a quarter-century after 1945. Increasingly, however, other criteria demanded attention. From the outset the inflationary dangers of full employment were recognized. An even closer watch had to be kept on the balance of payments. High employment meant high incomes, part of which were spent on imported goods and this could lead to a deterioration in the balance of payments. It was certainly the case that almost all the periodic economic crises in Britain took the form of containing difficulties with the balance of payments. Policies undertaken to ensure full employment were thus likely to increase or create difficulties over inflation and the external balance. These potential incompatibilities became more marked over time and were enormously heightened as, from the late 1950s, the public insisted not just on low unemployment, but also on a high rate of growth for the economy. Such a concern, pointing towards more expansion, seemed to contradict the requirement of constraining prices and the balance of payments.

The pressure towards adjustment both of the priorities and of the methods of government policy had been accumulating, then, for a long time. What was surprising was that it was contained for so long. Even in the 1960s the rate of inflation was modest. It was, however, continuous and this in itself eventually accelerated the pace through its effect on expectations. It became assumed that prices would increase by so many per cent in the following year and hence wage bargainers (employers as well as unions) took *that* increase as given and then haggled about how much *extra* should be added. This accelerated the inflation especially as what was added usually exceeded the general increase in productivity. Increasing inflation thus added to the attraction of alternative economic theories which seemed to be more directly related to price changes than was Keynesianism which was more associated with maintaining full employment.

It was natural, then, that during the 1970s increasing public attention was paid to so-called monetary economics. This represented the revival of an old tradition of economic ideas which had been much honed and refurbished by a group of scholars in Chicago, associated with Milton Friedman. The essential message was simple enough: that changes in the price level were caused by (in some versions, *only* caused by) variations in the money supply. If the supply of money was increased then (after a suitable lag) prices would rise; if the money supply was reduced, prices would be reduced. The theory thus seemed to be directly relevant to one of the most central economic problems of the 1970s, that of inflation. Its attraction for many, however, went well beyond this, since its basic political implication – in sharp contrast to Keynesianism – was that all that was required of a government was that it should control the money supply. In the pure form of the theory almost all other government activities were not only superfluous, but harmful. The monetary school was (and is) heavily attacked, of course, on both theoretical and political grounds. It provided the intellectual content of the Conservative electoral victory in 1979 and, as a result, was given an extended practical trial in an attempt to solve the problems of the British economy.

Monetarism was not, however, the only possible choice if Keynesianism was rejected. In the drastically changed economic climate of the 1970s, high unemployment, rapid inflation, stagnating output, there naturally emerged many attempts to analyse and prescribe for the British *malaise*.

But amidst the disagreement and confusion there was also a widespread acceptance of some of the basic ingredients of the problem: investment, especially in manufacturing industry, was too low; too much was imported and/or too little exported (and although, with North Sea oil, the balance of payments problem seemed much easier towards the end of the decade, the basic problem still lurked); and real incomes rose faster than output. Some of the responses were mostly pragmatic. One such was to revive the idea of adding a more or less permanent, more or less voluntary incomes policy to the basic Keynesian approach. If this kept increases in real incomes (in practice the discussion was about wages and salaries only) below those of output, it was hoped that resources could be released for investment and exports, though no obvious mechanism was provided to ensure such a transfer. Another approach identified the nation's economic difficulties with the growth of the public sector, and argued that not only funds but labour was directed to 'unproductive' public areas at the expense of 'productive' manufacturing industry. (This approach was mostly associated with Bacon and Eltis, 1976, and was well-publicized in a series of articles in *The Sunday Times.*) The reasoning was never very secure, nor did its message seem all that compelling when the proportionate size of Britain's public sector was compared with that (sometimes larger) of other countries who none the less seemed to be economically successful. It was, however, a popular viewpoint and it certainly helped to create an atmosphere more favourable to the pursuit of monetarist policies with their similar (though differently derived) emphasis on cuts in public expenditure.

Another view stressed that British economic growth since 1945 has been slower than that of most advanced industrialized nations because Britain's productivity growth has been slower. In part this was mere tautology: economic growth *is* productivity growth in the sense of increasing the output of an economy more rapidly than its inputs. None the less, to stress Britain's lagging productivity performance was to introduce a significant change of perspective. Most of the other diagnoses of Britain's economic difficulties tended to point towards the macro-economic aspects of the economy – that is, towards such broad aggregates as the *general* level of prices, the *total* money supply, the *overall* increase in wages. Concern with productivity, however, was also bound to involve greater attention being given to micro-economic elements – that is, to what was happening to the individual firm or industry. This was because productivity growth was clearly associated with technical development in which a critical stage concerns the pace and scale with which innovations are introduced into particular firms and factories. Some critics (e.g. Cairncross, 1975) claimed that Britain did very badly in the adoption of new technologies. It is a claim which could only be satisfactorily tested by looking at the micro-economic performance of the economy.

These various approaches of the economic analysts to the problems of the 1970s suggest that there was not just one British disease, but several. The most coherent theoretical exposition added to those of the Keynesians and the monetarists was that of the New Cambridge school. The theoretical details need not detain us: the approach was essentially Keynesian but inverted the relationships between some of the key variables (the balance of payments and the budget; aggregate demand and the exchange rate). For our purposes the most significant feature was that the writers of this school became increasingly associated with the case for imposing some form of import controls. It was asserted that the monetarist approach would simply entail a particularly severe form of old-fashioned deflation (high unemployment and reduced output), whilst conventional Keynesianism, if it aimed to reflate the economy would be endangered by a growing balance of payments deficit. There was much evidence that a very high proportion of any increase in income (demand) in Britain was spent on additional imports. The argument, therefore, was that steps should be taken to prevent, or limit, any additional imports resulting from a higher level of internal activity. The aim was said to be not to cut imports, but to reduce their rate of growth.

This is not the place to attempt to judge between the various policy proposals. The point being made is much simpler. The sharp changes in the economic climate which emerged in the 1970s did not fit clearly and easily into the existing dominant (Keynesian) pattern in Britain. A number of new approaches were developed or given greater prominence. If much of the discussion seemed to turn on complex problems of economic analysis, the implications were more wide-ranging and rather easier to grasp. In the face of the dismay at the growing confusion in the economy the long political consensus over the broad approach to be taken in economic policy was largely dissolved. In the maritime analogy beloved by politicians, at the beginning of the period governments knew how to sail the ship of state, and had good charts for their voyage. By 1980 they drifted blind across unknown seas.

Exercise 5

The British economy in the 1970s

5.1 Why was the 'Barber boom' a failure?

5.2 Were Britain's economic troubles in the 1970s caused by the world oil crisis?

5.3 What was the significance of the 1976 loan from the IMF?

5.4 What seemed to change in the 1970s in the relationship between wages and unemployment?

5.5 In what ways did post-war management of the economy differ from Keynes's concept of economic management?

5.6 Why were there large attempts to revise economic thinking in the 1970s?

Guide to exercises

1.1 Four broad characteristics are mentioned in the text. You need to consider these and perhaps comment on why they should be deemed important. But you might also think of others which might be mentioned (e.g. the level of taxes; the course taken by the balance of payments) and try to find out something about them. Remember the exercise is about *economic* characteristics.

1.2 The obvious approach to testing is to look for some indicators of the proportionate importance of government action in the economy as a whole. Some such indicators would be suggested by questions like: what proportion of gross national product is total public expenditure? of the total occupied population what percentage work in the public sector? Try to think of others (investment?). Each of the indicators carries with it problems of measurement. Thus, for example, total public expenditure includes large amounts which simply involve transfers from one group of citizens to another (pensions, family allowances etc.). Are they thus a good measure of the level of government intervention? Similarly, the employment figures may give an unreliable measure if the public sector happens to include many labour-intensive service industries (education, health etc.).

1.3 Prices and wages are given in the statistics on pp. 82–3. Do they run together or does one always (usually?) lag behind the other? Can it be said that changes in the one series *causes* the changes in the other? Have they risen steadily? Have they tended to accelerate?

2.1 If the main consideration was to be the proportionate burden borne by the British and American economies during the war then the answer would be yes. But was it? And was there any good reason why it should have been? If commercial considerations were the main consideration the terms then look generous and the answer would be no.

2.2 There was certainly very bad weather in the winter and spring of 1947. But why should this have had so drastic an effect? (Consider the crucial fuel shortage – how would this affect the economy?). When the economy is as desperate as was the case in 1947 almost anything that doesn't go just right is likely to create disproportionate problems – does this really amount to bad luck? And it's as certain as such things can be that there was no possibility – even under the most favourable circumstances – of Britain being able to have managed full currency convertibility in 1947 as the conditions of the earlier American loan required.

3.1 Rearmament can (arguably) be said to be economically useful if (as in the 1930s) there is high unemployment and low demand. But in 1951 the level of unemployment was very low (give figures) and there was clearly a high level of demand upon total resources. So the resources for rearmament had to come from other areas. Whether they should be so diverted was a policy question, and the health service *v.* defence argument simply dramatized the kinds of choices to be made. But that was only the superficial (financial) aspect. The real point – and Bevan's real point – was that the actual resources (steel, engineering products etc.) would have to be diverted from productive manufacturing uses. Defence, moreover, would lay claims to materials and skills which were especially short and especially crucial for general economic recovery.

3.2 'How' was mainly through the use of interest-rate policy (including control over hire purchase credit terms – why?). 'Why' was because it seemed increasingly foolish to put all the weight for adjusting and controlling the economy on fiscal (budgetary) measures. This partly reflected – but this would be a minor aspect – the presumed preferences of the Conservative governments of the 1950s for the more generalized monetary controls rather than the possibly more specific controls of fiscal measures favoured by Labour governments. But note that both parties would in the 1950s have used a mix of both methods; and that both parties were fully agreed on the right and duty of the government to control and adjust the economy.

3.3 The implication of the term is of a broad political consensus over both the aims and (even to a surprising extent) the means of economic policy. Largely this reflected the general satisfaction in the 1950s with the overall performance of the British economy. (Perhaps because contrasts were mostly being made with British inter-war experience).

3.4 Look at the balance of payments figures in the statistics on p. 85. Then consider the form taken by the economic crises of the economy which always seemed to be checked by external restraints.

4.1 Perhaps the central question to be discussed here involves an assessment of whether economic growth became prominent because the populace generally heavily desired material goods (effects of ITV?); whether the achievements of the 1950s (full employment and modest growth) had been digested; whether the performance of other advanced industrial nations became the indicator of economic success; or whether economic growth seemed a necessary prerequisite for radical (and peaceful) social improvements.

4.2 Much of this revolves round the obsession with growth, and with the concentration upon foreign (especially French) example. But modern technology often means that there is a long time-gap between making an investment and producing the final product (consider the development of a new car, for example). So private industry had good cause a) to plan ahead itself and b) to want some assurance that government will maintain a favourable general economic climate.

4.3 After describing stop-go you should consider whether the concern about it was just another aspect of the 1960s economic growth complex. And then say how stop-go would affect growth, and try to see what (if any) other harmful economic effects it might have (for example, creating uncertainty and instability).

4.4 The issue turns on the presumption that a Labour government elected to stimulate growth, to give a high priority to more explicit planning, to hasten social progress etc. was prevented or deflected or obstructed from such pursuits during its crucial early years in office (1964–7) by the need to maintain the value of the pound. If the pound had been devalued in 1964 a different set of priorities would, it is argued, have operated.

4.5 Much international trade was conducted by the use of sterling. Thus it was argued that any change in the value of sterling would make for instability and uncertainty in world trade. And the growth of world trade was considered an important source of economic growth. Also much foreign capital (private and government) was held in the form of sterling – devaluation would reduce the value of this. On these assumptions many (especially in the Treasury and the City) felt that Britain had a duty to maintain the value of sterling. This meant that much of Britain's internal economic policy was governed by this presumed need. Consider the implications (and justification) of these presumptions.

5.1 You need to set out the objectives of the boom – especially the intention to avoid stop-go and sustain economic growth so that an export-led boom could develop. Then consider whether this was realistic (for example, a rapid growth in exports required that British costs would be competitive – but would not the conditions of sustained growth produce pressures – via wage increases etc. – that would necessarily force up costs?).

5.2 This requires a setting out of the nature of the economic difficulties and a consideration of a) whether they had already taken shape before the oil crisis, and b) the extent to which they were worsened by that crisis.

5.3 The conditions of the loan vastly affected the kinds of policies which the British government could pursue. (How?) Part of the significance depends on the extent (if any) to which there was an alternative solution to the problems of the economy.

5.4 There was a general presumption until the 1970s that more unemployment would have the effect of slowing down the rate of wage increases. The empirical experience of the 1970s seemed inconsistent with this. Discuss the basis of the presumption and why it seemed to become inoperative at this time.

5.5 The requirement here is to discuss why Keynes suggested that a capitalist economy could be kept basically wealthy and maintain its virtues (which were?) by only occasional exercises of government intervention; then to consider why government intervention to manage the economy became much more continuous.

5.6 You need to set out the main ways in which the economic experience of the 1970s seemed much less favourable than that of the two previous decades. Then show whether and why the economy did not seem to respond to the earlier (reasonably successful) methods of controlling it based on Keynesian principles. And hence there was an incentive to search for alternative approaches – which required different economic analyses.

3 The British system of government since 1945

1 Change and continuity

Attitudes towards British government have changed more than the system of government itself. In the immediate post-war period élite opinion showed marked confidence in, indeed complacency towards, the system. By the 1970s following numerous and various attempts at reform, confidence had given way to distrust and cynicism. For the mass of people too, those not especially concerned in government, trust and loyalty had been eroded by years of apparent failure. In 1945 the legitimacy of government, that is, the government's right to loyalty and obedience, could be assumed. In the 1970s there was much talk, and some demonstration, of a condition of ungovernability. This was much exaggerated as a description of practice, but the change in attitudes was plain and profound.

The system of government so much admired in the earlier years had the unique virtues (so it was thought) of an unwritten constitution. It was indeed seen as a 'constitution', well-founded, solid and secure, respected if not revered; but 'unwritten', hence special and specially British, of an elusive and untestable profundity, above all 'flexible', to sway and bend in the winds of history. All this, clearly, was a myth as much as a constitution, but nevertheless a constitutional myth of great power, which still in 1980 worked to support and protect both the facade and the foundations of British government.

Behind the myth of the 1940s lay a set of understandings or notions about the constitution. It was unwritten in that it was not codified in a single document; some of its most fundamental working rules, like ministerial responsibility, were imprecise conventions; and the scope for litigation (appealing to law against the government) was limited. It was further a unitary constitution: there was no separation of powers because historically the Crown had merged with a sovereign (i.e. supreme) Parliament, and political parties for their own interests maintained the fusion of executive and legislature. The constitutional union of Crown-in-Parliament supported a centralized system of government. At the centre there was a small, closely related group of 'governors', ministers and civil servants, bound together by the conventions of the collective cabinet's responsibility and civil service monopoly; and unchallenged by any substantial system of local governments. This central power was enhanced, but also limited and legitimized, by a competitive two-party system, through which the two parties competed for, and alternated in, power. The parties were 'responsible': they presented a programme to the electors, and, if elected, could be held 'responsible' for their conduct in office, according to the electors' 'mandate'.

'Responsibility' was a key concept in this understanding of British government. For the constitutional myth, 'responsibility' had the advantage of conveying a vague sense of good behaviour and respectability. (It was used in this way at the end of the 1970s for 'free and responsible collective bargaining'.) But strictly 'responsibility' meant answerability to someone else. In this case it conveyed that the power of the centre was checked and controlled by answerability through Parliament to the people. Thus the British constitution was thought to have solved the problem of the incompatibility of strong and popular government.

In the 1960s and 1970s this account of British government lost some of its credibility. Broadly, the critics claimed (i) that the account was not an accurate guide to what actually happened; (ii) that in any case it was not deserving of the whole-hearted approval conveyed by the label 'democratic'; and (iii) that the system changed after 1945 in ways which weakened or destroyed the qualities claimed in the earlier account.

The following documents illustrate the myth of the constitution as it was in 1945, and some of the later criticisms.

Document 3.1
The constitutional myth in decline

(a) *The principles of the constitution*
From W. Ivor Jennings, *The British Constitution*, 1942, pp. 209–10

There is a close relation between the policies followed by the Government and the general ideas of the majority of the electorate. It is a consequence of the simple principles upon which the British Constitution is based. The Government governs because it has a majority in the House of Commons. It possesses that majority because the party which it leads secured a majority of seats at the last general election. The parties are . . . truly based upon competing political principles. In preferring one party to another, therefore, the electorate not only prefers one Government to another but prefers one line of policy to another. Its choice is of course made at infrequent intervals, but always the Government in power has the prospect of having to appeal to the electorate at no very distant date. If it wishes to remain in power it must continue to receive the support of a majority. It must be able to base a successful appeal on its past record. It must be able to explain away its mistakes and emphasise its achievements. Every mistake is an argument against it and every achievement an argument for it. Therefore it must not make obvious mistakes, and its achievements must be such as will meet the elector's approval. Since in fact the division of support between the two major parties is extremely small, any Government must have profound respect for movements of opinion. Nor can it fail to be aware of such movements, for every member of the House of Commons is in close touch with his constituency and is aware of the currents that tend to lose him votes. He will lose votes from every unpopular action by his leaders because he is elected not on his personality nor on his political record but on his party label. A vote against the Government is a vote against him. Accordingly, he expresses in the House or in the lobbies the fear that the Government policy induces in him. He sounds the alarm in the House when the bell begins to ring in his constituency.

(b) *Parliamentary Responsible Government*
From L. S. Amery, *Thoughts on the Constitution,* 1947, pp. 301–2

Our system of government is usually described as Parliamentary Responsible Government. It would be difficult to find a better description. But it must be remembered, first of all, that Parliamentary Government means government, not by Parliament, but to use the old phrase, government 'by the King in Parliament'. Secondly, that the responsibility is not merely one towards the majority in Parliament. Ministers on taking office accept a first and dominant responsibility to the Crown, as representing the unity and continuity of the life of the nation and of the Empire, for defending the wider national and Imperial interest. They accept . . . a corresponding individual responsibility towards the particular services over which they have been called to preside. As members of a Cabinet they accept, over and above their individual ministerial responsibility, a responsibility to and for their colleagues which is the basis of the collective responsibility of the Cabinet. As members of Parliament themselves they are responsible to Parliament as a whole and to the nation for the effective working of Parliament as the centre of our national life, for the maintenance of full and free discussion of every aspect of government policy, and for support of the Speaker in upholding the dignity and impartiality of debate. It is only subject to these wider responsibilities that, as party leaders, they owe a responsibility to their own party for promoting its particular views and forwarding its interests.

The word 'responsibility' has, however, two senses. It connotes not only accountability to an outside or final authority. It also connotes a state of mind, which weighs the consequences of action and then acts, irrespective, it may be, of the concurrence or approval of others. It is the strength of our constitutional system that it encourages and fosters responsibility in that higher sense. A British government is not merely responsible to those who have appointed it or keep it in office in the sense in which an agent is responsible to his principal. It is an independent body which on taking office assumes the responsibility of leading and directing Parliament and the nation in accordance with its own judgement and convictions. Members of Parliament are no mere delegates of their constituents, but, as Burke pointed out, representatives of the nation, responsible, in the last resort, to their own conscience.

Nor is the responsibility of the Opposition in these various respects any less than that of the Government and of its supporters. On the Opposition rests the main responsibility for what was once the critical function of Parliament as a whole, while at the same time it directs its criticisms with a view to convincing public opinion of its own fitness for office.

The combination of responsible leadership by government with responsible criticism in Parliament is the essence of our Constitution.

(c) *The Westminster model in decline*
From D. Marquand 'The Devolution debate', *The Listener*, 8 March 1979

The Forties and Fifties were in fact the apogee of the 'Westminster model'. Politicians, lawyers, academics, journalists and general public all seemed convinced, not just that the British system of government was the best for Britain, but that it was the best for everywhere else as well.

In the last 15 years or so, all this has changed. In the first place, the general public has become increasingly discontented with the 'outputs' of our system – and increasingly prone to demonstrate its discontent by kicking those who run the system in the teeth. Secondly, the system has come under increasingly fierce and sustained attack, occasionally from those who are actually operating it and very frequently indeed from those with recent experience of operating it.

All this activity, it seems to me – like the criticism which it is, in part, intended to answer – is a symptom of a much deeper malaise. The British system of government, like so much in this country, is a largely Victorian legacy, with a few 20th-century additions. But the 20th-century additions – governmental control of the parliamentary timetable, for example, or the growth of the cabinet office, or the development of the modern mass party – have not been assimilated into the Victorian structure. Meanwhile, new needs have grown up, and new things have had to be done to satisfy those needs.

At the same time, to an extent unequalled in any other country, Britain has suffered a sharp and painful decline, both in relative power and in relative prosperity. The result is burgeoning popular discontent, a steady decline in the moral authority of government, and a system which does not fit the society whose needs it is supposed to serve.

The implication is clear: further patching is not only useless but damaging. We are right to be discontented with the constitution as it is; we are right to want to change it. But we should now stop changing it piecemeal and ad hoc, buying off particular grievances here and satisfying particular party interest there, without looking at the structure as a whole and without having the remotest notion of the philosophical basis on which our changes rest.

Our Victorian ancestors had a theory of the state, and they based their structure on that theory. One of the reasons why it was so imposing and why it has lasted so long is that structure and theory coincided.

We have no theory; and one of the reasons why the changes we have made in the Victorian structure have so often been damaging and ephemeral is that we therefore have no clear idea of what we are trying to achieve.

(d) *Ungovernability*
From A. King, 'Why is Britain becoming harder to govern?', BBC, 1976, pp. 6–7

During the 1960s almost everyone took Britain's political institutions for granted. They needed to be reformed, of course. The civil service was thought to be too amateur; it was generally agreed that Parliament needed to be more responsive to the electorate and more capable of acting as a check on the executive. But no one advocated scrapping the constitution entirely, and most of us assumed, without really thinking about it, that our political system would remain essentially unchanged. Whatever else happened, the press would remain free, Parliament would go on sitting, the political parties would continue to contest elections. Britain would remain in the future what she had been in the past – a tolerant, liberal democracy.

Suddenly, in the mid-1970s, we are not so sure. We had got used to the crisis in our economy. Now we begin to wonder whether we are not also confronted with a crisis in our polity. Laws enacted by Parliament are not obeyed by the people. Elected Governments find that they have to share their power with unelected bodies like the Trades Union Congress and the Confederation of British Industry. Governments come and go with increasing frequency. Events are seemingly beyond their control. And the signs multiply of popular restlessness. Turnout at general elections has declined sharply since the early 1950s. So has support for both of the two major political parties. Men and women who have grievances, whether they be trade unionists or nursing sisters or dairy farmers, are far readier than they were a generation ago to take their grievances into the streets. Politically as well as economically, we in Britain can feel the ground shifting, ever so slightly, under our feet.

Talk of the end of liberal democracy in Britain is, of course, premature. Democratic norms are still almost universally accepted in Britain. Neither the extreme left nor the extreme right has anything remotely approaching either the mass following or the physical force that would be required to establish a dictatorship. Indeed serious talk of the end of British democracy is largely confined to American news magazines and television commentators. But the fact that the talk takes place at all is in itself remarkable. Britain is undoubtedly a much harder country to govern than it used to be – and is, if anything, becoming more so.

(e) *The British disease*

From N. MacRae, 'The People we have become', *The Economist*, April 28, 1973

. . . we have since 1945 had a unique test of whether our British system of government is proving appropriate to the modern age. During this period we have launched nearly a quarter of the present population of the world on to a course of national independence, with governments drawn up initially according to the Westminster model. They have been a nearly unmitigated disaster.

The countries of the new Commonwealth are now, almost without exception, among the few areas of the world where government is not succeeding in inspiring either economic growth or personal freedom or political stability.

Britain was the only major European country that did not have the decision-making bodies in its society ploughed through by defeat and occupation in war during 1940–1945. We are therefore left with a lot of institutions that no sensible country would have re-created, and Anthony Sampson is surely right in saying that the worst legacy from the Victorians to Britain has been 'the idea of permanence . . . railways, family firms, coal mines or regiments all acquired the safe, unchanging character of a country estate . . . our outdated Victorian conceptions are defended because they are there, or because "it's odd but it works."' The result is a surfeit in Britain of closed rather than open minds – of 'men whose thinking has been conditioned by the rules and atmosphere of a single institution, rather than those who see over the partitions and adapt institutions to suit their own ends.' In continental Europe, by contrast, the one usual closure of mind is the temporarily very useful one that hardly anybody is willing to think about what happened before 1945.

'The characteristic danger of great nations, like the Romans, or the English, which have a long history of continuous creation,' said Walter Bagehot a hundred years ago, 'is that they may at last fail from not comprehending the great institutions they have created.' The theme of this survey has been that this danger is now, for Britain, at possibly mortal crisis point. Almost all of the great institutions Britain has created –

parliament, the civil service, local government, the law enforcement authorities, the other public services, the nationalised industries, the trade unions – are not performing the functions which were their original purpose. Most are being operated mainly in order to allow the able top people in each of them to enjoy themselves by concentrating on doing the things that give them the most satisfaction. Almost all of the changes that are needed are therefore ones that would cause maximum disruption in what the most intelligent public men in the country have come insensibly to regard as their entirely reasonable sense of purpose. This is why they are the opposite of the changes that are likely to be put into effect. That is the British disease.

Exercise 1

The constitutional myth in decline

1.1 What are the principal features of 'the classic view' as represented by Jennings and Amery?
1.2 Is Amery's 'Parliamentary Responsible Government' democratic?
1.3 What do later commentators claim has gone wrong with British government?
1.4 Do the conditions described meet the description 'ungovernability'?
1.5 Marquand refers to a Victorian 'theory of the state'. What roughly do you think he has in mind?

2 Changes in the British constitution, 1945–80

The documents above show up the scope of the changes with which we are concerned – the constitution itself; attitudes towards it (which profoundly affect its working); theories about the state; the role of governments in the modern economy and expectations about that role; the number of participants in the processes of government and the nature of their behaviour. Thus changes in the institutions at the centre of the system of government are a part only of the whole process of political change. This section sets out the fundamental changes in the formal constitution since 1945; other institutional reform is dealt with in section 4.

Parliament

By the Representation of the People Act 1948, the remaining 'fancy franchises' (additional votes), those of occupiers of business premises and university graduates, were abolished; postal voting was introduced; and a general redistribution of seats was made. Thus the old Chartist objective of 'one man, one vote' was finally achieved. In 1969 the voting age was reduced from 21 to 18. The delaying power of the House of Lords was reduced to one year in 1949. In 1958 life peerages were introduced. This measure had quite radical consequences since life peers, together with the rapidly dwindling number of newly created hereditary peers, came to take a predominant part in the work of the House, and stimulated some of their hereditary colleagues to a more assiduous attention to business. The Life Peerages Act was thus much more significant than the Act of 1963, which permitted the renunciation of peerages (thus allowing Mr Wedgwood-Benn, Mr Quintin Hogg and Sir Alec Douglas-Home to pursue political careers in the House of Commons, the latter for a few months as Prime Minister). These changes completed the long series of 'parliamentary' reforms begun in 1832. In the Victorian sense, Britain became a formally perfect parliamentary democracy.

The government's responsibility

The first Parliamentary Commissioner for Administration (Ombudsman) was established in 1967. His job was to investigate complaints of maladministration (procedural, not substantive errors: for example, the ministry may do that to you, despite your objections, but they must first enquire into all the cirumstances, go through all the procedures). It is significant that Parliament jealously insisted that citizens must approach the Commissioner only through a Member of Parliament. Notwithstanding, the principle of redress of grievances outside Parliament was a constitutional novelty with radical implications. In practice the achievement of the Ombudsman was not spectacular, and the radical potential was not realized. But the redress of grievances in this way was valuable in itself, and the system was extended to the health service and local government.

   The two conventions of collective responsibility and ministerial responsibility survived, though not entirely unchanged. Under collective responsibility all ministers support in public the agreed policies of the government. The convention was specifically suspended prior to the referendum on Britain's membership of the EEC (1975 – the first time since 1932), and ministers campaigned openly against what had been, and became again, a major element in the Government's policy. The convention was suspended again in 1977 over the question of the method of election to the European Parliament. The secrecy, which was a necessary support to the collective responsibility of the Cabinet, declined in the 1960s and 1970s without any official blessing. Leaks to the press were quite common; individual ministers, it seemed, briefed the press about Cabinet meetings; and the publication of diaries by former ministers, notably Richard Crossman's massive volumes, displayed the disagreements, not to mention the jealousies and rivalries, of the Wilson Cabinet.

Crossman's publishers defied official disapproval. Other breaches of the Cabinet conventions were condemned and almost suppressed. In particular, Labour Prime Ministers upbraided Cabinet ministers who expressed their opposition to Cabinet policy in the National Executive of the party. Thus breaches of the convention perversely contributed to its reinforcement. It endured, not because it was regarded as part of the constitution, but because it served the political purpose of guarding the government's invulnerability towards hostile critics. The convention forces the Cabinet eventually to a more or less agreed policy (better perhaps than no policy at all), intensifies the secrecy at the centre of government, and gives a false impression of unanimity about matters on which disagreement is natural and likely.

The convention of ministerial responsibility lays down that ministers are answerable to Parliament for all matters 'within their responsibility'. In the famous Crichel Down case, 1954, (see Madgwick, 1976, pp. 93–5) the minister resigned because of the admitted errors of officials. However, neither this case, nor the absence of a similar case since 1954, is a guide to the significance of the convention. This has changed very little in this century and its chief consequence was that ministers, not officials, answer for the actions of their ministries. In practice this means the minister admits his error and apologizes to Parliament – or refuses to do so. The development of the Select Committees and of Parliamentary Commissioners provided new opportunities for answerability of civil servants and ministers, but had not by 1980 seriously dented the invulnerability of ministers. For behind the smoke of the constitutional convention lay simple propositions.

(i) The minister is responsible to Parliament for this matter, so he must retain full powers.
(ii) His civil servants cannot answer for him.
(iii) He will be protected by his party majority.

Thus the convention of ministerial responsibility drew power to the minister but could not make him seriously answerable for it. This was true throughout the period, but more evident at the end than in the beginning.

The government as a whole was 'responsible' to the House of Commons, and it exercised the Queen's commission to govern because it held the confidence of the House of Commons. In times of normal solid parliamentary majorities it was assumed that any defeat of the government, except on a trivial issue, led to the resignation of the government. But when defeat was always possible – as under the pre-war Labour minority governments – resignation followed only a specific vote of no confidence (as in 1924). This interpretation of the convention was followed in 1965, when the Labour Chancellor was defeated on a clause in the Finance Bill; and again from 1977 to 1979, when the Labour government was in a minority, and suffered frequent defeats on significant items of policy, including devolution legislation and the budget. For example, in December 1978 the government was defeated on what seemed a major item of policy, sanctions against employers breaking pay guidelines; the sanctions were abandoned, and the whole policy seriously weakened. The government finally resigned after losing a vote of confidence it had itself proposed. Thus the convention held only when it was not relevant, from 1945 to 1964, and was adjusted thereafter to suit the needs of the government – a nice demonstration that ultimately the constitution is what the government says it is, and can get away with. Even so, Parliament gained from this modification of the practice of collective responsibility, for government backbench Members were more willing to vote against the government's proposals, so long as the government itself was not in danger of falling.

Exercise 2

Constitutional responsibility

Would it be true to say that the constitutional responsibility of British governments was seriously eroded in the period 1945–80?

Referendums

There were two major referendums, on continued membership of the EEC (1975) and on elected assemblies for Scotland and Wales (1979, in Scotland and Wales only). There have been other referendums, in Northern Ireland and on local matters, including the Sunday opening of public houses in Wales, but these two referendums were a major constitutional departure. Nevertheless, there was little constitutional debate to accompany and justify the innovation. The referendum was seized on in both cases to save a Labour government from taking a firm line of policy in face of party and public disagreements. These espisodes illustrated and indeed extended the lauded flexibility of the British constitution, but raised a question whether flexibility did not lead to uncertainty and manipulation for sectional ends.

Such a constitutional innovation called for practical decisions and a justification. The practical problems were to do with the status of the referendum, the form of the question, and the mode of campaigning. The referendum was to be advisory only, and in the case of devolution approval of the Acts depended on a 'yes' vote by 40 per cent of the eligible electorate. The form of the question is crucial in referendums, since it has a marked effect on the response. In both cases the government chose specific questions, about staying in the EEC, and operating the Scotland and Wales Acts, and elicited conservative responses for continuing to belong to the

Common Market (1975) and doing without devolved assemblies (1979). Campaigning was a problem because the parties were divided. For both campaigns, 'umbrella' organizations were formed, alliances of parties, unions, the concerned public. Government provided financial assistance in 1975 but not in 1979. The campaigns were effective in presenting the issues, but could not transcend the limits of political circumstance, the deceptive calm of Britain's European relationships in 1975, the heavy unpopularity of the government in 1979 (encouraging the rejection of its proposals). It was evident that in the radically changed circumstances of 1980 – notoriously excessive contributions to the EEC budget, growing unemployment in Wales and Scotland – the referendum votes of 1975 and 1979 would have been quite different.

These considerations raise some doubts about the justification of the referendum. Very little was said in favour of this constitutional revolution. Document 3.2 illustrates some of the constitutional arguments against the referendum and makes an interesting assertion that there are 'rules' and 'political realities' above Parliament, of which the people are the best judge.

Document 3.2
The constitutional implications of the referendum

(a) Speech by J. P. Mackintosh in debate of 11 March 1975
In the last 400 years of its history this House has not only exercised sovereignty but has given away sovereignty – not just on the Common Market issue, which is arguable, but when it conceded independence to the Republic of Ireland, (and acquired and gave away an Empire) . . . these things were done – war, peace and the creation and ending of an Empire – by debate and decisions in the House of Commons. This therefore is the history of the matter. So one cannot argue that membership of the European Community is in any sense a unique occasion which merits unique treatment.

[In reply to the argument that democracy must be majoritarian.] This country has never believed (in simple majoritarian democracy). There has not been a majority on a head count basis for many of the greatest reforms that this House has been proud to pass. (Report, col. 411)

(b) Speech by B. Gould
No one disputes that our entry into the Common Market means a fundamental redefinition of our legislature . . . We have an unwritten constitution, so it is not possible to follow prescribed procedures. Nevertheless, we have a constitution. We have rules which define this Parliament, which govern our functions as members and so on. Those rules, logically take priority over the institution of this Parliament and

Government. They rest therefore not on the will of this Parliament, but on the political realities which underlie it. It follows that this Parliament alone cannot be sure that it has the competence to change these rules because it is a creature of them. We can be sure of changing the rules only if we can see that the political realities have changed. In a democracy how better to discover that than to ask the people. (Report col. 430)

Exercise 3

The referendum

3.1 Why do you think the referendum had not been used before the 1970s?
3.2 Why was it used in the 1970s?
3.3 Is it likely to be used again?

There are more practical and political arguments. It is difficult to arrange a 'pure' referendum. Low turn-out and unbalanced campaigning may make the result unrepresentative. The referendum issue is likely to be affected by current political events or conditions (as the devolution question in 1979 was caught up with the general standing of the government at the time). It is not easy to devise questions which admit of a simple 'yes' or 'no' answer. An informed citizen might wish to respond 'yes, but . . .' or 'no, not exactly . . .'

Further, popular opinion may not often favour 'progressive' change, for which governments may feel they must lead opinion. Hence, approval for British membership of the EEC was probably increased because Britain already belonged, and no change was involved. Roy Jenkins argued this when he resigned on the referendum issue from the shadow Cabinet. 'By this means', he wrote, 'we would have forged a more powerful continuing weapon against progressive legislation than anything we have known in this country since the curbing of the absolute powers of the old House of Lords. Apart from the obvious example of capital punishment, I would not in these circumstances fancy the chances, to take a few random but important examples, of many measures to improve race relations, or to extend public ownership, or to advance the right of individual dissent, or to introduce the planning restraints which will become increasingly necessary if our society is to avoid strangling itself'.

Against this must be set the arguments that constitutional change ought to be protected by special procedures (making it more difficult to enact and repeal); and that the arbitrament of the people, however formed, can never be wrong in a democracy. But the devolution referendum in Scotland (in which the electorate divided about equally for, against and abstaining) showed that it might be obscure. The precedents for the use of a referendum in the future remain, but that result is discouraging for governments looking for an unchallengable answer to an awkward question.

Accession to the EEC

British accession to the EEC was, after two rebuffs, finally legislated in 1972, 'renegotiated' under the 1974 Labour government and ratified in the referendum of 1975. It was hailed by its more enthusiastic supporters as an historic milestone in British and European history. There was some truth in this view. Western Europe had after all suffered two catastrophic wars in the previous sixty years, and was now looking toward economic and political union. More sceptical observers noted that the establishment of the Community was a consequence rather than a cause of the outbreak of peace; that the countries of the EEC and Europe were not identical geographically or historically, and that the scope and extent of unification was, and was likely to remain limited by the continuing pursuit of national interests by leading members of the Community, not least Britain. The EEC in fact had some of the character of an international alliance mixed with its supranational aspirations. Institutionally, the Commission (of administrators) and the Parliament (directly elected in 1979) were supranational but ultimately powerless. Power lay with the Council of Ministers, but it was power only to be exercised by agreement. This is not to say that the institutional weight and political impetus of the Community did not influence national governments and their ministerial representatives in Brussels.

Thus the impact of the EEC on the British constitution was potentially very great. The Community was a customs union, moving towards the harmonization of procedures for economic and social regulation. By the end of the 1970s Britain lived under EEC tariffs, and a system of agricultural support, the Common Agricultural Policy (CAP), designed in Brussels (for the benefit, so its critics said, of inefficient French and German farmers). Much of the work of the EEC was to do with agriculture – about three-quarters of its budget and even more of its legislation. EEC regulations penetrated a growing range of subjects, for example, safety in road transport and in food and drugs, vocational training and qualifications. While the Ministry of Agriculture increasingly looked abroad, the Foreign Office concerned itself with what had previously been domestic matters. But the shape and pattern of British government was changed more fundamentally. In crucial fields of taxation and financial assistance to industry – and potentially of exchange rates – British governments no longer exercised full sovereignty.

The institutions and processes of EEC regulation were plainly now part of the British system of government. Since they depend on legislation and treaties of a fundamental kind (difficult to reverse if not irreversible), they formed a new part of the constitution rather than an addition or alteration to the conditions in which the constitution works. The constitutional implications are set out in document 3.3. Parliament's response to this challenge lay through its direct relations with ministers concerned with EEC business; in the development of an adequate system for the scrutiny of EEC regulations, and in active co-operation with the elected members of the European Parliament. These were formidable new burdens to lay on Parliament. Some (including the Kilbrandon Commissioners) saw in this a further case for devolution; others saw in it the destruction of the centuries old work of constructing parliamentary sovereignty. (See the extract by Enoch Powell in document 3.10 below).

The impact of EEC membership on government was substantial. The perspectives and daily work of politicians and administrators were changed. Yet there was not by 1980 a radical change in the lives of the people. They paid more for their food, less for their newly favoured foreign cars. Inferior French apples drove the splendid Cox's Orange Pippin off the market stalls. This was the stuff of history.

Document 3.3
The EEC and the British constitution

(a) From Membership of the European Community Report on Renegotiation, Cmnd 6003, HMSO, 1975

134. Thus membership of the Community raises for us the problem of reconciling this system of directly applicable law made by the Community with our constitutional principle that Parliament is the sovereign legislator and can make or unmake any law whatsoever. That principle remains unaltered by our membership of the Community: Parliament retains its ultimate right to legislate on any matter.

135. The problem therefore has to be considered from two aspects: first, the general issue of whether the ultimate sovereignty of Parliament has been weakened, and secondly, whether Parliament can play an effective role in the making of any particular new Community law. On the general issue, Parliament by the European Communities Act 1972 authorised the application in this country of directly applicable Community Law and to that extent has delegated its powers. Parliament has however the undoubted power to repeal that Act, on which our ability to fulfil our Treaty obligations still depends. Thus our membership of the Community in the future depends on the continuing assent of Parliament.

136. At the level of the day-to-day legislative activity of the Community there is a range of legislative instruments, from the purely technical and

regulatory to items of major policy significance. Apart from the instruments made by the Commission in specific areas . . . all items of Community law are contained in instruments adopted by the Council, in whose discussions and decisions United Kingdom Ministers necessarily take part. Parliament, by passing the 1972 Act, in effect remitted to the Government responsibility for safeguarding United Kingdom interests in the Council deliberations which result in directly applicable Community law. United Kingdom Ministers remain directly answerable to Parliament, since the continuance of any Government depends on Parliament's support. Parliament thus operates in the Community law-making process by exercising its traditional role of controlling and restraining the Government against the background of the ultimate sanction of withdrawal of confidence. This applies to Ministers when they are sitting in the Council in Brussels as much as when they are taking decisions solely as members of the Government of the United Kingdom.

(b) From official referendum leaflet, 'Britain's New Deal in Europe', 1975

Fact No. 2. No important new policy can be decided in Brussels or anywhere else without the consent of a British Minister answerable to a British Government and British Parliament . . .

Fact No. 3. The British Parliament in Westminster retains the final right to repeal the Act which took us into the Market . . .

(c) From Royal Commission on the Constitution, Report, vol. II, 1973, pp. 445

The implications of Common Market membership for the United Kingdom machinery of government

101. The first and clearest consequence of Common Market membership is that in many fields (not limited to Agriculture, Finance, Trade and Economics) important areas of decision making will inevitably be moved still further away from the citizens of the United Kingdom. Major policies will now be determined in Brussels, not London. This has a second important implication for what hitherto has been a vital feature of our system of government – the clear-cut nature of political responsibility. Hitherto, Parliament and the electorate have, in theory, at any rate, been able to hold a particular Minister of Government fully responsible for major policy decisions. This will now be changed. In future major policy in many fields will emanate from the Council of Ministers by the complex bargaining processes. There will, inevitably, therefore, be many instances when United Kingdom Ministers will have to tell Parliament that a particular policy is the best they could get rather than what they really wanted. So, with decision making moving still

further away from the British people and with Parliament and the electorate unable in the future to hold Ministers or even the Government as fully responsible as now for major policy decisions, all this will give a still further impetus to the trend away from democratic control . . . unless we develop the appropriate countervailing forces.

Exercise 4

The EEC and the constitution

Do you see an inevitable conflict between membership of a body like the EEC, aspiring to 'supranationalism', and a) the British constitution and b) democracy?

These were the major changes in the constitution in the period 1945–80. Some other radical changes, devolution and reform of the House of Lords, were attempted but failed; another, proportional representation, was canvassed, but never tried. There were many other changes which are not strictly constitutional but which have affected the workings of the British system of government. This raises the question whether there is any purpose, or indeed validity, in attempting to distinguish between the constitution and other elements in the British political system. 'Standard' books on the constitution made such a distinction. The government's case for the two referendums was partly concerned with the fundamental constitutional significance of the issues. In the 1970s there were demands, notably from Lord Hailsham, for a 'Bill of Rights', that is constitutionally guaranteed rights for the individual. Rather more vaguely, the constitution figured in Conservative thought as a necessary foundation to political life. Sir Ian Gilmour complained that '(Labour) politicians have perverted the constitution . . . the idea of the constitution is more important than the constitution itself. And the constitution has lately been operated contary to that idea . . .' (1978, p. 198).

The British constitution differed from almost all other modern constitutions by being based on a comparatively few institutions and rules, not codified in a single document and not subject to a constitutional court. But this did not mean that there were no fundamental principles or institutions – plainly there were such. Parliament is in effect the historical and legal trustee for this constitutional fundament, and there was, and is, some virtue in making that trust explicit. The constitutional thinking of the 1960s and 1970s achieved little in this respect. In particular, the demand for a Bill of Rights raised the bogey of judicial power, which was unacceptable in a system based on parliamentary supremacy. The long argument over devolution did little to enhance thinking about the nature of the British constitution.

3 The extension and centralization of government

The extension of government

The extension of the activities of government is a characteristic of the twentieth century in the industrialized countries. All governments intervene in the life of the citizen, at least for the purpose of security; they organize, and have to recruit and pay for, police forces and armies. Even medieval governments were concerned with the protection and promotion of trade, and few rulers in history have been unconcerned about religion and morals. But the rapid growth of industry and towns in the nineteenth century confronted governments with new and difficult problems of public order, health, poverty and education. Laissez-faire individualism yielded in practice to state collectivism – slowly, often reluctantly, but with a cumulative effect which has fundamentally transformed economy, society and government. The nature and results of this process are set out in document 3.4.

There can be little dispute about the general nature of this historical process, but room for doubt about the pace, nature and consequences of the process in the period 1945–80. By the standards of the nineteenth century, government activity was already vastly expanded by 1945, the war having given a sharp push to the process. But the process of expansion continued and the government of the 1970s was arguably a stage further on the long march from laissez-faire.

One difference was that the new tasks taken on by government were inherently more difficult to accomplish, and so required greater intensity of government action. Thus it was comparatively easy to give money to the unemployed, more difficult to create jobs for them; it was easier to ensure that the elderly were fed and housed than to make them warm, healthy and happy. The new post-war responsiblity for full employment developed rapidly into a responsibility for prosperity, at which point the government's capacity to control the economy seemed to collapse.

Document 3.4 attempts to illustrate this development of government intervention. It is evident that the government spent both absolutely and proportionately to gross national product, far more at the end of the period than at the beginning, and that the range of its activity was wider. Britain was by no means out of line with other European countries in these respects. But it is also clear that the simple principle of government intervention had been established long before 1945.

Document 3.4
The extension of government

(a) *The view of the Kilbrandon Commission*

From Royal Commission on the Constitution Report, vol. I, 1973, pp. 76–8

232. The cumulative effect of government expansion on people's lives and activities has been considerable. The individual a hundred years ago hardly needed to know that the central government existed. His birth, marriage and death would be registered, and he might be conscious of the safeguards for his security provided by the forces of law and order and of imperial defence; but, except for the very limited provisions of the poor law and factory legislation, his welfare and progress were matters for which he alone bore the responsibility. By the turn of the century the position was not much changed. Today, however, the individual citizen submits himself to the guidance of the state at all times. His schooling is enforced; his physical well-being can be looked after in a comprehensive health service; he may be helped by government agencies to find and train for a job; he is obliged while in employment to insure against sickness, accident and unemployment; his house may be let to him by a public authority or he may be assisted in its purchase or improvement; he can avail himself of a wide range of government welfare allowances and services; and he draws a state pension on his retirement. In these and many other ways unknown to his counterpart of a century ago, he is brought into close and regular contact with government and its agencies.

233. Industrialists, too, are much more involved with government. An industrialist in the nineteenth century, if he wished to build a factory, could do so by entirely private arrangement, and government hardly needed to know about the project. In these days, however, a prospective factory developer is faced with a host of Acts and regulations – to do, for instance, with environmental planning, industrial development certificates, government grants, allowances and inducements, the welfare and training of employees, employee insurance and taxation, industrial relations, licences, waste disposal, air pollution and the collection of trade statistics – any aspect of which his nineteenth century forebear might well have regarded as an unwarranted interference.

The scale of government

The number of Ministers

234. As the scope of government has increased, so naturally has its size. This increase is well illustrated by the changes in the numbers of Ministers and civil servants and in the cost of government. For most of the nineteenth century the Cabinet consisted of twelve to fifteen

members and Ministerial appointments outside the Cabinet were few. In this century, there has been no great increase in the Cabinet, which usually includes about twenty Ministers, but the total number of Ministerial appointments of all kinds has risen to over one hundred, about three times as many as in the days of Disraeli and Gladstone.

The size of the public service

235. The corresponding increase in government organisation has ultimately been reflected in the size rather than in the number of separate government departments.

236. Increases in manpower give a clearer idea of the growth that has taken place in the departments. Up to the end of the nineteenth century, the strength of the non-industrial civil service (excluding the Post Office) did not exceed 50,000. In this century there has been a tenfold increase in that number, to around 500,000, while the population of the country has risen only by half. Employment in the public service generally has also greatly expanded. In October 1972, the total was about 6,400,000, including 691,000 industrial and non-industrial civil servants, 408,000 in Post Office, 1,900,000 in the other nationalised industries, 2,600,000 in local government and 775,000 in the National Health Service. Thus just over a quarter of the total employed population is now engaged in the various public services and industries, a proportion some six times as great as at the beginning of this century.

The cost of government

237. The rise in government expenditure has been even more dramatic, largely because transfer payments in the form of social security and other benefits to persons have risen at a much faster rate than direct purchases by government of materials and labour services. In 1870, total government expenditure was about £3 per head of population, whereas in 1970 it had reached some £400 per head; expressed as a percentage of national income (gross national product at factor cost), expenditure rose from 9 per cent to 43 per cent. The rise in transfer payments alone was from about 0.2 per cent, of national income in 1870 to 12.5 per cent in 1970, when the Government was claiming over 25 per cent of the annual output of resources for its own direct use.

238. The centralisation of government is reflected in the changing financial responsibilities of central and local government. More than half of total government expenditure in 1870 was undertaken by local authorities; but, despite the large increase in their functions, this proportion had fallen to less than one-third by 1970. Equally striking is the fall in the proportion of local authorities' expenditure financed by themselves. In 1870 probably about 80 per cent of local expenditure was financed by local rates, fees and charges, but this percentage had

fallen to around 45 per cent, a century later. Thus the changing size and structure of government viewed alongside the growth in population and incomes indicates its increasing domination over the management of the nation's economic affairs.

Document 3.4

(b) Assessing the extension of government, 1945–80

There were very few activities of government in this period which were entirely new in principle. The novelty lies in the breadth and penetration of government, the numbers employed, the high cost, the shift in assumptions.

Government and the economy
Governments before 1945 intervened in the following ways:

protection by tariff or promotion by free trade
taxation, direct and indirect, on individuals and corporations
regulation of standards
support by services
influence as customer
direct subsidy
ownership

In fact government was engaged in these activities by 1845. The one new activity after 1945 is economic planning in the full sense, providing for full employment, adjusting regional deficiencies and generally taking responsibility for the promotion of prosperity.

Some new concerns of government after 1945
noise abatement
the metric system
meals-on-wheels
drought
squatting
drug abuse
bicycle lanes in cities
air and river pollution
the Arts and Sports Councils
the EEC
new advanced technologies (nuclear; under-sea oil; natural gas, microprocessors).

Government and the motor car: new government functions after 1945
introduction of tests of vehicle safety (MOT)
penalties for worn tyres
tests and penalties for drunken driving ('breathalyser')

compulsory fitting of seat-belts (but not by 1980 compulsory wearing)

building, maintenance, regulation and policing of motorways; contracting of motorway services

restrictions on parking and provision of car parks

financial support of motor industry, including some direction of investment to depressed areas.

Again none of these functions was novel in principle. Indeed, nineteenth-century governments (representing horse riders and owners) had required the early motor cars to be preceded by a man carrying a red flag. Other means of transport, railways, canals, ships had long been regulated, restricted, supported. Even Gladstone had considered taking the railways into national ownership. So, in historical perspective, there was in the period 1945–80 not a revolution in government intervention but a massive development in its scope and extent.

Exercise 5

Attempt to discover all the ways in which governments (central and local) are concerned with the cinema and football.

Document 3.4

(c) Some measures of the extension of government 1945–80

The sum of consumption expenditure, capital expenditure and transfer payments (eg. social security) as a percentage of national income

	UK	W. Germany	Japan
1958	39	42	18
1974	55	54	29

(*Source:* OECD)

Expenditure on education

	At 1948 prices (£m)	As % of national income
1920	100.2	1.2
1940	154.9	2.0
1950	263.0	2.7
1965	451.4	4.1

(*Source:* Halsey, 1972, p. 168)

Public expenditure

	as % GNP	per head of pop'n
1870	9%	£3
1973	43 %	£400
1979	43 %	

(W. Germany and France 46 %, Holland 58%)

No. of civil servants	
1900	50,000
1973	500,000+

Growth in expenditure by local authorities 1949/50 – 1973/4
(Current and capital expenditure – Great Britain, at current prices, £m)

1949/50	1325
1959/60	2730
1969/70	7919
1973/74	14869

Proportions of income of local authorities derived from grants by central government and rates (local taxation)

	grants	rates
1964/5	51.1	48.9
1969/70	54.5	45.5
1974/5	61.9	38.1
1976/7	66.4	33.6

Employment in public services

All public servants, central and local, but excluding revenue-generating staff like postmen, railwaymen

(1979)	Britain	5.3m
	West Germany	3.6m
	France	3.1m

Employees in local government (Britain)

1959	1.6m
1979	2.9m

Non-teaching staff in education (schools)

1965	398,000
1979	717,000

Behind the statistical trends lie radically changed assumptions. In 1939 the Ministry of Health was worried about supplying blankets to homeless people after bombing attacks; this might encourage people to stay in the rest centres (with blankets) rather than coping for themselves (even without homes or blankets). In the 1970s persons adjudged in need might be given money for clothes and furniture as well as food. In 1939 there were no grants for university students, only a very few competitive scholarships which were not adequate to meet the costs of attendance at university. Some education authorities gave loans (still inadequate). In the 1960s and 1970s, a student gaining entry to a university secured a full grant (subject to means testing). Expectations rose: for example, the steel industry should be run, like the hospital service, as a public (non-profit-making) service; the government should insure holiday-makers against medical costs abroad; the government should provide parks for skate-boarders (a temporary craze of 1978). There was virtually no human activity which was not regulated or aided by the government. By 1980 the extension of government intervention appeared to some observers as excessive, and the limitation of government activity became once again a political cause.

There was general agreement that the government should 'manage' the economy and provide the services of a 'welfare state'. This was the great achievement of the post-1945 period – the expansion and consolidation of the social reforms begun in the early 1900s and pressed forward by the wartime coalition government. While there were differences of emphasis between the parties, there was a large area of agreement. But the consensus broke down in the 1970s. Some economists warned of the weakening of the economy through over-expansion of the public sector. Roy Jenkins, a leading Labour politician who had become President of the EEC Commission, declared that it was dangerous for public expenditure to absorb more than 60 per cent of GNP. Academics asked, 'can governments go bankrupt?', and answered, in effect, they can and they will. One section of the Conservative party, led by Sir Keith Joseph, rediscovered a philosophy in the individualism of earlier times. In thirty-five years the great thesis of 1945 (which was to do with government intervention) had become the antithesis of the 1980s. But by then this ideological struggle was at least a hundred years old.

The centralization of government

It was likely, though by no means inevitable, that this extension of the range of government activity in a system already centralized in character would intensify that character. Centralization meant the concentration of power in London rather than the regions and localities, in central rather than local government, and, within the centre, in the hands of a very few political leaders. Centralization was not motivated simply by the character and tendencies of institutions, or the imperialist arrogance of politicians or bureaucrats, though all these count. Rather, centralization was a response to the increased expectations, hence increased responsibilities, of government in matters in which local and small-scale action may be excluded by technical and financial demands. Only a central government could manage motorways, nuclear energy, investment for advanced technology; a co-ordinated fuel policy, relations with multi-national companies – and so on.

There seems to have developed in the 1960s and 1970s a presumption in favour of centralization, and a tendency for centralized institutions to favour policies for which they alone had the executive capacity. Hence, for example, motorways and high technology medicine were preferred to local roads and the community general practitioner; giant steel plants to small local mills. The centralizing forces were not confined to government, and they were driven within and outside government by the high professionals and experts, the 'technocrats'. Political institutions responded to pressures of this kind, but sometimes seemed to be driven along helplessly, applying no countervailing power, setting no limits. Critics maintained that British institutions did not resist but actively encouraged the process of centralization.

As the scope of government extended, so government became more complex and less accessible to understanding and control by politicians and people. Both ministers and Members of Parliament yielded power to civil servants, who could claim to be experts themselves or who had direct access to information and expertise. Hence, 'Parliament's relationship with government departments is an essentially unfruitful one. MPs by their negative criticism and search for information add greatly to the burdens of civil servants and thus impede efficiency without being able to exercise any positive democratic control.' For similar reasons, ministers were unable to 'exercise real (as opposed to nominal) control over more than a small fraction of the thousands of decisions that a civil servant makes in his name' (Royal Commission on the Constitution, Report, Vol. II, 1973, p. 8).

Similar arguments were heard throughout the period, but especially in the Labour party, and from the 1960s onwards – for example, Hugh Dalton in the 1940s, Peter Shore and Barbara Castle in the 1960s, Brian Sedgmore in the 1970s, Tony Benn in 1980. In the 1960s the argument was developed into a critique of the system of Cabinet government. The concentration of bureaucratic power was paralleled, so it was argued, by an increasing concentration of political power. Parliamentary sovereignty with a disciplined party majority focussed power on the Cabinet; but Cabinet power was transformed into prime ministerial power by the conditions of modern government. Thus the case against centralization in general turned into a case against the particular wielders of centralized power.

Documents 3.5 (a)–(d) illustrate these arguments. The extract from R. H. S. Crossman's introduction to his edition of Bagehot's *The English Constitution* was the first sharp statement of the doctrine of prime ministerial power. Significantly, it was written when Macmillan was Prime Minister, and reflected something of his style of leadership (if not the facts of his period of office). The immediate appeal of this view of British government fitted three other elements in the politics of the early 1960s: the attraction of presidential politics in Kennedy's America; the new and dramatic significance of television and the personal political combat it seemed to encourage; and the style of Wilson's first efforts to lead the Labour party after thirteen years of opposition, and with a tiny majority in Parliament.

The basic elements in prime ministerial power are well-known, though difficult to measure. These are: the power of appointment and dismissal of Cabinet and ministers; power over the structure and membership of Cabinet committees (any of which the Prime Minister may chair); the determination of the Cabinet agenda and the chairing of meetings; the central, overseeing non-departmental nature of the office; leadership of the party and high public visibility. Against this must be set the constitutional necessity of retaining the support of Parliament, hence the Prime Minister's own party and senior colleagues; the strength of the major departments represented by their ministers and their senior officials; and the sheer impossibility of carrying the highest office without consultation and support, which necessarily bring the constraints of collectivity. It is significant that Mrs Thatcher's clear preference for personal leadership could not consistently override the need for the support of her senior colleagues. She could defeat a majority in the Cabinet but not a preponderance.

These elements in prime ministerial power had not changed much in the twentieth century. But Prime Ministers in the 1960s and 1970s had one advantage over their predecessors in their wrestling with the constraints of their job. Prime Ministers needed help. All Prime Ministers had friends and confidants, not all chosen from among their senior colleagues (for example, John Wyndham for Macmillan, Douglas Hurd for Heath, Marcia Williams for Wilson). But until the 1960s there was very little official support for the Prime Minister. Wilson enlarged the Cabinet Office, created within it a Prime Ministerial Office, and introduced a group of 'political advisers' into Downing Street. In his second administration this 'Policy Unit' included about six people, appointed from outside the civil service, to give advice and support from a political point of view. At the same time most senior ministers acquired one or two advisers of the same kind. In 1974 there were thirty-eight such appointments, though the number was later reduced. The isolation of high office was thus relieved, and the Prime Minister armed with both official and political support against the opposition, but also against his colleagues.

Professor Mackintosh's study of the Cabinet (1962) had provided the academic basis for Crossman's thesis. When Mackintosh was elected to Parliament in 1964, he was astounded by the impotence of his position. However, academic opinion seemed in the end to reject the thesis of prime ministerial government in favour of an interpretation which stressed the importance of the Cabinet system (the Cabinet together with its elaborate ministerial and official committees) and the group of senior ministers within which Prime Ministers must work. But that group might in practice be quite small and its size and composition lay very largely with the Prime Minister. His power was further enhanced by the salience in this period first of foreign, then of economic policy; hence that salience was sometimes carefully contrived. In both fields the development of policy flowed naturally to the top – because of the international complications, the need (or claim) for secrecy, the potential for crisis, the obscurity of policy, the traditional apartness of the Foreign Secretary and Chancellor. (Examples are the decision to manufacture atomic weapons, the Suez intervention, Rhodesian peace negotiations, the 5 per cent wage limit 1978.)

One test of prime ministerial power is the persuasive counter-power of a threat of resignation, or the political damage of actual resignation. Resignation from the Cabinet was always a rare event, and there were few in this period. None had as great a political impact as Bevan's resignation in 1951. He had substantial support in the party and waged a prolonged and often ferocious offensive against the leadership (the ferocity was not limited to one side). But even in opposition, the leadership survived. Similarly, in the Conservative party, Lord Salisbury's resignation in 1957 hardly disturbed Macmillan's government, much to the surprise of observers. The following year, the three senior Treasury ministers resigned, and Macmillan spoke at London airport (a favourite stage for Prime Ministers) of 'little local difficulties'. Similarly, George Brown's resignation in 1968, often threatened, was received with relief.

Resignation by an individual minister was not in fact the terrible weapon supposed by the classical constitutionalists. It was generally a gesture of protest by angry people who felt they could no longer work with the Prime Minister, on grounds both of policy and personality. It marked the victory of the Prime Minister. A much more effective weapon against the Prime

Minister was the threat of resignation by a substantial group of Cabinet colleagues – a Cabinet split. That threat was a signal of persisting and profound opposition, a refusal to go along – a conflict to be resolved in the end by compromise, or by submission to a majority vote. Obviously, Prime Ministers were sometimes compelled to negotiate with colleagues. If the conflict came to a showdown, resignation by the minister meant the Prime Minister won. Similarly, a threat of resignation by the Prime Minister was in part signal, in part bluff. At the height of the 1969 crisis over trade union legislation, the Prime Minister threatened resignation. His colleagues seem then to have conceded him, if not victory, at least a face-saving retreat.

In the last resort, it seems, Prime Ministers could not be overthrown by their colleagues. Attlee and Wilson survived periods of serious discontent led by candidates for their office. Churchill remained in office long after his health had broken down. Only ill-health forced Eden from office. For the leader in opposition there was a different story, as both Douglas Home and Heath learned.

Altogether no Prime Minister in this period was less than very powerful indeed. But all were subject to some constraints, and none sustained a dominant position throughout his tenure of the office. Hence the more heroic styles of prime ministerial leadership were doomed to ultimate frustration.

The civil service was also much criticised: document 3.5(b) is but one of many complaints about civil service power.

These complaints were not accepted by the civil servants themselves (see document 3.5(d)). Indeed, Sir Brian Hayes's statement is a trenchant reaffirmation of the classical view. But, even allowing that ministers in the end must approve the big decisions, it is evident that senior civil servants were very powerful over a wide area of government. This was a natural consequence of the extension of government. In the British system a minister is a layman often with little previous experience of administration, or of the subject of his department. He is unlikely to stay in that department more than a year or two, and he cannot therefore challenge the knowledge and expertise of his civil servants. If he is wise, firm and lucky he may be able to make or influence policy in one or two matters; but the rest he must leave to his officials. Modern, extended, centralized government is perforce government by civil servants. But civil servants were, by constitutional tradition and practice, protected from outside pressures for change, hence masters in their own house, the house of government.

A major prop of executive power was secrecy. Policies were developed in secrecy. Civil servants and ministers alike were sworn to silence. When policy was finally announced to Parliament it was often too late to change. Sometimes it was not announced to Parliament. The most striking examples of government secrecy in post-war history were the decision to manufacture atomic weapons; the 'collusion' before the Suez intervention;

and the acquiescence in 'oil-swap' arrangements, which effectively broke the sanctions against Rhodesia, though these were, as far as Parliament and the Royal Navy knew, being strictly maintained by the government. How much the Cabinet or individual ministers knew about these matters is not clear, but Parliament and the public knew nothing.

In the 1970s the secrecy of government was modified by the issue of discussion papers ('Green' papers) setting out policy options, by a growing number of leaks even from the highest levels of government, and by a very half-hearted commitment by governments to 'freedom of information'. By American standards at least, British government remained closed and secretive.

All of these interpretations accepted that Parliament did little to modify central power. In relation to the people, Parliament was itself a central institution, unchallenged as a legislature in Britain, abolishing its only rival, the Northern Ireland Parliament, in 1972, and supported by the revered constitutional convention of parliamentary sovereignty. But that sovereignty was in effect wielded by the executive, and subject to comparatively weak parliamentary check or scrutiny. Normally, a government with a secure majority controlled the House of Commons, arranged its timetable, restricted its information and used it as a legislative machine for the processing of Bills already negotiated and revised through the departments and in consultation, or even negotiation, with interest groups. None of these conditions was new in the 1945–80 period. Party discipline and executive dominance had operated in the House of Commons since at least the turn of the century. The only novel features of the post-war period were the weight of government legislation, the clear party divisions, some narrow majorities and the extent of interest group pressure.

These understandings of government were familiar by the late 1960s. Earlier, the classic view was widely accepted. Herbert Morrison (document 3.5 (c)) dismissed the idea of prime ministerial power, and regarded civil service power as merely an occasional consequence of ministerial weakness. His views seemed by the 1960s a little complacent, but they represent both a significant myth about British government (which changes the substance) and at least one end of the spectrum of that substance.

Thus there were two kinds of arguments: about the degree and causation of the power of central government; and about the location of power within central government. When the two arguments are looked at together, the notion of centralization seems to require some qualification. First, ministers and civil servants at the centre often in practice complained about and seemed to be experiencing frustration and impotence. The reach of government was far less than was implied in the term 'centralization'. They too were powerless to control all they would have liked or were expected to control. The great interest groups acted as independent powers (see chapter 4 below). Individuals insisted on their 'rights'; organized groups made 'non-negotiable' demands. International commitments restricted national sovereignty. The symptoms of 'ungovernability' were entirely compatible with centralization, but not with unlimited central power. At the very end of the period *The Economist* suggested the traditional visage of British governments was 'beleaguered' – not at all the look of central domination. It seemed that government had extended its scope without increasing its power – 'big' government was not strong government.

Second, a modest revitalization of Parliament was evident in the second half of the period. Governments had to try harder to reach their objectives, and inevitably made concessions on the way. In 1968–9 the Labour government was forced by backbench pressures to withdraw its Bills on industrial relations and the reform of the House of Lords. The Heath government was defeated five times, 1970–4, by the opposition or abstention of its own backbenchers. Dissent and abstention, though never normal, occurred much more frequently – two-thirds of Conservative backbenchers voted at least once against their government, 1970–4. This relaxation of discipline continued. The Labour government was defeated on ten occasions, 1974–7, before it lost its majority. Thereafter it lost twenty-five divisions in two years, and was finally brought down by a vote in the House of Commons, the first government since 1940 to fall in that way (though Chamberlain's government was not in fact defeated in 1940).

The Whips of both the major parties came to accept that such widespread 'rebellion' could not be dealt with by formal discipline – a general lesson of the 1960s and 1970s in many aspects of life. More positively, there was a persistent effort, supported by members and even by governments to reform Parliament in ways which would enhance the influence of the backbencher – notably by changes in the system of select committees, and the provision of improved information and modest research assistance. The party backbench committees were taken more seriously. More members regarded membership of Parliament as a full-time profession and were less willing than some of their predecessors simply to march through the lobbies on the instructions of the Whips. However, the combination of rebellion, reform and professionalism could not much diminish the dominance of the executive in the system. This was supported by the constitution and the party system. No ambitious politician fought to destroy a system by which he might hope himself to wield great power.

Third, there was some evidence of countervailing pluralism in British government – a commitment to local government in principle, and, limited practical attempts, for example, through non-specific grants, to encourage local autonomy; the proliferation of boards, commissions and committees; the reluctance of the civil service to espouse particular lines of policy publicly; the traditional suspicion of bureaucratic and ministerial power. These amounted to a softening rather than simply a disguise for central power; but 'softening' did not much modify the overriding force of central power.

Finally, it cannot be assumed without argument that centralization was as damaging as the critics maintained. In particular, most of the great reforms of the 1945–80 period were achieved by central government, using its power to override the inertia of local government. (One pertinent example is assistance for university students: local autonomy may have been good for democracy, but in many areas it was not very helpful to students wanting to go to a university.)

If centralization was neither as intense nor as damaging as the critics of bureaucratic tyranny claimed, there was plainly some cause for concern. Government had grown bigger by the end of the period, but it was not plainly more effective, and it was not much loved. The active participating citizen of democratic tradition had, so it seemed, become a passive disgruntled citizen. This fundamental question about the health of British democracy was raised in a special form by the successes of the nationalist parties in Scotland and Wales in the 1960s and 1970s and the subsequent attempts to establish assemblies in Scotland and Wales. That episode suggested that the government was reluctant to yield any of its power, just as the critics claimed; but conversely (and taking into account the growing unpopularity of local government), that the people lacked enthusiasm for some of the alternatives to centralized power.

Document 3.5
Power at the centre

(a) *The power of the Prime Minister*
From R. H. S. Crossman, introduction to W. Bagehot, *The English Constitution*, 1963, pp. 51–2

The post-war epoch has seen the final transformation of Cabinet Government into Prime Ministerial Government. Under this system the 'hyphen which joins, the buckle which fastens, the legislative part of the state to the executive part' becomes one single man. Even in Bagehot's time it was probably a misnomer to describe the Premier as chairman, and *primus inter pares.* His right to select his own Cabinet and dismiss them at will; his power to decide the Cabinet's agenda and announce the decisions reached without taking a vote; his control, through the Chief Whip, over patronage – all this had already before 1867 given him near-Presidential powers. Since then his powers have been steadily increased, first by the centralisation of the party machine under his personal rule, and secondly by the growth of a centralised bureaucracy, so vast that it could no longer be managed by a Cabinet behaving like the board of directors of an old-fashioned company.

Under Prime Ministerial government, secondary decisions are normally taken either by the department concerned or by Cabinet committee, and the Cabinet becomes the place where busy executives seek formal sanction for their actions from colleagues usually too busy – even if they do disagree – to do more than protest. Each of these executives, moreover, owes his allegiance not to the Cabinet collectively but to the Prime Minister who gave him his job, and who may well have dictated the policy he must adopt. In so far as ministers feel themselves to be agents of the Premier, the British Cabinet has now come to resemble the American Cabinet.

From J. P. Mackintosh, *The Government and Politics of Britain*, 1970, pp. 65, 86–7

These then are the sources of the Prime Minister's strength – party loyalty, the support of his colleagues and of the machinery of government and his capacity, under most circumstances, to set the pace, tone and direction of governmental activity and thus to command public attention . . . the Prime Minister has a very strong position and . . . though it can become even stronger when he is successful and looks like remaining in office for a long time, much of his power and invulnerability remains even during periods of political adversity.

(b) Tony Benn on the power of the civil service: manifestoes and mandarins

From *The Guardian*, 4 Feb. 1980

My thesis is a very simple one and can be briefly stated. First, that the power, role, influence and authority of the senior levels of the Civil Service in Britain – especially now we are members of the EEC – have grown to such an extent as to create the embryo of a corporate state. This would threaten the workings of British democracy under which the people of this country are supposed to govern themselves through the Parliament they elect and the ministers who are accountable to it. . . .

If the Prime Minister retains real personal confidence in the ministers whom he or she appoints, then the permanent secretaries know it is in their interest to support them. But if the permanent officials have reason to believe that the Prime Minister has lost confidence in their departmental minister, it is in their interest to by-pass him and his policies.

Moreover, the permanent secretaries' network within Whitehall, in which the Secretary of the Cabinet is a key figure, can work very effectively to undermine the confidence of the Prime Minister in a minister whom the Civil Service dislike or distrust; and thus create an atmosphere favourable to bypassing in which the minister concerned can be slowed down, deflected, diverted, obstructed, or in the end, reshuffled or removed. . . .

Britain's membership of the Common Market has had the most profound influence upon our whole constitution and method of government. Whitehall is now busy adapting itself to these new arrangements and doing so with real zest. The Common Market is a Mandarin's paradise.

The permanent secretaries who masterminded the preparatory work for all these activities through the Cabinet Office and the Foreign Office have now got a legitimate excuse to bypass and override departmental ministers in the interests of co-ordination and the need to be good Europeans.

Unless this process is stopped in its tracks, Britain could be governed by a commission of permanent secretaries reducing ministers to ciphers only able to accept or reject what is put before them and the House of Commons will be a consultative assembly which can express its opinions but do little more. . . .

In October 1974 after the second General Election I was reappointed to the Department of Industry and one of the briefing sheets in the package was headed 'For an in-coming Labour minister – if not Mr Benn' – which indicated a premature hope of the reshuffle that occurred nine months later.

It however gave me a useful insight into the policy which the Department hoped my successor would follow – as indeed he did. I believe that academic research on the full set of briefs, prepared by the Civil Service for ministers in all departments in all governments when they enter office and throughout their term since the war would offer a more accurate explanation of policies followed and why, than a similar study of the manifestos upon which each government was elected.

(c) Herbert Morrison on prime ministerial power
From H. Morrison, *Government and Parliament*, 3rd edn 1964, preface

I have not thought it necessary to refer to exaggerated beliefs as to the role and status of the Prime Minister. He is clearly the most important member of the Cabinet unless – as has happened in some cases – he subordinates himself and prefers to leave the heavier burdens to some of his colleagues. It would be an illusion to accept the idea that the modern British Prime Minister has become as powerful as the President of the United States of America. And it would be wrong to assume that Gladstone and Disraeli were cyphers in the Governments over which they presided.

(d) *Civil servants on the relations of ministers and civil servants*
From 'No Minister', BBC Radio, 14 June 1981

Sir Brian Hayes, Permanent Secretary, Ministry of Agriculture, 1981
I think the job of the Civil Servant is to make sure that his minister is informed, that he has all the facts, that he is made aware of all the options

and that he is shown all the considerations bearing on those options. It is then for the minister to take the decision. That is how the system ought to operate and that is how I think in the vast majority of cases it does operate.

Sir Brian Cubbon, Permanent Secretary, Home Office, 1981
There's a store of wisdom about what the facts are, and what the implications are, and of changes in procedure; what the consequences are of certain statements of policies which might be used, and I dare say that you would find a collective and uniform statement in the department of what that assessment was. Whether that leads inescapably onto a policy, I very much doubt.

Exercise 6

Centralization

A simple historical change is indicated. Governments do more → Government power grows → Centralized power grows. Do you see this as an inevitable process in the period 1945–80?

Exercise 7

The power of the civil service and the Prime Minister

7.1 Do you see any reason to doubt Benn's thesis about civil service power? Is the thesis likely to be more true under Labour than Conservative governments?
7.2 Were post-war Prime Ministers more powerful than their predecessors? Or in the 1960s and 1970s rather than the 1940s and 1950s? Is it possible to pick out one Prime Minister as the most powerful?

4 Institutional reform, 1965–79

A characteristic feature of the second half of the period was the drive to reform the institutions of British government. This was done by government itself, and in some cases redone again by another government. The central departments were reshaped at least twice, the committee system of Parliament two or three times. A fundamental reform of the health service and local government was adjudged unsatisfactory, and further change mooted. All this seemed to end in the spring of 1979 with the rejection of devolution in Wales and (less certainly) in Scotland, and the election of a Conservative government pledged to reduce government activity.

But why did the reform movement start in the first place? It began with reports on the reform of local government – the Maud Committee on the management of local government was appointed in 1964; the more fundamental Royal Commission (Redcliffe–Maud) was appointed in 1966 and reported in 1969. By then the Committee on the Civil Service (Fulton) had reported and the Royal Commission on the Constitution (Kilbrandon) was about to start work. Thus, the initiatives originated with Wilson's Labour government. It was a reforming administration; the Prime Minister himself was interested in the working of government (and has written a good deal about it since). It seemed too that intractable economic problems might be approached in this way, indirectly. The government was urged on in its reforming zeal by political commentators and academics. The growth of politics as a subject of study in universities – and lately in schools – was relevant here. Keynes was right about the power of ideas: 'Madmen in authority, who hear voices in the air, are distilling their frenzy from some academic scribbler of a few years back' (Keynes, 1951, p. 383). It seemed that politics was to replace economics as the wonder science – but to little effect. At the end of the 1970s Callaghan claimed that he read biographies, perhaps hoping for inspiration where the social sciences had failed him.

For all the reports and commentaries, the institutional reforms of these years rested on no coherent theory of politics and government. The government resorted to committees and Royal Commissions for advice; or sometimes as a respectable way of postponing action. But committees of persons of eminence, experience, knowledge, interest or commitment are often neither wiser nor more harmonious than politicians or individual experts, and the need to present a more or less agreed report is inhibiting. In two cases at least, minority reports by one or two persons were better argued and more stimulating and helpful than the rather leaden majority reports which reflected compromises within the Commission. Mainly the government received back in the Reports a version of the conventional reformist wisdom it was familiar with at the outset.

The process was fragmented and illogical. In particular it was absurd to inquire into local government before considering devolution or the finance of local government. Still, it would be unfair to suggest that the government was not seriously interested in constitutional reform. Rather, it is in the nature of governments to pick up their problems one at a time as the problem or the need for action becomes urgent.

The major reforms were as follows. Some of the ideas and argument underlying the reforms are illustrated in the documents.

Reform of the central executive institutions

(i) The 'executive centre' of government was strengthened. The United

States Presidency with its powerful White House office provided an attractive model, which was much admired in the early 1960s when Kennedy was President. The model of a presidential system though beguiling to Prime Ministers, was of course misleading; and soon the love affair with the USA (much encouraged by television) faded as Johnson and Nixon succeeded to office. In the event the strengthening of the position of the Prime Minister, in so far as this happened at all, was part of a reinforcement of the Cabinet system and the Cabinet Office, so that the presidential possibilities of the office of Prime Minister were not realized.

The philosophy of much of this reorganization was set out in a paper, The Reorganization of Central Government issued by Heath's government in 1970 (document 3.6). The emphasis on reducing government activity was characteristically Conservative, and was repeated when the party next came to power in 1979. The rest, the new managerial style, was a continuation of the 1960s reformation, common to all governments.

The changes in detail were as follows.

- A proliferation of permanent secretaries. Until 1956 one permanent secretary headed the Treasury, the civil service and the Cabinet Office. By the mid 1970s each had its team of own permanent secretaries, five in the Treasury, two for the civil service, four for the Cabinet Office. The Secretary to the Cabinet headed the Cabinet Office but acted also as permanent secretary and chief civil service adviser to the Prime Minister. The holders of this crucial post were known to have been very close to the Prime Minister, and probably influential. One, Sir William Armstrong, acquired the reputation of being Edward Heath's deputy Prime Minister.
- Establishment within the Cabinet Office of the Prime Minister's Private Office. This is quite large (ten or more senior officials) and is concerned with government business, not personal and party-political affairs.
- Establishment, again within the Cabinet Office, of the Central Policy Review Staff or 'think tank' (1970). The intention of this small advisory and research staff ('multi-disciplinary', temporary, and mainly outsiders) was to think about priorities and strategies, to offer longer and sharper perspectives free from departmental prejudices. It did not in fact become the power-house that was perhaps intended. In some notable cases its advice was disdained – the CPRS report on the British motor industry was issued on the very day the Government announced an entirely contrary policy of aid to the Chrysler company; the report on the diplomatic service was brushed aside by the Foreign Office; and when the unit's first director publicly forecast (1973) that Britain might be the poorest country in Europe by 1985 (a prophecy that would not be regarded as wildly unrealistic by the early 1980's) he was sharply rebuked by the Prime Minister. The 'think tank' was characteristic of the

attempts to reform British government in the 1960s and 1970s, showing up an (excessive) confidence in the power of intelligence and expertise, and the advantages of institutional innovation, and too little appreciation of the massive inertia of the existing system.

– Establishment of the Civil Service Department (1968). This followed a recommendation of the Fulton Report on the Civil Service (see below). In effect the old Pay and Management side of the Treasury and the Civil Service Commission were taken to create a new department. This had its own minister but reported to the Prime Minister. The change was intended to give a new standing to the personnel function, and to assist the development of managerial skills. The achievement of these reformist aims was always in doubt; yet if the CSD was the most obvious achievement of the reform movement, ironically, by 1980 its dismantling was under serious discussion, and it was abolished in 1981.

– The recruitment of 'advisers' from outside the civil service, who would assist ministers by contributing independent advice and evaluating official policies. The adviser was typically a bright youngish man of academic brilliance or political commitment, or both. Most became temporary civil servants.

The numbers of such advisers increased rapidly under Wilson's government in the 1960s and again under Heath. In his second administration Wilson installed a Prime Ministerial Policy Unit but Mrs Thatcher replaced this with a small personal staff and three advisers in the Treasury. Ministers were rightly looking for a source of advice to balance the weight of departmental briefing. They were right too in the belief that civil servants tended to conspire together against ministers: in a crunch the official's loyalty was given to the service in whose ranks he hoped to prosper, not to the minister who would move on in a year or two. But ministers were probably mistaken in their hope that thirty or forty outsiders could do much to counteract the weight of departmental advice.

Exercise 8

'Outside' advisers

Outside advisers seem to have made comparatively little impact. Why?

– Changes in the Cabinet system. Not much is known about this. A system of Cabinet committees existed already in 1945 but was much extended thereafter. The whole structure, functions and membership were known only to the Prime Minister and his advisers. The Cabinet normally met only twice a week and much of its business was pre-digested in the committees. The Prime Minister controlled the agenda of the Cabinet and chaired whatever sub-committees he wanted to. But crises might force their way to the main Cabinet, and a persistent senior minister could press successfully for further discussion. The system of ministerial committees was shadowed by official committees. Thus the Cabinet had become by the 1970s an elaborate honeycomb of committees. It was not clear that it had become more efficient, just more complex to meet more complex problems. The distribution of power may have shifted slightly – away from individual ministers, towards the Prime Minister and the officials. Wilson's attempt to establish a more or less formal Inner Cabinet (1968–70) had no lasting significance, and looks like an attempt by the Prime Minister to exclude one colleague from the 'top table'. Most Prime Ministers make choices of that kind, though not usually in that way.

(ii) Departments were reorganized in order to secure greater relevance and coherence in central government. Partly this process was to do with fairly clear changes in government responsibilities – the India Office disappeared, the Welsh Office and the Northern Ireland Offices were, for somewhat different reasons, established. In 1970, a more thorough-going reorganization was carried out, resulting in four so-called 'giant' departments, Health and Social Security, Trade and Industry, Environment and Defence.

The change was part of the government reform movement and was justified in terms of the current managerial philosophy. The 'giant' department could 'develop its own strategy and decide its own priorities'; it would be less involved in interdepartmental negotiation; would have its own specialist services, and 'would support a clearer strategy at the centre' (quotations from Clarke, 1972, p. 3). 'Strategy' was a key word here. Co-ordination was also a perennial concern of administrators. Even Churchill had devised a system of 'overlords' (1951) – which quickly failed since the co-ordinating ministers were wartime cronies of Churchill and all peers. But there were disadvantages in the concentration of departments and the great reorganization of 1970 was partly undone in 1974.

(iii) Procedures for financial management were changed and formalized. The Plowden Report on the Control of Public Expenditure (1961) – the first harbinger of the reform movement – had stressed the need to control public spending by rational planning over a period of years. Two procedures were established – PESC and PAR. PESC (Public Expenditure Survey Committee) was in effect the machinery through which plans for public expenditure were developed, and provided for the making of bids by departments, interdepartmental negotiations conducted by the Treasury, and final decisions at Cabinet level. PAR (Programme Analysis and Review) was intended to apply the sharp tests of output budgeting to particular policy areas. This approach did not prosper, and the Conservative government of 1979 instituted in its place an inquiry by a businessman (the Managing Director of Marks and Spencer) assisted by civil servants and strongly backed by the Prime Minister, who even invited the business-man to address the Cabinet.

PESC remained as the central budgeting process, but its work was overtaken by the frequent crises of the 1960s and 1970s in which govern-ments, in practice the Prime Minister and the Chancellor in Cabinet, had to take hasty emergency measures to cut public spending. Thus, coherent planning was not characteristic of the process; nor was control. Public expenditure continued to rise. The introduction in 1975 of strict cash limits and in 1979 of a new and fundamental attack on public spending finally brought about a rather erratic control.

(iv) A reform of the civil service was attempted. The Fulton Report on the Civil Service (1968 – the committee was established in 1966) is a central document in the whole government reform movement. Its starting point and basic philsophy are indicated in document 3.7.

The committee made far-reaching recommendations. A new Civil Service Department should be established. The existing classes should be abolished, so that there could be much freer movement within the civil service, with specialists and non-graduates – and outsiders – moving into senior administrative posts. There should be a greater emphasis on training, including the establishment of a Civil Service College. These recommendations were accepted, but did not transform the service. The grading structure remained much less open than Fulton had wished. Recruitment to the administrative group continued to be dominated by Oxbridge educated arts graduates, while specialists (accountants, scien-tists, economists) remained in a minority in the higher levels. There were few exchanges with industry.

Many other recommendations were put on one side: the introduction of 'accountable management'; the establishment of departmental planning units and 'senior policy advisers'; the opening-up of the administrative process, including the modification of the convention of anonymity; the 'hiving-off' of government responsibilities (the Post Office and the Man-power Services Commission were major examples of 'hiving-off').

Fulton had some impact. The civil service of 1980 was different from that of 1966. But it was not fundamentally different, and the most optimistic of the reformers had apparently failed. It may be that the civil service reflects broadly the tasks demanded of it, and change can only come about by radically changing these tasks. Alternatively the reformers may have to accept that it is not possible to reform great institutions, only break them up or set competing institutions against them (some justification for the EEC and devolution). The civil service for its part could not be wholly complacent about its future. By the end of the 1970s, civil servants were regularly denounced as faceless bureaucrats, 'dictators', and so on while the rhetoric of popular journalism reflected genuine public lack of confidence. A new concern for pay comparability showed up the privileges of senior civil servants, including job security and inflation-proofed pensions (but not, it should be added, high pay). Even their admitted high ability was turned into a criticism – they were, it was suggested, far too able for the jobs they were given. Where in 1945 the future of Britain had seemed to lie with government and the public service, in 1980 it seemed that industry and commerce must be our salvation. The Elizabethan age was to give way to a new Victorian age.

Exercise 9

The post-Fulton reforms

Did the Fulton reforms meet the criticisms of the civil service made in document 3.7 below?

The management science and accounting techniques of the 1960s proved ineffective in disciplining government. By 1980 there was less confidence that the great Leviathan of the modern state could be controlled at all. The liberals and socialists, who had advocated massive public provision for social equity and justice, retreated a little. The great collectivist tide of the twentieth century checked and ran back.

Document 3.6

From *The Reorganisation of Central Government*, Cmnd 4506, HMSO, 1970

A new style of government: aims

2. This Administration believes that Government has been attempting to do too much. This has placed an excessive burden on industry, and on the people of the country as a whole, and has also overloaded the government machine itself. Public administration and management in central government has stood up to these strains, but the weakness has shown itself in the apparatus of policy formulation and in the quality of many government decisions over the last 25 years.
3. The Government intend to remedy this situation. The review of governmental functions and organisation which has been carried out over the last four months is intended to lay the necessary foundations. The aims in that review have been:
   (i) To improve the quality of policy formulation and decision-taking in

government by presenting Ministers, collectively in Cabinet and individually within their departments, with well-defined options, costed where possible, and relating to the choice between options to the contribution they can make to meeting national needs. This is not confined to new policies and new decisions, but implies also the continuing examination, on a systematic and critical basis, of the existing activities of government.

(ii) To improve the framework within which public policy is formulated by matching the field of responsibility of government departments to coherent fields of policy and administration.

(iii) To ensure that the government machine responds and adapts itself to new policies and programmes as these emerge, within the broad framework of the main departmental fields of responsibility.

The fulfilment of these aims will improve the efficiency of government. This does not mean an increase in State power, nor any sacrifice of humanity and compassion in public administration.

Indeed, the systematic formulation of policy and the presentation to Ministers of defined options for decision provides them with the opportunity for greater openness in government, and more responsiveness to the needs and wishes of the community and of individuals – in short, a new and better balance between the individual and the modern State. The Civil Service itself, as it is given clearer objectives and more sharply defined responsibilities, will find that the work of public administration will again become more satisfying and that relations with the public it serves will improve . . .

5. The product of this review will be less government, and better government carried out by fewer people. Less government, because its activities will be related to a long-term strategy aimed at liberating private initiative and placing more responsibility on the individual and less on the State. It will be better government, because the tasks to be done will be better defined and fewer in number, requiring fewer Ministers and fewer civil servants to carry them out. . . .

The analytical approach

7. The basis of improved policy formulation and decision-taking is rigorous analysis of existing and suggested government policies, actions and expenditure. This analysis must test whether such policies or activities accord with the Government's strategic aims and, indeed, whether they are suitable for government at all. And it must test whether they are of greater or lesser priority than other policies or activities at present carried out, or likely to be proposed in the future; what is the most efficient means of execution; and whether their long-term effects are likely to accord with Government priorities and policies as they develop.

Document 3.7
Fulton: the basic critique

From *The Civil Service, vol. 1 Report of the Committee 1966–68,* The
Fulton Report, Cmnd 3638, HMSO, 1968

1. The Home Civil Service today is still fundamentally the product of the nineteenth century philosophy of the Northcote – Trevelyan Report. The tasks it faces are those of the second half of the twentieth century. This is what we have found; it is what we seek to remedy.
2. The foundations were laid by Northcote and Trevelyan in their report of 1854. Northcote and Trevelyan were much influenced by Macaulay whose Committee reported in the same year on the reform of the India Service . . .
3. These reports condemned the nepotism, the incompetence and other defects of the system inherited from the eighteenth century. Both proposed the introduction of competitive entry examinations. The Macaulay Report extolled the merits of the young men from Oxford and Cambridge who had read nothing but subjects unrelated to their future careers. The Northcote – Trevelyan Report pointed to the possible advantage of reading newer, more relevant subjects, such as geography or political economy, rather than the classics. But as the two services grew, this difference between the two reports seems to have been lost. There emerged the tradition of the 'all-rounder' as he has been called by his champions, or 'amateur' as he has been called by his critics. . . .
7. Meanwhile, the role of government has greatly changed. Its traditional regulatory functions have multiplied in size and greatly broadened in scope. It has taken on vast new responsibilities. . . .

    All these changes have made for a massive growth in public expenditure. Public spending means public control. A century ago the tasks of government were mainly passive and regulatory. Now they amount to a much more active and positive engagement in our affairs.
14. In our view the structure and practices of the Service have not kept up with the changing tasks. The defects we have found can nearly all be attributed to this. We have found no instance where reform has run ahead too rapidly. So, today, the Service is in need of fundamental change. It is inadequate in six main respects for the most efficient discharge of the present and prospective responsibilities of government.
15. First, the Service is still essentially based on the philosophy of the amateur (or 'generalist' or 'all-rounder'). This is most evident in the Administrative Class which holds the dominant position in the Service. The ideal administrator is still too often seen as the gifted layman who, moving frequently from job to job within the Service, can take a

practical view of any problem, irrespective of its subject-matter, in the light of his knowledge and experience of the government machine. Today, as the report of our Management Consultancy Group illustrates, this concept has most damaging consequences. It cannot make for the efficient despatch of public business when key men rarely stay in one job longer than two or three years before being moved to some other post, often in a very different area of government activity. A similar cult of the generalist is found in that part of the Executive Class that works in support of the Administrative Class and also even in some of the specialist classes. The cult is obsolete at all levels and in all parts of the Service.

16. Secondly, the present system of classes in the Service seriously impedes its work. The Service is divided into classes both horizontally (between higher and lower in the same broad area of work) and vertically (between different skills, professions or disciplines). There are 47 general classes whose members work in most government departments and over 1,400 departmental classes. Each civil servant is recruited to a particular class; his membership of that class determines his prospects (most classes have their own career structures) and the range of jobs on which he may be employed. It is true that there is some subsequent movement between classes; but such rigid and prolific compartmentalism in the Service leads to the setting up of cumbersome organisational forms, seriously hampers the Service in adapting itself to new tasks, prevents the best use of individual talent, contributes to the inequality of promotion prospects, causes frustration and resentment, and impedes the entry into wider management of those well fitted for it.

17. Thirdly, many scientists, engineers and members of other specialist classes get neither the full responsibilities and corresponding authority, nor the opportunities they ought to have. Too often they are organized in a separate hierarchy, while the policy and financial aspects of the work are reserved to a parallel group of 'generalist' administrators; and their access to higher management and policymaking is restricted. Partly this is because many of them are equipped only to practise their own specialism; a body of men with the qualities of the French *poly-technicien* – skilled in his craft, but skilled, too, as an administrator – has so far not been developed in Britain. In the new Civil Service a wider and more important role must be opened up for specialists trained and equipped for it.

18. Fourthly, too few civil servants are skilled managers. Since the major managerial role in the Service is specifically allocated to members of the Administrative Class it follows that this criticism applies particularly to them. Few members of the class actually see themselves as managers, i.e. as responsible for organisation, directing staff, planning

the progress of work, setting standards of attainment and measuring results, reviewing procedures and quantifying different courses of action. One reason for this is that they are not adequately trained in management. Another is that much of their work is not managerial in this sense; so they tend to think of themselves as advisers on policy to people above them, rather than as managers of the administrative machine below them. Scientists and other specialists are also open to criticism here: not enough have been trained in management, particularly in personnel management, project management, accounting and control.

19. Fifthly, there is not enough contact between the Service and the rest of the community. There is not enough awareness of how the world outside Whitehall works, how government policies will affect it, and the new ideas and methods which are developing in the universities, in business and in other walks of life. Partly this is a consequence of a career service. Since we expect most civil servants to spend their entire working lives in the Service, we can hardly wonder if they have little direct and systematic experience of the daily life and thought of other people. Another element in this is the social and educational composition of the Civil Service; the Social Survey of the Service which we commissioned suggests that direct recruitment to the Administrative Class since the war has not produced the widening of its social and educational base that might have been expected. The public interest must suffer from any exclusiveness or isolation which hinders a full understanding of contemporary problems or unduly restricts the free flow of men, knowledge and ideas between the Service and the outside world.

20. Finally, we have serious criticism of personnel management. Career-planning covers too small a section of the Service – mainly the Administrative Class – and is not sufficiently purposive or properly conceived; civil servants are moved too frequently between unrelated jobs, often with scant regard to personal preference or aptitude. Nor is there enough encouragement and reward for individual initiative and objectively measured performance; for many civil servants, especially in the lower grades, promotion depends too much on seniority. . . .

24. One basic guiding principle should in our view govern the future development of the Civil Service. It applies to any organisation and is simple to the point of banality, but the root of much of our criticism is that it has not been observed. The principle is; look at the job first. The Civil Service must continuously review the tasks it is called upon to perform and the possible ways in which it might perform them; it should then think out what new skills and kinds of men are needed, and how these men can be found, trained and deployed. The Service must avoid a static view of a new ideal man and structure which in its turn

could become as much of an obstacle to change as the present inheritance.

25. We have sought to devise a form of management for the Civil Service that will ensure that it is better run and able to generate its own self-criticism and forward drive. One of the main troubles of the Service has been that, in achieving immunity from political intervention, a system was evolved which until recently was virtually immune from outside pressures for change. Since it was not immune from inside resistance to change, inertia was perhaps predictable.

Parliamentary reform

In the first part of the period it seemed to be generally agreed that Parliament was working well, though suggestions were made for modest improvements. In the 1960s and 1970s both élite and popular opinion turned against Parliament, and various attempts at reform were made. The earlier view is set out in document 3.8 (a). This is the traditional view of Parliament as the 'grand inquest of the nation', criticizing, probing, offering an alternative government to an attentive electorate, but always aware of the broad consensus and the higher duty. Modest proposals for improvement accompanied this wholesome account. Thus Amery in his 'Thoughts on the Constitution', more or less contemporary with Jennings, and agreeing with him about the nature of the system, had twenty pages on 'How to preserve Parliamentary Government'. These are summarized in document 3.8(b).

There is hardly any reform attempted in the 1960s and 1970s which is not included in Amery's list. The major reform carried through then was the reorganization of the committee system of the House of Commons beginning with the strengthening of the Estimates Committee under the title of Select Committee on Expenditure (1970); and the establishment of specialist committees, related from 1980 to the major departments of government. The intention was that these committees should play an active and effective part in challenging the departments. This depended on the willingness of backbench Members to review the work of ministers and departments critically, and to pursue their criticisms without regard to party loyalties. There was some evidence at the end of the period that a few backbenchers were determined to do this. No structural change was required: they had the power if they chose to exploit it. But it was much more usual for backbenchers to conform to party pressures and desist from challenging their own government. Hence, parliamentary reforms of the kind advocated throughout the period were largely cosmetic. It was in the nature of the system that this was so.

Document 3.8

(a) Jennings on the function of the House of Commons
From I. Jennings, *The Queen's Government*, 1954, pp. 86–93

Essentially, therefore, the Government consists of persons chosen from among the majority in the House of Commons. It is faced by an alternative Government which hopes to come into office at the next election. . . .

. . . The debate ebbs and flows across the floor. . . .

. . . It does not follow that there need be two parties only, but the machine works more easily if there are. One party thus takes the decisions under a fire of criticism from the other. The Government decides and the Opposition criticizes, both appealing to the opinion of the people whom they represent.

The Opposition is thus an essential part of the House of Commons. . . .

. . . opposition is usually formal. The Opposition's task is not to prevent the Government from carrying out its policy but to criticize that policy in the hope that the electors will choose a different Government next time. The Queen's service must be carried on, and so long as a party is in power it must be carried on by that party.

Once these principles are understood the scheme falls into place. The Government governs under criticism from the Opposition. The Opposition's functions are almost as important as those of the Government. . . .

. . . The real purpose of parliamentary debate is to bring home to the electorate the major conflicts of policy . . .

. . . A public servant works under a constant fear of parliamentary criticism, not of himself directly but of his Minister. Much time is spent in preparing answers to questions and briefs for public speeches. Action must be recorded in writing so that its consequences may be justified . . .

Though emphasis must be given to the function of the House of Commons as the forum for political debate, it also has less spectacular functions to perform. It is part of the legislature, and British legislation is lengthy and detailed . . .

The House also exercises, so far as it can, detailed control of public finance. The composition and procedure of the House are not well adapted for this purpose . . .

(b) Amery's thoughts on the reform of the House of Commons, 1947
From L. S. Amery, *Thoughts on the Constitution*, 1947

1 Improvements in procedure and the arrangement of business to make better use of time.
2 Leaving the detail of legislation to ministers (Amery had doubts).
3 Improving financial control (Amery suggested perceptively that the real remedy might lie in the Estimates themselves and . . . budget system as a whole) (p. 53).

4 Committees interested in the work of individual departments presided over by the ministers concerned.

5 Proportional representation at least in the larger cities, though 'it is more important that a government should be returned with a working majority than that it should represent any particular numerical proportion of the electorate' (p. 55). He added that 'an alternative method of strengthening the quality of the House would be to increase the representation of the universities and to add representatives from special professional organisations' (p. 56).

6 Reviving public interest in the House of Commons by distributing *Hansard* in cheap and popular form; better still broadcast its proceedings.

7 Devolution to Scotland and Wales, and to large provincial units in England.

8 Reform of the House of Lords, in particular the introduction of life peerages.

9 Functional representation – a House or sub-Parliament of Industry.

Exercise 10

The functions and reform of Parliament

10.1 In what respects, if any, would you say that Jenning's account was
  (i) fundamentally right?
 (ii) fundamentally wrong?
(iii) plainly complacent?

10.2 Which of Amery's proposals were implemented to some extent, which have been attempted but defeated, which not tried at all?
Explain the last category.

The most radical proposal for reform was the Labour plan to reorganize the House of Lords, 1968–9. The difficulty for Labour reformers was that their understandable objections to the existing unrepresentative House with its permanent Conservative majority were equalled by their distrust of any change which would make the House a credible rival to the House of Commons. Hence the proposals for reform were in fact not very radical – the hereditary peers were to remain as non-voting peers, and voting peers were to be nominated, like life peers, but with more regard for party balance. The Bill was defeated by an alliance of Enoch Powell, to the right of the Conservative party, and Michael Foot, a left-wing Labour Member – for rather different reasons.

This was one of the very few great triumphs of the House of Commons over the government in the whole period. One other was the defeat (in the same year, 1969) by Labour backbenchers of the Industrial Relations Bill.

Thus the House of Commons exerted its power against the government to preserve an institution which by the standards of every other advanced country was plainly obsolete and absurd. A cynic might well make a similar judgement about the Commons' defence of the trade unions – but this was a more complex and controversial subject (see chapter 6).

The system of parliamentary elections was changed in one modest way in this period of reform – the age for voting was reduced from twenty-one to eighteen (1969). A more far-reaching reform – the introduction of proportional representation – was actively canvassed, but predictably not taken up by governments owing their power to the existing system. The arguments for proportional representation are to do with the justice of proportionality, the allocation of greater political power to minorities and the easing of the rigidity of a party system arising from simple plurality voting. In this period these arguments gained some force from the failure of the first-past-the-post system in 1966 and 1974 to produce the strong governments it was claimed to do. A form of proportional representation was used in Northern Ireland for elections to the constitutional convention in 1975. The case for using it in the European elections of 1979 was especially strong, because of the distortions arising in the very large Euro-constituencies. The distortions duly arose (Labour won 22 per cent of the seats for 33 per cent of the vote). PR seemed to be a lost cause; whether it is a good cause depended on an evaluation of equity in the abstract and the existing party system in practice; for there is little doubt that PR would tend to fragment that system.

While the election system remained almost unchanged, the electoral process was transformed by changes outside the constitution, especially by the development of television and opinion polls. The techniques of marketing were introduced to the political market in ways unknown to the great popular leaders of earlier times.

5 Government outside London

The period of constitutional reform included a massive assault on local government, as well as an attempt to establish elected assemblies in Scotland and Wales. The latter would have amounted to a constitutional revolution, and, perhaps for that reason, failed. A reshaping of local government did take place. This was preceded by a flurry of major reports – Maud, Redcliffe-Maud, Mallaby, Layfield, Bains – mostly far more ambitious than the reforms actually carried through.

The movement of ideas about local government reform through the period was again an interesting guide to the broad flow of political ideas. Until the early 1960s, reform was confined to the redrawing of boundaries, and occasional upgrading of the status of a particular authority. By the

1960s local governments had about doubled their expenditure (at current prices) in a decade, and an increasing proportion of their funds came from central government (see document 3.4(c)). There was growing concern for their efficiency and to some extent, their democratic quality. Thinking about local government moved from minor adjustment of boundaries and status (the old Boundary Commissions) to general problems of size, efficiency and relationship to local communities (the Redcliffe–Maud Report, also Maud and Mallaby) to questions of democracy, raised sharply by the Layfield Committee, which insisted that this was inherent in its allotted subject, local government finance.

The Redcliffe–Maud Report broke down the age-old boundaries of country and town, county and county borough. It went on to argue the virtues of single large 'all-purpose' authorities, which would remedy the weaknesses of the existing system of small units: fragmentation, inefficiency, domination by the centre, public apathy. Research did not wholly support this (or indeed any other) view, but the case was argued with force and conviction.

The Commission recommended a structure of local councils based on an operational level which would be 'unitary' except in the conurbations. In addition there would be community councils (to represent local communities), and provincial councils to 'set the strategic framework'. The Report conveys a particular admiration for the all-purpose authority, like the old county boroughs, and a clear distrust of smaller authorities. The Commission regarded 250,000 as the minimum population for efficient administration of education, housing and the personal social services. For transportation and planning a population of up to one million would be appropriate. This redrawing of the map of local government and the division of powers was in practice too complex to be firmly based in research or argument; nor was it clear that this kind of reorganization could bring about the fundamental revitalization of local government which the Commission rightly desired.

The Report was delivered to the Labour government in 1969, but finally acted on by the Conservative government in 1972. The reorganization enacted in that year represented a considerable modification of the Redcliffe–Maud proposals. In particular the unitary authority gave way to a two-tier system (counties and districts). But the new counties were much larger than before, in some cases being amalgamations of former counties with other counties or county boroughs. Some of the Metropolitan Districts fell below the population regarded by Redcliffe–Maud as appropriate to their powers. There was limited recognition in the new Metropolitan areas of the value of a provincial or strategic level of government (another of the Royal Commissions recommendations). This was more marked in the separate reorganization of local government in Scotland. In Wales the reorganization followed English lines. The most striking feature of the reorganization was the extinction of many local government units – especially the county boroughs and some counties. A reform intended to revitalize local government was carried through by a remarkable demonstration of the supremacy of central government.

Redcliffe–Maud believed that the new authorities they envisaged would enhance local democracy. In the 1970s their argument (or hope) was challenged in two ways. First, the Layfield Committee, established to consider local government finance (illogically following the reorganization), argued that local taxation was not an administrative impossibility. The principle could draw much support from history, the practicality from the experience of other countries. The choice they posed is summed up in document 3.9.

For all the turmoil of local government reorganization, the story of 'devolution' was the most extraordinary episode in British constitutional history in the period. Devolution was not in fact a novelty in modern British history. The movement for Home Rule had dominated the later years of the nineteenth century and was extinguished only by the outbreak of war in 1914, and the subsequent granting of near-independence to Ireland, outside six of the counties of Ulster. Home Rule for Scotland and Wales had also been seriously discussed. But for nearly fifty years little was heard of the constitutional or national aspirations of the people of Scotland and Wales (and very little too of the Irish people). In the late 1960s the national questions were raised again.

For Wales and Scotland the issue arose with by-elections in 1966 and 1967 in which Labour seats were captured by Nationalists. The Labour government set up a Royal Commission on the Constitution (Crowther, later Kilbrandon, Commission, 1969–73). It is difficult to resist the judgement that this move was intended to fend off the problem, or even, optimistically, to solve it by simple postponement. In the event the Nationalists did badly in the election of 1970, but very well in the 1974 elections, especially in Scotland.

By then the Royal Commission had reported. Its specific recommendations were confused but the majority recommendations and the general argument of the Report pointed toward some measure of devolution of power to Scotland and Wales. A Minority Report by a political scientist and an economist argued a more forceful case for a thoroughgoing scheme of devolution to English regions as well as Scotland and Wales. They took nationalist discontent in Scotland and Wales as a symptom of a wider dissatisfaction with the whole system of government throughout Britain. They wrote: 'There has been a decline this century in the extent to which we as a people govern ourselves . . . Government appears to be, and is, remote from the people . . . Everywhere there is a growing "we-they" syndrome . . . and people are increasingly alienated from the political process . . .' (Report vol. II, pp. xii-xiii).

There was a good deal in these arguments, though sceptics might question whether Britain's poor economic performance was not the major cause of discontent with government. There must be doubt too whether many citizens really wanted to participate intensively and continuously in political activity. Still, the democrat could respond that there might well be a link between political participation and performance, even economic performance; moreover, some of the evidence of discontent, notably in the frequency of direct action, was difficult to push aside. The government might well have been persuaded by the force of the arguments and the electoral showing of the Nationalist parties. But – a sharper argument – the Labour government's majority in Parliament was so thin that the support of the Nationalists seemed worth securing. The Labour party itself both in Parliament and in the country was divided. The government decided to go ahead with legislation to establish elected assemblies in Scotland and Wales. The first Bill (1977) met such resistance in Parliament that it had to be abandoned. A second attempt (with two slightly amended separate Bills) succeeded largely because opponents insisted on a referendum with a 40 per cent minimum vote for approval.

The Bills proposed elected assemblies in Scotland and Wales. The Scottish Assembly was to have legislative powers, and a Cabinet-type executive. The Welsh Assembly was given executive powers (in the weak sense of 'executive'), and a 'power-sharing' local government type of executive committee. The Assemblies were to exercise their powers in the fields of health and personal social services, education, housing and so on, in effect overseeing the traditional field of local government, but having only restricted power in economic policy. The Assemblies were to be financed through a block grant. Ultimate sovereignty rested at Westminster and the Scottish and Welsh offices would remain.

These proposals reflected the difficulties of attempting to devolve power while retaining sovereignty at the centre (implying a formal division of sovereignty). The devolution schemes were designed as elaborate attempts to establish centres of power in Scotland and Wales, without subtracting any power from London. In consequence the Bills, already disliked, for different reasons, by Nationalists and loyal Unionists, met opposition on technical grounds: the scheme was an unstable 'half-way house'; conflict would arise from the overlapping and competing jurisdictions of centre, assembly and local government; the United Kingdom Parliament would be left in an anomalous position in dealing with England. A less technical, more easily grasped objection was that the assemblies would aggravate not mitigate the problem of overgovernment, adding a sixth tier to the system which ran from EEC through Westminster to the three levels of local government.

In the end, this distaste for government, for politicians and bureaucracy and government expenditure, was probably the chief motive behind the electorate's rejection of the Scotland and Wales Acts in the referendum of March 1979. The voting was as follows:

	Turnout	Yes % electorate	No % electorate	Yes % vote	No % vote
Wales	58.3	11.8	46.5	20.3	79.7
Scotland	62.9	32.5	30.4	51.6	48.3

The massive rejection of devolution in Wales expressed the greater integration of Wales with England, the disunity of Wales itself, and the special tensions arising from the issue of the Welsh language. In Scotland, an ambivalent result showed the confusion of Scottish national feeling, its strong and historical separateness, the elusive economic promise of North Sea oil (not that the government would have conceded that the oil belonged to Scotland).

For both Scotland and Wales the referendum vote marked the end of a brief era (1966–79) of Nationalist vitality. In the subsequent general election (May 1979), the Nationalist vote slumped.

The Nationalist vote, 1966–79

Nationalist vote as percentage of total vote
in Scotland and Wales respectively

	1966	1970	1974(F)	1974(O)	1979
Scottish National party	5.0	11.4	21.9	30.4	17.3
Plaid Cymru	4.3	11.5	10.7	10.8	8.1

The new Conservative government repealed the two devolution Acts, and thus brought to an end the period of intense institutional reform. The sudden end of the government's proposals for devolution hardly did justice to the complexities of the discontents which gave rise to them. Nor generally did the achievements of the period of reform match the intentions of the reformers, the quality of the debate and the substance of the problems to which reform was addressed.

Document 3.9
Central power or local autonomy

From Committee on Local Government Finance, Report, Cmnd 6453, HMSO, 1976

Making the choice

58. We have suggested that the main responsibility for local expenditure and taxation should be placed either upon the government or upon local authorities . . .
59. First, introducing LIT (local income tax) is a necessary condition of greater local responsibility . . .
61. The second main issue is the implications for economic management . . .
63. The third, and perhaps the most important, issue is whether all important governmental decisions affecting people's lives and livelihood should be taken in one place on the basis of national policies; or whether many of the decisions could not as well, or better, be taken in different places, by people of diverse experience, associations, background and political persuasion. Local authorities are able to consider the needs and circumstances of their areas as a whole and respond to the preferences of people living there. There has been a growing demand for decisions to be taken closer to the people who are affected by them. We have pointed to the essential role of local authorities in enabling people to take part in decisions about the services and amenities in their areas, in promoting democracy, in acting as a counter-weight to the uniformity inherent in government decisions, and in providing a vehicle for formulating new policies and pioneering new ideas.
64. Governments on the other hand are elected with a programme to carry out national policies which may cut across local preferences. There are powerful pressures in society for more uniformity of provision, stimulated and expressed by well-organized and informed bodies of professional and other interests. From the point of view of organisations concerned with the welfare of the aged, the disabled or the homeless, variations in standards between one area and another are seen not as the legitimate outcome of local choice but as anomalies in the provision of services which happen to be administered by local authorities. Ministers who are subject to these pressures and who are anxious to implement their electoral commitments are also impatient of local choices which do not accord with their policies.
65. The pressures for uniformity are felt by local authorities also. While local responsibility would allow scope for the provision of services in some areas to advance faster than in others, it would not necessarily lead to wide disparities. But the standard or extent of local services and

the level of local taxation would be determined to a much greater extent than now by the decisions of individual local authorities and could vary more widely between areas of differing social composition and political control.

66. Much turns on the value which is placed on local democracy itself. Central responsibility would tend to undermine the role of the local councillor. Most of the contact between government departments and local authorities would probably be between officials. Local government officers would therefore tend to regard themselves as increasingly answerable to government departments rather than council committees . . . it is likely that the main role of councillors would be to press the government for more grants to meet the needs of their areas. Shortcomings in local services could be blamed on the inadequacy of the grant, as they are increasingly at present. Ministers and their officials would become answerable to Parliament for local services

67. The choice we have posed is a difficult one. There is a strongly held view amongst us that the only way to sustain a vital local democracy is to enlarge the share of local taxation in total local revenue and thereby make councillors more directly accountable to local electorates for their expenditure and taxation decisions.

Exercise 11

The local income tax

Successive governments rejected the local income tax. Why?

A second challenge to the Redcliffe–Maud approach was based on the fashionable slogan 'small is beautiful' and the accompanying enthusiasm for the values of community and participation. Arguments of this kind were often overstated, and in the end they proved as difficult to substantiate as the Redcliffe–Maud proposition that (large) size was related to efficiency and democracy. But there was a humane and common sense quality about the community argument: people related to people not institutions. Reinforcement came from concurrent arguments about participation and the new and fashionable concern for the environment. People should be able to decide for themselves, influence what was done to them, or in their name. The cost-benefit analysis of, say, a motorway which destroyed part of a forest should rate the costs to local residents very high against the benefits to motorists passing through. The climate of opinion moved on in the 1970s, leaving reorganization of local government based on 'size means efficiency' looking decidedly inept.

The reorganization was carried through in 1974. Like all changes in the organization or technology of industry, it was exploited by the major staff unions to secure compensation for disturbance, promotion, better pay (size = greater responsibility = higher pay). At the same time the rate of inflation began to rise rapidly. The resulting increases in rates (local property tax) made local government very unpopular; and raised doubts whether the Layfield local choice option was really what the British people were longing for.

Indeed, the period of local government reform seems to have been a period of decline in local democracy. A chronic shortage of finance pushed local government sharply against the political constraints imposed by its ungenerous masters, the central government and the ratepayers. The centre pursued its own policies, notably in education and urban planning, with little regard for local autonomy. The reformed health service was left outside the local government system, and water supply was removed from local government control. The voters, if they turned out at all, voted in accordance with their view of the national government; and the local authority associations also came to reflect national party loyalties. Few national political leaders had the grounding in local government which marked earlier figures like Morrison and Attlee. From many points of view the high tide of local democracy had passed by the 1960s.

Exercise 12

The uses of Royal Commissions

Why did governments so often establish Royal Commissions and similar commissions of inquiry? and did they prove valuable?

6 The end of the age of reform

Britain's accession to the EEC has been dealt with above as a fundamental change in the constitution. But it was too, by its timing and political dynamic, a part of the reform drive of the 1960s and 1970s. It had economic rather than political objectives, but the latter were part of the general reaching out for a new direction, a new theme, which began with Macmillan in 1957, went through the 1960s with Wilson and ended with a truly committed European, Heath.

Common Market and devolution taken together seemed in the 1970s to be pushing Britain into a fundamental reformation of the territorial basis of government. Power seemed to be moving away from Westminster – to Brussels but also to Edinburgh and Cardiff. Plainly the change nicely met the arguments of the Kilbrandon Report. It also fitted the vaguer prescriptions of the 'small-is-beautiful' school, and the arguments of some

Nationalists, that the fragmentation and isolation of the small units could be compensated within the larger umbrella of Europe. The shift in power was revolutionary in its implications, and a few critics reasserted the constitutional principle of parliamentary sovereignty – notably Enoch Powell (document 3.10). But by 1980 devolution had been removed from the agenda by the referendums and general election of 1979; and the supranational claims of the EEC seemed to lie beyond the will of its member states, and hence beyond the Community's political capacity.

Document 3.10
The erosion of parliamentary sovereignty

From a speech by Enoch Powell in February 1977 printed in R. Ritchie (ed.), *Enoch Powell, a Nation or No Nation? Six years in British Politics*, 1978, pp. 134–6

There can I believe be no dispute as to what for Britain has been the central institution which has embodied our national values, and whose history has been essential to our perception and acceptance of those values. That institution is Parliament. Our national experience has been unique and our national values are unique because there is no other nation of which the statement I have just made can be predicated . . . The British are a parliamentary nation; internally and externally they are conditioned and defined by that institution and that historical experience. If our values are in danger, and if our freedom and our independence are in danger, it is because Parliament is endangered, and endangered in the only way an institution can be – by inner loss of conviction . . .

The loss of conviction to which I refer manifests itself internally, in the attitude of the institution towards itself, and externally, in the attitude towards it of the nation at large.

Internally, Parliament is increasingly coming to regard itself not so much as the supreme and unchallengeable arbiter and inquest but rather as a part of the machinery of government and even of administration, and hand in hand goes a growing disposition to see its membership more as a career with appropriate emoluments, perquisites and security than as a unique distinction, to be purchased if necessary – and cheap at the price – with personal sacrifice. Here are some of the symptoms. There is the enormous growth of committees of all kinds, to a point where they not only conflict with one another's demands but are more and more normally expected to take priority over the Chamber, where the diminution of true debate proceeds apace with such changes as the officially acknowledged obsolescence of the prohibition against reading speeches. The parliamentary salary has not merely been maintained in purchasing power, but substantially increased, . . .

If I had to single out one symptom as especially significant, it would be the tapping of public funds in order to finance parliamentary activities on a party basis . . .

Parliament is being ground – indeed, has voluntarily offered itself to be ground – between the upper and the nether millstones. The upper millstone is the European Economic Community, to which the Parliament of 1970 ceded overriding power to tax and make laws and policies for the British people – something for which there has not been the remotest precedent since the Middle Ages, and only dubiously then. Without as yet any sense, upon the part of Parliament or people, of the total and revolutionary effect of this abnegation, it is now anticipated that in no more than two years hence we shall have concurred in furnishing the superior taxing and legislating authority of the EEC with an elected parliament of its own, thus renouncing in the most explicit manner the political authority and independent existence of the British parliament and its constituency.

The nether millstone is the process – euphemistically called 'devolution' – of setting up within the United Kingdom directly elected bodies or anti-parliaments which purport to represent nations and which, being in principle endowed with the right to make or change the law, cannot logically be subordinated to Parliament itself or denied the power of taxation. Ironically, perhaps because the perspective is shorter, the consequences in this case have been perceived sooner and seem in Parliament itself to have aroused quicker antagonism. Those consequences are a conflict which could only be resolved by either dividing the United Kingdom into separate states or converting it into a federation.

What I have called the upper and nether millstones revolve upon an axis. It is the fact that the same electorate – or, if I may use the older but more expressive term, the same constituency – cannot be represented upon the same principle by two bodies without the one dominating and eventually ousting the other. Parliament is at this time involved in a struggle for its existence not less real and not less dangerous than if it were threatened with extinction by violent usurpation or aggression . . .

Exercise 13

Enoch Powell on the erosion of sovereignty

How convincing do you find Mr Powell's argument?

In the 1970s the movement for the reform of government turned sour. Some reforms seemed to have been aborted, checked or emasculated by the constraints of a tradition-bound system. Parliament had not been transformed by the reformers, though minority governments and looser party discipline had wrought some change. The civil service had responded only modestly to the main thrust of the Fulton Committee's criticisms. Where reform had plainly forced radical change in the shape of institutions – in local government – the changes, coinciding, and not totally unconnected, with rapid rises in local taxation, were widely regarded as changes for the worse. Accession to the EEC also failed conspicuously to yield the benefits its advocates had promised. At the same time the government's devolution proposals were spurned in the referendums in Wales and Scotland.

Confidence in the capacity and general beneficence of governments seems to have been high from the 1940s to the early 1960s, and to have sagged in the 1970s. In economics, laissez-faire in general, monetarism in particular, replaced the confident Keynesian interventionism of the 1940s to 1960s. Running the economy appeared to be beyond the capacity of the political system. Hostility to the welfare state in general grew, alongside attachment to particular measures from which an individual benefited. Libertarian and environmental movements challenged the government's right to do good, preferring individual freedom, individual judgement, the individual's familiar amenity to the planner's grandiose plans.

In this climate of distrust of government, the judiciary was seen as a counterweight to a tyrannical government. A few people, including Lord Hailsham, and Lord Scarman (and indeed a Select Committee of the House of Lords in 1977), called for a Bill of Rights, to provide the citizen with constitutional and judicial guarantees of liberty. The judiciary made one or two notable forays against the executive. For example, in the Laker Airways case (1976) the High Court, and subsequently, the Appeal Court, held that the Secretary of State for Trade could not intervene to reverse the decision of the Civil Aviation Authority to permit Laker to operate a scheduled, low-fare, transatlantic service (what became the famous 'Skytrain'), In the government's dispute with the Tameside education authority (1975–6) the Appeal Court, and subsequently the House of Lords, ruled that the Education Minister could not compel the Authority to introduce a scheme of comprehensive secondary education (prepared by their Labour predecessors) since the education authority could not be regarded as having acted unreasonably. Shortly afterwards the Labour government secured legislation which gave them powers of 'requirement' of plans for comprehensive reorganization. But the possibilities of delay were substantial. The incident illustrates the uneasy and sometimes antagonistic relations that arose between central and local government in the 1960s and 1970s. Central governments of both parties consistently preferred their own versions of policy reform or efficiency to the virtues of local or individual choice; and there was little scope for resistance in the courts. In the British system, parliamentary sovereignty virtually excludes judicial intervention, except when the law is unclear. There was in fact no great political role for the judges to take on, and little support in democratic theory for them to do so.

The shift in opinion against government was a popular as well as an élite movement – as the election of 1979 showed. But, as in all such movements of opinion, articulate élites exaggerated the change in popular mood. Thus surveys showed that high taxation, bureaucracy and indolence were unpopular; but the masses still, reasonably enough, strongly favoured provision by the state of the major public services and (with less enthusiasm) welfare benefits. The reaction against government in the 1970s was in historical perspective simply one more episode in the endless tension between individualism and collectivism, which had marked British history – indeed Western history – since the eighteenth century. In that perspective, the rhetoric often went beyond the limits of actual policy. Britain like every civilized society in the late twentieth century was profoundly committed to government action in economic and social spheres. The lesson of the 1930s was that governments could do more for the welfare of the people. Arguably the lesson of the 1960s and 1970s was that there were limits to government action. Thus, the high collectivism of 1945 gave way to a new individualism by 1980.

The shift in ideas may be seen in the political parties too – Labour as well as Conservative. The massive twentieth-century state was not about to be abolished, but within its complex web of power and against its concern for the public interest, the citizen's right to assert his or her private interest was modestly enhanced. Perversely the major attempt within the reform movement to assert citizen power against central government – the devolution proposals – failed completely. Mainly the reform movement was concerned with the efficiency of government. Its one undoubted achievement was to demonstrate that efficiency was not enough.

Conclusion

For all the turmoil of this period, the British system of government did not change in fundamentals. Jennings and Amery would have recognized the Cabinet and parliamentary systems they admired. Two conditions were new (i) the extension of the scope of government to a point regarded by critics as 'overload' (ii) the decline of confidence and consent to a point of alienation or even 'ungovernability'.

But these conditions were symptoms of a more fundamental weakness in the constitution – the erosion of responsibility. That was the central concept in the old theory of the constitution, but it had been corrupted by executive power supported by party discipline and civil service anonymity. The doctrine of collective responsibility had become a system of collective security, and ministerial responsibility a thin disguise for ministerial prerogative.

This corruption of the constitution was not simply a post-war phenomenon. The test of the doctrines of responsibility had always been resignation, and these had never been frequent on grounds either of collective or ministerial responsibility. The trickle almost dried up by the 1970s. The last cases of resignation on policy grounds by a senior minister under ministerial responsibility were in 1954 (Sir Thomas Dugdale) and under collective responsibility in 1968 (George Brown and Ray Gunter) and 1976 (Reg Prentice).

The prop of irresponsible power was secrecy. Jennings and Amery would have accepted that as a necessary condition of government. What they did not see, and what political history since 1945 has demonstrated, is that executive secrecy annihilates the responsibility of government to Parliament.

Guide to exercises

1.1 The line of 'responsibility' which they thought ran from Cabinet through Parliament to the people. Parliament is crucial in this process of responsibility, and, within Parliament, the political parties and, in particular, the opposition.

1.2 If 'democracy' connotes some responsibility to the people, then the answer is yes, indirectly through representation in Parliament. The system has a potential for democracy, but much depends on the representative character and processes of Parliament.

1.3 People are dissatisfied with the performance of governments; and have lost confidence in the institution of government. Mainly the commentators are concerned with symptoms, but Marquand emphasizes the loss of a sustaining constitutional theory; King, the condition of 'ungovernability'. MacRae attempts a more subtle diagnosis, of the nature of the governing class.

1.4 'Ungovernability' is a useful sharp term to sum up a condition. But the condition falls short of ungovernability. It is the 'erosion of consent', being harder to govern. This much seems to have been true of the 1970s. There is a danger, however, of exaggerating comparatively unrepresentative but well-publicized incidents of dissent, disruption, law-breaking and defiance. (On the other hand, publicity may spread the condition).

1.5 A state of more limited scope than the modern state; and with a less tightly controlled, 'top-heavy' government machine; hence a freer and more effective Parliament. (This is in part an interpretation of what he actually writes.)

2 No. That responsibility had been weaker in practice than in theory, since the mid-nineteenth century when governments had first been based on organized parties (i.e. almost since they had ceased to depend on the support of the monarch). But tradition counts in these matters, and it does seem that the traditional idea of responsibility weakened in the period, as faith in the classic view of the constitution weakened.

3.1 The referendum really does not fit the British tradition of representative and responsible government. Members of Parliament may reasonably object, and governments normally would wish to retain decision-making in the field they dominate. Awkward issues, like abortion, could be left to private Member's Bills, or, like hanging, to free votes.

3.2 The issues of membership of the EEC and devolution were awkward, in cutting across party lines, but also not peripheral. So governments felt they must act, but wanted to avoid responsibility for acting.

3.3 See 3.1 above. But the precedents are there, ready for another 'awkward' issue.

4 Membership of the EEC must conflict with the fundamentals of the British constitution, the supremacy of Parliament and the responsibility of the government to Parliament. This may be avoided, or diminished, insofar as governments retain the ultimate right to veto the decisions of the EEC.

In theory, there is no conflict with democracy. In practice there may be doubt about the extent of power of the European Parliament, and the possibility of effective accountability to the people. Size and remoteness inhibit democracy. (See document 3.10 for Enoch Powell's views on the threat to sovereignty)

5 This is for you to do by research and inquiry. If possible you should try to date the beginnings and development of involvement. The implication of the text is that you will find a great deal of involvement, both negative (regulation and control) and positive (promotion).

6 It was inevitable that governments would do more, once the war had extended government economic and social activity, and raised expectations. The Labour victory in the election of 1945 ensured that government activity would not contract as it had done in 1918–19 during Lloyd-George's return to 'normalcy'. It was also inevitable in the British system that the power accruing to government from this expanded activity would be, formally at least, centralized power, for the British system knows no other.

7.1 Of course the civil service has immense power. But Benn attributes a greater skill, cohesion and organization to the civil service than is likely to be the case. Departments develop their own ethos or outlook, have their own favourite policies, so they are not consistently available for concertation against the minister. There is evidence that able ministers, sure of themselves, and with Cabinet and party backing, make their own policies.

Little evidence, and not much reason to accept that civil service power will vary with the party in power. In Benn's view, the civil service pursued a consensus of its own, which was not inherently closer to one party rather than another. A simple class judgement would be that senior civil servants are middle class, hence inclined toward the Conservative party. But the highly-educated middle class, employed in the public service, is not quite as predictable as that.

7.2 A case that post-war Prime Ministers were more powerful than their predecessors is based on the development of centralized parties and a centralized bureaucracy. See the extract from Crossman. Neither of these was new in 1945, but it might be argued that both have intensified since then. The impact of television might also be adduced.

This factor applied in the 1960s and 1970s, not earlier. In other ways, there is no reason to believe Prime Ministers were stronger in the later period. Indeed, the 'ungovernability' argument, if it is valid, suggests the opposite.

Hence, it seems unlikely that one Prime Minister could be picked out as 'the most powerful'. But if we looked for 'personal dominance', then the choice of Macmillan, 1957–62, could be defended; and perhaps Wilson 1964–7.

8 'Outsiders' were successful mainly as advisers close to the minister, but were never absorbed into the main work of the departments. 'Outsiders' lacked the expertise of the career civil servant, and their position cut across departmental lines of responsibility. If the 'outsider' fitted in, there was little point in having him; if he did not, there were problems. It is not the way of large organizations to be flexible, but perhaps government departments ought to have tried harder?

9 Those criticisms focussed on civil service power and the frustration of ministers; but Tony Benn suggested civil service power was used to pursue the politics of a 'Whitehall consensus' which proved disastrous. The Fulton proposals were designed to produce a different kind of civil servant, more professional, more often technically qualified, skilled managers, in touch with the community. These new civil servants might have been even more powerful than the old; more vigorous, less concerned with the consensus, more ready to press policy recommendations on the minister. The problem of relations with ministers might have been resolved by the Fulton proposals for planning units and senior policy advisers. These were not implemented, and of course only limited change was brought about through recruitment and training.

10.1 Jennings is right in seeing Parliament as the essential arena for the transaction of government business – it is the junction, the exchange, the registry. He is wrong to emphasize the 'ebb and flow' of debate, 'the constant fear of parliamentary criticism'. He exaggerates the vitality of Parliament as a popular forum. In that way, he is complacent. But if he was wrong about the actual condition of Parliament, he may well have been right about its proper function (see exercise 13).

10.2

Implemented to some extent: 1, 2, 4, 6, 8.
Attempted but defeated: 7
Not tried at all: 3, 5, 9.

Financial control was improved in detail. In particular, by the end of the 1970s government was releasing far more information about its spending programme and its general economic planning, so that the annual budget could be set in context. But financial control remained with the government, as a central part of the executive power it drew from its majority in the House of Commons.

Proportional representation was accepted for Northern Ireland, but not for the European Parliament or the projected assemblies for Scotland and Wales. Parliament itself remained firmly based on the simple plurality system, mainly because it served the interests of the two 'major' parties.

Functional representation was contrary to the historic principle of territorial representation. But Parliament itself, and the parties, increasingly represented 'functions', groups, interests and activities, as well as constituencies. Bodies like the National Economic Development Council provided informal representation of the major interests, industry and the trade unions.

11 The reasons usually given were difficulties of administration; competition with central government's need for revenue; and interference with central government's overall management of the economy and procedures for equalizing resources between one area and another.

By 1980 central government's financial contribution to local services was so large as to be irreversible. The financial basis for local democracy had then to be: modest resources raised locally for modest local variations in policy; and/or local responsibility for spending money raised by central government. A local income tax might have been important as a break with the old pattern and a shift in perceived responsibility.

12 There were almost thirty commissions in the period. It is noticeable in the cases with which we are concerned that the government did not adopt the recommendations of the commissions. The main argument of Redcliffe–Maud for unitary authorities was rejected by the Conservative government, though the amalgamation of boroughs and counties met the Report's case. The challenge of the Layfield Report was left unanswered by governments. The recommendations of the Kilbrandon Commission were so diverse that they could not be followed precisely, though the general tendency of the report was accepted.

So why did governments set up commissions? They could have acquired advice in other ways, through civil servants, research staff, consultants. The sceptical answer would be that the government wished to evade a problem while appearing in public to be concerned. Governments are entitled to feel beset by too many problems at once, and there is no doubt some truth in that interpretation. But British governments since 1945 have also become committed to government by consultation – so much so that *The Economist* referred in 1980 to the trade unions' 'constitutional right of consultation'. The Royal Commission fits this mode of government well, without delivering the government into the hands of any one group. It engages a wide range of interests, expertise and authority in the consultative process, through the commissioners themselves and by means of hearings, the submission of evidence and, in the later commissions, research reports.

This process of consultation, deliberation and report certainly provided the government and the concerned and attentive public with some valuable material. Some of the reports proved to be best-sellers. The Beveridge Report (1942) sold 280,000 copies, the Robbins Report on Universities (1963), 50,000. In some cases minority, dissenting reports proved more valuable than the majority report, which either tended toward a low common factor of blandness and predictability, or showed the undue influence of one or two commissioners (eg the Donovan Report on Industrial Relations). But that does not affect the point. Nor does it matter that governments do not follow the commission's recommendations. If they did so consistently, that would be a strange shift of responsibility from the government to an unrepresentative body. The influence of the commissions was often indirect, identifying choices and creating a climate of concern.

So there was in fact a good deal to be said for the commissions – but a lingering suspicion that governments might more often have thought out major policy for itself; or reacted more vigorously to the reports of the commissions.

13 Powell was a passionate advocate of the historic sovereignty of Parliament. Note that he has none of Jenning's complacency. Jennings said in effect, this is how it is, this is how it should be. Powell says this is how it should be, but people do not recognize the shift away from the historic ideal.

Powell is surely right in claiming great merits for the ideal form of parliamentary sovereignty. He may be wrong in believing that the system could be restored – for executive power based on disciplined political parties lies in the logic of the system and is at least a century old.

Again he is right to see membership of the EEC and the proposed 'devolved' assemblies as restrictive, hence destructive, of the sovereignty of Parliament. The more difficult question is whether the restrictions were harmful and avoidable. In a pluralistic, fragmented, transnational system, can sovereignty itself be maintained?

4 The representation of the people

1 The two-party system under stress

In the 'classical' view of the British constitution, the two-party system played an essential part – competition, challenge, criticism, scrutiny, the continuing presentation of choice, an alternative form of government. Political parties have never looked fully equal to these high constitutional functions, and their inadequacies have been apparent in the period since 1945.

Broad continuities in the system of political parties hide both temporary fluctuations and more fundamental change. In 1945 two major parties dominated the system; in 1980 this was still true, despite some apparent crumbling. The Conservative party remained united in principle, deferential to its leaders, and dedicated to the principles of 'private enterprise', limited government and a strong foreign policy. By comparison, the Labour party was throughout the period deeply divided and critical of its leaders, stressed by the illogicality of its structure, uncertain of its doctrine but opposed to the basic orientations of conservatism.

Within these elements of continuity both parties shifted their ground and their style. First, movement between government and opposition wrought temporary transformation in both parties. Governing parties shifted towards the middle ground, opposition parties moved away, reasserting their fundamental ideologies. Some shifts were tactical rather than ideological: notably, both parties opposed an enforced incomes policy in opposition, only to adopt one when in government. This 'Jekyll and Hyde' approach to politics was a marked feature of the period after 1950. It reflected the sharpness of electoral competition; the wide span of opinion on which the parties were based and their adaptability in face of the actual problems of government. A cynic might add that it showed the capacity of partisans for self-deception and hypocrisy.

A second feature of shifts in party position moderated these Jekyll and Hyde transformations. In the middle of the period, roughly from 1955 to the late 1960s, the parties moved closer together, in a shaky and only half-avowed consensus, an 'era of good feeling' (sometimes disguised by bad temper) between the abrasiveness of the post-war period, and the 'conviction politics' of the early and late 1970s. This was the period of the chancellorship of R. A. Butler, and the Labour leadership of Hugh Gaitskell – hence 'Butskellism'. The consensus owed something to the personal and intellectual qualities of these two men, and Macmillan too, but was based on a genuine political foundation of agreement on the broad objectives of prosperity and peace, achieved through a managed, mixed-economy, welfare state, committed to collective security (in its post-war formulation). In the early 1960s, the Conservatives accepted economic planning and first tried out an incomes policy. Harold Wilson picked up and developed some parts of a new mood, an enthusiasm for youth, technology, vitality – and joining the EEC. Everybody could agree on economic growth as the objective – so everybody would win and all would have prizes. By the end of the decade that dream had collapsed and the two parties (Labour while in opposition, the Conservatives all the time) turned again to their ancient philosophies. Even so, the differences between the two parties remained narrower than party rhetoric suggested.

The two-party system prevailed throughout the period, but its weakening in the 1970s, notably in the elections of 1974, showed both the continuing appeal of the Liberal party and the new and surprising strength of Nationalist parties in Scotland and Wales. At the same time, the Unionists of Northern Ireland, under the pressure of civil war, abandoned their unwavering loyalty to the British Conservative party. It seemed for a time that Britain was on the way to developing a multi-party system, like many of its European neighbours, and like them it acquired a weak form of coalition government in the period 1976–9 when Labour governed without a majority.

The success of the 'minor' parties was in fact quite limited. The electoral system was weighted against small parties. Below a threshold of about 30 per cent of the vote, the reward in seats was small. The Liberals suffered particularly from this inequity. In February 1974, they won only fourteen seats for 6 million votes. The Nationalists, being more concentrated, fared better, and the Scottish National Party until its defeats in 1979, seemed about to exploit the system by breaking through the threshold of votes.

Both the Liberal and National parties gained support to some extent by the ill-success of the major parties. The 'protest' or disillusioned vote against the major parties showed up especially at by-elections, in which government-held seats were invariably at risk. Thus, the Labour government of 1945–51 did not lose a single by-election; in 1974–9, Labour lost five seats, and in eight elections the swing to the Conservatives was over 10 per cent (21 per cent at Ashfield in 1977). Surveys suggested that many more voters might have voted Liberal in a proportional voting system. But the Liberals never quite developed an alternative outlook or set of policies or 'image' or leadership to rival the rough polarities of the two big parties. The two-party system may not have reflected political differences very accurately; but it seemed the degree of misrepresentation was not so acute as to cut through the inertia of voters locked into the old system.

Table 4.1 Votes for third parties, 1945–79

(a) Votes for third parties in general elections (1945–79)

	1945	1951	1964	1970	1974(F)	1974(O)	1979
% of poll	12.4	3.2	12.5	10.5	24.9	25.0	19.2

(b) The Liberal vote and seats, 1945–79

	1945	1951	1959	1964	1966	1970	1974(F)	1974(O)	1979
% of poll	9.0	2.6	5.9	11.2	8.5	7.5	19.3	18.3	13.8
Seats	12	6	6	9	12	6	14	13	11

For a while – between 1966 and 1979 – the Nationalist parties in Scotland and Wales challenged that inertia with a positive, readily identified appeal. In both countries nationalism had a long history, but a weak political presence. Nationalism was about history and institutions and culture, and had less to say about the bread-and-butter questions which agitated the contemporary voter. But the economic problems of the 1960s and 1970s combined with other factors – North Sea oil in Scotland, the crisis and resurgence of the Welsh language in Wales – to offer political opportunities to revitalized nationalist parties. They won a modest victory in the elections of 1974, and returned altogether fourteen Members to Parliament – a strategic base in what became a minority Parliament. Meanwhile the government's first panic-striken reaction to Nationalist gains had yielded the Report of the Kilbrandon Commission and plans for elected assemblies in Scotland and Wales. The rejection of these proposals in the referendum of March 1979, and the subsequent electoral losses of the Nationalists brought to an end the greatest threat to the two-party system since 1945. (The 1980s brought a renewed threat.)

2 The character of the major parties: support and ideology

These shifts within a continuing pattern suggest some fundamental instabilities in the political parties; and, indeed, despite the continuities, the party system of 1980 differed from that of 1945–50. Notably, the two major parties were much weaker at the end of the period. Table 4.2 shows how the two parties' share of the support of the electorate had declined – significantly but not catastrophically. In part voters turned away from politics altogether – average turn-out declined by about 7 per cent in the second half of the period; in part (notably in 1974) voters gave their support to third parties which challenged the major parties in a rapidly growing number of constituencies. At the same time, individual membership of the parties declined from a peak in 1953. The Conservatives lost at least one-third to one-half of their members from 1953 to 1975 (2.8million to 1.5 million) but rallied thereafter. Labour in the same period lost at least two-thirds of its individual members (1.0 million to 0.3 million or less). A consequence was a loss of income, which left both parties dependent on their industrial supporters (business firms and trade unions).

Table 4.2

(a) **Two-party share of vote**

	Votes	Electorate
1945	87.6	72.6
1951	96.8	79.9
1964	87.5	67.5
1970	89.5	64.6
1974 F	75.1	59.2
1974 O	75.0	54.7
1979	80.0	61.3

(b) **Proportion of electorate regarding themselves as (very) strong Conservative or Labour 'identifiers'**

1964–70	1974	1979
40%	26%	20%

(Source: Gallup)

This decline in support for the parties – in votes, membership and money – reflected fundamental if obscure shifts in the social structure and political outlook of the electorate. At the beginning of the period a simple explanation of the party system in terms of social class seemed valid. There was a rough division in British society between a working class and a middle class. The middle class voted largely Conservative; the working class inclined towards Labour. Prophecies of a permanent Labour majority based on this analysis proved wrong – because the analysis was imperfect, and the Conservatives managed to win about one-third of the working-class votes.

In 1959 the Conservatives won their third election in a row, and handsomely. A new class analysis was put forward. The workers had been recruited by their new comparative affluence into the middle class: they were 'bourgeoiseified'. Permanent prosperity had arrived; the Marxist critique of society was plainly irrelevant; and Labour would not come to power again (unless, like the West German Social Democrats, the party abandoned its ideological baggage). This analysis again proved wrong. Labour came to power in 1964 and spent eleven years altogether in office between 1964 and 1979; although this was based on only one decisive election victory, in 1966. The theory of 'enbourgeoisement' was shown in further research to be not so much false as oversimplified.

It still seems likely that the simple class analysis was at least part of the explanation of politics in 1945. But economic and social change, and the perplexities of governments in face of economic problems, complicated and weakened the social bases of the parties by the 1970s. Other issues, notably the EEC and devolution, cut across party lines. The following are the major explanations of voting in the period.

(i) Social class. This remained significant for those voters – probably less than one-half in the 1970s – who were fairly certain where they belonged in a class division of society. Thus, unskilled manual labourers living in council houses, working in large factories, belonging to a trade union and thinking of themselves as working-class were likely to vote Labour. Stock brokers, lawyers, business 'executives', and small businessmen, especially if they were educated in private schools, tended to vote Conservative. This still left out all the people who did not fit so obviously into these class patterns. There seemed to be a large new intermediate or service class, or lower middle class, which was neither bourgeois nor proletarian in its interests or outlook, and tended to make pragmatic judgements about political parties. Class was more complex. Some issues cut across old class sympathies. The link between class and party was much less clear than in the 1920s and 1940s. Voting was no longer a response to a clear choice between 'them' and 'us', but to a more practical demand, 'what can that party do for me?'

(ii) Geography. Differences of class and economic interest were reflected in, and reinforced by geography. Indeed, while the relationship of class to voting grew more complex and obscure during the period, the geographical division grew simpler and more evident. Broadly, the Southeast of Britain and especially the countryside and small towns, was inclined towards the Conservatives; the Northwest, and the large cities, to Labour. In areas where one class was predominant, voting disproportionately reflected the inclinations of that class, as if there were a climate of opinion, derived from class and affecting votes.

(iii) Age. Voters tend to become more conservative as they grow older. But age reflects the voter's experience of politics. Thus, the number of voters who rememberd a Liberal government declined rapidly after 1945. Labour voters who remembered the great victory of 1945 might have a stronger loyalty to the party than those who recalled only later electoral misfortune.

(iv) Religion was once a powerful element in British politics. The Liberals were the party of 'the nonconformist conscience'; the Church of England, it was said, was 'the Tory party at prayer'. It is clear that religious affiliations affected voting in Northern Ireland, Scotland and Wales. Research suggests that still in England, even in the Midlands and Southeast, there remained throughout the period some association between Anglicanism and Conservative voting, and between religious dissent and Liberal voting. For example, in 1963 middle-class Anglicans who hardly ever attended church were more likely than more frequent attenders to vote Labour; and, conversely, working-class Anglicans, attending church frequently, were much more likely than infrequent attenders to vote Conservative. (Butler and Stokes, 1974, p. 160). It is not really surprising that the profound effects of religion on society and politics throughout history have not ceased in a more secular climate. At the same time the precise meaning of religious affiliation and non-affiliation in terms of beliefs, ideas and attitudes were obscure.

These social factors were prominent in accounts of voting in the 1960s and early 1970s. This reflected important truths about voting in a period of stable two-party competition. But it also reflected the rapid development of research by sample survey into 'electoral behaviour'. The revised picture of the average voter emphasized the determination of the voter's choice by social background, and the stability of his choice. The floating voter was regarded as comparatively uninterested in politics and ill-informed and not very numerous. Many politicians seemed to reject this revision of the classical picture of the thinking voter, and obstinately continued to fight elections as if the campaign and the issues counted, and the voter was interested. Their obstinacy turned out to be wise. Issues continued to have some significance in the voters' choice; many more voters 'floated' or at least wavered in their party commitment; and the campaign was still worth fighting.

'Peace and prosperity' were the political themes of the 1950s elections. In the 1960s peace was taken for granted, while prosperity began to seem insecure. Hence economic issues came to dominate politics – problems of unemployment, prices, incomes and the power of the trade unions – and replaced a more general identification with a class interest. The responses of government to these problems varied, but not according to a clear party pattern; neither party seemed to have effective solutions. In consequence, voters grew restless and volatile, unsure of their party preference, concerned for particular issues, and much affected by immediate events, shifting climates of opinion, and the ebb and flow of party appeals. While in the 1960s it may have been true that most voters voted most of the time for the same party, in the 1970s it became clear that party loyalty of that kind had sharply diminished, third-party voting had increased, 'wavering' in party loyalty was normal and the 'floating' voter quite common. Even during the period of the election campaign a substantial proportion of voters changed their minds – one-third in October 1974, one-quarter in 1979.

In close elections the campaign itself could be crucial, particularly if a news 'event' happened or could be made to happen – a sensational speech, a gross blunder, good or bad trade figures, even a sports success or failure. Polls of electoral intentions played an important but obscure part in the campaign, and their results were headlined almost as if the election were over. In the elections of 1974 and 1979 Independent Television News used stories about polls on three-fifths of the days of the campaign. But the polls confirmed that voters changed their minds during the campaign. A general election became one of the great gambling events of the season. This horse-race approach to politics seemed to suit the British voter – but it hardly comforted the parties seeking their support.

Table 4.3 The pattern of class voting

Proportion of each class voting for party

Class (% of pop.)	Solid middle (15%)		Lower (non-manual) middle (20%)		Upper (manual) Working (30%)		Solid working (35%)	
	1950s	*1979*	*1950s*	*1979*	*1950s*	*1979*	*1950s*	*1979*
Conservative	85	65	70	57	35	44	30	31
Labour	10	17	25	21	60	45	65	53
Other	5	(Lib) 15	5	(Lib) 20	5	(Lib) 10	5	(Lib) 12

The 1950s figures are based on surveys from M. Abrams, *Class distinctions in Britain*, Conservative Political Centre, 1958; the 1979 figures are based on a survey commissioned by the BBC, published in *The Economist*, 12 May 1979.

Exercise 1

Does this table suggest that British politics was class politics?

Table 4.4 The geography of voting in Britain

| *Members of Parliament elected* | | | | | | |
	1950		*1974 (Oct)*		*1979*	
	NW	*SE*	*NW*	*SE*	*NW*	*SE*
Labour	173	142	183	136	173	96
Conservative	98	190	73	204	89	250

NW = Scotland, Wales, three standard regions in North
SE = Five standard regions in the Midlands and the South

Exercise 2

Does this table suggest the development of 'two nations'?

In face of declining support and an unstable electorate, both parties modified their public image, and to a limited extent, their private character. But these changes in the nature of the parties, evident by their leaders and activists and their ideas, did not bring the parties much closer together, and showed rather the distinctiveness of their composition and outlook.

The Conservative party was characteristically an aristocratic party, governing on behalf of the middle classes. But this was less so by 1980. Mrs Thatcher's Cabinet included six old Etonians (and four more from Harrow or Winchester), but she herself, like her predecessor, came from a lower-middle-class family, going to Oxford University by way of a local grammar school. The Conservative Parliamentary party showed some change in social background too. There were fewer sons of peers and fewer men of 'private means' and without an occupation, a marked change from the pre-war period; fewer Old Etonians, and more Members educated at universities (predominantly Oxbridge). By the 1970s the representative Conservative Member was a public school and university educated businessman, not an Old Etonian lawyer or former army officer. At party conferences the lower middle classes and even trade unionists began to appear. It was very far from being a party of the poor, but neither was it just the party of the rich: it was increasingly the party of people with something to lose.

Ideologically the Conservative party has not shifted so far since 1945. It had come to accept the managed economy, the welfare state and a limited external policy. But, even during the Butskellite period, that acceptance had been reluctant at least on the right of the party. 'True' Conservatives still stood for the virtues of free enterprise, private property and a strong defence policy. Edward Heath's government reasserted these principles in

1970 but retreated in face of growing economic difficulties. Margaret Thatcher's government in 1979 hoisted the principles to the masthead in triumph, encouraged not only by the election victory of May 1979 but the apparent failure of the opposite principles. Even so there were differences in emphasis among Conservatives, some glorying in the rediscovered foundations of the party, others regarding the policies as temporary and regrettable expedients. Document 4.2 offers some illustrations of Conservative ideas which relate, with differing emphasis, to the whole period.

Like the Conservative party, the Labour leadership differed in social background from Labour voters and from party activists. Attlee's first Cabinet (1945) included twelve members of working-class origin; Wilson's eight in 1964; four in 1974. Labour Cabinets were increasingly dominated by Oxbridge graduates (often brilliant academics). About half of Attlee's Cabinet in 1945 were university educated; and about four-fifths of Wilson's cabinet of 1970. The Parliamentary party also gained university graduates (in the main not from Oxbridge) at the expense of businessmen. The party still differed socially from the Conservative party – by its still substantial number of Members who could claim a working-class background, by its lack of businessmen, and by the distinctiveness of its professional class (teacher rather than lawyer, state not public school and so on). The Labour party had rather more women MPs than the Conservative party (almost twice as many through the period). But there were never more than twenty-nine women MPs. In that way both parties were strikingly unrepresentative.

Ideologically, the Labour party was divided at its birth between socialists, trade unionists and 'reformers', and had been divided ever since. There have been periods of apparent unity – after 1945 and in the mid-1960s – but at other times the divisions were all too clear. During the 1970s the Parliamentary Labour party moved significantly to the left (i.e. towards the socialists), and this reflected a shift among activists in the constituencies, at a time of falling membership. The ideological difference between socialists and reformers (or revisionists) were not always profound or intense, since socialism is itself an ambiguous and much revised term. In any case the earlier divisions in the party – in the 1950s and associated with Aneurin Bevan – were mainly to do with foreign policy, the rearmament of West Germany and the British atomic and nuclear weapons. It was not until the late 1960s that the evident weakness of the British economy brought fundamental economic questions once again to the forefront of political argument. In these ideological battles the trade unions did not pursue a consistent line. In the 1950s they threw their substantial weight to the right. In the 1960s and 1970s they were more inclined to the left, but their consistent care was to protect and pursue their trade union interests. Hence they have opposed incomes policies, except for short periods. Whether that was a left or right policy, socialist or not, was not their concern.

Judged in this way, by leaders and activists and ideas, the distinctiveness of the parties was clear enough. But this was often not appreciated by the electorate. Partly this can be explained by the political insensitivity (or weak partisanship) of the voters; they did not appreciate and enjoy political difference. But partly the voters were correct in their understanding. First, each party was a coalition of various tendencies, and at the inside edges the parties were not so distinctive. Second, in policies and programmes (as distinct from attitudes and ideology) there was at times less to choose between the two parties. What they did in office differed less than their war cries; on some issues the differences lay in the relative enthusiasm and reluctance with which they pursued similar policies. The litmus test of party difference throughout the period lay in attitudes towards private education and perhaps policemen. But most voters do not expect to have much to do with either.

Document 4.1

Information from D. E. Butler, *The British General Election of 1951,* 1952; and D. E. Butler and D. Kavanagh, *The British General Election of 1979,* 1980

(a) Occupations of Members of Parliament, 1951, 1964, 1979
(Main groups shown as a percentage of all Members of that party.)

	Conservative			Labour		
	1951	*1964*	*1979*	*1951*	*1964*	*1979*
Professional	45	55	55	46	49	49
Business including Farming	43	40	40	14	15	12
Workers	0	1	0	37	31	35

(Columns do not add up to 100 due to omission of groups not falling under these heads, and unclassified members)

The table shows one major difference between the parties and remarkably little change. But the very broad categories hide other characteristics and distinctions. Thus, at least 30 per cent of Members of the House of Commons were lawyers; there were always 6 per cent or so Conservative MPs claiming an armed services background, and about that proportion were farmers. The category 'private means' included 8 per cent of Conservatives in 1951, none in 1979 (i.e. none who did not claim some occupation). Teachers and lecturers became the largest single occupational group on the Labour side. The honourable profession of housewife is hardly represented on either side.

(b) The educational background of Members of Parliament, 1951 and 1979

(The categories are shown as percentages of all Members in that party)

	1951		1979	
Education	Labour	Conservative	Labour	Conservative
All universities	41	65	57	68
Oxford and Cambridge	19	52	20	49
All public schools	20	75	17	73
Eton	1	24	0	15
Elementary only or elementary and adult	26	1	5	0

Document 4.2

The ideology of the Conservative Party – some illustrations

(a) From Quintin Hogg, *The Case for Conservatism*, 1947, pp. 10, 11, 13, 14, 97

(a) Conservatives do not believe that political struggle is the most important thing in life. . . . The simplest among them prefer fox-hunting – the wisest religion.

(b) The Conservative does not believe that the power of politics to put things right in this world is unlimited.

(c) Conservatism is not so much a philosophy as an attitude . . . Indeed history records no example of a fixed political theory, however successful, which does not appear wrong, and even ridiculous, in the eye of succeeding generations.

(d) . . . private property is to the interest of the community since the desire to obtain it provides an incentive for work which is morally legitimate, and at the same time sufficiently material to operate on natures which in most of us contain certain elements not entirely spiritual or unselfseeking . . . private property – including some large fortunes – is the natural bulwark of liberty because it ensures that economic power is not entirely in the hands of the State.

(b) From Ian Gilmour, *Inside Right*, 1978, pp. 170–1

Yet surely there are still available themes and ingredients of Conservatism sufficient to make an appealing whole: leadership, security (both national and personal), authority and freedom, consensus and constitutionalism, national unity encompassing diversity not uniformity, a tempered attitude to free enterprise, state welfare as an aid not a burden, common sense not party dogma. These are not merely Conservative aspirations. They are shared by the bulk of the British people.

Soon after becoming Prime Minister, Baldwin said he wanted 'to be a healer', and at home he largely succeeded. Later, he said he would like to be the leader of those who did not belong to any political party. Those are the right ambitions of all Conservative leaders.

(c) Prime Minister Macmillan to the Queen, 1959
From Macmillan, 1972, pp. 18

The most encouraging feature of the Election . . . from Your Majesty's point of view, is the strong impression that I have formed that Your Majesty's subjects do not wish to allow themselves to be divided into warring classes or tribes filled with hereditary animosity against each other. There was a very significant breakdown of this structure of society, which, in spite of its many material advantages, was one of the chief spiritual disadvantages of the First Industrial Revolution. It will be curious if the Second Industrial Revolution, through the wide spread of its amenities of life to almost every home in the country, succeeds in destroying this unfortunate product of the first.

(d) Peregrine Worsthorne, 1959
Quoted in Gamble, 1974, p. 62

The Right is acutely aware that the kind of Britain it wishes to preserve very largely depends on Britain remaining a great power. Certainly the Conservative party's main appeal to the great mass of the voters is its close association with national greatness. It is as the 'conserver' of the Land of Hope and Glory . . . that it wins elections . . . The decline of Britain as a great power, therefore, would undermine the basic Conservative appeal far more effectively than socialist legislation . . . Everything about the British class system begins to look foolish and tacky when related to a second-class power on the decline.

Peregrine Worsthorne, 1966
Quoted *ibid.*, p. 103

(the Tory party's) whole purpose is to make it possible for a governing class to get on with the job of governing, within the context of universal franchise; to relate the practical requirements of good government to the contemporary circumstances of majority rule, to translate the idea of aristocratic rule into terms which make sense in a democracy, which means organizing mass support for what is basically an elitist or paternalist system of government.

(e) From Ian Gilmour, 1978

Conservatives do not favour the imposition of economic equality, but they can easily imagine a distribution of income that would be intolerable and would require adjustment. (p. 114)

Popper has suggested 'the principle that the fight against avoidable misery should be a recognised aim of public policy, while the increase of happiness should be left, in the main, to private initiative'. 'Work', he advises, 'for the elimination of concrete evils rather than for the realisation of abstract goods. Do not aim at establishing happiness by political means. Rather aim at the elimination of concrete miseries'. This principle is wholly congenial to Conservatives. (p. 153)

There are three fundamental things wrong with the British system of government at present. Firstly some social forces in Britain today are stronger than the country's political institutions and are not adequately represented in the constitutional process. The trade unions are over-mighty subjects who are not fully subject to control by the ballot box. (p. 197).

(f) From Timothy Raison, *Why Conservative?*, 1964

It is the peculiar Tory contribution to show that it is people rather than politics that must tackle [problems]: the job of politics is to try to create the conditions which will give scope to the courage and resourcefulness of man. (p. 17)

The fundamental injustice of class comes when it deprives any man of the right to make the most of the talents which he may possess.

Gradually, we are breaking away from its dominance. The sons of the poor are coming slowly into their own in industry and learning – and they do so not by overthrowing the old order but by being incorporated in the particular community, whether it be boardroom or high table. (p. 24)

One sometimes gets the impression that Professor Titmuss and his disciples are more interested in making the rich miserable than in making the poor happy. There are times, even, when they act as if making the rich miserable were identical, with making the poor happy. That is, of course, an error, as poor people know even if academic ideologues do not. (p. 26)

the Tory Party has an instinctive understanding that a government must have authority. Democracy does not work if there is weakness in the centre. (p. 30)

As the government's sphere has ramified and extended so the element in the party whose main concern is good administration has increased. The other new element, which is in some ways similar to and a part of, the managerial trend, is the growing tendency to apply intellectual analysis to political problems. (p. 42)

. . . true strength comes from giving the individual his freedom rather than from directing him. The burden of proof should lie with paternalism. (p. 43)

Thus the modern Tory must think in terms of the search for national greatness – not by brute force or simple material wealth, but in some way which justifies his claim to influence the world. And linked with the greatness of his own nation will be the greatness of the Commonwealth, which is still potentially Britain's greatest contribution to history. (p. 44)

Document 4.3
The ideology of the Labour party – some illustrations

(a) The constitution of 1918

To secure for the workers by hand or by brain the full fruits of their industry, and the most equitable distribution thereof that may be possible, upon the basis of the common ownership of the means of production, distribution and exchange, and the best obtainable system of popular administration and control of each industry and service. (Clause 4.4.)

(b) From Labour party manifesto 'Let us face the future', 1945

On the slumps of the interwar period:
They were the sure and certain result of the concentration of too much economic power in the hands of too few men. These men had only learned how to act in the interest of their own bureaucratically-run private monopolies which may be likened to totalitarian oligarchies within our democratic state. They had and felt no responsibility to the nation. (p. 2)

On the Tory enemy:
The anti-controllers and anti-planners desire to sweep away public controls, simply in order to give the profiteering interests and the privileged rich an entirely free hand to plunder the rest of the nation as shamelessly as they did in the nineteen-twenties. (p. 2)

On socialism:
The Labour party is a Socialist party, and proud of it. The ultimate purpose at home is the establishment of a Socialist Commonwealth of Great Britain – free, democratic, efficient, progressive, public spirited, its material resources organized in the service of the British people. (p. 6)

On nationalization:
The basic industries were 'ripe and overripe for public ownership and management in the direct service of the nation'.

(c) Aneurin Bevan, 1952

From Aneurin Bevan, *In Place of Fear,* 1952, references to Quartet edn, 1978

Society presented itself to us as an arena of conflicting social forces and not as a plexus of individual striving.

These forces are in the main three: private property, poverty and democracy. They are forces in the strict sense of the term, for they are active and positive. Among them no rest is possible.

I imply here no narrow definition of poverty although heaven knows there is enough of that. I mean the general consciousness of unnecessary deprivation, which is the normal state of millions of people in modern industrial society, accompanied by a deep sense of frustration and dissatisfaction with the existing state of social affairs. It is no answer to say that things are better than they were. People live in the present, not in the past . . .

The issue therefore in a capitalist democracy resolves itself into this: either poverty will use democracy to win the struggle against property, or property, in fear of poverty, will destroy democracy. (pp 22–3)

It is the practice of many publicists to sneer at the Labour Party for clinging to what are called 'doctrinaire' principles. You would imagine from the manner of these attacks that lack of principle is a suitable political equipment. (p. 125)

But the boards of our nationalized industries, in their present form, are a new and potentially dangerous problem, both constitutionally and socially. We have still to ensure that they are taking us towards Democratic Socialism, not towards the managerial society.

There is a disposition in some quarters to believe that the latter is the next stage in social evolution. That would be to surrender to the worst feature of the Great Society – its impersonal character. Over and over again I have laid stress on the need to make the citizen the master of his social environment. No real progress is made if the new order leaves him the passive creature of a class of supposed supermen, even though these present themselves in the guise of public servants. (pp. 127–8)

Until we make the cross-over to a spirit of co-operation, the latent energies of democratic participation cannot be fully released; nor shall we witness that spiritual homogeneity that comes when the workman is united once more with the tools of his craft, a unity that was ruptured by the rise of economic classes. The individual citizen will still feel that society is on top of him until he is enfranchised in the workshop as well as at the ballot box.

Indeed, vital though it is, ballot-box democracy at municipal and national elections is limited and only partially satisfactory, because it is occasional and remote instead of continuous and intimate. (p. 129)

(d) Gaitskell, November 1959
From P. M. Williams, *Hugh Gaitskell: a political biography*, 1979, p. 554

Gaitskell set out seven basic principles: concern for the worst-off; 'social justice, and equitable distribution of wealth and income'; a classless society without snobbery and privilege; equality of all races and peoples; belief in human relations 'based not on ruthless self-regarding rivalry but on fellowship and co-operation'; precedence for public over private interest: freedom and democratic self-government. Public ownership was 'not itself the ultimate objective; it is only a means to achieving the objective'. But it was necessary for a better distribution of wealth; for controlling 'the commanding heights of the economy' in order to plan; for ensuring accountability to the people.

(e) The politics of group interest
From S. Beer, *Modern British Politics*, 1965, pp. 241–2

. . . the policy statement in which the Gaitskellite period of rethinking culminated, *Your Personal Guide to The Future Labour Offers You*, was conveniently thumb-indexed with references to 'Your Home,' 'Your Job,' 'Education,' 'Health,' 'Age Without Fear,' and so on, as if to enable tenants, workers, patients, and other groups to turn directly to the promises beamed to them. Putting the matter in a historical perspective, one could say that, broadened in scope, the 'interests of labour,' which had given the party its purpose at its foundation, continued to provide it with goals of policy when its ideological commitment was obscured and enfeebled.

(f) The collapse of the historic support of the Labour Party
From M. Abrams and R. Rose, *Must Labour Lose?*, 1960, p. 119

This book asks the question 'Must Labour Lose?' On a first reading of the survey, the answer would appear to be 'Yes, it must – at least in the near future'. Support for its two great appeals of the past is waning. Its class appeal is being undermined, because the working class itself, even the lower categories within it, is emerging from its earlier unhappy plight; manual workers are gradually moving over into the white-collar category, which does not identify itself with the unskilled or semi-skilled labourers; and many, particularly among the young, are now crossing the class frontiers into the middle class. The ethos of class solidarity is beginning to crumble in the face of the new fluidity of our society, the new opportunities for advancement through individual effort. The socialist idealists from other sections of the population are no longer drawn to the support of 'the workers' as they were when the workers were downtrodden and despised.

The second appeal of Labour is also fading. Its promises to conquer economic distress and crises by planning based on public ownership mean little now that the terrible economic depressions of the past appear to have been left behind. The experience of public ownership has been insufficiently successful or inspiring to arouse a desire for more. On the contrary, the majority of people seem positively to dislike the idea of further experiments in this direction. To make matters worse, while these appeals diminish the Party is divided. There are many within it who find it too difficult to adjust themselves to a new age, and bitterly accuse those who try of 'betraying their principles'.

(g) Crosland's revised socialism
From A. Crosland, *Social Democracy in Europe*, 1975

Anthony Crosland, former Oxford economist, was a member of the Labour governments of 1964–70 and 1974, until his death in 1977. This extract from a Fabian pamphlet of the mid 1940s reflects the position he first set out in 1956 in his important book, *The Future of Socialism*. He argued that socialism should be about ends not means, specifically about equality, not public ownership; and that equality was no longer primarily an economic quality but to do with social justice, the diminution of social antagonism and barriers to mobility. In this extract he re-emphasizes a concern for the poor, and adds a concern for the environment – both reflections of the 1970s.

'Socialism . . . describes a set of values, of aspirations, of principles which socialists wish to see embodied in the organization of society. What are these values? I believe that essentially they are these.

First, an overriding concern for the poor, the deprived and generally the underdog, so that when considering the claims on our resources we give an exceptionally high priority to the relief of poverty, distress and social squalor.

Secondly, a belief in equality. By equality we mean more than a meritocratic society of equal opportunities, in which unequal rewards would be distributed to those most fortunate in their genetic endowment or family background. We also mean more than a simple redistribution of income. We want a wider social equality embracing the distribution of property, the educational system, social-class relationships, power and privilege in industry – indeed, all that is enshrined in the age-old socialist dream of a 'classless' society. To us, the fundamental divide between Left and Right, socialists and non-socialists, has always been about the distribution of wealth, power and class status.

Thirdly, strict social control over the environment – to enable us to cope with the exploding problems of urban life, to plan the use of our land in the interests of the community, and to diminish the growing divergence between private and social cost in the whole field of environmental pollution. (This is also an aspect of social equality, since the rich can often buy themselves a good environment; only social action can give the less well-off the same protection.) . . .

It is a thesis about means as well as ends. In particular, it rejects the Marxist thesis that Socialism requires, depends on, and indeed can be defined as, the nationalization of the means of production, distribution and exchange. The ownership of the means of production is not now, in our view, the key factor which imparts to a society its essential character.'

(h) From Labour party manifesto 'Let us work together', February 1974

. . . It is indeed our intention to:

(a) Bring about a fundamental and irreversible shift in the balance of power and wealth in favour of working people and their families.

(j) From Jim Northcott, *Why Labour?*, 1964

However rich we become as a nation, there will always be too little money for education and for social services so long as we leave things to a system which has a bias against the goods and services which need to be provided on a social basis rather than a commercial one. (p. 154)

If we are in earnest about tackling our problems, therefore, we must be prepared to spend more Government money, which in turn means raising more revenue in taxes.

And if we really mean to get the economy moving again we cannot expect to get far without the use of controls. (p. 158)

We shall need an extension of public ownership. We cannot begin to re-plan our cities until we bring building land into public ownership. We cannot hope to overcome the housing shortage without more council houses and housing co-operatives. We cannot prevent expansion being held up by bottlenecks and restrictive practices unless we are prepared to set up new competitive public enterprises to fill awkward gaps and revitalize backward industries. (p. 159)

Belief in the dignity of man implies a belief also in the equality of man and a concern for the personal fulfilment of each indidivual. But the individual cannot live a full life in isolation. We are all interdependent in that we each depend for our personal fulfilment on the adequacy of certain things which cannot be achieved individually, such as social services and economic expansion. And the only way these things can be secured on an adequate scale, and made available equally to all, is by means of Government initiative in various forms, particularly through public expenditure, public controls, and public ownership.

Thus concern for fulfilment of the personality implies more equality, and concern for freedom of the individual implies more planning and public initiative. That is the essence of socialism. (pp. 162–3)

(k) Socialism without the state, 1979
From M. Goyder, *Socialism Tomorrow*, 1979

Mark Goyder argued, in a Fabian pamphlet, that the Labour party should react to the 'popular mistrust of the apparatus of officialdom . . . dislike for the facelessness of large organisations, with their inability to respond in a human way to an individual problem; the growing acknowledgement that the formalities of public ownership are a far cry from the substance of social ownership; the search for something more creative than the oppositional stance of traditional collective bargaining.

A new philosophy is needed, based on self-regulation, not external imposition; a philosophy of change initiated from the outside, not from the centre; a decentralized social ownership, and not national, almost notional, ownership of an uninspired and slowchanging industrial sector. The co-operative ideals of the Labour Party must not be lost in a pre-occupation with dispossessing the privileged, or of substituting one oligarchy for another.'

Exercise 3

3.1 There is a tendency in these extracts for Conservatives to claim that Conservatism is different from other political creeds, something more or less than an ideology. How valid is this claim?

3.2 What do these extracts reveal to be the distinctive attitudes of Conservatives and Socialists to (i) equality (ii) poverty (iii) the role of government. Would you expect these attitudes to have changed between 1945 and 1980?

3.3 Is there any evidence that Bevan was the extreme Communist fellow-traveller and bogeyman pictured in the Conservative press (see below)?

3.4 Construct a table briefly summarizing the outlook of the Conservative and Labour parties, under the following headings:

    Economy
    Taxation
    Welfare
    Equality
    Foreign policy and defence

Try to discover whether there is a consistently distinctive Liberal party position related to these differences.

Exercise 4

Are the Conservative and Labour parties class parties?

Document 4.4
Differences in outlook of voters and Members of Parliament in each party c. 1970

Derived from R. Rose, *The problem of party government*, 1976, pp. 302, 307)

Matters on which Conservative and Labour voters differed most (1966–72):
Steel nationalization; union power; EEC; comprehensive schools; earnings related state pensions; internment in Northern Ireland.
Matters on which MPs differed most (1970, 71):
Comprehensive schools; military east of Suez; Rhodesia; legally enforced prices and incomes policy; immigration.

These extracts are intended to be broadly representative of political ideas associated with the Conservative and Labour parties. Such a small selection is inevitably very rough in its representativeness. Moreover, political ideas are not as central to political life as reactions to problems and suggestions for action accompanied by traditional rhetoric. A cynic might think that politicians have postures not principles or even policies. Even so, British politics is related to some fundamental political ideas, and a modest shift in these ideas took place in the period.

Thus, Socialist thinking produced two major variations, Crosland's 'revisionism' and 'socialism without the state'. These were responses to the achievements and the failures of the times. Many of the old objectives were achieved in the period 1945–50; but the results were disappointing. But the more significant feature of Socialist thinking is still its absence in the Labour party. While Marxism in many forms flourished in groups on the fringes of politics, the Labour party lapsed into the politics of group interest (see documents 4.3 (e)), and subsequently the politics of the trade union interest. This was not of course a betrayal of its historic mission, rather the reverse.

The Conservatives managed a greater consistency. Quintin Hogg's book, published in 1947, might stand as an exposition of conservatism in the 1980s. There were changes of emphasis during the period, largely related to changes in external influences affecting foreign and economic policy. In particular, the struggle against nationalization, the core of the Socialist evil, was waged consistently, though much of Labour's work in this field was accepted; and, with admirable pragmatism, the Heath government nationalized Britain's most prestigiously named company, Rolls-Royce. The new outlook of the Thatcher government was similar to the outlook of the Heath government in its early years (associated with the Selsdon Park Conference). Indeed, a leader in *The Times* in August 1970 declared that the post-war consensus had ended, and a new era was beginning. The same new era began again in 1979. The only novelty was the monetarist economic theory of Milton Friedman, which gave a new style and self-confidence to a government inclined to allow the forces of the market to rule.

3 The structure of the parties

Both parties were coalitions. The Conservatives were comparatively cohesive, courteous and united in face of the enemy, and in the prospect or exercise of power. The Labour party was altogether more unruly and divided; a 'broad church' in its more fraternal moods, but sometimes bitterly sectarian. These differences between the parties seemed to be continuing characteristics of the two parties, not peculiar to the 1945–80 period.

The divisions in the Labour party expressed the range and intensity of its members' beliefs, and their concern for ideas. But the divisions were expressed in and reinforced by the constitution of the party. Historically, the Labour party was a working-class and socialist movement based on the trade unions. The Parliamentary Labour Party was the parliamentary arm of this organization. But constitutionally, and in practice, the PLP represented also, indeed primarily, the Labour voters in the constituencies. The constitution of the Labour party reflected the complexities of this position. The Annual Conference and the National Executive Committee represented the movement outside Parliament, especially the trade unions. The trade unions were further represented by a majority of the NEC. The PLP in practice managed its own affairs, more or less independently; and Labour Prime Ministers and Cabinets assumed that the British constitution, not the Labour Party constitution, defined their powers. But the PLP nurtured its own divisions, so that the leader could not count consistently on the support of his own forces in the constitutional struggle; they were not always his to command. This was not a stable constitutional framework and it was entirely within its logic that the pre-eminence of its parliamentary wing (the PLP) was successfully challenged in 1981 – in the most sensitive area of the election of the party leader.

These problems, inherent in the structure and history of the party, existed throughout the period. In the first half of the period – into the 1960s – the trade unions generally supported the party leadership, despite the apparent crisis of 1960 (caused by the defection of the TGWU leader, Frank Cousins). In the later years, profound disagreements developed between unions and party over economic matters, especially incomes policy. The fissures in the structure of the party opened. By the end of the period both sides, parliamentary leadership and NEC, seemed to believe that they could no longer muddle along with an illogical constitution. But that illogicality was essential to the Labour party as it had developed between 1900 and 1980.

The structure of the Labour party was federal. Of the several points of power – the Conference, the National Executive Committee, the PLP, the leadership – none could assert unequivocal authority. The constitution itself reflected fundamental divisions of ideology and interest divisions within the party, and shaped a struggle for power related to those divisions. The contestants were the leaders (based on the PLP and, when in office, the Cabinet); the backbench Members of Parliament (in the PLP); the trade unions (Conference and NEC); constituency 'activists' – not to be taken necessarily as a pejorative term (Conference and NEC); the voters (represented indirectly in the PLP).

These contestants all claimed democratic authority, but some with more justice than others. The party leader was elected by the PLP, the members of which were themselves elected by 'the people'. The Conference was dominated by the massive 'card' votes of the unions, about five-sixths of the total vote. A majority of the twenty-nine places on the NEC, twelve trade union seats, and five women's seats, were also controlled by the trade unions. Of these a critical but not unsympathetic commentator wrote:

> It is doubtful if more than a couple of thousand people in all have influence on the selection of these 17 NEC members out of a total of 29. Arguably they represent the largest rotten borough since the 1832 Reform Act. Yet with the power that flows from them Bevin tamed Lansbury; Deakin, Williams and Lawther preferred Hugh Gaitskell to Nye Bevan or Herbert Morrison; and Cousins, Jones and Moss Evans have broken the long hegemony of Labour's Right. (J. Cole in *The Observer*, 7 Oct. 1979)

The constituency parties formed another element in the internal structure of the Labour party. Like most voluntary organizations the local parties were run by a handful of activists. In the 1970s these were often well to the left of the constituency voters. Every level of the party was divided thus between right and left. The 'right' was dominant in the leadership and, to a less extent, in the PLP. Conference and NEC went the way of the unions, strongly right in the 1950s, equivocally left in the 1970s.

The objective of the contest was power to influence the direction of the party (left or right, socialist or 'moderate' – the latter not to be taken necessarily as a term of approval). Hence the constitutional debate shifted according to the current political tendencies of each part of the organization. The ostensible objectives were the relative powers of Conference and NEC as against the PLP and the leadership, and in particular the procedures for the selection of the leader, the approval of the party's programme; and the selection and reselection of Members of Parliament. Both, or all, sides fought in the name of democracy. By the principles of democracy the part of the trade unions in conference and NEC was also open to questioning, but it remained virtually unquestioned until the 1970s, because the unions backed the leadership in the 1950s and 1960s.

Examples abound of the uneasiness, even acerbity, of the relationship of the leader with the NEC and Annual Conference, and with backbench Members of Parliament in the PLP.

For example, in 1945 Attlee, the leader of the Labour party, clashed with the chairman of the NEC, Professor Harold Laski, over the powers of the leader. During the abnormally long interval between voting and the declaration of the result, Allied leaders were to meet at Potsdam. The Prime Minister, Churchill, invited Attlee to attend, in case he should become Prime Minister within a few weeks. Laski hastened to declare that Attlee could attend only as an observer, and could not commit the Labour party. Churchill made much of this pronouncement, but Attlee conceded only that as leader he must consult the NEC. A few weeks later, Laski and some of Attlee's parliamentary colleagues challenged the leader's right to accept the King's commission to form a government. Again Attlee brushed aside these objections, claiming his undoubted right under the British constitution to accept the royal commission, and thus submit himself to the judgement of the House of Commons. Thus, Attlee, with five years service as Deputy Prime Minister behind him, asserted the primacy of the British constitution over the Labour party's constitution, and behaved as if the holding of a great state office transformed his position in the party. This was the Conservative, and probably the popular view of the party, but it has never been accepted wholeheartedly within the Labour party.

Every Labour leader had to fight similar battles within the party, often in terms of bitterness which belied the fraternity to which the Labour party was dedicated. In the late 1940s and throughout the 1950s, disputes arose from rivalry for the leadership between Morrison, Bevan and Gaitskell, and serious disagreements over foreign policy. Bevan lost the Labour Whip and was almost expelled from the Labour party in 1955, and his relations with Gaitskell remained cold despite Bevan's restoration to high position in the party after 1957. Gaitskell challenged the Annual Conference in a famous confrontation in 1960 over nuclear disarmament (see document 4.5). It was significant that the Conference vote against him reflected the switch of the 800,000 votes of one union (TGWU). During similar struggles Wilson raised the possibility of Labour candidates standing as PLP candidates, independent of the party organization. Often he simply did not attend meetings of the NEC. In the elections of 1974 and 1979 the party's manifestoes plainly diverged from the views of Conference and NEC. Callaghan described his attendance at meetings of NEC as 'like going to purgatory – being cross-examined and vilified' (31 Oct. 1979). His attitude, and that of his predecessors was summed up in 1978, when he told the NEC: 'You may be right and I may be wrong; the difference is that I have to carry the responsibility' (reported in *The Observer*, 3 Dec. 1978).

Document 4.5
Gaitskell at the Conference, 1960

From P. M. Williams, *Hugh Gaitskell*, 1979

'I would not wish for one day to remain a leader who had lost the confidence of his colleagues in Parliament. It is perfectly reasonable to try to get rid of somebody . . . who you think perhaps is not a good leader . . . What would be wrong . . . and would not be forgiven, is if, in order to get rid of a man, you supported a policy in which you did not whole-heartedly believe.'

Furious interruptions began, especially from the galleries packed with his implacable foes. 'I have been subject to some criticism and attack,' he shouted back. 'I am entitled to reply . . . It is not in dispute that the vast majority of Labour Members of Parliament are utterly opposed to uni-lateralism and neutralism. So what do you expect them to do? Change their minds overnight? . . . There are other people too, not in Parliament, in the party who share their convictions. What sort of people do you think they are? What sort of people do you think we are? Do you think we can simply accept a decision of this kind? Do you think that we can become overnight the pacifists, unilateralists and fellow travellers that other people are? How wrong can you be? As wrong as you are about the attitude of the British people.'

This passage brought continuous boos and shouts, reaching a crescendo at the words 'fellow travellers'. It was a fantastic scene, unprecedented as the party leader's remarks were lost in the howls of protest.

Gaitskell suggested that the system by which most votes were pre-determined before the executive recommendations were known 'is not really a very wise one . . . the result may deal this party a grave blow . . . but . . . There are some of us, Mr Chairman, who will fight and fight and fight again to save the party we love. We will fight and fight again to bring back sanity and honesty and dignity, so that our party with its great past may retain its glory and its greatness.'

Then the votes were announced. The Executive had lost four times. The official policy went down by just under 300,000. Slightly bigger majorities carried the AEU's unilateralist motion and defeated a Woodworkers' resolution endorsing the official statement and supporting NATO.

These examples do not represent a continuous conflict of the leadership and the party outside Parliament. Conference was often on the side of the leadership and the centre/right of the party. Thus Conference voted in favour of German rearmament in 1954, the Common Market in 1967, the US action in Vietnam in the 1960s, incomes policy in the late 1960s; devolution in 1976. The left, and in some cases, the NEC, then fought against the Conference. The true issue was the policy not the institution;

and the crucial relationship was with the trade unions. The relations of the leader and the trade unions were conducted directly with top trade union leaders (who never sat on the NEC). Thus, in 1976, the Labour government made use of a new Labour-TUC liaison committee to negotiate the Social Contract, which was later rejected by the NEC, but, of course, adhered to by TUC and government. The leadership never complained openly about trade union influence in the party because

   (i) in the 1950s, and from time to time thereafter (as in the period of incomes policy), the top trade unions supported the leadership:

  (ii) the trade unions had substantial powers, despite any provision of the constitution:

 (iii) the trade unions provided well over three quarters of the central income of the party. Appearances were deceptive here. The comparative calm of leader–trade union relations reflected the strength of both sides. The anger which often affected leader–NEC relations reflected the weakness and consequent frustrations of the NEC, which lacked the capacity to use its apparent constitutional power.

During the whole period, constitutional conflicts within the Labour party were never resolved, but fluctuated with changes in electoral fortunes, issues and personalities. A new crisis was precipitated by the party's heavy defeat in the election of 1979, fought on a bland programme over which Callaghan had exercised substantial personal influence. In particular Callaghan had attempted to impose a 5 per cent income limit in the autumn of 1978, and the party was divided both on the policy and its electoral consequences, some thinking the policy itself heresy for a Labour government, others that trade union resistance to the policy had finally brought the government down. The 'left' of the party (meaning those who believed in socialism, high wages, high social spending, and trade union 'rights') were strongly represented in the party in the 1970s, at every level except in the Cabinet and leadership, and were notably active in the Conference. Hence it was possible for the NEC and the Annual Conference 1979 to vote in favour of a compulsory reselection process for Members of Parliament (which carried with it the possibility of dismissal), and NEC control of the manifesto. A proposal for the election of the leader by an electoral college representing the local parties was narrowly defeated. A commission of inquiry was established, from which the PLP was excluded. In 1980 – unlike 1945 – the leader could not call to aid the royal invitation, the British constitution, and the promise of five years of power.

In 1981 a special conference of the Labour party at Wembley finally voted to take the choice of leader from the PLP to an electoral college of trade unions, constituency parties and the PLP – with the latter in a minority. This precipitated the split in the Labour party and the formation of the Social Democratic party. This was neither inevitable nor predictable but plainly explicable in the history of the Labour party.

The Conservative party was comparatively more cohesive than the Labour party. This is not to say that the party was wholly united. The span of its ideology was probably as wide as Labour's; and there were organized groups, the Monday Club, the Bow Group, attacking the centre from the wings. But the persistence, intensity and acerbity of Labour's left wing was lacking – or, at least, much less publicized. Moreover, there was a strong tradition of deference to the leader, and substantial constitutional provision for the authority of the leader, who was not elected until 1965 and appointed his Shadow Cabinet, controlled the party central organization and promulgated the Manifesto. The party did not suffer the divisiveness nor benefit from the democratic potential of the Labour party's federal system. Even so, twice during the period, the Conservative party showed its capacity to replace leaders in whom they had lost confidence. (Douglas Home, 1965; Heath, 1975).

In policy matters, the Conservatives were most vulnerable to division over foreign, especially imperial or post-imperial, issues, questions of law and order, and race. Thus, the withdrawal from 'east of Suez', and the imposition of sanctions on Rhodesia after the unilateral declaration of independence led to substantial rebellions in Parliament and the Annual Conference. In the Conservative party the ranks closed quickly after such divisions. In that way the party always acted like a party of government, rightfully holding power; while Labour behaved like a party of principle, anxiously seeking the truth.

Exercise 5

Was the Labour party more or less democratic than the Conservative party in this period?

4 The condition of party government

While the problems of structure and of ideas and policies were not entirely new, they contributed to a general weakening of political parties during the period. Voters and members fell away. Financially the parties grew more dependent on their industrial backers. The Houghton Committee on Financial Aid to Political Parties (1976) recommended some form of state assistance to political parties (as in Italy, Denmark, Norway, for example). The government provided funds for research and administrative support, but not on a scale sufficient for a modern party in an age of mass media. The Labour party, despite the subventions of the trade unions, was much worse off than the Conservatives. For example, it was employing only seventy agents in 1979 compared with nearly 300 in the 1950s and over 300 for the Conservatives. On these inadequate resources, the political parties had to cope with new perplexing and unsettling political conditions. Expectations rose, problem-solving capacity fell. Television, with its instant and cruel exposures came to dominate political communication by the 1960s. Issues waxed and waned while voters switched their allegiance with increasing rapidity. (In the 1979 election the overall national 'swing' was the highest since 1945; and in over 150 constituencies the swing was higher than 7 per cent). Third and fourth parties attracted substantial votes. Extreme parties attracted more publicity, and occasionally more votes. In the Labour party, various radical groups took over constituency parties by the simple and constitutional device of attending and taking part in meetings (the phenomenon known as 'entryism').

The weakening of parties showed up too in Parliament. Party loyalties were notably less stable in the 1970s in both parties, and abstention and cross voting, while never normal as in the US Congress, became less a matter for headlines and formal discipline. Members of Parliament themselves reflected some of the uncertainties of the times, and the frequent artificiality of party conflict. Criticism of 'adversary politics' was fashionable. It represented an opposition of interests, particularly class interests, which was no longer significant for the people. Governments, it was pointed out, adopted in office policies they had denounced – and would again denounce – in opposition. The 'U-turn' became a regular (but deniable) political manoeuvre. Governments played Jekyll and Hyde as they advanced from the euphoria of election victory to the hard realities of government. Faced with these changes in policy, it was difficult for intelligent and independent minded Members of Parliament to maintain uncritical loyalty. Some notable figures left politics. A few changed party. One of these was Christopher Mayhew, a former Labour minister who resigned and was later to join the Liberal party. He commented, 'A certain degree of humbug is inevitable in politics, but the amount required of us now to keep the party system going is becoming excessive.'

In fact, the party system appeared to crack in the 1970s, with the increase of voting for third and fourth parties, and a period (1977–9) of minority government, in which Labour had to bid for the support of the Liberal and occasionally the Nationalist and Irish parties. The 1979 election seemed partially to restore the two-party system. But the Labour party was seriously divided; there was much talk of the establishment of a new centre party; and evidence enough from sample surveys of popular support for such a venture. Indeed this had been true throughout the 1970s. In 1981 the much predicted finally came about. A few prominent Labour politicians on the right of the party notably David Owen, William Rodgers and Shirley Williams (all former Cabinet ministers) set up a Social Democratic party, and sought an arrangement with the Liberal party.

This may or may not turn out to be an historic realignment in British politics. The case for such a change, in relation to the Labour party, rests on the view that the Labour party had moved sharply to the left in the 1970s and was no longer representative of its voters or its central traditions. The case for a realignment, in terms of British democratic politics, was based on the contention that the two major parties no longer represented the interests and outlook of the British people. The election of 1979 showed that the two parties represented at least 61 per cent of the people, though some of these might well have been reluctant supporters. Whatever the justification, the chances of a realignment taking root were not high. The barrier to realignment, and hence the enduring support of the two major parties, was the electoral system which effectively discouraged small parties. Nevertheless, surveys showed just over one-third of respondents favouring a centre (Lib–Lab) party in 1972 and over one-half a centre party of some kind in 1980.

In the light of all the problems of party cohesion and operation, it still seems remarkable that the two major parties survived the period still with over 60 per cent of the electorate supporting them, and more or less effective parliamentary organizations. A survey conducted for the Committee on Financial Aid to Political Parties (1976) found 86 per cent of respondents agreed that parties were 'essential to our form of government'. The comparative weaknesses of the parties reflected no discredit on them but rather the political complexities of the period. The parties did not fully achieve the ideals set out above but they did contribute to the necessary and difficult arguments of the period, and in a halting, confused and sometimes devious way, they promoted changes in the direction of goverments by democratic means. It may be that the simple model of two-party competition is too coherent, deliberate and directive to portray the subtlety and complexities of the relations of government and people as mediated by the parties in this period. To understand the movement of politics it is necessary to understand the periods of unavowed coalition between parties which link the periods of classical confrontation across the party divide.

Exercise 6

In democratic theory political parties are a crucial link between government and people. Did the parties carry out this function adequately in this period?

5 Political forces

Governments are influenced by forces which are clearly political in nature, political parties and political ideas; but they are also affected by forces which exist for other purposes or are not exclusively or persistently, and by clear intention, political. These include interest groups, protest or 'cause' groups, and the media.

Interest groups

The influence of interest or pressure groups in British politics was discovered by observers in the 1950s. Professor S. E. Finer claimed in 1958 that he had been able to trace the origin among the respective interest groups, of every significant amendment tabled to the Transport Bill of 1946–7 (1963, p. 130). In the same year Professor R. T. McKenzie wrote: 'There can be no doubt that pressure groups, taken together, are a far more important channel of communication than parties for the transmission of political ideas from the mass of citizenry to their rulers' *Political Quarterly*, XXIX 1, pp. 8–10). But such groups had been at work long before the 1950s. Consider the influence of the Church throughout history, or the landowners, or, in the nineteenth century, the railway interest. In some cases, these interests were 'built in' to the political system, so that pressure from a body external to government was not apparent. Indeed, it is in the nature of governments that some interests are built in, as it is with political parties. But organized and clearly external groups have operated in the modern form since the eighteenth century; and twentieth-century governments have dealt as a matter of course with bodies like the National Farmers Union and the British Medical Association, or their predecessors, which originated before 1900.

Nevertheless, there were some significant changes in interest groups in the period since 1945. The new awareness of the influence of the groups was in part a recognition of undue and secret influence. Professor Finer ended his path-breaking study, *Anonymous Empire* (1963, first published 1958) with a clarion call to accountability. '. . . through this (secrecy) the lobbies – as far as the general public is concerned – become faceless, voiceless, unidentifiable; in brief, anonymous. Light! *More* light!' (p. 133).

In that passage Professor Finer was referring especially to the unacknowledged submission of Parliament to the secret pressure of the interest groups. Prudent men, observing this, concluded that it would be wise to join the system and acquire for themselves the evident benefits of this supplementary means of representation. So, as government activity extended, interest group activity extended and intensified too and, so far as it was possible, grew more expert. The groups needed the benevolence of governments, and for their part governments often needed the co-operation of the groups. Government by consultation had arrived.

Alongside, sometimes within, the interest groups, there was a growth of advisory and expert groups. Governments were increasingly called on to act in fields where only experts could guide them, notably in the high technology of nuclear energy, supersonic flight, computers and so on. This was not novel in the defence field, and in industrial matters even nineteenth-century governments had sometimes depended on difficult scientific advice. What was new in the post-1945 period was the extent of government involvement and the complexity and uncertainty of the technologies involved. Governments were forced to make judgements on matters they could not fully comprehend. Inevitably experts acquired a power of recommendation, and naturally (as in the case of the Concorde supersonic passenger aircraft) tended to overvalue the products of their own expertise. (Professional people from generals and judges to university teachers rarely advise that their own profession is obsolete or redundant.)

Besieged by interested and expert groups, governments in effect opened the gates to the besiegers. Government changed its shape and its self-image. It was no longer a citadel under attack, a unique institution under pressure from outsiders; instead, the more powerful of the outsiders were invited in, and incorporated in the government process. Occasional consultation became permanent consultation. Indeed, consultation with the unions was referred to by *The Economist* (February 1980) as 'a constitutional principle'. Consultation in some cases amounted to negotiation, with the interest group claiming a right to a veto over, even consent to, policy. This position seems almost to have been conceded to farming and medical associations, and, at least by the Labour governments in the 1970s, to the trade unions. It would be appropriate to describe this as the private government of the public domain, if it were possible realistically to distinguish public and private.

This process of 'incorporation' was often referred to in the 1970s as the creation of the corporate state. But that term implied a more formal and inclusive system for the representation of the major interests. Other commentators referred to 'tripartism', which conveyed some kind of arrangement between government, industry and unions, with the complication that government might have to accept that its position in relation to the others was special but not superior. Professor G. Ionescu described the process accurately but called it 'the politics of concertation': 'faced with the prospect of increasingly ungovernable societies . . . the representative governments relinquish their positions as unique national policy-makers and seek "partnerships" or "contracts" with . . . corporate forces . . . the politics of concertation is the technique of policy-making in which the horizontal process of consultation-commitment replaces the vertical process of command-obedience' (Ionescu, 1975, pp. 1–2, 8).

The notion of incorporation conveys a general view of the power of the major groups. More exact assessment depended on the bargaining leverage of the group – its power to damage or enhance the interests of government, the countervailing power of competitive groups, and the overriding authority governments might derive from popular support, party and parliamentary opinion, and constitutional standing. But the latter, the historic authority of government, the traditional legitimacy of government power to uphold a national or public interest, seems to have diminished after 1945. Thus in the period 1947–51 the steel industry, under threat of nationalization, refused all co-operation with the Labour government. In the 1970s, trade unions resisted legislation on industrial relations. Governments learned the extent of their own impotence, and the consent of the governed took on a new significance as a condition of, not a desirable accompaniment to, government action. Governments after 1945 were in theory no weaker than nineteenth-century governments in face of the major interests of the time. But post-war governments attempted to do much more, in face of a larger number of better organized groups, who were no longer deceived by the element of bluff inherent in government authority.

The two major interest groups most deeply entrenched in government and in the parties and Parliament were industry and the trade unions. Each was closely identified with a major party. Industry was well-represented in the Conservative party in Parliament and in the leadership, and contributed heavily to Conservative party funds. The Conservative ideology fitted the interests of industry. This alignment of party and interest was often informal and discreet, 'built-in' so that the service of interest seemed like the service of country. Industrialists did not need to make speeches at the party conference, or wait on MPs at the House of Commons. However, the relationship was more complex than this simple alignment might suggest. The Conservative party sought power, and needed to attract millions of popular working-class votes. For that reason the party accepted in the 1950s the basic goals of the Managed Economy Welfare State. Hence Conservative governments could not consistently serve the interests of industry except 'incrementally' by modifications and adjustments. Moreover, the interests of industry ranged widely and included many conflicts of interest. In particular, the interests of small business and big business, retailing and manufacture did not coincide. Document 4.6 on the Conservative government's move to abolish Resale Price Maintenance in 1963–4 shows some of the complexities of the relationship of the party and small business.

Document 4.6
The abolition of Resale Price Maintenance 1963

Resale Price Maintenance (RPM) is the agreement between manufacturers and distributors not to cut prices.. It was made illegal (with some exceptions, including books) by an Act of 1964. By then competitive price cutting had already begun, notably in supermarkets. But in other areas RPM was replaced not by price competition, but the 'Recommended

Retail Price', and non-competitive discounting. While the consumer may gain from price maintenance, which encourages the retailer for example to hold slow-selling stocks and to offer good service, generally RPM was in the interests of retailers and to the disadvantage of his customers. The movement to protect the consumer developed in the late 1950s with the establishment of the Consumers Association and the first publication of its magazine *Which?* (1957). The Conservative party had close links with industrial rather than consumer interests, but its voters were of course consumers too. Traditionally the party preferred the operation of the market to legislative intervention. A market arranged to avoid competition was against their principles but in the interests of their friends. The Labour party tended to favour the consumer, though not without some hesitation induced by its allies in the retail unions, and the co-operative societies. The most persistent advocate of the abolition of RPM was the Board of Trade, which had been concerned since the 1940s with government action against monopolies and restrictive practices.

This account of the forces favouring and opposing RPM indicates why very little had been done since 1945 despite occasional initiatives by the department and ministers. How can the legislation of 1964 be explained?

(i) It was passed only after a long struggle in Cabinet and with Conservative Members of Parliament, including a substantial revolt on the floor (over fifty Conservative Members abstained or opposed the Bill on Second Reading, and on one vote the government's majority was just one); and after some amendment of the Bill. The RPM interests launched vigorous action against the bill, and worked closely with a committee of Conservative back-benchers. Over 100 amendments to the Bill were moved, and the final Act incorporated significant modifications to Heath's first proposal. (The Act was thought to be still quite effective, though it did not prove so).

(ii) It was pushed through by Heath, newly appointed as Secretary of State for Trade. This marked a novel high status for that department, and indeed for Heath, who had been Chief Whip since December 1955. Douglas-Home had just replaced Macmillan as Prime Minister, and a general election was less than a year away. Heath, looking for a dramatic new theme, took up the fashionable idea of modernization, to be accomplished by a programme of regional development. The RPM Bill fitted into the idea of industrial regeneration. Heath fought for his Bill with determination, threatening resignation at one time. He had crucial support from the Prime Minister.

(iii) Accident played a part. The introduction of trading stamps had raised the question of price competition. At the same time a private members' Bill against RPM was introduced by a Labour member (on behalf of the co-operatives), and the Cabinet had to take a view – the issue could not be avoided.

Note. A detailed account of this episode is in Bruce-Gardyne and Lawson, 1976, pp. 80–117.

Exercise 7

7.1 What does the case of RPM suggest about the relative power of the organized commercial interests, a departmental minister, Parliament and the civil service?

7.2 Does it appear that the Conservative Members of Parliament were the instruments of the interests?

7.3 How characteristic would you say this episode was of the politics of the period?

The case of Resale Price Maintenance showed that there is no simple alliance of the business interest and government, each seeking identical objectives. Similarly, under a Labour government, there was not a simple pattern of conflict between two opposed groups, recognizing and pursuing irreconcilable interests. The business interest tried to live with Labour governments. Thus, in 1945–46, 'the reaction of employers' organisations . . . was surprisingly meek and law-abiding' (Finer, 1963, 121). But the steel industry, threatened with nationalization, refused to co-operate with the Labour government unless it obtained a clear majority in the general election of 1950. Such incidents occurred only when industry recognized a clear and present danger to itself. The relations of trade unions and governments followed a similar pattern.

The trade unions, like the industrial interest, were built into government as the third element in tripartite power. The incorporation of the unions was more recent and less discreet; the exploitation of power in the service of self-interest was more open, obvious and occasionally brutal. The trade unions had attained a position of acknowledged influence by 1945, a long historical development but much hastened by co-operation with government during the war when conflicts of interest were not pressed. In 1946 a trade union leader told the TUC Conference that they had moved from an 'era of propaganda' to 'responsibility'. At the previous conference, the *Times* correspondent had said: 'You have no longer any need to thunder; you have only to whisper and Ministers tremble and Field-Marshals bend their knees.' This 'social contract' between government and unions was extended and consolidated through the period after 1945. By 1948–9 the unions were represented on sixty government committees, compared with only twelve in 1938–9. In 1948 the unions co-operated with the Labour government in the first of many post-war attempts at concerted wage restraint. In 1962 the unions joined with industry and the Conservative government in a deliberative and mildly planning body, the National Economic Development Council. In the 1970s, the unions were established in government bodies dealing with industrial relations, like the Advisory Conciliation and Arbitration Service. From time to time, for short periods, the unions co-operated with governments in restraining wages (1948–9, 1966–7, 1975–7).

Over the period as a whole despite the conflicts of the 1970s, co-operation between unions and government was more characteristic than conflict. There were two crucial elements in that co-operation. The first was a division of labour: the unions were responsible for wage bargaining and would not for long accept government interference in 'free collective bargaining'. This, their inheritance from Victorian laissez-faire capitalism, was regarded as sacred. Second, the Labour party was particularly favoured with their co-operation, since it was their party. Historically they helped to found it, financed it, sponsored up to 40 per cent of its Members of Parliament, dominated its conference and National Executive Committee and ensured that its ideas and policies served their interests. Trade union leaders such as Deakin, Cousins, Jones were no longer marginal figures in the pages of political history.

From the late 1960s this unwritten contract between the unions and government fell apart, even when Labour was in power. Both Labour and Conservative governments were defeated in attempts to establish a tighter legal framework for trade union activity, and an 'incomes policy' (i.e. formal control of wages). Arguably, the unions helped to bring down governments in 1970, 1974 and 1979. Commenting on the Labour government's attempts to secure the co-operation of the unions in a new social contract in the mid 1970s; *The Economist* had this to say:

> The essence of Britain's dying social contract was that government policy was warped in various undesirable, uneconomic and slightly illibertarian ways in order to secure the signing of pieces of paper by Mr Jack Jones and other trusted trade union leaders, who from now on will not greatly affect the wage demands tabled by their members anyway.
>
> Even while the wage restraints agreed by the Joneses were being loyally obeyed, and while Britain was therefore hobbling along with an inflation rate only twice that of its competitors, there was a cost in this. In economic policy the trade union leaders have demanded the sheltering of old inefficient industries at the expense of preventing adequate profits in new employment-creating ones, thus temporarily diverting unemployment from the redundant Leylands towards the unrecruited young. In the more important non-economic fields, legislation has increased the privileges of trade unions at some cost to civil liberties, the attorney-general of England has felt constrained not to enforce the full rule of law, and nobody can feel happy about picketing that has escalated into intimidation. (*The Economist*, 16 July 1977)

These comments may seem a little unfair, given that the unions had supported quite severe restraint in wages in 1975–7, though this followed and preceded periods of massive wage inflation. However, the sourness of this criticism was reflected in opinion polls at the time, showing the trade unions to be the least popular institutions in Britain (even among trade unionists). The unpopularity of the unions was evident again in the election of 1979, when many trade unionists voted for a Conservative party committed to further restraint of the unions.

By 1980 the 'union problem' had become a major anxiety for governments, where in the 1940s and 1950s governments had expected and received at the least grudging and uneven co-operation. Anthony Crosland, writing in the mid-1950s had built his revision of socialism on the assumption of continued economic growth, negligible inflation and the co-operation of the trade unions. The change after the late 1960s had many causes. Unions had expanded, both among manual workers and among new white collar and public service groups. The latter enjoyed low pay and unexpected opportunities for disruption. Trade union officials were more professional, more concerned for their own standing as national union officers, and with a sharp appreciation of the realities of power. The potential for disruption and damage by trade unions had grown through the centralization and interdependence of industry, and the development of carefully calculated disruptive tactics, e.g. the banning of overtime (when maintenance was carried out), the stopping of computers, the lightning strike, 'flying pickets'. This new militancy in trade unions is itself associated with the general spread of militant protest in Western societies in the 1960s and 1970s; the decline of the British economy so that workers' claims could no longer easily be met by economic growth; and the loss of control by central union officials of their local leaders, based on the shop stewards movement. But while militancy grew, the union leaders learned to speak with moderation, and disruption was renamed 'industrial action', thus acquiring a spurious air of normality.

For all the turmoil, militancy and violence of industrial relations in the 1970s, the power of the unions was not unrestrained. They fought for limited objectives – trade union 'rights' or 'privileges' (strictly their historic legal immunities) and continuous rapid improvement in their members' standards of living. They were remarkably successful until 1980 in the first objective; successful in the second only in maintaining the growth of money wages, but in an inflationary and declining economy. On more general objectives of economic and social policy, union pressures on governments were markedly less successful. This was true for Labour almost as much as for Conservative governments. Thus the assessment of the power of the unions over government and in the Labour party is complex. Over the period as a whole, the unions were powerful within a narrow field, though that was perhaps of major significance for the economy. In that field the Labour party was rarely able to move far without union agreement; beyond it the party had more freedom. But historically and constitutionally the Labour party of the period was a political expression of working-class interests as represented by the unions, and it could not for long alienate the trade unions. (*Note*: Chapter 6 includes a section on the unions and the Industrial Relations Act of 1972.)

The corporatist relationship of industry, unions and government was a special form of interest group activity, promising greater rewards for both sides to the arrangement. There is no easy general measure of the impact of interest groups in this period. On one side it may be argued that interest groups were both weak and wholesome; rarely getting their own way, forced to take account of competitive interests, and educated in the public interest by a stern unbending government – in short, tamed, captured and civilized by the system. On the other side, it may be contended that the major groups were powerful and harmful, pressing private interests against the public good, ruthlessly exploiting their capacity to 'hold the community to ransom', upsetting the balance of constitutional representation, and setting at a disadvantage the groups who could not easily be organized for political pressure – old people, children, consumers, the unemployed. (Document 4.7 offers a corporatist view of government).

Historically, it is clear, first that there are powerful interests in society, and these by definition influence government; second, that there has always been some competition for influence and that over the years the hold of some interests on government (notably the Church and the land) has been weakened and others have taken their place and, third, that government in Britain has retained some capacity for resistance to group pressure. But the ultimate power of government to contain and control the interests was more evident from 1945 to the mid-1960s than in the 1970s.

Document 4.7

A corporatist view of British government

From D. Marquand, *Taming Leviathan: social democracy and centralisation*, 1980, pp. 10–13

. . . Above all, it has become clear that the Leviathan on which social democracy has relied to put its values into practice is not the kind of animal on which it is safe to rely. The state, we have learned, is not a neutral instrument after all. Indeed, it is not an instrument at all; it is a collection of men and women (more men than women, it ought to be said) with interests to pursue, jobs to protect, pension rights to defend, empires to build. These men and women want what is best for the society they serve: there can be no question about that. But they are bound to believe that they can serve society best by continuing to do the jobs they already do in the way they already do them. Inevitably, they have their own views of the public interest, and of the proper functions of their departments. Inevitably, they try to make their views prevail. Inevitably, they resist what they see as misguided or dangerous views, even if those views happen to be held by the politicians set in temporary authority over them. Inevitably, they often win . . .

That is only one of the flaws in the Victorian view of the state, on which present-day British social democracy has implicitly rested. A more fundamental flaw is that the whole notion of parliamentary sovereignty and parliamentary government and the conception of the policy-making process which springs from that notion, now conceal more than they illuminate. It may or may not be accurate to describe present-day Britain as a 'corporate state': that is a question of semantics rather than of substance. What is beyond dispute is that the corporatist elements in our polity are now so pronounced that the terminology of our pre-corporatist past no longer helps to explain how we are governed. In the first place, it no longer makes much sense to think of Parliament as a legislature. Its function is to approve, and to a diminishing extent to legitimate, the legislation hammered out in a complex, largely secret process of consultation and bargaining between the ministers, officials and interest groups concerned. It is not even clear that it makes sense to think of Governments as governing. They preside, with varying degrees of aplomb, over a loose, informal, constantly shifting and only half-acknowledged form of power sharing between the state, on the one hand, and organised labour and the organised employers, on the other . . .

But their responsibility is nominal, not real. In reality, the 'outputs' of the system frequently bear little resemblance to their preferences – or, for that matter, to the preferences of the parties which sustain them or of the voters who put them in office . . .

The notion that public expenditure is necessarily redistributive, and therefore inherently desirable, collapses in ruins once it is realised that, because ministers are not in full control of the state machine, the composition of public expenditure is determined less by ministerial choice than by a haphazard combination of *ad hoc* pressure, departmental politicking and bureaucratic inertia.

6 The protest groups

Beyond the institutionalized and comparatively civilized persuasions of the incorporated interest groups lay the territory of the protest groups. By the 1960s these were more numerous than ever before, concerned with a greater range of issues, and armed with more elaborate strategies. This is not to say that protest groups were unknown in pre-war Britain. While the unemployed between the wars had been remarkably docile, there had been unemployed workers' movements, and some protest demonstrations to match the militancy of the 1960s and 1970s – for example, marches, blocking the traffic in Oxford Street, London, mock fishing in the air raid trenches. The 1930s were notable too for protests and agitation related to the growing European crisis, and especially the civil war in Spain. In the earlier part of the century the trade unions had developed the general strike as a major weapon of protest; and before the 1914 war the Suffragettes had exploited the potential of civil disobedience, disruption and modest violence in drawing attention to grievance.

But the Suffragettes ceased their activity on the outbreak of war, achieved some recognition of their claims in other ways, and on the whole brought little credit to the tactics of militancy ('sawing at the very bough on which its members were demanding the right to sit' as the historian and journalist, R. C. K. Ensor, wrote). The general strike of 1926 failed, and the unions retreated into quiescence. The war of 1939 did not bring all protest to an end. In particular, there was a lively campaign for a second front in 1942–3, organized by the Communist party but drawing on far wider support for Britain's beleaguered ally, Russia. (The slogan, 'Open a Second Front Now' may still be seen on some walls and bridges). But for two decades after 1940, Britain seemed a moderately contented country, saving and digging for victory, coping with the rigours of war and post-war, and expressing its sometimes bitter post-war conflicts through the constitutional medium of Parliament and party politics.

This happy scene was transformed by the Campaign for Nuclear Disarmament which organized its first march in 1957. A brief account of the Campaign is set out in document 4.8. The Campaign marks a turning point in post-war politics, the moment when politics moved into the streets and the age of militant protest began. CND set a pattern imitated abroad and inspiring many a village Hampden at home to protest over a whole new range of minor grievances, the siting of a gas tank or a trunk road, the withdrawal of a school bus or a crossing patrol, the closure of a hospital. The methods of protest ran quickly from meetings, letters and petitions to disruption and direct action, occupation, squatting, blocking traffic, work-ins, keeping children away from school, digging up cricket pitches, releasing rabbits in a sports ground, hunger strikes. Some of these tactics came very near to violence, and certainly violence against property and against the police took place. The media were a necessary accompaniment to these tactics. Indeed the point of the tactic was often simply to engage the interest of television, which magnified the protest and transmitted it to a mass audience. This extension of protest activity was supported and strengthened by new versions of political theory which stressed the virtue of participation in democracy, and even the necessity of confrontation with a state which, for all its formal apparatus of representation, was for the ordinary citizen irresponsible and repressive.

Document 4.8
The Campaign for Nuclear Disarmament

The Campaign was a protest against the possession by Britain of nuclear weapons, and, for a section of the movement, against all nuclear weapons. The characteristic method of the Campaign was the mass public demonstration, in particular, the Easter marches from Aldermaston in Berkshire (the site of an atomic weapons establishment) to Trafalgar Square in London. At its peak, in the early 1960s, CND's major annual demonstration was supported by perhaps 100,000 people, counting those at the final rally, as well as the marchers.

The Campaign marks a turning point in post-war politics The old technique of the protest march was revived and modernized by efficient organization and the attraction of media coverage. It was the first post-war protest to attract young people in large numbers and to elicit support and imitation in the Western world. It acquired an international flavour and a moral fervour. Nevertheless CND had only limited immediate practical success. The Labour Party's Annual Conference in 1960 voted for unilateral nuclear disarmament; but this was reversed in the following year, and later Labour governments maintained the nuclear programme. Insofar as governments showed any reluctance they seemed more affected by the technical, strategic and economic problems of sustaining nuclear armed forces than by the moral and political case made by CND. Yet there is little doubt (and surveys confirmed this) that CND succeeded in making public opinion more sensitive to the issue, and it came alive again in the 1980s.

Some of the new protest groups did much more than just engage in protest campaigns. There was a rapid growth of 'self-help' protest organizations which aimed to tackle a problem themselves, as well as campaigning for government action. These groups worked mainly in the welfare field, and were heirs to the old and honoured tradition of charitable work among the poor – but joined to a hard modern political objective. Examples were Shelter, Age Concern, Mind.

Explanations for this growth of the new politics of protest are necessarily speculative. It was a phenomenon common throughout the Western world and, within strict limits, in the Communist countries too. Protest was intense in some years, notably in 1968. This had something to do with the Vietnam War and racial tension in the USA, while protest elsewhere was carried on by an international student class (of graduates rather than under-graduates) in which North Americans were prominent. But this cannot explain the events in Paris in 1968 (nor in Hungary or Czechoslavia); nor the extreme violence of some radical movements in Germany, Italy and Japan. But in Britain, most of the time, protest was scattered and sporadic, and the numbers involved quite small. Explanations have to take into account the fact that most people did not engage in protest.

Insofar as it is possible to measure such matters at all, it does not seem likely that there was more to protest about in the Britain of the 1960s and 1970s than say the 1930s. But this is irrelevant. Protest arises from a subjective sense of grievance which might be as strong in 1970 because a man could not afford a car as in 1930 when he could not afford to feed his children. There was a greater dependence on government and a great resentment of its failings (hence much criticism of impersonal government, 'faceless bureaucrats' and so on). Standards of contentment changed; there was a lower degree of tolerance of misfortune, and economic performance lagged behind higher expectations. But that lower tolerance itself requires explanation. It would seem to be associated with the lifting of the intense fear of poverty and the ending of the disciplines of war and military service. It was also associated in time with the rebellion of youth referred to in chapter 1, a break-out from dependence, subordination and discipline. Evidence of participation and leadership of protest movements suggests too that the highly educated and the unemployed (sometimes the same people) were likely protesters. Finally, one indisputably new element in British politics, race, and another which had only briefly appeared before, women's liberation, added objectives, motives and willing demonstrators to the protest movements.

For all their vigour, rage and ingenuity, protest activity did not often change the course of governments. Indeed, protest on the streets meant that the group lacked an entry to the corridors of power. So government could brush aside the protest, unless it had a good deal of public sympathy, some support in party and Parliament or high places, or an awkward capacity to disrupt. For these reasons, in varying proportions, strikes were by far the most effective weapon of protest. In other cases governments sometimes made concessions which carried virtually no economic or political cost; for example, the government's retreat from motorway building in the late 1970s in response to an effective if unscrupulous campaign of disruption of planning inquiries was not very painful for a government desperately short of money.

There is and was a justification in democratic theory for such protest activity. A major argument is expressed in document 4.9. There is still some room for doubt whether the quality of British democracy was always served by the protest activity of this period. Protest movements were not always representative, since people vary in their willingness and capacity to take part in protest and the variation is not in proportion to the grievance. The young and the middle classes were often overrepresented; and the issues fought over were of a special kind. Nuclear weapons, and later nuclear power, Vietnam and South Africa, abortion and the Welsh language were frequent subjects for militant activity, but not poverty in old age or the community care of the mentally ill. Perhaps these priorities are right but a concern for priority was not characteristic of protesters.

The balance is difficult to strike. Governments had taken immense powers to influence the lives of ordinary people in countless ways. The constitutional machinery for ordinary people to talk back to governments was not, or was not thought to be, adequate. The protesters seemed to give voice to the voiceless, power to the powerless. But the politics of protest was in practice much cruder than that neat and comforting formulation suggests. Protest was a necessary element in freedom of speech, a proper complement to parliamentary processes. But the power which militant protest sometimes gave was unevenly distributed, and challenged the minimal order and authority on which all governments must depend. In general, therefore, the assessment of protest groups is similar to that of interest groups. But militant activity on the streets raised another issue, the role and power of the police. By the end of the period this was, for better or for worse a matter of political concern, and the 'law and order' issues appeared in election debate in the 1970s.

Document 4.9

(a) Justification of disobedience in a democracy
From P. Singer, *Democracy and Disobedience*, 1973, pp. 133–4

In a model democratic society, there would be important reasons for obeying the law which do not exist in other forms of government. Apart from the general consideration that any preference we have for one form of government over another is a reason for obeying the laws of the preferred form of government, there are two special reasons for obedience which are peculiar to democracy. The first is based on the fact that a democratic society, in which all have equal power and there is no tendency for the majority to treat the minority with less than equal consideration, is a fair compromise between competing, otherwise irre-solvable, claims to power. The second stems from the fact that participat-ing in a decision-procedure, alongside others participating in good faith, gives rise to an obligation to act as if one had consented to be bound by the result of the decision-procedure . . . These reasons for obeying laws in a democracy apply only when no rights essential to the functioning of a fair compromise decision-procedure have been infringed . . .

There remain some forms of limited disobedience which do not run counter to the democratic reasons for obedience. Disobedience de-signed to gain publicity for a point of view which has not received a fair hearing, and disobedience aimed at inducing reconsideration of a decision, are compatible with fair compromise, and may assist in restoring a fair compromise when a basically equal decision-procedure is not working properly. Normally such disobedience ought to be non-violent and those disobeying ought to accept the legal penalties . . .

Although our investigation had, up to this point, suggested that there is a great deal of truth in the view that there are much stronger reasons for obeying the law in a democratic society than in a non-democratic society, when we sought to transfer this conclusion from a model democratic society to the sort of society in which we live, we found less truth in it. The modern form of 'Western democracy', as described by leading political theorists favourable to it, is not a fair compromise between competing groups. Although more diverse and more numerous groups influence decisions than in a dictatorship, some groups have less than an equal share of influence, while many people are not effectively represented by groups at all. Elections, it is generally agreed, do not rectify this inequality.

(b) Compatibility of direct action with parliamentary democracy

From April Carter, *Direct Action and Liberal Democracy*, 1973, pp. 139, 146

Direct action is not necessarily subversive of the existing political system. At a certain level it may be seen as a way of plugging gaps in the system due to inadequate administration, lack of imagination or normal bureaucratic inertia. The squatting campaign fits into this interpretation. Second, direct action can be understood in terms of a pressure group model – as a means of the poor and disadvantaged exercising pressure to protect and forward their own interests because they are denied access to the accepted channels of influence.

But the general tendency of direct action methods is to promote alternatives to the existing parliamentary model and existing modes of administration in the workplace or the university . . .

Direct action can therefore be incorporated into an acceptance of parliamentarianism, if it is seen as a means of setting limits to compromise, and of altering the context in which decisions are taken. It may do both by altering the configurations of power, and by changing certain beliefs, attitudes and interpretations of the situation. In contrast with the resort to guerilla warfare, a direct action campaign is usually open at all stages to a negotiated settlement which involves a degree of compromise; though where a head-on confrontation like the general strike occurs, one side has to accept defeat.

Apart from its potential for effecting social change direct action is also a means of asserting the importance of certain values in politics. Idealization of compromise in general obscures the fact that whilst adjudication of two legitimate sets of interests may be necessary and desirable, there can also be an undesirable compromise of basic values or principles.

Exercise 8

These excerpts are valuable in setting out the justification of disobedience and direct action within a democracy. As such they are characteristic of the intellectual support for the protest politics of the 1960s and 1970s. But the case is not without some weakness. How would you counter these arguments?

7 The media

Television seemed to dominate politics by the mid-1960s. The statistics of television ownership (chapter 1) show over 10 million television licences in 1960, over 15 million in 1968; by 1960 the evening audience for television had jumped to almost 30 per cent of the population (aged five and over). Politics seemed increasingly to take place on television, and to be received by the people through television. While television itself was new, the influence of the communication media on politics was not at all novel. Radio was almost universally available by the late 1930s, and came into its own as an instrument of communication for wartime governments. News broadcasts then reached up to a half of the population. Churchill's political impact in the critical years of the war, especially 1940–2, and again in a different style in the election of 1945, depended on broadcast speeches – great set-piece occasions for powerful appeals to the people. The cele-brated radio comedy programme, ITMA, ('It's That Man Again', starring Tommy Handley) had a regular audience of about 40 per cent of the adult population (home audience) in 1944. The newspapers too had been comparatively influential conveyors of political information and appeals. Prime Ministers from Gladstone to Lloyd George and Baldwin had courted their favour. Indeed it was assumed that a serious political party needed its 'own' newspaper, to carry on its political work. By the 1920s the circulation figures of the popular newspapers clearly put them in to the modern class of 'mass media'.

In this perspective television was not a revolutionary novelty either as arena or medium for politics; but it was significantly different from its predecessors and competitors as a mass medium. First the existing tendencies to massiveness and monopoly in the press and radio were quite surpassed by television. Its audiences were truly massive by any previous standards. This was dramatically demonstrated when the television broad-cast of the Royal Wedding in the summer of 1981 was viewed by 39 million people in Britain and an estimated total of 750 million people – an awesome landmark in the history of communication. Television also tended to monopoly. Although the BBC's monopoly was broken in 1954 by the establishment of independent (commercial) television, collaboration or networking by the formally separate commercial companies reduced the competition. In effect, there was a choice of two national news programmes on television each night throughout the United Kingdom, supplemented by regional news coverage. By contrast, the slowly diminishing number of national daily newspapers still amounted to ten in 1980.

Second, television was based from its inception on the BBC's public service tradition of broadcasting, in which the objectives of information and education preceded the newspapers' objectives of catching attention and persuading. In practice, the BBC offered no editorial judgements of its own (though judgements might be implied), and kept a strict balance in the time allowed to each of the parties. Commercial television was enjoined by statute to follow this tradition of impartiality and balance. Television time could not be purchased for political purposes, so, unlike USA, this most powerful of advertising media could not be exploited by the wealthy.

Third, television broadcasting by its very nature – people talking to or at you in your living-room – seemed to have an immediacy, a reach and penetration, an impact beyond that of the humbler newspaper. Television filled one-third of people's leisure hours; television comedy programmes fed on other television programmes; books linked with television programmes filled the lists of best-sellers; events in television fiction were reported in news bulletins. By the 1970s it seemed life was lived in, by and for television. In politics, fortunately, television did not have the influence that this saturation suggests. Reflection suggests that television can be watched as idly as a newspaper may be flicked through. Research showed that television was not capable of instant brainwashing, and that the processes of communication were complex and subject to barriers of interest, attention and need. Most people were as they had always been, not very interested in politics. Nevertheless, television had an unrivalled capacity to project political messages, and the politics of the 1960s and 1970s were marked by the intense but uneven impact of the medium. Thus, for example, it seemed that some politicians gained in popularity through television – Wilson in 1964 compared with Douglas-Home. A small party like the Liberals was projected notably in the elections of 1970 and 1974 by one skilled television performer, a kind of stage army of political leadership; industrial unrest became a nightly television drama in 1972, 1974, 1978–9; no sensible demonstrator moved until the cameras had arrived; in the strange landing by a 'force of British policemen' on the Island of Anguilla in 1969, the first boat ashore was of course that of Independent Television News.

Despite the competition of television there was in most respects remarkable continuity in the history of the press in this period. The tendency of the press to monopoly was maintained. The industry was dominated by three large groups, whose interests covered national and provincial newspapers, magazines, and commercial broadcasting. Britain had a very few daily and Sunday papers, sold throughout the country, hence with massive circulations unknown elsewhere in Western countries (though rivalled in Japan and Russia). In 1964, 16 million copies of eight newspapers went into four out of five British homes. The distinction between 'quality' newspapers and the rest was, if anything, more obvious, as the non-quality papers, yielding news to television, turned themselves partly into general interest magazines. The tendency of the non-quality press to selection, bias and sensation in its treatment of news was modified only by the general retreat from news. Overall, the Conservative party regained the traditional advantage over Labour which it had lost in the 1940s as the *Daily Mirror* and the *Sun* moved to the right in the 1960s and 1970s.

The impact of television showed up in this retreat from news and politics. But a still more serious consequence of television was the loss of advertising revenue, a further blow, mortal in some cases, to the economic viability of the press. In the first half of the period, and for two Royal Commissions, the major concern for the press focussed on questions of ownership and quality. By the 1970s the concern was with newspapers as an industry in decline. Few papers made profits; some such as the *Daily Herald* and the *News Chronicle* collapsed; others such as *The Times* were cross-subsidized from the profitable non-publishing activities of the owning group. Partly this commercial failure was due to the nature of the industry, collecting and distributing a highly perishable commodity, depending on advertising revenue and now in competition with television. But the industry was without doubt inefficient, bound into nineteenth century forms of production by the most powerful unions in British industry, unable to adopt the new technology of printing, or to moderate chronic overmanning based on what one editor described as 'a bizarre series of frauds'. *The Times* ceased publication for almost a year (1978–9) in an ill-rewarded attempt to change these practices. The situation was nicely summed up by the trade union leader who said to Lord Thomson, the Canadian businessman who had become proprietor of *The Times*, 'You own it, I run it'.

In the 1940s press lords still presided over an apparently buoyant if highly competitive industry, and walked the corridors of power, as arbiters of public opinion, and friends of Prime Ministers. By 1980, newspaper proprietors were hard-running businessmen, coping desperately with the rising cost of newsprint and unco-operative trade unions; not directly involved in politics, nursing few political ambitions, and much less likely to be lords. Cecil King of the *Daily Mirror* looked to be the last newspaper-man to seek a direct part in national politics, using his newspaper as his power base. He tried (in 1968) to dislodge the Prime Minister, and was himself dislodged. But in his time King had been wooed by politicians; he claimed he had been offered a peerage no less than five times.

Cecil King said that it was impossible to govern without press support.

Labour governments proved this was an exaggeration. Nevertheless, few politicians neglected to cultivate and influence both press and television. The diaries of politicians and newspapermen (Crossman's and Cecil King's are good examples) show the anxieties of politicians, and the occasional closeness of their relations with media men. One experienced lobby correspondent (James Margach) described Harold Wilson as 'Britain's most media-obsessed Prime Minister' (Margach, 1978, p. 140). He records a series of incidents amounting almost to a private war between Wilson and various newspaper and television men, and angry interviews between the Prime Minister, armed with press cuttings, and editors. In some cases Wilson was plainly justified in believing that newspapers had determined to exploit trivial personal matters for political purposes. (This was notably the case in stories relating to land dealings by relatives of Wilson's secretary; in nine days in April 1974, the national press devoted 6000 column inches to reports, comments and photographs related to this 'Land Affair'.) Nevertheless, Margach conceded that 'Harold Wilson, notwithstanding his obsessional nightmares about the press and his state of siege war with the political correspondents, made more significant advances towards informed discussion than did Heath' (p. 171).

The most serious clash between government and the media rose in 1956 during the invasion of Suez. The government took the view that the country was at war and the BBC must fall into the supportive, patriotic role of the BBC in wartime. But the country was deeply divided, and the BBC insisted that it must allow criticism of the government, including a talk by the leader of the opposition, to be broadcast. The government came very near to taking over the BBC. The BBC won in the end, though not without some punishment – including a reduction in its funds for overseas broadcasting. This was a crucial stand for independence. In the next few years broadcasters won some modest freedoms – the abandonment of the fourteen-day rule which, incredibly, forbade broadcast discussion of matters to come before Parliament for a period of fourteen days; and the coverage of elections by ordinary news programmes; and in 1978 the broadcasting of Parliament on radio. Civil war in Ulster raised new problems, both political (the presentation of the case of groups engaged in terrorism) and military security. The BBC's relationships with the government were made less easy by rapid inflation, which meant that the Corporation had to seek frequent increases in its licence fee.

Governments clearly had some political resources to employ against the media. But the relationship was not continuously warlike. In the long run of day-to-day working, politicians and media need each other. Governments could not control the way the media dealt with news but they could manage the flow of news, create it or suppress it. News management again was not novel – it was invented in its modern professional form by Lloyd George – but it was developed through the period, and by the 1970s the government employed 1300 public relations officers. One Conservative minister in Heath's government complained that the only civil servant who seriously restricted him was the press relations officer.

Further, this news management was reinforced by the tradition of secrecy of British government. This arose from the conventions of Cabinet government – unity, secrecy, the anonymity of civil servants, the weakness of parliamentary scrutiny – as well as the operation of the Official Secrets Act, which makes it a criminal offence to disclose any official information however trivial unless authorized to do so; the so-called Estacode of the civil service which reinforces the Act; and the restrictions of the libel laws. Thus the press kept silent on the Profumo affair (1963 – a sex and security 'scandal' involving a minister) long after information was known to them; and press comment on the partial collapse of Ronan Point, a system-built block of flats (1968) was limited. It was argued that the press revelations which uncovered the Watergate scandals in the USA would have been impossible in Britain. In the 1970s successive governments committed themselves to more 'open government' and the eventual reform of the Official Secrets Act. In practice, governments issued occasional consultative papers setting out policy proposals and options. But the Cabinet system – and the instinct of self-preservation for both ministers and civil servants – ensured that the keenest and most pressing differences of view were not revealed. Britain remained a long way from the liberties of the American Freedom of Information Act.

The response of the media to news management and closed government was occasionally to carry out what became known as investigative journalism, a serious attempt to discover the truth about government, making use of all sources of information including the readiness of ministers to keep diaries and to justify themselves; and a greater frequency of 'leaks' to the press, partly due to the invention of cheap photo-copying.

Some of the material on which this book draws testifies to the fair success of the media in half-opening the closed book of government. For the earliest years of the period Cabinet minutes and other papers are made available under the thirty-year rule, but much good was done by Crossman's publication of his massive diary and its serialization in *The Sunday Times*, partly in defiance of the rules. (The effect of the Cabinet diarists on the mutual trust of Cabinet ministers was perhaps less beneficial.)

It is not at all easy to sum up the influence of the media in the politics of the period. Document 4.10 shows the partisanship of the press and offers one measure of its influence. By the 1960s television had become a more significant source of information and opinion, countervailing the highly partisan messages of the national newspapers, and contributing to the fluidity of opinion and weakening of partisanship evident in the 1970s. (See document 4.13.) In the 1950s interviewing of politicians on television was deferential. By the 1970s a few political interviewers, Robin Day and Brian

Walden, for example, subjected politicians to a severe test of the grasp of their case, before an audience of perhaps 2–3 million. Still, most politicians would have judged that television offered them opportunities which much of the press denied them. Newspapers were certainly more partisan than the broadcasters, and often much more aggressive. They had to their credit some distinguished 'investigative journalism', instant history of high quality. Newspapers helped to expose some major injustices, for example, the devastation wrought by the drug thalidomide, and the rack-renting in London known as Rachmanism (both in the 1960s). On the other hand, a story about a 'worldwide bribery web' run by British Leyland, which made headlines in the *Daily Mail* in 1977, turned out to be based on a carelessly accepted forged letter.

The overall tendency of the media was probably, and inevitably, both conservative and sensational, and so unsettling and destabilizing. 'Events' were reported, but 'conditions' not investigated; hence, the frequent claims by trade unions that they only appeared in the news when they were on strike. (Both the reporter and the citizen suffering from the strike have obvious answers to this claim.) Similarly, dramatic events in the health service, the closure of a hospital, or a heart transplant operation, were treated sympathetically and without critical concern for priorities in health care. The undramatic and the non-visual, including the old and the poor, were neglected. A new materialism was encouraged, and popular expectations grew: inequalities were noticed and contested. Disasters occurred twice nightly. London was assumed to be the centre of interest for the British people, indeed the centre of Britain itself, and the world outlook was markedly transatlantic.

In the background the media generally failed to question the basic assumptions on which British society was built. The media were not constructively radical; so the basic structure was not challenged fundamentally, but it was often treated with derision or disrespect. Politicians suffered a good deal from facile criticism. Some of them gained too from the media promotion of the elusive qualities of 'leadership'; while the people they were expecting to lead became less governable. Altogether, the history of the media in Britain between 1945 and 1980 demonstrated the price that politicians must cheerfully pay in a democracy for the erratic vitality of a free press. In this respect the media reinforced the tendencies of the interest and protest groups towards political volatility, the instant salience of single issues, the sudden promotion of protest, high expectations and low trust.

This discussion assumes that the media acted as largely independent influences on opinion. But the media cannot be separated from the society in which they operate. They necessarily reflected the views and interests of journalists, the immediate pressures of government and the heavier weight of a structure of information created by government and public and private corporations. News and opinion were increasingly manufactured goods, and, as Professor Beer pointed out (document 4.14), the economy of information is deeply penetrated by government itself.

Document 4.10
The partisanship of the press

There are many examples of the intense partisanship of the press in the 1940s and 1950s (see Madgwick, 1976, pp. 352–3). The following are notable examples:

(i) The General Election of 1945. The *Daily Express* seized on statements by Professor Laski, Chairman of the Labour party's NEC about the importance of the NEC in a Labour government, and about the use of violence to achieve socialism. These statements were significant but were not endorsed by leading Labour politicians. Nevertheless, the *Express* gave nearly one quarter of its whole election coverage to the matter. This was characteristic of the blatant campaign by the *Express*, led by Lord Beaverbrook, to persuade its readers to vote Conservative. The *Daily Mirror* campaigned with equal vigour for Labour.

(ii) In the 1951 election the *Mirror* ran what turned out to be the last of the great newspaper election stunts, and one almost entirely of its own making. The paper tried to suggest that the Conservatives might lead the country to war over Persian oil. On election day itself the paper had on its front page a large drawing of a pistol, pictures of Attlee and Churchill, and the banner headline 'TODAY YOUR FINGER IS ON THE TRIGGER'. The *Mirror's* style seemed to belong to the world of advertising rather than politics (since then these worlds have moved closer together). An observer at the time commented 'One can hardly doubt that, judged purely as a Labour propaganda sheet, (the *Mirror*) must have had an appreciable impact on its five million purchasers in the vital last days before the poll' (Butler, 1952, p. 134).

(iii) In that election and again in 1955 and 1959, Conservative newspapers endeavoured to make Aneurin (Nye) Bevan into a bogeyman, the red menace. In an election broadcast of 1951, Charles Hill, former 'Radio Doctor' and a popular broadcaster, warned: 'The end is Nye.' In 1955 the *Daily Sketch* ran the headline 'PRIME MINISTER BEVAN'. Doubt was cast on the loyalty of a Labour government, particularly in dealing with Russia.

(iv) During the Suez crisis of 1956 the *Daily Mirror* opposed the military intervention, suffered a substantial loss of circulation (70,000 copies – about 2 per cent), and began to revise its editorial attitudes.

(v) There is some evidence that Conservative papers in 1962–3 and Labour papers in the late 1960s reflected disenchantment with the government, and drew voters away from the party they normally supported.

(vi) From 1945 to the late 1960s the popular press was about equally divided in readership between Labour and Conservative. In that period, Labour won four elections (two very narrowly); the Conservatives three. Thereafter, the balance of the press was tipped towards the Conservatives (for example, in 1979 the national newspapers ran four times as much anti-Labour as pro-Labour material). But television with its political balance had replaced the press as the major medium of political communication. In that period the Conservatives won two elections, Labour one, and one was 'drawn'.

Document 4.11

(a) *Partisanship of newspaper readers, 1963*
Adapted from D. Butler and D. Stokes, *Political Change in Britain*, 2nd edn 1974, p. 116

Readers' partisanship	Conservative[a] papers	Labour[b] papers	Less committed Times	Guardian
Conservative	57	13.5	60	23
Labour	26	74.5	20	33
Lib/Other	17	12.0	20	44
	100%	100%	100%	100%
	n=783	n=573	n=10	n=30

[a] *Telegraph, Sketch, Mail, Express*   [b] *Mirror, Herald/Sun*   n=number of respondents

(b) *The influence of the press on partisanship, 1963*
Based on Butler and Stokes, 1974, p. 118.

Family	Newspaper	Party
Conservative ⟶	Conservative ⟶	79% Conservative
	Labour ⟶	44% Conservative
Labour ⟶	Labour ⟶	86% Labour
	Conservative ⟶	62% Conservative

The percentage is the percentage of respondents in the two categories indicated in the first and second columns, e.g. respondents with a Conservative family, and taking a Conservative newspaper.

Exercise 9

9.1 Does the press treatment of politics indicated in Cases (i), (ii) and (iii) above amount to gross irresponsibility, sensationalism or what?
9.2 What do cases (iv), (v) and (vi) above suggest about the influence of the press?

Document 4.12
The triumph of the picture

In the 1979 election campaign, the Conservative leader, Mrs Thatcher, followed an elaborate 'campaign media strategy' designed by her professional publicity advisers. The aim was to 'soften' Mrs Thatcher's image, to present her 'relating to' ordinary people, housewives, skilled workers and young people. The method was the 'controlled walk-about' which produced pictures of the desired kind, suitable for the lighter evening magazine programmes.

In the course of the campaign Mrs Thatcher was filmed tasting tea in a tea-repository, having her heart beat tested electronically, sewing clothes in a garment factory, and, in a grand climax, holding a calf in the middle of a Suffolk field, surrounded by eighty journalists and about fifty of her entourage. All this had almost nothing to do with meeting people in the locality, nor indeed with the serious issues of the election.

In the same election, the Labour leader, James Callaghan followed a similar strategy from time to time, but with less enthusiasm and less careful planning. In the 1970 election the emphasis of the parties was the other way about as Wilson engaged in walk-abouts and Heath made long serious speeches.

Document 4.13
Political significance of the transformation of the media

From D. Butler and D. Stokes, *Political change in Britain*, 2nd edn 1974, p. 419

. . . the British public of a generation ago was more habituated to the printed media than the electorate of any other large democracy. The national morning newspapers held strong partisan commitments and these were closely reflected in the party affiliations of their readers. If readers were not in the first place converted by their newspapers their continued exposure to a heavy flow of politically slanted information helped to reinforce existing party alignments.

But this pattern has been sharply altered by the transformation of the media themselves. The monopoly of a partisan press, weakened by the coming of radio, was broken completely by television which for the mass of the people became the prime source of political information. British governments, unlike some others, felt constrained not to exploit the air waves for party advantage, and the broadcasting authorities have broadly sought to be politically neutral. Thus as television reached saturation coverage by the end of the 1950s, the British electorate became exposed to a quite different kind of political information. The public showed that it clearly perceived the difference in bias between the broadcast and the printed media.

There can hardly be any doubt that this revolution in the media helped to prepare the way for the much more fluid changes of party preference in recent years. The electorate by no means stopped reading newspapers. But the angling of politics by the press was somewhat muted and was now overshadowed by a treatment of events on television and radio that was almost ostentatious in its presentation of the several sides of any issue. It should occasion no surprise that the years just after television had completed its conquest of the national audience were the years in which the electoral tides began to run more freely.

Document 4.14

Government and the formation of opinion

From S. Beer, *Modern British Politics*, 1965, p. 349

. . . the fact is that not only political parties, but indeed the whole vast apparatus of modern government and politics has a role in forming the opinion by which it is supposed to be governed. In this respect the mixed economy is paralleled by the mixed polity. In the era of Collectivist policy, we cannot separate the sphere of government from that of the production of material goods and services. Neither can we in the era of Collectivist politics separate the sphere of government from that of the formation of public opinion – the sphere of 'ideal production'. As government policy has deeply penetrated the economic market place, so also have the massive concentrations of contemporary politics invaded the market place of ideas.

Conclusion

There is much more movement in the 'politics' described in this chapter than in the constitutional matters treated in chapter 3. Four major trends in British politics may be discerned.

(i) Britain was harder to govern in the 1970s than in the 1950s. The extent and cause of this condition are indicated in the text.

(ii) The contest between collectivist intervention and laissez-faire government was at the heart of political conflict. The 1950s marked a settlement only in the sense that the Conservative party did not engage in sweeping denationalization or dismantling of the welfare state. The public learned to love the National Health Service and public education, to hate unemployment and to be indifferent to nationalization.

Ideologically, the Conservative party moved towards the centre in accepting the broad lines of the Managed Economy Welfare State, but to the right through its discovery of monetarist economics. Meanwhile the Labour party seemed for the most part to take the Managed Economy Welfare State as a satisfactory substitute for, or even the reality of, socialism.

(iii) The party system was weakened but not disrupted by many factors: the poor performance of the economy; the complication of social classes; the discontent of Scotland and Wales; the impact of the media.

(iv) Loss of confidence in politics led to more aggressive pressures on government through lobbying and direct action.

Two new forms of government emerged in response to these political trends.

(i) Corporatism, meaning the conversion of governing to a process of formal and informal negotiation between the government itself and the two major industrial interests, management and the unions.

(ii) Coalition government as an ideal rather than a practice. The classical two-party system was denounced as 'adversary politics' leading to exaggerated partisanship, and the development of policies in opposition which had to be abandoned after engagement with the realities of office. Coalition government would, so it was argued, diminish partisanship, neutralize the extremes and provide a steadier middle-of-the-road government.

The Lib–Lab Pact of 1977–8 might have demonstrated the virtues of co-operation between the parties. But it was for Labour an expedient brought about by their minority position in Parliament, and it was banished with the return of a majority government in 1979. Coalition government, like party realignment, awaited the adoption of proportional representation.

Guide to exercises

1 Yes, especially in the tendency for the middle classes to vote Conservative. Note, however, that these amount to only 35 per cent of the population, and that the association of class and vote diminished from the 1950s to 1979. See also Exercise 4.

2 Yes, with some qualification. It is more evident when the Conservative vote is high (1979). The number of seats held by each party roughly reflects the number of votes – but except in a few 'one-party' areas like South Wales, both major parties have substantial support, and there are also large numbers of non-voters and minor party voters. So the 'two-nations' diagnosis must be regarded as a little over-dramatic. Some other factors reinforce it (e.g. the distribution of heavy industry and unemployment); others modify it (e.g. the culturally unifying impact of the media).

3.1 Quintin Hogg says conservatism is an attitude, rather than a philsophy; Gilmour refers to 'national unity', 'common sense not party dogma'; Worsthorne is concerned with 'national greatness', and 'the job of govern-ing'. It may be argued that these are either so vague as to be meaningless; or substantial and significant enough to constitute a philosophy. In support of the Conservative claim it can be argued that this feeling that some vague general conditions are desirable is very different from the precise theory and prescriptions of ideologies like socialism. But the distinction does depend on taking an extreme view of the ideologies and the non-ideologies – on the one side socialism; on the other almost a refusal to hold political principles at all. In practice, however, socialism is a minority view within the Labour party; and Conservatives by implication base their programmes on some specific political principle.

Does this argument matter? Plainly the attitudes, philosophies and ideologies produce differing political objectives, and different political styles, the ideologue confident, positive, intolerant, the Conservative non-ideologue unsure, undirected, tolerant. But the Conservative cannot claim a monopoly of this approach to politics. Indeed, the Labour party could well be seen as a working-class and union *movement*, rather than a party with an ideology.

3.2 (i) Conservatives favour equality of opportunity, rather than equality. This implies a competition in which the successful gain the prizes, and there is a governing class (Worsthorne). Macmillan is opposed to animosity between classes. Gilmour expresses the 'moderate' view that equality should not be imposed, but gross inequality would be intolerable.

Labour in contrast stands for equality. But this is more evident in Crosland than in Bevan and Gaitskell. The latter were particularly concerned with the destruction of evident poverty and injustice. In practice, Bevan and Gaitskell still concentrated on means (state welfare and nationalization). Crosland's 'revisionism' took the achievements of the Labour government as a starting point for the setting of new goals.

(ii) Attitudes to poverty were affected by attitudes to equality. For the Conservative, poverty must be relieved; for Socialists, the gap between rich and poor must be eliminated or much reduced. The Socialist argues that poverty was not simply an unfortunate necessity, but the inevitable and cruel product of an unjust system, capitalism. Hence the elimination of poverty required a radical change of economic system. For Socialists like Bevan, attitudes were coloured by the personal experience of poverty – just as for Conservative thinkers, the relief of poverty is always a little like Oxfam, doing good to strange and distant people.

(iii) Plainly, Conservatives see a more limited role for government than Bevan and Gaitskell. Crosland's revised socialism also assumes a highly interventionist government, managing the economy, securing equality, and, in his later writing, controlling the environment. But at the end of the 1970s, socialism was influenced by the 'small is beautiful', 'community values', individualist thinking of the time.

3.3 No. In particular, he was fundamentally a democrat; he was not especially 'doctrinaire'; and his socialism was not very precise. Bevan was intellectually a product of the between-war period, angered by poverty, and afraid of fascism; and personally he was a volatile man, sometimes moved to anger (as he said, people in a minority often had good reason to be angry).

Bevan's differences with his party in the 1950s were mainly over foreign policy. His differences with Gaitskell seemed to have been personal as much as ideological. They were intensified by the activities of the Bevanite group, from which Bevan himself was at times somewhat detached. The ferocity of the Bevanite period seems to be related to the natures of the party and the contending leaders rather than to profound ideological differences. (3.4 below).

4 This can be answered in relation to voters, Members of Parliament and leaders, ideology and programme. By all measures it is correct to argue that both parties are class parties. But the social classes they relate to are complex; and both parties try to be national parties too. In sum they are

3.4 The basic differences between the Conservative and Labour parties 1945–80

	Conservative party	*Labour party*
Economy	For private property and free enterprise: hence outright opposition to nationalization and a lack of enthusiasm for planning. Hostile to power of trade unions.	For common ownership, planning – enthusiastic planners. Accepted the power of trade unions as proper if sometimes inconvenient, in a modern social democracy.
Taxation	High taxation regarded as discouraging enterprise.	'Robin Hoods' (robbing the rich to feed the poor).

	Conservative party	*Labour party*
Welfare	Unenthusiastic, especially about 'universal' welfare schemes, i.e. irrespective of need; aims to work welfare state efficiently, cut costs, encourage self-dependence.	Enthusiasm for 'fair shares', helping the weak, concern for a reasonable standard of living for all.
Social equality	Favoured private education and selective grammar schools: hence saw the ideal society as based on distinctions of merit and wealth, a society in which there must be leaders and led.	Against both private and selective schools. This was one of the sharpest distinctions between right and left, and is related to fundamental ideas about social equality, as against Conservative notions of a society which is necessarily unequal to some extent, because this reflects natural inequalities and encourages enterprise through competition and rewards.
Foreign policy and defence	Strongly patriotic, favouring a world role for Britain; willingly high spenders on defence; suspicious of USSR. Strong attachment to NATO and USA, early suspicions of UNO. Ambivalent towards EEC.	Tendency to split on this, particularly when the party was in power. Strong tendencies to 'little Englander' policies, colonial withdrawal, distrust of NATO and nuclear weapons. Suspicious of Germany in 1950s and 1960s; and of USA. Early enthusiasm for UNO. Tending to hostility to EEC.

The Liberal party is opposed to nationalization, more critical than Labour of trade union power, and on other measures tended in the 1960s and 1970s to be nearer to Labour. But an alternative short answer could be there is not!

both coalitions based on one class (or sector of society) but reaching out for support across class divisions.

But it would also be fair to argue that the term 'class' is too broad and vague to have a precise meaning, so full of meaning that it is meaningless, but plausible and easily adapted to suit almost any argument. Like 'democracy' and 'freedom' it has become a term to be used only with the greatest caution. (This applies to exercise 1 too)

5 It depends what you mean . . . The traditional view was that the Labour party was a popular movement rather than a parliamentary organization. Its peculiar structure reflected this and made the leadership responsible to 'the movement'.

Attlee's conduct of the post-war Labour government showed that Labour once in power tended to act like a government, in the British mode of 'responsibility' (i.e. now we're here we'll do the job, talk to you, even consult you, occasionally but not accept direction), and with the PLP not the Conference as the representative of the electorate.

So, in office, Labour was similar to the Conservatives, but in opposition, power swung some way towards Conference and NEC. That was more democratic according to Labour tradition, but, objectively, perhaps less so.

The Conservative tradition was certainly less democratic by these measures. The leader was not restricted by the constitution of the party; he controlled the party organization and his responsibility to the Annual Conference was a matter for his political judgement only.

During the post-war period the Labour party was impelled by seventeen years of office away from its tradition of party democracy. The Conservative party moved the other way, adopting a system for the election of the leader in 1965 (after the near-fiasco of 1963) which was used ten years later to change the leader. By the 1960s the leader attended the Annual Conference, and took part in the debates, where previously an inspirational speech after the end of the Conference had sufficed.

When all this is said, there remains a difference in style and tone between the two parties. The Conservatives are essentially a party of government and the 'stupid' (i.e. not intellectual) party; Labour is a party of protest, and of ideas. Conservatives when they disagree have usually employed the courtesies of the drawing-room and the board-room; Labour the rougher, blunter style of the public bar and the union committee. Labour is the angrier party. This raises the question, is anger an emotion making for democracy?

6 Parties relate to voters and to members. Both parties have structures for keeping in touch with members, which might be regarded as adequate, given the difficulties of the task. But neither party built up a large mass membership, and the Labour party's membership fell substantially. It would seem that the advantages of membership were simply not attractive.

Voters are linked to parties through the ballot box. There is evidence, reviewed in the text, to suggest that the voter's support for the major parties fell away to some extent during this period. This decline in the vote for the major parties, together with an increase in voting for third parties or not at all, and for taking action outside parliamentary channels, point to some dissatisfaction with the performance of the major parties as government–people linkages. This argument may be developed as a case for the realignment of parties – to which the party system failed to respond.

7.1 The organized commercial interests seem to have been influential in resisting legislation on RPM for so long; losing the battle only in exceptional conditions; and still succeeding in moderating the consequences of defeat. The departmental minister would have been powerless without the backing of the Prime Minister, and even so he was almost defeated by backbench Conservatives. Parliament was unusually influential in this case because of an unusually solid alliance in defence of a party interest threatened by the leadership. The civil service was influential only in having policies ready for a willing minister to take up.

7.2 Almost so. But Conservatives were concerned especially for the small shopkeeper, who, they argued, needed the protection of RPM in order to offer his valuable services; public and private interest coincided. Hence, so it could be argued, the Conservatives were not simply protecting a sectional interest.

7.3 Consumer protection was a secondary political issue from about this time. Backbench rebellions became more frequent in the 1960s and 1970s. Interest group activity of this intensity was evident throughout the period since 1945.

8 It must be admitted that the justification of disobedience and direct action raises difficult problems for the democrat. The general thrust of the case set out in the document cannot be denied: it is likely, indeed, inevitable, that society and democracy are imperfect, so the aggrieved citizen must be allowed political action outside the constitution. If that is not allowed, a great deal of desirable change would have been frustrated – don't make a fuss, things are quite good as they are.

But if the argument for disobedience is pressed too far it disrupts and may destroy the system. Moreover, the capacity for direct action is not equally distributed. A miner or a student with a grievance has more scope for protest than an old age pensioner. If you take a radical view of the system, believing there is much injustice etc., then you may often believe yourself to be justified in disobedience and direct action. If on the whole you approve of the system, then you will need to justify your disobedience very carefully indeed, assessing the extent of your grievance, the possibilities of remedy within the system, and the effects on your grievance, and on the system, hence on other people, of your disobedience.

There is no general principle which will guide you beyond the point that disobedience may sometimes be justified.

9.1 None of these cases involved complete fabrication; but some of the interpretations were hardly reasonable, and were much inflated by the press. (But remember that Bevan was denounced by his colleagues too in exaggerated terms.) 'Sensationalism' is a matter of taste as much as objective judgement. The *intention* was to achieve a quick, unthinking shock effect, and that may have been the consequence; and that roughly is what is conveyed by 'sensationalism'.

'Irresponsibility' is another difficult word. Strictly, the press is answerable only to the market and to itself. The question could be rephrased, for example, did the press in these cases fail to meet the needs of an informed democracy? But many newspapermen could regard that, rightly, as a loaded question. They could go on to make a case for the communication style of the popular press (for example, the *Daily Mirror* has claimed that its readers are much more likely to read its leading article than are *Times* readers to read the *Times* leader).

9.2 These are rough measures of the political influence of the press. In particular, case (vi) shows only that the outcome of elections is not determined simply by the press. Case (v) seems to show newspapers and electors moving in the same direction, but perhaps the newspapers confirm and hasten the move. Case (iv) is an example of the press adjusting to its readers – but in unusual conditions, with the country on the edge of, or even into, war. It has been said, 'The reader will always be King': but this applies only when the reader knows his own mind. Altogether, it is safe to conclude only that there was a complex interrelationship between newspaper and reader – and in the period of 1945–80 this was almost pushed aside, and certainly diminished in political significance, by television.

5 British foreign policy since 1945

1 Britain in 1945

Winston Churchill, called somewhat unexpectedly to the office of Prime Minister in May 1940, rallied and united the British people with his determination to fight on, whatever the cost, until final victory had been achieved. He described the performance of the British people in the summer and autumn of 1940 as 'their finest hour', and the phrase can, with much justice, be applied to Britain's performance throughout the whole of the Second World War. The United Kingdom was the only major power to fight from the beginning in September 1939 until the end in August 1945, and she was the only combatant to sustain major offensive operations in all the main theatres of conflict – European, Atlantic, Mediterranean, Middle Eastern, Southeast Asian and Pacific. She fought until fascism and aggressive militarism had been destroyed, in Europe and the Far East.

Moreover, she ended the war with her territorial influence and control at its greatest extent ever, greater even than in 1919. She continued to administer the former Italian colonies in Africa, she was dominant throughout much of the Middle East, her forces controlled most of Southeast Asia and had a leading role to play in any settlement in French Indochina and the Dutch East Indies, and she was the leading power in Western Europe. On this last point, it was clear in 1945 that the United States had every intention of retreating from Europe as soon as she decently could, and Stalin was on record as accepting a British sphere of influence in Western Europe.

All in all Britain's performance in the Second World War was an impressive one. However, while tributes are in order, there is another side to the story, probably more significant in the long run and less fortunate. With the advantage of hindsight the wisdom of British policy can be questioned, the awful cost of Britain's contribution can be assessed, and the hollowness of Britain's triumph can be exposed. While it is probably going too far to describe Britain's performance in the Second World War as a rather lingering and painful form of suicide, nevertheless the costs of victory in human, economic and social terms were very high: in effect the country was bled white by its exertions between 1939 and 1945.

It is true that Britain was a leading member of the Grand Alliance that had won the war, and that Churchill, or Attlee after the election of July 1945 was rightfully one of the 'Big Three'. But compared with her allies, Britain's power in 1945 was more like that of France in 1918. In 1918, France was one of the then 'Great Powers' but from 1917 onwards she was increasingly carried to victory by Britain and the United States. In 1945, Britain was one of the 'Great Powers' but from 1943 onwards she was increasingly carried to victory by the United States and the Soviet Union. In 1945 the United States and the Soviet Union were on the way to a new 'superpower' status, Britain in contrast, while hankering after the status of a superpower and certainly with the commitments of one, was in a state of virtual bankruptcy and was slipping towards the relegation zone in the rapidly shrinking league of great powers.

At the end of the war realists (and pessimists) thought in terms of power. Stalin had asked bluntly, 'How many divisions has the Pope?' and Churchill at least understood and accepted an international order based on power. Idealists (and optimists) placed greater faith in the newly established United Nations Organization. This was designed to remedy some weaknesses of the old League of Nations; in particular, the USA was fully committed and the major powers were permanent members of UNO's 'Security Council'. But the capacity of the new organization to keep the peace depended on agreement among the great powers. If they agreed and acted in concert, UNO would work, but would not be needed. If the great powers fell into conflict, UNO would not be effective, though it would be needed. Over the years UNO proved inevitably a great disappointment, though its diplomatic and economic work was valuable. But as the new ex-colonial nations joined, UNO became a platform for the denunciation of 'imperialism'. Even the Labour party's initial enthusiasm for UNO failed.

Wherever the British government looked in 1945 it faced serious problems. In Europe, despite victory in the war, Britain's position was weaker than it had been in 1939. The United Kingdom had gone to war to uphold the sovereignty, independence and integrity of Poland, and more generally, to prevent German hegemony in Europe. She had gone to war in the company of France, a strong ally, at least on paper. By 1945, Poland's sovereignty and independence were at the mercy of the Red Army, France was broken, and at least half of Europe was now threatened with domination by the Soviet Union. German hegemony had been prevented, but Britain had weakened herself almost beyond recovery to do this, and the process had opened the way to a potential Russian hegemony in continental Europe.

Outside Europe, Britain's commitments had never been greater but she no longer had the power – and was beginning to lose the will – to cope with the half of them. India demanded urgent attention, so did Palestine, so did Southeast Asia. Long-standing positions of influence in Turkey, the Eastern Mediterranean and the Persian Gulf were about to come under attack. The African colonies were for the moment quiet for Africa was late in developing anti-colonial nationalism and in attracting Russian interest.

Britain's position in the extra-European world, especially in Asia, was further complicated by the loss of prestige following the humiliating defeats at the hands of the Japanese in 1941–2. Much of colonial authority rested on prestige rather than the use of force. Britain, despite her victories in 1944 and 1945, never really recovered that prestige, and certainly did not have the extra force necessary to replace it.

It is clear therefore, even from this brief survey, that Britain's victory in 1945 was a flawed one, a twentieth-century example of the classical Pyrrhic victory, which brings defeat in its train. Victory is indeed questionable if the economy is badly run down, the treasury is empty, threats appear greater at the end of hostilities than they did at the beginning, commitments have been extended and almost everywhere are under attack, and, there is some danger of a loss of the will to go on. It is interesting – and very heretical – to advance the proposition that the victory had been achieved at too great a cost, that possibly the advocates of a compromise peace with Nazi Germany in 1940 were right, that Churchill's advocacy of total war and unconditional surrender was wrong, and that at the very least some effort should have been made by 1943 at the latest to have withdrawn from the war, leaving Germany, Japan, the United States and the Soviet Union to knock each other around if they so wished.

Christopher Mayhew, parliamentary under-secretary at the Foreign Office from 1946 to February 1950, reflected on some of the consequences of the war and on Britain's position in 1945 and the years following, in an address to the Royal Institute of International Affairs in June 1950. The address was subsequently published.

Document 5.1

From *International Affairs*, vol, XXVI, no. 4, Oct. 1950, pp. 477–8

First let me comment on the extent to which the United Kingdom has had freedom of action in foreign affairs since the war. I remember when, to my astonishment and alarm, I was appointed a junior minister at the Foreign Office, one of my first actions was to approach a certain very shrewd and experienced official to ask innocently for some document which would tell me just what the current foreign policy of His Majesty's Government was. I received the disappointing reply, not merely that no such document existed – a deficiency which has since been amply remedied – but also that it was really rather doubtful whether we had a foreign policy in the proper sense at all. Personally, I think that was rather a gloomy and defeatist attitude; but it was a healthy jolt. Pursuing a foreign policy implies having power and independence – enough of both to make, of one's own free will, a consistent impact on world events. The more a country gets tied up with its neighbours (either because through weakness, it must lean on them, or because it has voluntarily allied itself with them), and the more powerful the outside events are which it is required to influence; so much the less can a national have a foreign policy of its own.

Since the war, Britain has undoubtedly had her freedom of action in foreign affairs curtailed by all these factors. To the extent that our hands have been tied by voluntary association with our friends, we welcome it. To the extent that they have been tied by our weakness – or by the intractability of external events – we deplore it. In the early stage it was our economic weakness resulting from the war, spilling over into the field of defence, which seemed a particularly impelling factor. The close association with the United States was a pleasure, but also a necessity. Similarly, the grant of freedom to India and Pakistan was a moral duty, cheerfully undertaken: but any other policy would undoubtedly have proved before long to have been beyond our strength. More recently, our hands have been increasingly tied by voluntary associations with friends and allies. Constant consultation with the countries of the Commonwealth; with the Brussels Treaty Powers; under the Atlantic Pact; at O.E.E.C.; and elsewhere – all this has meant that important acts of policy which previously we should have made unilaterally, now have to be cleared with many countries, at many levels. Mr Bevin said in the House of Commons on 28 March this year, 'The day when we, as Great Britain, can declare a policy independently of our allies, has gone'. And then, on top of all this, we have had to face an active, aggressive, and appallingly intransigent Soviet foreign policy, which has, inevitably, dictated to us as to most of the non-Communist countries the general direction of our foreign policy.

Bearing all these things in mind, I think it is remarkable how much influence Britain has exerted in world affairs since the war. The war reshuffled the cards, and we have played our rather meagre hands with great shrewdness, owing much to the strong personality of our Foreign Secretary and also to the wide support he has received from Parliament and from the public.

The most notorious, and probably the most able, exponent of what can be described as the heretical view of Britain's performance in the Second World War was Sir Oswald Mosley. In his autobiography *My Life* (1968) he has a long chapter, 'Why I opposed the war', in which he sets out his views. It is impossible to reproduce the whole chapter, but the following extracts present the essence of his arguments:

Document 5.2
Sir Oswald Mosley, *My Life* (1968)

Chapter 'Why I opposed the war', pp. 377–97

The declaration of war in 1939 risked three consequences: the disaster of defeat, the triumph of communism, the loss of the British Empire despite victory. The only power which could in no circumstances benefit from that war was Great Britain. The complete disaster of defeat was averted by the heroism of the British people, the European triumph of Russian communism was partially averted by the scientists, and the loss of the Empire and reduction of Britain to the position of an American satellite remain the only clear results of the Second World War. We escaped entire destruction, but much of Europe did not. Evil was the inevitable result of entry into that war, and we are fortunate to live only with the least of the possible evils . . . We were well and truly hoist with our own petard; the chief example of self destruction in all history. The heirs and beneficiaries we had introduced to the scene were ready and willing to take over; America appropriated straight away the world-wide trading and financial position of Britain, and Russia prepared in its own fashion for the ultimate take-over of our Imperial trusteeship by the preliminary employment of American liberalism. Their action in Europe was even more direct: Europe was divided into two satellite powers, with Britain attached to America as the only alternative to death under Russia.

. . . The result of a war fought in the name of freedom was to subject ten non-Russian peoples to the Soviets, at least seven of them not even Slavonic peoples . . .

. . . A few men in the seats of power had ruled Britain throughout my political life. I opposed their policies from start to finish and invariably advanced constructive alternatives. When I contrasted the Britain they inherited from their forebears with the Britain they bequeathed to their successors, was I unfair to write: Has so much greatness ever before been brought so low by the errors of so few men, without defeat of its people in war? . . .

. . . I maintain the validity of the alternative policy: rearmament of Britain to the point of equality in the air with any power in the world, coupled with a strong fleet and a mechanised army which could have struck directly on the Continent in defence of France; this strength to be combined with a clear firm foreign policy which renounced all intervention in eastern Europe and western Europe. I am still convinced the policy was right . . .

Exercise 1

Britain was the only major power to fight throughout the Second World War from September 1939 to August 1945, and she was a key member of the victorious alliance. List the benefits that she gained from the war and also the losses she incurred. Was the war worth it?

2 Britain and the cold war

The new Labour government faced a whole series of problems and challenges when the war ended in 1945. The underlying problem was to fit Britain into the post-war international system, particularly in relation to the United States and the Soviet Union. More immediately, there were a number of lesser and more practical problems to be dealt with, all more or less direct consequences of the war. One was the political need to get the boys – and girls – out of uniform and back home as soon as possible. By the end of the year demobilization was proceeding at the rate of 12,000 a day, still much too slow for many of the men and women overseas. Other problems that had to be faced ran counter to speedy demobilization, for they demanded the maintenance of manpower overseas. Order and authority had to be maintained in Europe and the Middle East and restored in Southeast Asia; enemy countries had to be occupied, governed and fed; war criminals had to be tried and the survivors among their victims provided for; and peace treaties had to be drawn up after discussion with our allies.

These problems took up time and used up scarce resources, and were more than enough for any government to cope with, especially one whose first priority was a massive programme of social reform at home. But, in addition, the new government was faced almost immediately with more problems, partly the result of the war but increasingly the product of post-war factors. There was no neat dividing line between the two sets of problems, no breathing-space, however short, between end-of-war and post-war issues. One example, which will be returned to later, will make the point. Attlee replaced Churchill as Prime Minister towards the end of July 1945, the atomic bombs fell on Hiroshima and Nagasaki in early August, the war in the Far East ended in mid-August. On the 31 August, almost before the guns had cooled down, President Truman wrote to Attlee urging the British government to open the gates of Palestine for Jewish entry. The Palestine problem had arrived to plague the government for something like three years.

The new problems related to a number of issues and regions, and they make a convenient framework for a treatment of British foreign policy between 1945 and the present day. Briefly, there were problems with regard to Britain's role in the cold war, problems relating to British interests in the Middle East, problems relating to the future of the colonies and dependencies especially in Africa and Asia, with which are associated the question of Britain's subsequent post-colonial role 'east of Suez'.

Finally – and in the long term probably the most significant – problems arose from Britain's relationship with Europe.

Before discussing what became the central problem in the years immediately after 1945, namely the developing cold war, it is necessary to say something about the politicians, Labour and Conservative, who were significant in making foreign policy. It is difficult for something like twenty years after 1945 to find great differences of principle over foreign policy between the leaders of the two governing parties, although of course some of their followers clashed passionately over a variety of issues. Suez in 1956 is a possible exception to this statement. Some members of the Labour government in 1945 appear initially to have entertained the notion that they could get on better with the Soviet Union than could a Conservative administration, but Stalin and Molotov soon disabused them of such idealism. It was not really until the 1960s when Britain's attitude to Europe became a matter of nationwide debate that the political élite may be said to have split on an issue of principle, and then the split was across rather than on party lines.

One of the main reasons for the absence of major clashes of principle over foreign policy between the two frontbenches was that both sets of leaders had shared the same experiences – meeting the challenges of the 1930s and the Second World War – and had responded in much the same way. Indeed until the retirement of Harold Macmillan in 1963, British foreign policy was dominated by a group of men – Attlee, Bevin, Morrison, Cripps, Churchill, Eden, Macmillan – who had all served in the wartime coalition government together. The Labour leaders, after playing major parts in the wartime coalition, won general elections in 1945 and 1950, and were to hold office until the autumn of 1951. When Churchill's government succeeded Attlee's and Eden replaced Morrison as Foreign Secretary there was no revolution in foreign policy; the differences were of personality and method rather than of principle. As D. C. Watt puts it in an essay, 'Britain and the Cold War in the Far East 1945–58' in Nagai and Iriye (eds) 1977, referring to British policy in the Far East but applicable to British foreign policy as a whole:

> Where differences are discernible, they can be ascribed mainly to differences of personality and political method between Bevin and his successor in the 1951 Labour government as foreign secretary, Herbert Morrison, on the one hand, and Eden, on the other, Eden being much more instinctively inclined to negotiation than either of his Labour predecessors.

Whatever Britain's interests elsewhere, her security in Europe and the recovery of that continent remained her major preoccupations. Initially the possibilities of a renewal of German aggression were considered quite seriously by policy-makers, but such possibilities were soon seen to be negligible, and were replaced by consideration of the looming menace of the Soviet Union. The notion of a renewal of German aggression after 1945 now seems absurd, but for men and women in London and Paris with long memories – and some in Paris had very long memories – Germany had appeared as the main threat to peace and stability for eighty years or so, and had recovered from one crushing defeat (1918) in a remarkably short space of time and embarked on another war of conquest. So when Britain and France concluded a Treaty of Alliance and Mutual Assistance in March 1947 – signed rather oddly at Dunkirk, not perhaps the best example of Anglo-French co-operation – the preamble talked about 'the object of preventing Germany from becoming again a menace to peace', and the articles of the Treaty spelled out what the two signatories would do if they became again involved in hostilities with that country. One year later Britain, France, Belgium, Luxembourg and the Netherlands concluded the Treaty of Brussels (March 1948). This included a ritual reference to steps to be taken in the event of a renewal by Germany of a policy of aggression but the treaty referred in more general terms to the threats, political, military and economic, to be faced, talking about an 'armed attack in Europe' (Article IV), and 'a threat to peace, in whatever area this threat should arise' (Article VII). A further year later, when the five signatories of the Treaty of Brussels joined with other powers in concluding the North Atlantic Treaty (April 1949), all reference to Germany was dropped, and the signatories merely agreed that 'an armed attack against one or more of them in Europe or North America shall be considered an attack against them all' (Article 5). Indeed, by 1949, statesmen in London and Washington, though not as yet in Paris, were beginning seriously to think about the need for German military assistance in Europe in meeting the new common foe.

British hostility to the USSR went back to the successful Bolshevik revolution of November 1917. A new and profound distrust of communism (even in the Labour party) was added to older suspicions of Russian power in Western Europe. British apprehensions of a Russian threat to her own security and to the stability of Europe grew during the course of the Second World War – certainly by the time of the Conference at Yalta in 1945 – and British concern at Russian imperialism outside of Europe became serious as evidence mounted in 1945 and 1946 of Russian ambitions at the expense of China, Iran and Turkey. By the end of the 1940s the British government regarded the Soviet Union as actively promoting revolution on a worldwide basis, and in particular as having ambitions to take over much of Europe by military force or political infiltration. In 1948, for example, as the recently opened Foreign Office papers show, there was a whole stream of memorandums from Ernest Bevin, the Foreign Secretary, warning the Cabinet that Russian communism was on the march and that the West had to act swiftly and determinedly to stop it.

With the advantage of a thirty-year perspective, historians – especially in the United States – can argue about the events of the late 1940s, and specifically about Russian motives and the offensive or defensive aims of Russian policy. Policy-makers in the 1940s were dominated by the example of German aggression in the 1930s, and inevitably did not have much time for reflection. Mounting evidence of direct Russian activity, and what was regarded as Russian-inspired activity, gave substance to the fears of the British Government and the warnings of the Foreign Secretary. The war ended with Russian armies camped across much of Central and Eastern Europe, and the Russians appeared to be in no hurry to go home. East of the Elbe in the period 1945–7 there was the systematic establishment of friendly governments, the process reaching its climax with the imposition of a Communist government in Czechoslovakia in February 1948. Nothing so brutal had occurred in the West, where non-Communist governments had emerged more or less naturally. Attempts to negotiate with the Russians, particularly at a succession of foreign ministers' meetings in Moscow, Paris and London, over such issues as the peace treaties to be imposed on the minor enemy powers and German reparations and the future government of Germany, led to acrimony, accusations of betrayal and ultimately to breakdown. In 1948 the Russian government, dissatisfied with what was happening in Germany, blockaded the Western sectors of Berlin for almost a year, from June 1948 to May 1949. In August 1949 the Russians successfully tested an atomic bomb. Beyond Europe, there was Russian pressure immediately after the war on Turkey and Iran. Then, in the late 1940s, there were a series of uprisings in Southeast Asia, in Indochina and Malaya, and in the newly independent countries of Burma, Indonesia and the Philippines, all of which appeared to draw encouragement if not direct assistance from Moscow. Finally, in 1949 the Communists triumphed in China, and in June 1950 North Korea invaded South Korea, a case of aggression that was certainly encouraged if not actually sponsored by the Soviet Union.

A typical example of Bevin's analysis of the Soviet threat is provided by his speech in the House of Commons in January 1948.

Document 5.3
Bevin's speech in House of Commons, 22 January 1948

From Margaret Carlyle (ed.), *Documents on International Affairs, 1947–1948*, 1952, p. 202

The story begins with a series of conferences which were held during the war, and at which many ideas were formed. Some were crystallised. Some were not. In this connection, of the political developments that have taken place, one of the main issues at that time affecting the line of subsequent policy was connected with the future of Poland. The solution arrived at at Yalta was looked upon by His Majesty's Government at that time as a sensible compromise between conflicting elements, but there is no doubt that, as it has evolved, it has revealed a policy on the part of the Soviet Union to use every means in their power to get Communist control in Eastern Europe, and, as it now appears in the West as well. It therefore matters little how we temporise, and maybe appease, or try to make arrangements.

It has been quite clear, I think, that the Communist process goes ruthlessly on in each country. We have seen the game played out in Poland, Bulgaria, Hungary, more recently in Rumania, and, from information in our possession, other attempts may be made elsewhere. Thus, the issue is not simply the organisation of Poland or any other country, but the control of Eastern Europe, by Soviet Russia, whose frontiers have, in effect, been advanced to Stettin, Trieste and the Elbe. One has only to look at the map to see how since the war, Soviet Russia has expanded and now stretches from the middle of Europe to the Kurile Islands and Sakhalin. Yet all the evidence is that she is not satisfied with this tremendous expansion. In Trieste we have difficulties. We had hoped that the method of international agreement would be allowed to work; but it has not been allowed to work, and so what should have been a great experiment in postwar international collaboration has only been a continuing source of friction and bother.

Then we have the great issue in Greece, which is similar to the others I have mentioned . . . So, it is not a question of what sort of elected Government there is in Greece – Liberal, Coalition, or whatever it might be – but it is a ruthless attempt, constantly maintained, to bring that country in the Soviet orbit.

The response of the British government to this Russian challenge was on the whole realistic, and in retrospect can be described as successful. The performance of the government was particularly impressive in the years 1945–7, when, beset with a host of problems at home and abroad, it had to take the lead in Europe, and was desperately conscious of a waning of American interest and involvement. The British approach rested on four propositions. First, the question of priorities: it was accepted that in terms of British security and military involvement, Europe was foremost followed by the Middle East, Southeast Asia, and then the Far East, in that order. It was accepted that the Far East would be an area of American primacy. Historically this marked an abdication of British responsibility, and the ending of an historic role. Second, there was a realization, which grew steadily in the period, that Britain could not 'go it alone' in Europe: she was too weak, the costs were too high and she had too many commitments elsewhere. Third, there was a determination to retain

American participation in any post-war security system. Fourth, an attempt was made to secure Soviet membership in such a system. This rested on the well-founded principle that would-be adversaries are better included in the system than left to languish outside it. This attempt had manifestly failed by 1947.

The year 1947 saw the ending of Britain's leadership in Europe, and that year, even more than 1956 with the catastrophe at Suez, marked the end of Britain's role as an independent great power. In the early spring the British government was compelled to inform the United States that it could no longer fulfil Britain's traditional and leading role in the eastern Mediterranean. The American response was first the Truman Doctrine in March 1947, and later in the year the more general European Recovery Programme, the Marshall Plan, announced in June and accepted by sixteen nations in September. The nightmare of American disengagement and a return to isolationism was over, the gain was a multilateral approach to the problems of security in Europe and to the question of European economic recovery, the cost was the loss of British leadership in Western Europe and of some independence. The American initiatives in the spring and summer of 1947 transformed the cold war in Europe, led to the formation of NATO two years later, provided stability and security for the countries of Western Europe including Britain, and made 'containment' (of communism) a possible and effective policy. The American initiatives and the British response deserve attention at some length, for they formed the basis of British foreign policy in the whole post-war period.

Document 5.4

(a) President Truman's message to the Congress: The Truman Doctrine, 12 March 1947

From Margaret Carlyle (ed.) – *Documents on International Affairs, 1947–1948*, 1952, pp. 2–7

The gravity of the situation which confronts the world today necessitates my appearance before a joint session of the Congress . . . . The United States has received from the Greek Government an urgent appeal for financial and economic assistance . . .

. . . The British Government, which has been helping Greece, can give no further financial or economic aid after March 31. Great Britain finds itself under the necessity of reducing or liquidating its commitments in several parts of the world, including Greece . . .

. . .Since the war Turkey has sought additional financial assistance from Great Britain and the United States for the purpose of effecting that modernization necessary for the maintenance of its national integrity . . . . The British Government has informed us that, owing to its own difficulties, it can no longer extend financial or economic aid to Turkey . . .

. . . I believe that it must be the policy of the United States to support free peoples who are resisting attempted subjugation by armed minorities or by outside pressures.

I believe that we must assist free peoples to work out their own destinies in their own way.

I believe that our help should be primarily through economic and financial aid which is essential to economic stability and orderly political processes . . .

(b) Speech at Harvard University by Secretary of State, George Marshall on 5 June 1947

From Margaret Carlyle (ed.), *Documents on International Affairs 1947–1948,* 1952, pp. 23–6

It is logical that the United States should do whatever it is able to do to assist in the return of normal economic health in the world, without which there can be no political stability and no assured peace. Our policy is directed not against any country or doctrine but against hunger, poverty, desperation and chaos.

. . . Any government which maneuvres to block the recovery of other countries cannot expect help from us. Furthermore, governments, political parties, or groups which seek to perpetuate human misery in order to profit therefrom politically or otherwise will encounter the opposition of the United States.

It is already evident that, before the United States Government can proceed much further in its efforts to alleviate the situation and help start the European world on its way to recovery, there must be some agreement among the countries of Europe as to the requirements of the situation and the part those countries themselves will take in order to give proper effect to whatever action might be undertaken by this Government. It would be neither fitting nor efficacious for this Government to undertake to draw up unilaterally a program designed to place Europe on its feet economically. This is the business of the Europeans. The initiative, I think, must come from Europe. The role of this country should consist of friendly aid in the drafting of a European program and of later support of such a program so far as it may be practical for us to do so. The program should be a joint one, agreed to by a number, if not all, European nations . . .

(c) Speech by the British Foreign Secretary, Ernest Bevin, to the Foreign Press Association 13 June 1947

From *The Times*, 14 June 1947

Notwithstanding that we are the centre of a great Empire and Commonwealth we recognise that we are more than ever linked with the destinies of Europe. We are . . . a European nation and must act as such . . .

. . . We welcome the inspiring lead given to us and the peoples of Europe by Mr Marshall, the American Secretary of State. His speech at Harvard will rank, I think, as one of the greatest speeches made in world history . . .

. . . this great new and wonderful country, with all its great and potential wealth, is acting in the most unselfish manner in an endeavour to use her capacity to save Europe from another ruin and to rehabilitate Europe as urgently as possible. We in this country are exploring urgently and actively how best to respond to that lead, and must in this work consult France . . .

. . . We have decided to consult her and other European nations to see how best we can take advantage of this great proposal of the United States. Personally, I think we must proceed, so far as Europe is concerned, on a functional basis with problems of coal, food and transport . . .

. . . We feel that the duty falls upon us, situated geographically as we are, to take the initiative in trying to get this great machine of Europe working again on a sound basis . . .

The results of the events of 1947 were that leadership of the Western alliance passed firmly to the United States and that Britain participated fully alongside the United States in efforts to contain the Soviet threat. The attempt to force the Western powers out of Berlin in 1948–9 was overcome, and in April 1949 the new Western relationship was formalized by the setting up of the North Atlantic Treaty Organisation (NATO). In the early 1950s NATO was transformed from a paper organization to a formidable military alliance, with unprecedented permanent and close working relationships. By the mid-1950s the new, Western sponsored state of West Germany participated in NATO. The pattern of wartime alliances was thus completely broken. This diplomatic revolution widened a deep split in the Labour party (see chapter 4). The realignment of the Western countries in face of Russia and her allies marked the onset of the condition known as 'cold war' – armed hostilities short of actual warfare. The cold war, in varying forms and intensity, was the central condition of British foreign policy for the rest of the period.

The British government supported American efforts to counter aggression in Korea by participating under the flag of the United Nations in the Korean War. An attempt to extend containment to Southeast Asia was made in 1954 when, following the Geneva Conference, the Manila Pact brought the Southeast Asia Treaty Organization (SEATO) into existence with Britain as a member. But this new form of 'treaty organization' did not suit the uncertain international politics of the Far East. There was confusion from the very beginning as to what exactly SEATO was supposed to be doing or containing: communism, Chinese aggression, a conventional attack, subversion, an Indian threat to Pakistan, or what.

Containment worked well in Europe, and the Anglo-American relationship was a close and generally successful one. Outside Europe, while Communist expansion was checked in Korea, containment was less effective, and the Anglo-American relationship was less harmonious. There were major differences of attitudes and policies over how the new People's Republic in China should be treated, over objectives in the Korean War (especially after the Chinese came in on the side of the North Koreans) and over what should be done in Southeast Asia as the French position in Indochina deteriorated in 1953–4. In each case the British position was more moderate and pragmatic and certainly less idealistic and heroic than that of the Americans.

Britain suffered much less than the USA from hysterical anti-communism, though without falling into the opposite sin (in American eyes) of 'being soft on communism'. Whether Britain could have done more at that time to build a sympathetic understanding of Russia seems doubtful. Russian actions discouraged it.

A controversial aspect of Britain's policies in the cold war period was the decision to make her own atomic bomb and eventually become a nuclear power. The decision was taken by a Cabinet Committee in January 1947, announced in the House of Commons in May 1948, and the first British atomic weapon was tested in Australia in October 1952. This was a significant move but not Britain's first step into atomic armaments, for Britain had been associated with the development and use of the first atomic bombs used against Japan in 1945. That casual first step was taken in wartime when atomic weapons were seen as a terrifying but economical extension of an already massive bombing offensive. After the war the USA excluded Britain from further full co-operation in the field; hence the British decision to manufacture her own atom bombs was made in a peculiar context. It was not seen by the government, or the commentators or public opinion, as the historic move it undoubtedly was, a move into the proliferation and normalization of atomic and nuclear armaments. The move did not buy British independence; for her new armoury was dependent still on American technology and strategic co-ordination. Britain's strategy was therefore based on an uneasy relationship of 'interdependence' (which a sceptical observer might think indicated more dependence than independence). It was indeed indicative of Britain's rapidly declining position that the British atomic bomb test in October was followed in November 1952 by the American hydrogen bomb test at Eniwetok.

In her research into the government archives of the period for the officially commissioned history, *Independence and Deterrence: Britain and atomic energy, 1945–1952* (1974), Professor Margaret Gowing found only one memorandum which dissented from the idea that Britain should develop atomic weapons. It was written by the Nobel physicist, Professor P. M. S. Blackett. As she says in an essay, 'Britain, America and the Bomb' (Dilkes, 1981):

> He [Blackett] had originally supported the bomb as a deterrent, but by the end of 1945 he had changed his mind and wrote to the Prime Minister urging that if Britain made bombs this would decrease rather than increase security. He feared that Britain would spend a disproportionate effort in building up a stock of bombs too small to be of military value. A year later he wrote another memorandum urging a neutralist policy in atomic energy as part of a neutralist foreign and defence policy . . . Blackett's papers were closely argued and, however unacceptable their thesis, they merited at least an equally closely argued commentary, but they were met in Whitehall either with silence or by contemptuous minute writing. 'He should stick to science', wrote Mr Bevin, the Foreign Secretary.

The theory of nuclear deterrence was originally quite simple. The powers in conflict had a capacity to inflict 'unacceptable damage' on each other; therefore they would refrain from war. Though there were problems about 'first strike' and 'second strike' capacity, the theory required only that a country even after attack would possess just sufficient capacity to retaliate – hence the deterrent effectiveness of Britain's comparatively tiny nuclear force. However, the theory did not work as well as its proponents hoped. First, it became clear that nuclear deterrence prevented big wars but not small wars, occupations, infiltrations, intimidations. Nuclear weapons turned out to be irrelevant to most actual conflicts. Second, continuing development of weapons was not only fearsomely expensive, but also threatened to upset the delicate 'balance of terror', giving to one side an advantage which might encourage aggression. Third, nuclear war, which was at first 'unthinkable' came to be accepted as tolerable, provided some survivors remained after the holocaust, and life of some kind was possible. Fourth, it seemed likely, particularly as small 'tactical' nuclear weapons were developed, that Europe would be the site of a nuclear war fought chiefly by the USSR and USA. Fifth, it seemed also likely that nuclear weapons would 'proliferate', and negate the comparative stability which was to the credit of deterrence and superpower predominance. Once again the great powers were likely to find that they could not determine the pattern of international relations, because of the independent actions of smaller countries.

At first, few people seemed to challenge the theory of deterrence. There was plenty of debate about foreign and defence policy in the years after 1945 but the bomb hardly featured in this discussion. It was not until 1957, with the coming of the Campaign for Nuclear Disarmament, that there was any large-scale public protest at Britain's possession of nuclear weapons.

The timing is significant for there is little doubt that the wartime and post-war generations had endured too much themselves to be immediately sensitive to the question of the morality of bombing.

Britain became a nuclear power as the result of a deliberate act of policy, and British foreign and defence policy never wavered from that commitment for over thirty years since 1947. The act of policy was and remains controversial; it may be said to reflect something basic and primitive, a nostalgia for a past greatness, and a determination to be independent. Margaret Gowing has some perceptive comments on the British decision, and it is interesting to compare these remarks on 1947 with an article in *The Times* on the commitment to the nuclear deterrent in 1981.

Document 5.5

(a) From Margaret Gowing, *Independence and Deterrence. Britain and Atomic Energy, 1945–1952. Volume I: Policy Making*, 1974, pp. 184–5

The British decision to make an atomic bomb had 'emerged' from a body of general assumptions. It had not been a response to an immediate military threat but rather something fundamentalist and almost instinctive – a feeling that Britain must possess so climacteric a weapon in order to deter an atomically armed enemy, a feeling that Britain as a great power must acquire all major new weapons, a feeling that atomic weapons were a manifestation of the scientific and technological superiority on which Britain's strength, so deficient if measured in sheer numbers of men, must depend . . .

. . . The decision was also a symbol of independence. It had not been taken as a result of the breakdown in 1946 of Anglo-American atomic cooperation . . . As it was, American atomic attitudes in this period hardened Britain's resolution not to be bullied out of the business and not to acquiesce in an American monopoly; it encouraged her determination to be a nuclear power for the sake of the influence this was expected to give her in Washington . . . there was at this time – in 1946 and 1947 – no United States military commitments to come to Britain's help in war. If Britain wanted to be sure of being covered by an atomic deterrent, she had no option but to make it herself.

(b) Article by Peter Hennessy in *The Times*, Tuesday, 27 January 1981

. . . in the defence community there is a devotion to the idea of a British deterrent that goes deeper than mere reason would allow . . .

. . . Deterrence theorists in the ministry, when asked why a British force is so vital, emphasize the need for a 'second centre of decision making' in NATO to keep the Russians guessing about the consequences of moving an inch forward on the central front in Europe. Outside critics argue that it is a hangover from imperial days, a consolation for the loss of world power.

Could it not be something simpler that lies behind the impulse to deterrence in the early 1980s? The five ministers who sat on Mrs Margaret Thatcher's Polaris replacement Cabinet committee, MISC 7, are of an age where 'standing alone' in 1940 was a personal and formative experience.

Is not their devotion to the deterrent, and the feeling of those of a similar background in the defence community, an instinctive wish for insurance against a rerun of the Battle of Britain summer? For clever 'boffins' applying radar and breaking the Luftwaffe's codes one can read 'eggheads' at Aldermaston and communications experts in bunkers beneath the Chilterns, and for brave young men in Spitfires substitute youthful commanders in submarines lurking beneath the North Atlantic as all that stands between a British bereft of allies and the enemy along the Channel ports.

Whitehall would never resort to using the 'national sovereignty' argument, unless it looked like losing the debate once and for all, for fear of upsetting the United States. But it was uncertainty about our allies in the future that lay behind the decision of MISC 7 on Trident as surely as it was the imperative guiding Mr Attlee's Cabinet committee when it decided to build the first British bomb in 1947.

Britain acquired thermonuclear weapons (the hydrogen bomb) in 1957, thus, more or less, keeping up with the Americans, and securing a negotiating position as even Aneurin Bevan claimed. In that year, too, Britain's V-bombers came into service. The V-bombers – Vulcan, Valiant and Victor – had been commissioned for the carrying of atomic and hydrogen bombs. They were good aircraft, but by the time they came into service in 1957 bombers were being replaced by missiles, and aircraft were on the way to being obsolete. They are symbolic of much of the story of British defence policy after 1945 – good of its kind but too little and usually too late. The defence policy of 1957 placed great reliance on the deterrent effect of the bomb, and provided for cuts in conventional arms. In particular conscription was to be ended – the last conscript was to be out by 1962 – and the total numbers in the armed forces were to be sharply reduced; overall, services' manpower was to be cut from 690,000 to 375,000 by 1962. Thus Britain's nuclear strategy had the virtue, for the moment, of saving money.

The problem, however, was to stay in a rapidly accelerating arms race based on high technology. Britain's attempt to acquire missiles at the end of the 1950s is a story of false starts and expensive and abortive projects before the provision of Polaris by the Americans in 1962. At first there was a plan for a British missile – Blue Streak. This failed, marking the end of British nuclear independence, and in 1960 the Americans promised to supply Skybolt. In 1962 much to Britain's dismay the Americans cancelled Skybolt because of soaring costs, and at Nassau Kennedy felt obliged to offer Macmillan Polaris. With four Polaris submarines Britain remained a nuclear power for the next twenty years, and the question of what to do after Polaris did not become an urgent one until 1980.

Exercise 2

2.1 What were the main issues that faced the new Labour government in foreign policy in 1945?

2.2 What do you think of the idea of bipartisanship in foreign policy after 1945?

2.3 Why was 1947 such a critical year for Britain in its relations with the United States and the Soviet Union?

2.4 Why did the Soviet Union appear as the most likely foe for the states of Western Europe by 1949?

2.5 Discuss the reasons why containment worked well in Europe after 1949 but less well in East and Southeast Asia in the 1950s.

2.6 Do you consider that the British government had much of a choice over whether or not to become a nuclear power in the late 1940s?

2.7 Attempt a justification of the British government's decision to become and remain a nuclear power.

3 British interests in the Middle East

British interests in the modern Middle East go back to the nineteenth century, and Britain's position was firmly established by a series of events and agreements in the First World War. There was some modification during the inter-war period, notably the conceding of independence to Iraq and a change in relations with Egypt; but Britain's position remained essentially intact at the beginning of the war in 1939. The main British concerns may be described very easily: Britain was the responsible mandatory power to the League of Nations for Transjordan and Palestine, she had a special position in Egypt, she controlled the Suez Canal and a number of bases such as Aden, and further east she had a large interest in the oil produced in Iran and Iraq and along the Persian Gulf.

In the short-term the war enhanced the British presence and power in the region, and she emerged in 1945 as the paramount power from Libya in the west to the border of Afghanistan in the east, from Turkey in the north to the Horn of Africa in the south. However, appearances were deceptive, and the war had three consequences, which combined to undermine Britain's position in the region and to inflict considerable humiliation on British policy-makers in 1947–8, 1951 and 1956. Of the three consequences, one was directly attributable to the war, the other two were the product of other factors but were seriously affected by events between 1939 and 1945. The direct consequence of the war was, of course, Britain's economic weakness in 1945. She was therefore unable to devote the attention, resources and energy to the region that were vital if her position was to be maintained.

The other consequences, the products of many factors but much affected by the war, were the development of Arab nationalism and the deterioration of the situation in Palestine. Arab nationalism developed in the years immediately before the war of 1914–18 and it was actively encouraged during that struggle by the British. However, it was by no means sympathetic to Britain, and by 1945 the Arabs tended to see British imperialism as a major enemy. The Arab League, formed in March 1945, provided a focus for Arab aspirations. It supported Egypt's demands in 1946 for the early withdrawal of British troops, and in 1947 for union with the Sudan. The League was weakened by a number of political and dynastic struggles within the Arab world, notably that between the more progressive states, like Egypt and Syria, and the more reactionary states, like Saudi Arabia and Iraq; also by the rivalry between the Hashemites who ruled Jordan and Iraq and the family of King Ibn Saud of Saudi Arabia. This disunity prevented the League from mounting a sustained challenge to Britain's position until 1956. Britain attempted to weaken the Arab cause by supporting Iraq against Egypt in 1955 through the Baghdad Pact, and by supporting Jordan against Egypt and Syria in 1958. These moves failed in the long run to preserve Britain's position in the region.

Britain had played a large part in creating the modern Palestine problem by its actions during the war of 1914–18, encouraging Arab aspirations on the one hand and promoting the idea of a Jewish National Home in that country on the other. It was therefore unfortunate but not unjust that after twenty years of repeated efforts to solve the Palestinian question she was as far as ever by 1939 from a final settlement of the Arab-Jewish conflict. The war made the problem even more intractable. Britain needed oil and bases in the Middle East, Arab solidarity was growing, and the Arab League supported the cause of the Palestinian Arabs. The British government was compelled therefore to give careful consideration to Arab demands. On the other hand intensive Zionist propaganda, the appalling sufferings of European Jews at the hands of Hitler and the Nazis, the determination of a million or more remaining European Jews to find refuge in Palestine, and the strong support of the Jewish cause in the United States, all made it difficult for the British government to do what British national interests demanded, namely to give wholehearted support to the Arab cause while insisting on safeguards for a Jewish minority in Palestine.

The result was something like three years of intense diplomatic activity on the part of the British government, mounting anger on the part of the

British people, bad relations with the United States, a moderately successful campaign of terror by Jewish extremists in Palestine, and tortuous
intrigues by Palestine's Arab neighbours. Finally Britain gave up and left
the country in somewhat humiliating circumstances in the summer of 1948.
All attempts at a reasonable solution, whether for a unitary state with
safeguards for the minority, or for some kind of federation, or for partition
with or without the backing of the United Nations failed. The issue was put
to the sword, the first of the Arab-Israeli wars that have been a feature of
Middle Eastern politics since 1948.

It is easy to blame Bevin and the British government. The withdrawal
from Palestine was certainly less than glorious, but given her weakness and
preoccupations elsewhere it is difficult to see what else Britain could have
done. She was beset by strident and occasionally hysterical Zionism on the
one hand and aggressive Arab nationalism on the other. The one hope was
support from the United States, but the Truman administration, conscious
of the 5 million Jewish votes in the United States, could never be relied on
to pursue a consistent policy. Britain emerged with her prestige throughout
the Middle East weakened, and with nothing much to show for thirty years
of patient endeavour in Palestine. The new Jewish state of Israel considered that it owed Britain nothing, while the Arabs felt that Britain, after
betraying their interests from the Balfour Declaration of 1917 onwards,
had finally abandoned them.

The withdrawal from Palestine eased but did not end Britain's troubles
in the Middle East. Relations with Egypt continued on a very troubled
basis after 1945, a sequence of events best considered as part of the
background to the Suez affair in 1956. Then in 1951 Britain's oil interests in
Iran were taken over. It should be emphasized that with the granting of
independence to India in 1947 the British government became less
concerned with the protection of the historic imperial route to India and
the Far East through the Middle East, and more concerned with the
defence of its oil and other interests in the region. The main priority was
stability in the region, the policy chosen was to support the status quo,
backing the Persian Gulf sheikdoms and the royal governments in Jordan,
Iraq and Iran. Of these last three, it is intriguing that Jordan, the one
regarded as the least stable, survives until the present day, while Iraq and
Iran succumbed to revolutionary forces in 1958 and 1979 respectively.

The nationalization of the Anglo-Iranian Oil Company in April 1951 was
the work of Dr Mohammed Mossadegh, the would-be revolutionary Prime
Minister of Iran. The United States tried to persuade the British government to accept the nationalization and work out a settlement in Iran, but
the British believed that too ready acceptance of the Iranian takeover
would encourage extremists in other Arab oil-producing countries. The
British government did promise not to use force without prior consultation
with the United States, and took its case to the International Court of

Justice and to the Security Council of the United Nations. These bodies were of little value in settling the affair, for the former ruled that the dispute was outside its jurisdiction, while the latter failed to come to any decision. Direct Anglo-Iranian negotiations failed. In late 1951 Iranian troops seized the Abadan refineries, and the following year Iran broke off diplomatic relations with Britain.

Diplomatic relations were restored after the fall of Mossadegh in 1953, and by August 1954 a settlement of the dispute was arrived at. An international consortium of which the Anglo-Iranian Oil Company was a member, was to operate the oil fields, although ownership remained with the Iranian government. Iran was to receive 50 per cent of the profits on all oil exported, and was to pay the Anglo-Iranian Oil Company adequate compensation for the nationalization of its property.

The centre of British power and interests in the Middle East was the British presence in Egypt and control of the Suez Canal. Unfortunately for Britain, Egypt was probably the most advanced politically and certainly the most restive of the Arab states, very much in the vanguard of the new mood of nationalism. Anglo-Egyptian relations quickly deteriorated after 1945. Egypt attacked the Treaty of 1936 that governed those relations, and demanded that British troops be withdrawn and negotiations begin on the future of the Sudan. The British government, preoccupied elsewhere and increasingly worried about a possible Soviet threat to the Middle East, was unwilling to abandon the Treaty but was ready to contemplate some revision. However all attempts at revision failed in the late 1940s, a major stumbling-block ironically being Egypt's own imperialist designs on the Sudan. One of the factors that handicapped Bevin in the negotiations was Britain's indebtedness to Egypt. Britain wanted bases, or the right to maintain troops, or the right to re-enter Middle Eastern territory in the event of the threat of hostilities, but she could offer little in return. At a conservative estimate she probably owed Egypt nearly £400 million.

Egypt, together with all the other Arab states with the exception of Iraq, refused to be too worried about the cold war, and the possible Soviet threat. For the Arabs, the main enemies were the new state of Israel and Western imperialism. Consequently British attempts to solve her problems with Egypt in a general Middle East Defence Organization in 1951 were rejected by the Egyptians. In 1952 a *coup d'état* by a group of army officers led by General Neguib overthrew the monarchy in Egypt, but the new republic, whether headed by Neguib or after 1954 by Colonel Nasser, proved even more intractable as far as the British were concerned. Egypt refused to accept that the Baghdad Pact of 1955, bringing together Turkey, Iraq, Pakistan, Iran and Britain, had any real value for the peoples of the region, regarding it as an attempt to split the Arab League and play off Iraq against Egypt as the leading Arab state.

In the early 1950s successive Egyptian governments, royalist and republican, began to encourage sabotage and guerrilla warfare against the British in the Canal Zone. All Egyptian labour for the base was withdrawn, and the 80,000 troops there had to spend much of the time on their own protection. The military base on the canal became a liability rather than an asset. Negotiations in 1953 and 1954 finally led to agreements over the Sudan and the Suez base, and offered a prospect of better Anglo-Egyptian relations. The new Egyptian government agreed in 1953 that the Sudanese must be free to choose their future, and in 1954 Britain agreed to withdraw its troops from the Canal Zone, with the right of re-entry in certain conditions. Churchill and Eden had to contend with opposition from their right-wing supporters to what was regarded as 'scuttling from the Canal Zone', and this opposition is probably a factor in Eden's later anti-Nasser fixation. He felt that he had laid his reputation on the line by concluding an agreement with the Egyptians, and he took it as a moral – and a mortal – offence when Nasser appeared to trample on it.

The comparative calm that descended on Britain's position in the Middle East following the 1954 agreements with Iran and Egypt did not last for very long and was a prelude to the great Suez crisis of 1956. This is considered as a case study in some detail in chapter 6. Briefly, the USA refused to make a loan for the building of a dam at Aswan; Nasser took over or nationalized the Suez Canal; Britain and France arranged with Israel to intervene after an Israeli attack on Egypt. The intervention – the bombing of Egypt, followed by an invasion – was called off mainly under pressure from the USA. Nothing was gained by the Anglo-French action, and more was lost, including the use of the canal (closed by blockships in retaliation for the invasion), and Britain's reputation, such as it was, for fair-dealing. Incidentally, the Prime Minister, Eden, collapsed from a long-standing illness and left office and politics in January 1957.

It is often argued that Suez signalled the decline of Britain as an independent great power and destroyed Britain's position in the Middle East. With regard to the first point, 1947 and the admission of weakness then is probably a better indicator of Britain's post-war decline, while as to the second, after the immediate humiliation had been overcome, Britain's position did not appear to be greatly affected. Britain continued to have important territorial, strategic, and economic interests in the west (Cyprus), in the south (Aden), in the east (the various states along the Persian Gulf) and in the north (the Baghdad Pact). In 1958 British troops could be flown into Jordan from Cyprus to sustain a friendly monarch, King Hussein, and his government. But appearances were deceptive. From 1957 it was the United States rather than Britain that began to take the lead in the region. In 1958 a faithful ally was overthrown with the Iraqi Revolution and the murder of Nuri Pasha, in 1960 Cyprus became independent after some years of trouble; in the late 1960s there was increasingly serious trouble in Aden, and by the early 1970s British interests were mainly restricted to the Persian Gulf. It was not until the late 1970s that Britain aspired to play a major role again in the Arab–Israeli question, and it was not as an independent power but as a member of the European Community.

Exercise 3

3.1 What were the main factors undermining Britain's position in the Middle East after 1945?

3.2 Can you suggest an alternative policy for dealing with the problem of Palestine between 1945 and 1948?

3.3 Describe Britain's interests in the Middle East in the early 1950s. Why was the region so important in British foreign policy?

3.4 To what extent did the Suez crisis wreck Britain's position in the Middle East?

4 The retreat from empire

Britain was at the peak of its authority and prestige as an imperial power in the ten years or so before 1914. About one quarter of the people of the world owed allegiance to the British crown, and were ruled directly or indirectly by the British government. Political control allied to immense economic and commercial power made up a formidable empire. By 1914, however, a number of strains and weaknesses in the imperial structure were already beginning to appear – the military problems highlighted by the Boer War, for example, or the dangerous over-stretching of naval resources after the Germans embarked on a policy of naval expansion, or the developing tension in India with the growth of nationalism. But overall the empire looked strong and its future assured. Further imperial gains were made at the expense of Germany and Turkey at the end of the First World War and the empire reached its greatest territorial extent in 1919. Minor territorial adjustments took place in the inter-war period, but the British empire that began the Second World War and that emerged victorious in 1945 was almost identical with that of 1919.

The next two decades saw the rapid collapse of the empire 'on which the sun never sets' and by 1965 only a number of minor but niggling problems remained, for example, Aden and Rhodesia; some other territories which were difficult to dispose of (Hong Kong, Gibraltar, British Honduras, the Falkland Islands) remained in Britain's charge. The empire as an institution and an idea was replaced by the commonwealth, an entity of a very different kind, arguably a liability rather than an asset to post-imperial Britain, and at best of limited usefulness.

Before considering the process of decolonization and the reasons for it, it is interesting to compare Britain's position with that of the other great imperial powers of the twentieth century. In 1900 there were eleven major territorial empires either in being or in the process of being acquired. In rough order of size and importance, these were the British, Russian, French, Chinese, Turkish, German, Japanese, Austro-Hungarian, Portuguese, Dutch and Italian empires. By 1981 only two of these remained: the Russian empire, now described as the Union of Soviet Socialist Republics, and the Chinese, somewhat modified as the Chinese People's Republic. Of the other nine empires, five disappeared as the result of defeat in the major international wars of the century: those of Turkey, Germany, and Austria-Hungary after the First World War, and those of Japan and Italy after the Second World War. One empire, the Portuguese, collapsed in 1974 after a domestic revolution, partly caused by the excessive strain of expensive colonial wars. The remaining three empires, British, French and Dutch, all disintegrated in the period 1945–60. The French fought long and bitterly, and of course ultimately unsuccessfully, to hold on to Indochina and Algeria, and the Dutch fought briefly, and equally unsuccessfully, in the late 1940s to hold on to the Dutch East Indies. The British, by contrast, did not fight at all to hold on to the bigger or more important (economically or strategically) parts of their empire, but became involved in military activity over the retention and control of what were regarded as key bases, like Suez or Cyprus in the 1950s or Aden in the 1960s, and over territories the future of which was uncertain and for which there were competing claims, like Palestine in the 1940s and Kenya in the 1950s. This military activity while always minor was often prolonged and costly and was a substantial drain on Britain's limited economic and military resources.

Britain shared with France and with Portugal the problem of what to do about colonies which had a substantial white settler population with influential political friends back in the mother country. The settlers wanted, naturally enough, but against natural justice and the tide of history, to retain control over the immensely larger native population. In the early years of empire the question was resolved in favour of the settlers, in Australia, New Zealand, Canada and South Africa the natives were destroyed or at least dominated. After 1945 the question was resolved in favour of the indigenous population, though not without struggle and bloodshed. The French fought hard in Algeria but finally conceded independence in 1962. The British became involved in a bitter racial struggle in Kenya in the 1950s, scene of the Mau Mau uprising, but after this had been suppressed Kenya gained an African-controlled government in 1963 and the promise of full independence a year later. The future of the colonies in Central Africa posed a more complicated example of this problem for Southern Rhodesia, which contained the bulk of the white settlers in the region, had been to all intents and purposes independent since 1923. Attempts to solve the problem of control in a larger Central African Federation broke down in the early 1960s, Northern Rhodesia and Nyasaland became independent as Zambia and Malawi respectively, and the problem of Southern Rhodesia remained. The white Rhodesians felt that they had been tricked by Macmillan's government over the Central African Federation, and in November 1965 with a unilateral declaration of independence tried to make formal their previously informal independence. The constitution allowed the small White settler community to continue to dominate the much larger African population. Fifteen years of humiliation for successive British governments, and of unrest and war for the peoples of Rhodesia, followed. Finally, in 1980, after bitter fighting, difficult negotiations, and a hazardous election, an African-dominated state, Zimbabwe, emerged. The Rhodesian problem is a splendid example of the perils of responsibility without power, which was the position of the British government from 1965 onwards.

Turning from a consideration of Britain's imperial position in comparative terms to the question of why the empire disintegrated so rapidly after 1945, it is fairly easy to produce a list of reasons to explain the sequences of events. What is not so easy is to put those reasons in any order of relative importance, and it is even more difficult to assess how they affected the timing of the retreat from empire. After the general statements have been made and the conclusion drawn, it must be emphasized that the case of each particular piece of territory, India or Burma or the Gold Coast or Tanganyika, should be examined separately.

The two fundamental causes of the retreat from empire were first that the eventual independence of the colonies, dependencies and protectorates had always been a part of British imperial thinking. The preparation of the various parts of the empire for eventual independence through a process of economic and social development and of education was seen as an important aspect of the 'white man's burden'. What was at issue was the question of when, conservative imperialists always thinking on a much longer time-scale than more progressive politicians. Various parts of the colonial empire were in fact beginning to approach independence before the Second World War, two good examples being India and Burma. It can be said with confidence, however, that not even the most progressive and anti-imperialist politician imagined that the process would happen so fast after 1945.

The second cause of the retreat from empire explains its surprising speed. The steady but rapid growth of nationalist movements in various parts of the empire meant that in the long run it could only be kept in being by a policy of repression and murder on a massive scale, a policy that no British government of whatever political persuasion was ever willing to countenance, at least in the long term. The example of Britain in this respect affords a pleasant contrast to the short-lived attempts of France and Portugal to retain their colonies and the more sustained and successful efforts of Russia and China.

The fashion of the 1960s and 1970s was to denounce imperialism and to damn all imperialists – especially if they were Western ones! Imperialism certainly had its less attractive side: there was at times racial prejudice, there was often economic exploitation and the skewing of local economies in the interests of the mother country, and, perhaps above all, there was the destruction of local social, cultural, legal and educational patterns. But over against this academic fashion it is perhaps useful to quote two opinions, one by a politician and one by a historian, that put the motives of British imperialism in a different perspective. Imperialism had a nobler side.

Document 5.6

(a) A comment on the end of the Indian empire in John W. Wheeler-Bennett, *King George VI; his life and reign*, 1958, p. 714

Thus passed, on August 15, 1947, the glory that was the Indian Empire – that 'bright jewel' which Disraeli had presented to Queen Victoria not quite seventy years before. On that date ended also the much longer rule of the British in India; that long and honourable record of men who, before and since the Mutiny, gave of their unselfish best in generations of dedicated service to the Indian peoples. Of these men Lord Radcliffe has written: 'It may.be of some service to think of them at those times when one falls to wondering whether those who are given power must always use it for selfish ends or forget its purpose in the pride of its possession. When one asks whether there must always be a "governing clan" to whom power is to be entrusted, it may help to recall the origins and training of these men. What was their secret? Pride of Race? Sense of duty? Sound Schooling? All these things were present, and yet the quality that strikes one most is a certain unaffected readiness to be themselves.

(b) Extract from a speech by the Foreign Secretary, Mr Selwyn Lloyd, to the United Nations General Assembly, 17 September 1959. Reprinted in W. N. Medlicott, *British Foreign Policy since Versailles, 1919–1963*, 2nd edn 1968, p. 343

In those territories where different races or tribes lived side by side, the task is to ensure that all the people may enjoy security and freedom and the chance to contribute as individuals to the progress and well being of these countries. We reject the idea of any inherent superiority, of one race over another. Our policy therefore is non-racial. It offers a future in which Africans, Europeans, Asians, the peoples of the Pacific, and others with whom we are concerned, will all play their full part as citizens in the countries where they live and in which feelings of race will be submerged in loyalty to the new nations.

As for the growth of nationalist movements, India set the pace even before the First World War, and the inter-war period saw developments in Egypt, Palestine and Burma to name perhaps the three most significant. The nationalist movements used the political principles of European democracy – self-determination, one man one vote – against European colonialism. Their cause was greatly assisted by the humiliating defeats to which Britain and other colonial powers were subjected in the Second World War. The Labour party had long been sympathetic to the cause of Indian freedom, and with a Labour government in power the countries of Southern Asia, India, Ceylon and Burma, moved rapidly to independence after 1945. In India the problem was to choose between one nationalism or two. In the event after the deaths of thousands of people in violent conflicts between Hindus and Moslems before and after the British withdrawal, two states, India and Pakistan, emerged. Anti-colonial nationalism began in Asia and moved westwards: China and India before the First World War, Southeast Asia and the Middle East in the inter-war period, Africa after the Second World War. The successful example of countries like India, Indonesia and Egypt accelerated the process of 'decolonization' in Africa. Nationalist movements began, developed and achieved independence in little more than a decade, an achievement which had taken India something like seventy years.

Apart from the fundamental reasons, the third most important reason for the retreat from empire was, as has been indicated, the Second World War itself. The war had three consequences for the future of the empire. First, it left Britain victorious but more or less bankrupt, quite unable in the short term to sustain the cost of empire, particularly if the imperial authority was to be challenged. Second, the humiliating defeats suffered by the British early in the war in the Middle East and particularly in Southeast Asia had disastrous consequences for British imperial prestige, a vital factor in running the pre-war empire. Britain fought her way back in Burma and returned in 1945 to Malaya, but this could not eradicate the impression of 1941–3 that the British Lion was no longer the king of beasts and that the European idol, the white man, had feet of clay. The consequences were felt in Southeast Asia, in India and throughout the Middle East. Empire had been run on the cheap before 1939, a handful of civil servants, police and soldiers responsible for millions of people. Prestige was a key factor in this process and after 1945 that prestige had gone. Third, the war left Britain tired and consumed by self-doubt, the old values were under attack, and there was a loss of will and a loss of confidence. Moreover the prevailing view after 1945 was inward-looking: social reform at home was a more attractive cause than taking up the 'white man's burden' abroad. And as with the loss of prestige, the loss of confidence in an imperial mission was crippling for the maintenance of empire.

Further causes of the retreat from empire may be found in the post-war international situation. One that very much affected the timing of events was the cold war confrontation between Russia and the West which dominated international relations between about 1947 and the Geneva Conference of 1954. The cold war meant that Britain's attention was firmly fixed on Europe, that the priorities for the allocation of manpower and resources were, in the order in which they occurred, NATO, the Korean War, rearmament after 1950, containment in Southeast Asia and then the Baghdad Pact. Imperial considerations had no priority unless, as is the case with Malaya or with the issue of bases in the Middle East, they could be related to the wider international conflict. Moreover, after the early stages of the cold war from 1945–7 Britain became closely tied to and dependent on the United States, politically, economically and militarily. This had consequences for Britain's imperial position, for the attitude of successive American governments to empire was hostile. In so far as the Americans exerted an influence on British policy it was critical and unsympathetic to imperial problems. The United States was certainly not willing to help the British maintain their imperial interests. This comes out very clearly in the United States' attitudes to British actions at Suez in 1956. It was only when a colonial struggle could be portrayed as part of the cold war confrontation with international communism, as happened to the French struggle to hold on to Indochina after 1950, that the Americans were prepared to help. The question of American hypocrisy in all this, given the United States' own imperial ambitions admittedly of a largely non-territorial kind, is an interesting and important one, but it has no real bearing on the point under discussion.

Finally, rapid decolonization was a consequence of the prevailing anti-imperial atmosphere that is a feature of the period after 1945. Empire had become a source of guilt not pride. This atmosphere was the product of anti-colonial nationalism; but it was also the logical culmination of the idea of self-determination proclaimed with fervour at the Paris Peace Conference of 1919 and afterwards; it was a European invention, propagated by both the United States and the Soviet Union. It may be thought that both countries were somewhat hypocritical in their denunciations of imperialism, but this possibility hardly affected the tide of anti-imperialism. The forum for the expression of the new anti-colonial idealism was the United Nations Organisation, and the Western colonial powers – but not the Soviet Union – were repeatedly pilloried in its debates. The anti-colonial atmosphere of the times hastened the process of decolonization. What began as a trickle in the 1940s become a flood by the end of the 1950s, and every session the United Nations welcomed a number of newly independent, ex-colonial territories. Britain and the other Western colonial powers were in no position to resist the pressure, given their other problems and preoccupations. The best that could be done was to use delaying tactics. Only Portugal tried positively to swim against the prevailing current and ultimately failed.

It can be said that on the whole the British retreat from empire was conducted skilfully and with some grace. Problems of the kind that arose in Kenya, Cyprus or Aden were only slight disturbances in an otherwise very smooth process. Moreover, with the possible exception of Suez, there was no great domestic upheaval over the loss of empire such as occurred in France and Portugal. Both the major parties can be praised or blamed, depending on your point of view, for the retreat. The Labour government was mainly involved in the sequence of events in Asia, the Conservatives in Africa and with the residual problems of the Middle East. Africa in fact achieved its independence very rapidly and was the main beneficiary of the decolonization process. In 1955 it contained only five independent states – Egypt, Ethiopia, Liberia, Libya and the Union of South Africa. By 1960 the number had risen to twenty-seven, and by 1965 the entire continent was free with the exception of Rhodesia and the Spanish and Portuguese territories. The important dates for the British colonies were 1957 when the Gold Coast became independent as Ghana, 1960 when Nigeria achieved independence, and 1961 when Tanganyika in East Africa followed suit.

Africa provoked the most famous official statement of Britain's approach to the end of empire – Macmillan's 'wind of change' speech to a joint session of both Houses of the South African Parliament in February 1960. George Hutchinson, Macmillan's most recent biographer in *The Last Edwardian at No. 10* (1980) says of the speech:

> Contentious at the time (and offensive to his hosts), it has remained contentious: Macmillan's critics accuse him of having contributed to a weakening of white authority, to the encouragement of black nationalist demands and the abdication of European responsibilities in Africa, the surrender of Western interests, not least in Rhodesia. To others it seemed, and still seems, a speech of reason, realism and moderation.

The speech can be seen as an expression of the final phase of British colonial policy, the realization that the 'white man's burden' could, indeed must now be laid down; it can also be seen (as in a savage comment by Sir Roy Welensky, a Rhodesian leader) as showing a tendency to quit, 'to run before the tempest' of black African nationalism. The speech merits detailed consideration.

Document 5.7

Macmillan's speech to both Houses of the South African Parliament in February 1960. Extracts taken from George Hutchinson, *The Last Edwardian at No. 10: an impression of Harold Macmillan* , 1980, pp. 109–10

Ever since the break-up of the Roman Empire one of the constant facts of political life in Europe has been the emergence of independent nations. They have come into existence over the centuries in different forms, with different kinds of Government, but all have been inspired by a deep, keen feeling of nationalism, which has grown as the nations have grown.

In the twentieth century, and especially since the end of the war, the processes which gave birth to the nation States of Europe have been repeated all over the world. We have seen the awakening of national consciousness in peoples who have for centuries lived in dependence upon some other power. Fifteen years ago this movement spread through Asia. Many countries there of different races and civilisations pressed their claim to an independent national life. Today the same thing is happening in Africa, and the most striking of all the impressions I have formed since I left London a month ago is of the strength of this African national consciousness. In different places it takes different forms, but it is happening everywhere. The wind of change is blowing through this continent, and, whether we like it or not, this growth of national consciousness is a political fact. We must all accept it as a fact, and our national policies must take account of it.

Of course, you understand this better than anyone. You are sprung from Europe, the home of nationalism, and here in Africa you have yourselves created a new nation. Indeed, in the history of our times yours will be recorded as the first of the African nationalisms, and this tide of national consciousness which is now rising in Africa is a fact for which you and we and the other nations of the Western World are ultimately responsible. For its causes are to be found in the achievements of Western civilization, in the pushing forward of the frontiers of knowledge, in the applying of science in the service of the human needs, in the expanding of food production, in the speeding and multiplying of the means of communication, and, perhaps above all, the spread of education . . .

Much of the process of withdrawal from empire does not make an entirely happy story. The retreat was forced and even hurried. There is at least one exception, Malaya, where Britain contrived to manage if not quite master events. The Malayan 'emergency' (1948–60) was the most prolonged and effective use of force by Britain in an imperial setting in the post-war period. The operation can be favourably contrasted with the

French failure in Indochina between 1946 and 1954 and the American failure in Vietnam between 1964 and 1975. Britain, despite her other pre-occupations and diminished resources, found an answer to Communist insurgency, while at the same time bringing Malaya and Singapore to independence by 1957. It was a considerable political and military achievement. Following independence and the ending of the emergency, the Federation of Malaya was expanded into the Federation of Malaysia in 1962, bringing into one state Malaya, Singapore, Sarawak and British North Borneo. The new state was immediately threatened by Indonesia practising an imperialism of its own; and British military support enabled 'confrontation' between 1963 and 1966 to be resisted successfully. The successes in Malaya, and over confrontation meant that Britain's imperial role in Southeast Asia ended very much with a bang rather than a whimper!

Britain retreated from empire after 1945, but the empire was replaced by the commonwealth. Until 1947 Britain's partners were the old white dominions. Thereafter the commonwealth became multi-racial. In 1949 at the Commonwealth Prime Ministers Conference provision was made for membership by states with republican constitutions, recognizing the King as head of the commonwealth. It is easy both to exaggerate the importance of the commonwealth and to minimize its usefulness. As the numbers have grown so the old intimacy has disappeared, and sentiment for the British connection has steadily weakened even in the old dominions such as Canada and Australia. Two members of the commonwealth, India and Pakistan, went to war with each other in 1965, and it was the Soviet Union that mediated the dispute. The commonwealth tried to assist in resolving the Rhodesian problem, failing in 1965–6 and helping to bring about a settlement in 1979–80. The peculiar flavour of the commonwealth can be appreciated from the following document.

Document 5.8

From George Woodcock, *Who Killed the British Empire? An Inquest*, 1974, p. 333–4

Today the Empire is no more. The Commonwealth remains. It is a body without structure and without sanctions, with no unified political philosophy and no homogeneity of political aims. Its members have warred with each other, and it has not even acted as a court of arbitration, preferring to leave such tasks to the United Nations. There is no longer, since the British Nationality Act of 1948, a common citizenship, though Commonwealth citizens are usually allowed to travel without visas in each other's territories. There is no common legal system; some members still accept the judicial committee of the Privy Council in London as a final court of appeal, and some do not. There is no common defence system;

some members belong to NATO and similar Western alliances, some have mutual assistance treaties with Communist countries, and some are completely neutral. There has never been a Commonwealth bloc in the United Nations, and there has been no attempt to establish a common approach in foreign affairs. The Commonwealth, indeed, has its Secretariat, it continues its regular meetings of Commonwealth Prime Ministers in Westminster, it bows to the past by accepting the Queen of England as its head (but not its sovereign), it operates certain committees relating to common interests in economic matters and communications. It does little else that is concrete and tangible.

Its real functions, indeed, are probably the intangible ones. It recognizes that all the countries which adhere to it have shared a common experience of immersion in the Empire, that they have derived their common language from Britain, and with it some of the cultural attitudes which a language transmits. Most have shaped their political systems, their legal systems, their armed forces, their civil services and their educational systems on the British model, though each has made its own variations. The Commonwealth, in so far as it is a formal organization, maintains contact among peoples whose problems, because of a common recent past, may be similar even if their aims are not always so. The fact that it demands no exclusive loyalty, that it seeks to establish no political orthodoxy, that it encourages its members to join in other associations of peoples, is an advantage, for today the world needs not rigid, all-inclusive international organizations, but a multiplicity of contacts, of circles of association to dissolve its antagonisms on many levels.

In the 1950s the commonwealth loomed large in Britain's view of the world. As Mr Attlee, while Prime Minister, put it in a debate in the Commons in May 1948:

> . . . [he] was disturbed by the suggestion . . . that we might somehow get closer to Europe than to our Commonwealth. The Commonwealth nations are our closest friends. While I want to get as close as we can with the other nations, we have to bear in mind that we are not solely a European Power but a member of a great Commonwealth and Empire.

The 1950s was to see the steady erosion of support for this point of view; in the 1960s it was abandoned. But the sentimental ties remained strong and were reinforced by a growing awareness of the responsibility of the advanced countries towards, indeed their interdependence with, the poor and underdeveloped countries of the Southern Hemisphere, most of them former colonies. The tensions which made the commonwealth difficult to sustain indicated precisely its political value.

Exercise 4

4.1 How important was the Second World War in bringing about the decline and fall of the British empire?

4.2 Why have the Russians, unlike the British and the French, been so successful in retaining control of their empire?

4.3 The documentary extracts tend to show the empire and imperialism as a good thing. Write a critical anti-imperialist counter to these documents.

4.4 Do you consider that Britain conducted its retreat from empire smoothly and successfully in the period 1945–65?

4.5 Why were Algeria, Angola, Kenya and Southern Rhodesia such awkward territories to dispose of in the process of decolonization?

4.6 Write a critical assessment of Macmillan's 'wind of change' speech.

4.7 Is the commonwealth worth keeping?

5 Britain's relationship with Europe

There is nothing particularly new about the idea of European unity, and at different times over the centuries, and for different reasons, a variety of men and movements have advocated some form of union. In more remote times the names of Charlemagne, Charles V and Napoleon spring to mind, and in the twentieth century, the French statesman Aristide Briand was advocating a United States of Europe in 1930 and of course Adolf Hitler had his own particular vision of a united Europe. The Second World War, which can be seen perhaps above all as a European disaster, provided a great stimulus to nations for unity or union, if only to prevent a recurrence of the catastrophe, and Churchill in 1943 suggested that a council should be set up to provide a framework for some sort of political unity in Europe.

After 1945 the movement for European union gathered momentum. When the causes of this momentum are examined it is easy to see why Britain's attitude was always equivocal, why successive British governments dragged their feet, and why finally the West European states went ahead in 1957 without Britain. Britain was left trying to scramble aboard the rolling bandwagon, a somewhat undignified and indeed humiliating spectacle in the 1960s, finally making it in the early 1970s. The irony of the whole sequence of events is that Britain appeared to be the natural leader of at least Western Europe in 1945, and was so recognized both by the United States and the Soviet Union.

The fundamental cause of the enthusiasm for European union after 1945 was the Second World War and the catastrophe it brought to Europe. It is rather more than coincidence that the six founder members of the European Economic Community had all been defeated and occupied during or after the war, and understandably were disposed to question the virtues of the nation state. Britain, by contrast, had not been defeated or occupied, the war seemed to have demonstrated the value of the nation state in general and the British state in particular. The differing wartime experiences created a psychological barrier that was far more significant than the geographical barrier of the English Channel (though that remained).

Following the shattering experience of the war, post-war Europe found itself in a state of economic collapse and apparently the prey of Russian imperialism. Eastern and part of Central Europe succumbed to Russian pressure, but the West European states with American backing saw in unity a chance for survival and recovery. The post-war situation and the perils of the cold war provided the second major impetus for European union. Britain shared in the collapse and by 1947 was well aware of the Russian threat, but her response was significantly different to that of the continental European states. She wanted American help through the Marshall Plan for economic recovery, but she wanted it on an individual state basis. Britain was, however, willing to accept, and indeed anxious to encourage, joint action on defence whether through the Brussels Treaty of 1948 or NATO in 1949. For Britain the nation state was the accepted vehicle for economic recovery and – with the 1945–51 Labour government – for economic progress and social reform – and old-fashioned alliances were the preferred choice for meeting the threat of aggression.

A third factor in the impetus for union was the encouragement of the United States. It is easy to be carping or cynical about the Americans: they were never quite sure what they were encouraging, they had no clear conception of what was meant by European union, they tended to support all unification movements indiscriminately; but the sincerity and the value of their encouragement cannot be denied. It was of course enlightened self-interest, for the Americans were afraid that Russia might absorb Western Europe with its great resources and individual skills, and they could not afford this. Moreover by 1947 they began to realize that they needed allies in Western Europe, a key area in the cold war. American encouragement took the form both of economic support – the Marshall Plan; and military backing – NATO. The American policy-makers were concerned, as John Foster Dulles put it to the Senate Foreign Relations Committee in 1947, with the idea not of merely rebuilding pre-war Europe, but of building a new Europe which would be more unified, a better Europe.

The emergence of the superpowers by the end of the 1940s was another factor in the movement for greater co-operation and possibly union, and here again Britain's appreciation of the consequences of this was significantly different from that of the continental powers. For the latter, the emergence of the superpowers signalled the end of European pre-eminence (by which of course was meant Western European pre-eminence) in international relations. A rather horrid new world – certainly not a brave one – was coming into existence. A weakened Europe was compelled to adjust to this new world, no longer providing the main actors although probably, and unfortunately, providing the main stage for the action. Economic, political, military co-operation and possibly union offered a way of safeguarding Europe's interests, and even, conceivably, of keeping up with the United States and the Soviet Union. Britain shared some of the apprehensions of the continental powers, but her appraisal of the new situation and of her place in the new scheme of things was different from theirs. To begin with the initial British view was that she could survive independently and learn to live with the superpowers, obviously not as powerful as they were, but very much in the same division of the league, and able to play an independent role at the centre of things. The evidence against this British view was pretty overwhelming after the events of 1947, but this did not prevent such a view from being held until well into the 1950s, and in some quarters even after Suez. Again the British held the view for a long time that in a rather peculiar and hard to define way they had a 'special relationship' with one of the superpowers, which put them in a different category from the other Western European states. It is a matter of controversy as to whether there ever was a 'special relationship', and if there was what it consisted of; but, special relationship or not, the idea certainly affected Britain's attitude to the United States and to Europe for something like twenty years after 1945. At the level of personal sentiment there was a warmth of feeling between Truman, Acheson, Eisenhower and Dulles on the one hand and Attlee, Bevin, Churchill, Eden and Macmillan on the other. Eisenhower in particular, after becoming President in 1952, seems to have welcomed the opportunity of working once again with Churchill, and after 1957 with Macmillan, with whom he had enjoyed good relations in North Africa during the Second World War. But whatever the warmth of feeling, this did not prevent major differences over Palestine in the 1940s and over China, Indochina and Suez in the 1950s. After 1960 the new generation of American policy-makers had a bias more towards Western Europe as a whole and less towards Great Britain.

The problem of what to do about Germany was another factor in the drive towards union, and on this issue Britain's appreciation of the problem was not very different from that of her continental neighbours. Germany was divided, and the fear was either that at some stage in the future Germany might be reunited and once again dominate Central and Western Europe, or that the Germans might go east towards Russia in the search for reunification. This option had a respectable historical precedent from the Treaty of Rapallo in the 1920s. Either possibility was a nightmare to other states in Western Europe, and economic and political union provided a way of escape; the task was to fit Germany in, not to leave the Germans in an isolated position where they might do something dangerous.

Finally, there was idealism. It is easy to be cynical about this. Hard analysis encounters a great deal of rather empty rhetoric. Nevertheless men of all parties and countries, many of them extremely hard-bitten politicians, felt the pull of the European idea, based on a shared history and common culture. The trouble on the British side was that the idealism tended to be at its greatest when the person concerned was in opposition; on taking office other considerations came to the fore. Moreover, in both the major parties there were dominant figures such as Bevin and Eden who rarely if ever seemed to have idealistic impulses about Europe.

The British Labour party, in power from 1945 to 1951, along with the Scandinavian Socialist parties, did not share the enthusiasm of Socialists in France, Germany and the Benelux countries for a united Europe. This was partly a result of the dominating position of Ernest Bevin in the councils of the party, and partly it reflected a suspicion that European union was a device by the Right and Centre to prevent the achievement of democratic socialism. Bevin was not so much anti-European, as massively pro-British in a rather nineteenth-century way, with a healthy suspicion of all foreigners and of all theoretical schemes of political organization. He wanted a Western European Union against the Soviet threat, but he intended this to be a limited defensive agreement with no wider implications. He was a blunt and practical man and made no attempt to conceal his distrust for what he called 'ambitious schemes of European unity'; he was contemptuous of the efforts of intellectuals (for whom he never had much respect) to produce elaborate constitutions for a federal union.

The Labour party was always willing to pay lip-service to the idea of internationalism, but it had no intention by the end of the 1940s of putting at risk the steady progress it was making in Britain in building socialism. It was basically concerned with using its political power to improve the lives of British working people, and it had no intention of jeopardizing the economic and social advances being made in Britain by permitting decisions to be transferred to some supra-national European Assembly. Thus it was very suspicious of the plan sponsored by the French Foreign Minister, Robert Schuman, in 1950 to establish a supra-national authority to run the coal and steel industries of Western Europe, and was unwilling to join the newly nationalized British steel industry to the Coal and Steel Community that was eventually established in Europe.

The Conservative response to Europe after 1951 was much the same as that of Labour, although the reasons were different. There was certainly more of a difference between the Conservative party in opposition and in power than was the case with Labour. Churchill in opposition was one of the most inspiring advocates of the closer union of Europe and was forever prodding the Labour government for its slowness in moving into Europe. His speeches were littered with phrases such as 'if Europe is to survive it must unite' and Britain 'must be prepared to take her full part in European unity'. But Churchill in office dragged his feet, although it must be said that he was old and preoccupied, and his first lieutenant, Eden, shared many of Bevin's prejudices about Europe. Oddly enough, it was Eden, usually described as luke-warm about Europe, who in 1954 gave a major push towards greater European unity with his successful attempt at rescue after the collapse of the European Defence Community, an attempt that led to West Germany coming into an enlarged Western European Union and into NATO as a full member.

The Conservatives were not worried about Europeans sabotaging socialism, but they were at this stage (the 1950s) much more concerned about Britain's role outside of Europe, and of Britain's links with the United States and commitments to the commonwealth and empire. These were perhaps the main inhibiting factors for many in the Conservative party about closer European union. Harold Macmillan was one of the more enthusiastic advocates of closer links with Europe, but when schemes for European economic integration were being considered in 1956 he felt obliged, as former Foreign Secretary, to point out to the House of Commons that Britain had to react to the pull of three distinct forces: the Commonwealth, the American alliance, and Europe. He argued that Britain had to support greater unity in Europe but not at the expense of her other interests. Britain could not accept a customs union which imposed a single common tariff on all goods from the world outside. Britain could not expect the countries of the Commonwealth to continue to give preferential treatment to British exports to them if she had to charge them full duty on their exports to Britain. Apart from that, British interests and responsibilities were much wider. Macmillan did not believe that Parliament would ever agree to Britain's entering arrangements which, as a matter of principle, would prevent the treatment of the great range of imports from the Commonwealth at least as favourably as those from the European countries. This position was understood by the Governments of the countries who were then negotiating their customs union in Brussels. However, what Macmillan ruled out in 1956 soon became more acceptable. By the end of the 1960s the House of Commons was willing to agree to most things in order to get into Europe, whether they were matters of principle or not.

Britain's attitude to the earlier moves towards European union after 1945 was usually sympathetic but detached. She accepted the Customs Union among the Benelux countries in 1948 and a similar Franco-Italian customs arrangement in 1949. She did her best to ensure that the Organisation for European Economic Cooperation set up in 1948 as a result of the Marshall Plan remained a forum of nation states rather than becoming some kind of supra-national body, and in this she was largely successful. She was mildly hostile to the European Coal and Steel Community which came into existence in 1952, seriously underestimating its chances of success and its long-term importance. Dean Acheson argued that Britain's failure to join the Coal and Steel Community was a turning point in her relations with Europe, and it has been pointed out that this was the first occasion after 1945 that the French took a major successful European initiative without Great Britain. The Labour party was suspicious of the Community, and both Labour and the Conservatives still thought in terms of Britain as a world power, with an oil dispute in the Persian Gulf, participation in the Korean War, and the handling of the Malayan Emergency, all being of greater significance. Britain gave further evidence of her detachment by not participating in the European Defence Community, although, as indicated previously, Eden moved rapidly in 1954 to repair the damage caused by the French refusal to ratify the agreement setting up the EDC.

The mix-up over the Defence Community did not seriously impede the movement towards European unity and, following a conference at Messina in Sicily in 1955, the Treaty of Rome in 1957 formally set up the European Economic Community or Common Market as it was more popularly called. The six original members were West Germany, France, Italy, Belgium, the Netherlands and Luxembourg. Britain did not join the Community for a variety of reasons, most of which can be identified in her attitude towards Europe in the previous decade. There was considerable scepticism in Britain about the ambitious nature of the Economic Community, especially after the shambles of the European Defence Community, and allied to this was a feeling of smug superiority that the continental powers could not handle supra-national organizations, and once again they would have to look to Britain – and Britain would respond in her own good time of course – to get them out of the mess they had created. Moreover there were serious reservations in both the major political parties about the threat to sovereignty posed by the Community, with its plans for eventual economic integration and the transfer of political and legal authority from the individual members to the Community. Further as an emotional underpinning to the opposition to the Community there was the need to safeguard commonwealth interests and the hankering for a special position as against Europe on the one side and the United States on the other. Britain would have been happy with an organization with more restricted aims – free trade, no common external tariff, no common agricultural policy, and no nonsense about eventual political developments. In 1960 she tried to organize an alternative group, the European Free Trade Association, comprising most West European states not included in the Common Market.

Britain missed the boat. She was taken back by the speed with which the Community was created and moved into action and she was disturbed by its obvious and rapid success. The preferred alternative, EFTA, was only moderately successful in contrast; the commonwealth hold weakened rapidly, and the new American administration from 1961 had a less sentimental view of Britain and a different perspective on Europe. By then President de Gaulle was in power in France and he took a decidedly cool, if not hostile, view of Britain. In 1961 Britain applied for membership, rather cap-in-hand, but also affirming stoutly that she could honour existing obligations to the commonwealth and to her EFTA partners despite taking on new ones to the Community. The decision of the Conservative government was generally welcomed by its own supporters, enthusiastically endorsed by the Liberals, but met with a mixed reception on the part of the Labour party. Negotiations on Britain's application to join the Community began in the autumn of 1961 and proceeded steadily through 1962. The negotiation appeared to be close to success but in January 1963 President de Gaulle vetoed the application. Critical to de Gaulle's decision to block the British application was his view that Britain was still not genuinely European, and that she still rated her special relationship with the United States above any commitment to Europe. This view was confirmed for him by the 1962 Kennedy–Macmillan agreement at Nassau over the supply of Polaris nuclear missiles to Britain.

The man in charge of the detailed negotiations for Britain's first attempt to enter the Community was Edward Heath, then Lord Privy Seal in Macmillan's government. His statement to the EEC Council of Ministers in October 1961 at the opening of the negotiations sets out well the arguments for European union and for Britain's place in that union. However, it was some fifteen years too late.

Document 5.9

Extracts from a Statement by the Lord Privy Seal, Mr Edward Heath, to the EEC Council of Ministers, Paris, 10 October 1961. Reprinted from D. C. Watt (ed.), *Documents on International Affairs 1962,* **1971, pp. 444–60**

The British Government and the British people have been through a searching debate during the last few years on the subject of their relations with Europe. The result of the debate has been our present application. It was a decision arrived at, not on any narrow or short-term grounds, but as a result of a thorough assessment over a considerable period of the needs of our own country, of Europe and of the Free World as a whole. We recognise it as a great decision, a turning point in our history, and we take it in all seriousness. In saying that we wish to join the EEC, we mean that we desire to become full, wholehearted and active members of the European Community in its widest sense and to go forward with you in the building of a new Europe.

Perhaps you will allow me to underline some of the considerations which have determined our course of action. In the first place, ever since the end of the war, we in Britain have had a strong desire to play a full part in the development of European institutions. We, no less than any other European peoples, were moved by the enthusiasms which gave birth to the Brussels Treaty, the Council of Europe, the OEEC, the Western European Union, and the North Atlantic Treaty . . .

. . . The second consideration has been the increasing realisation that, in a world where political and economic power is becoming concentrated to such a great extent, a larger European unity has become essential. Faced with the threats which we can all see, Europe must unite or perish. The United Kingdom, being part of Europe, must not stand aside . . .

. . . The third factor determining our decision has been the remarkable success of your Community and the strides which you have made towards unity in both political and economic fields. This has been in many ways an object lesson. You have shown what can be done in a Community comprising a group of countries with a will to work closely together. Our wish is to take part with you in this bold and imaginative venture . . .

In the debate in the House of Commons following the French veto in 1963, Edward Heath said, on the 12 February, referring to the negotiations: 'But it has been the great debate of modern times, and the debate will continue, because the relationships between ourselves and Europe are bound to be of the greatest concern both to ourselves and to the Continent'. The debate did continue not least because of the success of the Common Market in the 1960s, and the widespread and growing feeling of alarm in Britain at being left outside this prosperous and dynamic organization, with which Britain had an ever-increasing proportion of trade. While the Conservative party remained committed to Europe, although not very enthusiastic, the Labour party was more divided; nevertheless it was Harold Wilson's Labour government that promoted Britain's second attempt to join the Community in 1967. The attempt failed with a second French veto in 1969.

By 1971 Britain had a new Prime Minister, Edward Heath, who was an enthusiastic European, and France had a new President, Georges Pompidou. Heath did the sensible thing by obtaining assurances in advance from Pompidou that France would support British entry, and a third British attempt to join the Community began in the summer of 1971. It was a case of third time lucky. The treaty was signed in January 1972 and Britain along with Ireland and Denmark became members of the Community in January 1973. The main threats to Britain's closer relationship with Western Europe thereafter came not from France or from any other of Britain's new partners, but from a large body of irreconcilables to the new commitment in Britain, particularly in the Labour party, and from a growing public awareness that the costs of membership, economic, social, political, possibly outweighed the benefits. The new Labour government of Harold Wilson after March 1974 was badly divided over membership of the Community but, after some renegotiation of the terms on which Britain had joined in 1972, recommended continued membership of the Community to the electorate in a referendum held in June 1975. There was a good deal of the cosmetic in the renegotiation process, but Wilson and his foreign secretary, James Callaghan, did secure concessions on the method of assessing national contributions to the Community's budget. The result of the referendum was a massive two-to-one vote in favour of continued membership of the Community. It cannot be said that this settled the question, for doubts about the costs and benefits of membership continued to grow and the irreconcilables remained irreconcilable.

In particular, the freeing of trade between Britain and her European partners opened British markets to Europe, rather than the reverse. Even less defensible by 1980 the agricultural support programme took up about two-thirds of the Community's budget, and much of this went to the subsidy of farmers in France and Germany.

As in other spheres it seemed current policy was designed to solve the problems of the last generation. The EEC had a special appeal to those who deplored the diplomatic disarray of Europe in the 1930s. This broader but slightly antique vision of Europe was put (in a broadcast marking his 85th birthday) by a grand old man of the European cause, Harold Macmillan, the man who made the first application to join in 1961. It remained to be seen whether the vision would commend itself to the people of Britain.

Document 5.10

Extracts from a broadcast by Harold Macmillan in February 1979 to mark his eighty-fifth birthday. Reprinted from George Hutchinson, *The Last Edwardian at No. 10*, 1980, p. 149

Since it is purely an economic body or more or less a free trade area with a lot of bureaucratic system, we are getting all the troubles without any of the advantages. We argue about fish, about potatoes, about milk, on the periphery. But what is Europe really for? The countries of Europe, none of them anything but second-rate powers by themselves, can – if they get together – be a power in the world, an economic power, a power in foreign policy, a power in defence equal to either of the superpowers. We are in the position of the Greek city States: they fought one another and then fell victim to Alexander the Great and then to the Romans. Europe united could still, by not niggling about the size of lorries, but by having a single foreign policy, a single defence policy and a single economic policy, be equal to the great superpowers. For the moment, the future is very uncertain. Nobody is really facing this; nobody is coming out with this great demand, even the French or the Germans. Somebody must arise, somebody who, like Churchill, is not just an echo but a voice.

Exercise 5

5.1 Why was Britain's attitude to the cause of greater European unity so lukewarm in the years after 1945?
5.2 Contrast the differences in attitude and approach to the cause of European unity between the Conservative and Labour parties in the 1940s and 1950s.
5.3 Can you justify Britain's rather negative attitude towards the establishment of the European Economic Community in 1957?
5.4 Why did Britain fail in her first and second attempts to join the European Economic Community?
5.5 Make a case that Britain should remain in the European Economic Community in the 1980s, *or* make a case that Britain should withdraw from the Community.

6 Thirty years of foreign policy – the decline of Britain

By 1975, Britain's foreign policy dilemmas seemed to be ending. The withdrawal from east of Suez was almost complete, the agonies of decolonization were almost over, a limited measure of détente seemed to be ending the cold war, and the 1973 entry into the European Economic Community was overwhelmingly confirmed in the 1975 referendum. The indications were of a strong commitment to Western Europe as the basis of British policy. By 1980, however, the future was once again uncertain. The EEC itself was in a state of disarray, Britain's economy remained weak and seemed to be getting weaker, and there was a tendency to place much of the blame for this on membership of the Community. Europe was unpopular, and there were many irreconcilables, especially in the Labour party, who refused to accept the verdict of 1975. The irreconcilables did not agree on the several alternatives, a special relationship with the United States, an understanding with the Soviet Union, the strengthening of bonds with the commonwealth, neutralism or 'Little Englander' isolationism.

From the perspective of the 1980s it is now possible to assess Britain's record in foreign affairs in the years after 1945. The theme of the period both at home and abroad was gradual transformation from a leading world role to diminished status and limited responsibilities, a transformation that was a matter of necessity rather than of free choice, and a process that was often painful. At home for something like twenty-five years the key feature was the continuity of Britain's post-war arrangements. The Attlee government made huge strides towards a welfare state and a mixed economy. It began the orderly withdrawal from the empire, it inaugurated the nuclear and NATO strategies, it rejected the leadership of Western Europe.

Succeeding Conservative governments between 1951 and 1964 did not stray very far from this path. In foreign policy there was a greater emphasis on Europe after 1957, and a greater inclination to assert Britain's interests abroad. The Labour governments between 1964 and 1970 continued the main lines of established policy. The Labour party was less enthusiastic about NATO and nuclear weapons, and the maintenance of strong military forces 'east of Suez'. The Suez affair itself divided the parties. But policy itself differed less than the enthusiasm with which it was pursued. However, towards the 1970s more significant differences emerged, especially over the central policy of confrontation with Russia. This repeated two central themes in British thinking about foreign policy over much of the period. The first was the interpretation of Russian motives and aims. The death of Stalin in 1953 and the subsequent 'de-Stalinization' in Russia had suggested a new liberalism in Russia and the possibility of what came to be called 'détente', an easing of the tension of the East–West confrontation. But events threw doubt on this interpretation: the crushing of the Hungarian rising in 1956, and of the Czech reform movement in 1968, as well as massive Russian armaments. The second theme related to armaments in general and nuclear arms in particular. The old historical question was raised in the 1960s, and again in the 1980s: did arms races lead to war? The new question was the nuclear one: was nuclear deterrence effective and moral? By 1980 the Labour party leadership was less sure of the principles of foreign policy laid down by Bevin in the late 1940s.

It is clear from the history of the post-war years that there was a great loss of power and influence between 1945 and 1980. Britain in 1945 was broken, but she was one of the 'Big Three', she was the centre of a vast empire and commonwealth and she was expected to dominate Western Europe. By 1980 all this was but a dream, Britain's sovereignty and her capacity to control her own destiny let alone influence the destinies of others was severely weakened, and her relative status as a power, an ally or an enemy, was challenged by the greater growth in capabilities of a number of other states: Japan, West Germany, China and France. In 1945 Britain was a respectable third to the United States and the Soviet Union. By 1980 she was not even in the premier division but was trying to hold on to a position as a leading power of the second rank.

By 1980 there were few delusions of grandeur, and there appeared to be in the main political parties an acceptance of an international role which generally matched Britain's capabilities. The mood of the 1970s in foreign policy was realistic, certainly unheroic, possibly lacking in idealism, reflecting a sober awareness of the limitations of power. This realism can be seen on a number of issues: the fishing disputes (cod wars) with Iceland, the attitude to the Arab world during and after the 1973 war, the failure to fulfil treaty obligations in Cyprus, the refusal to do anything dramatic and heroic over Rhodesia. Arguably unheroic realism was carried too far especially in Southeast Asia and the Persian Gulf. Britain could have sustained a role, and local powers wanted her to remain in both regions, but she chose to withdraw. She remained of course one of the leading economic and military powers of Western Europe, with a vital role in NATO.

The loss of power and influence after 1945, and the realistic acceptance of this by the 1970s, were matched by the gradual revision of the assumptions that governed thinking about British foreign policy. First, there was the central assumption in 1945 that Britain could and would continue to operate as an independent political unit at the centre of the international system. This assumption was held in varying degrees by Bevin, Churchill and Eden, but was finally accepted as untenable. Sir Henry Tizard, then chief scientific adviser to the Minister of Defence, questioned this assumption as early as 1949. He wrote:

> We persist in regarding ourselves as a Great Power, capable of everything and only temporarily handicapped by economic difficulties. We are *not* a Great Power and never will be again. We are a great nation but if we continue to behave like a Great Power we shall soon cease to be a great nation. Let us take warning from the fate of the Great Powers of the past and not burst ourselves with pride. (See Aesop's 'fable of the frog'.)
> (Quoted by Margaret Gowing in 'Britain America and the Bomb' in Dilks, 1981).

Second, there was the assumption that Britain would continue to have a world role. This held in the 1940s and 1950s, but in the 1960s it was grudgingly accepted that because of limited capabilities it would have to be abandoned. Third, there was the assumption of the central importance of the commonwealth. This began to be questioned after Suez, and did not survive a series of hammer blows in the 1960s from issues such as the withdrawal of South Africa, migration to Britain, and Rhodesian UDI. Finally, there was the assumption that while Britain was a European power it was also detached from Europe. This assumption began to be challenged in the mid-1950s, but there was reluctance to abandon it until the early-1960s, and by then the bus had been missed. To change the metaphor the bandwagon was already rolling, and a weakening Britain had to try and climb on, finally succeeding at the third attempt.

In the light of a history of rapid change in Britain's place in foreign affairs, the general principle of a British foreign policy may be discerned. Lord Trevelyan, a British diplomat of great distinction, outlined the prospects for British foreign policy at the end of the 1970s in the twenty-sixth Stevenson Lecture to the Royal Institute of International Affairs on 29 November 1977.

Document 5.11

Extracts from 'Towards a British Role in Foreign Affairs', *International Affairs*, vol. 54, no. 2, April 1978, pp. 203–19

An examination of our foreign policy will, of course, start from the premise that British policy should serve British interests. This is not a purely selfish concept. It is a British interest, for instance, that the peace should be secure, that the strong should not gobble up the weak, that international disputes, even if they cannot be settled, should at least be talked over until the danger point is passed, that atomic weapons should not get into the hands of any country which might be tempted to use them, that the nuclear balance should be firmly maintained, that relations between the capitalist and communist countries should become gradually easier, that the less-developed countries should be able to raise the living standards of their people, that raw materials, including oil, should be generally available on terms equally reasonable for supplier and consumer, that governments should keep their word, in particular their treaties and other international agreements (at least so long as they have the power to do so) and should generally observe the principles of international law and treat in a civilized way those of their own citizens who question their ideology or behaviour. A citizen of the United Kingdom cannot forget that he is also a citizen of the world and that this shrinking world's interests are his own.

To be effective our policy should of course be founded on a clear understanding of the world as it is and on an objective assessment of the balance of political, military and economic forces, not on sentimental recollections of a vanished past. It should be one that we and our allies can back up effectively by the economic and military power which we can together apply to a particular situation. It must be determined in the light of its influence on other policies and of their influence on it – as Bevin remarked, the conduct of foreign affairs is like keeping a lot of balls in the air at the same time – and since there is never an absolutely correct answer to any problem of foreign policy, we can only choose what appears to be the least disadvantageous course open, however unpalatable it may be. Rhodesia is a case in point. The principles which should govern foreign policy are clear enough, but at the moment of decision, emotion, ideology or plain politics are sometimes stronger than rational thought.

A British Foreign Secretary will know that he no longer has the responsibilities of a power of the first rank but is enmeshed in an immense variety of complex relationships. He is confronted by struggles of ideologies and nationalisms and by all the complications arising from history, political instability and tribal rivalries in a host of new states having leaders with little political experience and an uncertain power base. He will reflect that there have been few periods of British history when Britain could act effectively on the world stage without allies. He must resist the temptation to be too active or to overplay his hand, but must use every bit of influence which the country inherits from the past and which it can still exercise effectively in spite of its relative loss of power. He must bear in mind that a country which appears to have lost confidence in itself will lose the confidence of others. And he must reconcile himself to the knowledge that there are no victories to be won in foreign affairs. In that sphere, with persistence and patience over a long period, a situation can sometimes be improved; but though you can lose sensationally, you never seem to win.

After four decades of post-war diplomacy, Britain holds on to the position of a leading power of the second rank. She remains one of the small number of nuclear powers, and plays a leading role in the defence, politics and economics of Western Europe. Her independent world role is over, except possibly in the Far East where possession of Hong Kong and memories of a historic role in the opening of China leave her with special interests. Britain remains densely populated, short of resources, very dependent on overseas trade. Her resources are limited, her horizons narrow, her aims unambitious. Dean Acheson, a former American Secretary of State, said in December 1962 that Britain had lost an empire and had not yet found a role. The remark was resented, but it was true in 1962 and it remains true in the 1980s – except that there is no certainty that a role is there to be found (or is even worth the seeking?).

Paul Kennedy summed up the British experience in the following document.

Document 5.12

Paul Kennedy, review in *The Times Literary Supplement* on 20 March 1981

Taken overall, it is remarkable how gentle and regular the British retreat from power has been. The traumas which occurred were generally short-term and limited in extent: even the fall of Singapore, described by Churchill as 'the greatest disaster in our history', was a regional and not a global defeat; and even the Suez crisis, much though it troubled the nation, could not compare with France's agony over Algeria.

There has been no invasion, no Hiroshima, no unconditional surrender, no sack of Rome; nor has there been any significant right-wing backlash at this steady, inexorable retreat. More than any other empire in its final throes, Britain has come closest to Toynbee's aphorism that a declining power is like an old man, shuffling down the back-stairs in his slippers as the rising powers ascend the front-stairs in their jack-boots.

Exercise 6

6.1 List what you consider to be the successes and failures of British foreign policy since 1945. Do you think that the successes outweigh the failures?

6.2 Make a case for an alternative policy for Britain after 1945 towards (a) the cold war, *or* (b) the Middle East, *or* (c) Europe.

Guide to exercises

1 There are various ways of approaching this question, most of them of a comparative nature. Consider Britain's position – political, military, territorial, economic – in 1939, and her position in 1945. You can, as the question suggests, try to draw up a balance sheet: the benefits or profits – mainly political and military – against the losses – mainly economic and territorial. Think about alternative courses of action open to the British government in say 1940 or 1943, and the possible consequences of those courses of action.

2.1 Try to distinguish between short-term and longer-term problems. Draw up a rough order of priority – as it looked to the policy-makers at the time, and as it now looks to historians. There are some interesting differences.

2.2 The approaches of the two main parties – Labour and Conservative – to the major problems facing Britain should be compared. Points for consideration include: the extent to which both parties were bound by their membership of the wartime coalition and by the decisions made by that coalition; the important differences – on paper – between the two parties over such questions as the future of the empire and attitudes to Russia; the sharp differences within the Labour party over such issues as approaches to Russia and what to do about Palestine.

2.3 Your answer should include a mix of factors, domestic and international, political, military and economic. Give some attention to Britain's admission of weakness, to Soviet moves in Eastern Europe, to the Truman Doctrine, and to the European Recovery Programme.

2.4 Take into account what the Russians and their supporters were doing and saying in the years 1945 to 1949 – the imposition of friendly or 'puppet' governments in Eastern Europe, the activities of the French and Italian Communist parties, the 1948 takeover of Czechoslovakia, the Berlin Blockade, revolutionary activities in Eastern Asia, and the acquisition of an atomic bomb. Note that for some years after 1945, many contemporary observers in Western Europe still regarded a resurgent Germany as the most likely threat to peace and stability.

2.5 A difficult and complicated question. Take three approaches: (i) the sharp differences in political and economic stability that existed in the two regions under discussion; (ii) the policies and attitudes of the major military powers, such as the United States, Britain and France, who had to make containment work – they were generally united in Europe, often divided in East and Southeast Asia; (iii) the differing nature of the threats in the two regions, and how those threats were seen by the states in the regions.

2.6 Your answer should include some discussion of a number of factors; Britain's role during the war in developing the atomic bomb; the British government's view after 1945 of Britain's continuing role as a great power with worldwide interests and commitments; the (not unreasonable) determination to have the best weaponry available; the fear of Russia and apprehensions about American reliability; the secrecy of all discussions about nuclear power and the absence of a clear alternative policy with any measure of public support.

2.7 The factors listed for the previous question are obviously of great relevance. In addition, a number of other bureaucratic, political and economic factors are important, particularly in considering why Britain chose to remain a nuclear power. For example, once Britain had *become* a nuclear power, vested interests and bureaucratic inertia in political and military circles combined in favour of her *remaining* a nuclear power. Again, nuclear weapons were politically popular, helping to reduce both the financial burdens and the manpower needs (ultimately including conscription) of a more conventional defence policy. These points explain the policy: its justification depends on a balance of the problems of national security posed under question 2.6.

3.1 Consider the more pressing problems facing Britain – such as the state of the economy, stability and security in Europe, the question of India – which prevented the British government from giving a high priority to the Middle East, and then look at the particular factors in the region: the withdrawal of British military power, the growth of Arab nationalism, Jewish determination to set up a state in Palestine, the equivocations of American policy, Soviet bloc involvement after 1950.

3.2 A speculative question. There were a number of alternative policies theoretically available to the British government, from standing firm in Palestine to getting out much earlier. You need to consider the pros and cons of a number of these. It is easy to see why they remained 'theoretically available'!

3.3 A description of Britain's interests – economic, political, territorial – will demonstrate the importance of the region for British foreign policy. Such factors as bases, treaty commitments to various states in the region, and, above all, dependence on oil should be considered.

3.4 Britain's prestige obviously fell to zero in much of the Arab world, but apart from this and the actual physical losses at Suez, the crisis does not in the short-term seem to have had much effect on Britain's interests and commitments in the region. Britain was able 'to bounce back' in the 1958 crisis. You need to examine in some detail British interests and commitments in the summer of 1956, and then see what had happened to them by say 1958–60. Changes in Britain's position by 1960 were increasingly determined by other factors – Cyprus, Iraq 1958, Aden – although of course these problems were all affected by what had happened in 1956.

4.1 The effects of the war on the empire – the growth of a sense of national identity in parts of the Middle East, the loss of British prestige in Southeast Asia – have to be assessed. This has to be related to the many other factors, both before and after the war, domestic and international, economic, social and political, that brought about the decline of the empire and the emergence of the commonwealth. The war was 'the last straw', but without the last straw the camel's back remained unbroken!

4.2 The contrasting imperial experiences of Russia, Britain and France are the result of a number of factors such as military and economic strength, ruthlessness in putting down opposition, differing attitudes to minorities and indeed majorities in the territories of the empire, response to outside pressures, and perhaps above all differing philosophical or ideological approaches to empire. All these deserve some consideration, particularly the different attitudes to empire. The Chinese – no mean imperialists themselves – assert that the whole thing is racial: Russians cannot be anything other than imperialists!

4.3 Three major arguments in the anti-imperialist case are (i) that imperialism encouraged attitudes of racial superiority, on the part of the colonizing power, for the 'lesser breeds without the law'; (ii) that the colonizing power at best neglected and at worst destroyed the social and religious values and the culture of the colonial peoples; (iii) that the economy of the colony was developed and exploited in the interests of the imperial power rather than of the people of the colony. You need to provide some examples to illustrate these arguments.

4.4 Consider a number of cases of decolonization both from the point of view of Britain and from that of the newly independent country. You might take India, Malaya, Ghana, Cyprus and Northern Rhodesia as examples. Look at the economic and military costs, the loss of human life, the stability or otherwise of the new state, and its continuing relations with the United Kingdom. You might also compare how the British managed decolonization with the performances of France and the Netherlands.

4.5 Examine the problems resulting from a substantial white settler population in these countries; and consider also the differing approaches to the problem of Britain, France and Portugal.

4.6 A critical assessment should take various points of view: African nationalists, white settlers, the government of South Africa, the Colonial Office, anti-colonial members of the United Nations.

4.7 The benefits of a free association amongst peoples and countries of varying histories, geographical positions, stages of economic development and differing political philosophies need to be assessed, and balanced against the costs. On the credit side there are social, educational, economic and diplomatic factors. On the debit side there is some loss of liberty of action, especially on the part of Great Britain, and a good deal of humbug and hypocrisy.

5.1 The differing impacts of the Second World War on Britain and on the other major states of Western Europe should be contrasted. Consider how successive British governments saw Britain's role after 1945: a power with global commitments, the centre of a commonwealth and empire, a special relationship with the United States, interests in Europe.

5.2 In some ways the comparisons seem more important than the contrasts! Both major parties tended to say different things out of office from what they said when in office. Both had a rather stand-offish attitude combined with a suspicion of enthusiasts for European unity – although for different reasons! These reasons need to be spelled out together with their consequences for the parties.

5.3 Two possible lines of justification seem to emerge. First, a feeling that the attempt was premature and bound to fail – it was too soon after the rather painful collapse of the European Defence Community. Second, Britain still accorded her relations with Europe a lower priority than her relationship with the United States and her role in the commonwealth.

5.4 The simple answer is to blame the French on both occasions. But you should examine other possible factors, such as the complex Anglo-French-American relationship that bedevilled the negotiations in the early 1960s, and the fact that British policy on both occasions was confused, the result of a muddle over objectives and priorities. It can be argued that French objections were the result of the failure of British policy rather than the cause of it.

5.5 An interesting debate that often reveals more about the prejudices of the debater rather than the reasons for his choice! Questions of national identity, loss of sovereignty, the security of Western Europe, and economic benefits and losses must feature prominently in the arguments.

6.1 A long list either way, and you should try to justify your selections. In your assessment of success and failure you must try to distinguish between the contemporary view – that is success or failure in terms of what the policy-maker was trying to achieve – and the view of the historian – that is trying to relate success and failure to some larger pattern of British history and policy-making. The decisions to cut down British commitments east of Suez in the 1960s and early 1970s must be considered as successes at the time, but to the historian, even with the perspective of less than a decade, they begin to look less successful in terms both of the maintenance of British interests and the stability of the regions involved.

6.2 A very speculative question whichever topic you choose. It is easy to suggest alternatives, the difficult part is to make a case for them without taking liberties with the evidence!

6 Topics and problems

1 Government and the trade unions, 1969–80

The relations of trade unions and government in the 1970s were often stormy, and the unions were plausibly accused of bringing down three governments (1970, 1974, 1979). This study examines the validity of that accusation, and the nature and extent of trade union power.

The development of the trade unions, 1945–80

The proportion of trade union members in the labour force was about 44 per cent in 1950 and the same in 1969. This proportion expanded rapidly to 52 per cent in 1976. The increase reflected a large rise in union membership in the 'public sector' and in 'white collar' unions, and a fall in the declining heavy industries. In the 1970s NUPE expanded from about a quarter of a million members to almost three-quarters, and the expansion of NALGO was on a similar scale. By then the TGWU had over 2 million members and the Engineers (AUEW) almost 1.5 million. However, few unions spanned whole industries and in most large plants employers faced a plurality of unions.

Co-operation between government and unions

It needs to be emphasized at the outset that the relations of government and trade unions over the whole period were characterized by co-operation as well as by conflict. In the late 1940s the unions accepted wage restraint for three years, 1948–50. This was a fully negotiated agreement (equivalent to the Social Contract of the 1970s) by which the TUC on behalf of the unions agreed with the government and the major employers' organizations to accept a wage freeze in return for the limitation of profits and the control of prices.

This agreement and the later Social Contract reflected the greater willingness of the unions to work with Labour. But the unions were not continuously antagonistic towards Conservative governments, and their friendliness toward Labour collapsed in the face of strict incomes policies.

Strikes

In 1945–67 there were only three years when days lost exceeded 4 million (1957, 1959, 1962) and only one above 8 million (1957). In 1968–78 there was only one year with less than 4 million (1976) and six above 8 million.

These figures are a rough guide to the state of industrial relations and of the government–union relationship. Comparison with other countries does not show Britain to be unusual in the frequency of strikes – its record was often surpassed by Italy and the USA for example. Only West Germany, with its centralized and disciplined trade union organization (imposed by the Allies in 1945) was comparatively free from disruption. It should be added that trade unions in the Communist countries did not strike, except in near revolutionary circumstances.

The British record was worse than the figures suggested because British industry suffered forms of disruption which make little mark on the statistics – short but disruptive strikes by a comparatively few people, 'wild-cat' strikes, strike threats, go-slows, overtime bans, 'working to rule' – but which had disproportionate effects on production. On the other hand, the British record was much better than it seemed to those who experienced it, because strikes were highly publicized, and their extent sometimes exaggerated. Even in the 1970s being on strike was an unusual experience for most British workers, and being absent for sickness was much more common (although absence for sickness reflects morale and motivation too). Yet strikes were frequent enough to indicate a damaging lack of co-operation and good will in labour relations, involving a defensive resistance to changes in manning and technology.

Explanations of the increase in strikes in the 1970s

  (i) Discontent of workers, related to the poor performance of industry, hence low wages, and fears for future living standards. In inflationary times workers wanted more money – a want intensified by the rapid rise in deductions from pay for tax and insurance (from almost nothing in the 1950s to about 25 per cent in the 1970s). Discontent was probably related too, to boredom with repetitive work and a lack of motivation for the job, more significant while full employment reduced the economic motivation.

  (ii) Ineffective procedures for collective bargaining, related to the conflict between the official union organization and the shop stewards on the factory floor, and leading to frequent unofficial strikes (rare in the 1930s).

(iii) The growing professionalization of unions, so that officials were highly motivated to do the central work of unions – getting more money. Further, competition for members raised militancy.

(iv) The tradition of British industrial relations, which, while not as violent as in the USA for example, are marked by adversary, indeed antagonistic, relations between 'masters' and 'men'; and in which the strike is an absolutely legitimate procedure, not a weapon of last resort.

(v) The realization by trade unions that they possessed power which had hardly been used before. The concentration and interdependence of industry meant that strikes could be very effective very quickly. This power was used now in accordance with the simple logic of the British system: 'it is the brute instrumentality of British trade unionism, its disorderly, competitive but highly effective pursuit of wages, which makes it so lethal' (P. Jenkins, *The Guardian* 26 January 1979). This was the less acceptable face of the trade union principle of 'free, collective bargaining.'

(vi) The calling of the bluff inherent in the old wages sytem. As Harold Lever said, 'Few coal miners believe that there's a moral law that says a High Court Judge should earn five times as much as they do.' Of course, there was no law and not much reason either.

(vii) The wider political background of the late 1960s and 1970s – the growing acceptance of protest and direct action.

(viii) The influence of television in promoting material acquisitiveness, encouraging comparisons of living standards and making compromise and accommodation more difficult (because more public).

(ix) The hostility of public opinion to trade unions was modified by particular sympathies for miners, for the unemployed and for workers likely to lose their jobs; and a general sympathy for the protection and raising of living standards.

The Donovan Commission, 1968

The Donovan Commission was set up in 1965 by the Wilson government which had great faith in Royal Commissions. By the time it reported (1968) the climate had much changed, and incomes policy – a fundamental restriction of trade union activity – had become a major concern of the government. In that perspective the Report seemed tame, for it endorsed the existing 'voluntary' style of industrial relations, and its main contribution towards 'doing something about' the unions, was the recommendation of an Industrial Relations Commission to examine disputes. The Conservative Iain Macleod called it 'a blue print for inaction'.

The case for 'bringing unions within the law' was made in a note of reservation by Andrew Shonfield:

The main Report addresses itself to the immediate situation in British industrial relations and proposes a number of remedies which I heartily support. But it barely concerns itself with the long-term problem of accommodating bodies with the kind of concentrated power which is possessed by trade unions to the changing future needs of an advanced industrial society. There are a number of questions that ought to be asked at this stage about the degree of regulation which should properly be applied to organisations wielding great authority in communities where the average citizen becomes progressively more vulnerable to what they do. With the growing dependence of people on the reliable performance of services required for tolerable living in crowded urban communities, the employment of collective power of groups of producers to disrupt the lives of people who have no means of helping themselves raises new problems. One has to contemplate a situation in which the typical city dweller has been forced into relying on collective services for things that he is no longer able to provide for himself privately. This has happened, or is happening, with light and heat, and is likely to happen with transport and other services. It will become less possible in the circumstances which are unfolding to distinguish, in the sharp traditional style of the English Common Law, between public authority and power and the 'private' power of organisations with collective functions, which control the supply of essential goods and services not obtainable from any alternative source . . . It is no longer possible to accept the traditional notion of the individual workplace as a separate and largely autonomous estate, where employers and employees are able to conduct their quarrels with little or no regard to the effects of what they do on other workplaces. In recent years we have seen how a large complex of interrelated industrial operations located in different concerns may suddenly be placed at the mercy of the impulse of some small work group somewhere along the line. The degree of industrial interdependence is certain to increase . . . the distinction between labour organisations which explicitly accept certain responsibilities towards society as a whole, as well as towards their own members, and those which refuse or are unable to do so, needs to be pressed further. This should be done by demanding of trade unions, the fulfilment of certain minimum standards of behaviour as a condition for being registered . . .

It seems inconceivable in the long run that in a society which is increasingly closely knit, where the provision of services to meet the elementary needs of a civilised daily life depends more and more on the punctual performance of interrelated work tasks of a collective character, trade unions will be treated as if they had the right to be exempt from all but the most rudimentary legal obligations. This is the traditional view, which has bitten deep into the British system of industrial relations. It is what the TUC in their evidence to the Royal Commission referred to as the principle of 'abstention, of formal indifference' on the part of the state (paragraph 174).

I start from the proposition that the deliberate abstention of the law from the activities of mighty subjects tends to diminish the liberty of the ordinary citizen and to place his welfare at risk. If organisations are powerful enough to act the bully then very special grounds are necessary to justify the decision not to subject their behaviour to legal rules. The legal rules need not be much brought into play in practice; if such organisations enforce their own systems of rules and these work in the public interest there will be little actual labour for the law to do. But the content of the rules and the way that they operate in particular cases must not be allowed to escape from close public surveillance. I therefore regard the principle which is stated in paragraph 471 of the Report to be characteristic of the British system, that collective bargaining should remain 'outside the law', to be wrong . . .

Historically the doctrine of the 'licensed conspiracy' served a useful social purpose. The trade unions were weak and vulnerable at the time, and the respectable prejudice against them, which was shared by judges, would almost certainly have meant that legal decisions on matters affecting their affairs would have tended to inhibit their growth. The removal of these matters from the purview of the courts therefore helped the British trade unions to establish themselves as the large and influential bodies which they are today. But now that they have evolved to this dominant role, it would be highly anomalous if the legal prejudices of an earlier generation were to continue to be used to encourage them to avoid undertaking ordinary contractual obligations in their relations with employers or to permit their actions to escape the public regulation which has come to be accepted as the common lot of corporate bodies wielding economic power. (Report, pp. 288–91)

'In Place of Strife', 1969

This was an engagingly titled White Paper produced by Barbara Castle, Secretary of State in the new Department of Employment and Productivity (also engagingly titled). Mrs Castle was a senior member of the Cabinet, usually associated with the left wing of the party. Her paper was developed with the backing of the Prime Minister, and the foreknowledge of the TUC. For the Cabinet it was more of a surprise – which proved to be its undoing.

'In Place of Strife' proposed *inter alia* the establishment of a Commission on Industrial Relations (CIR) and an Industrial Board; a compulsory ballot before strikes; a 28-day 'conciliation pause' in the case of unofficial strikes; the imposition of settlements in inter-union disputes; the possibility of fines (but not imprisonment) as a sanction for these provisions. Legislation based on these proposals was introduced. Opposition in the unions, the Labour party and, finally, in the Cabinet forced the withdrawal of the Bill. To save the dignity, indeed credibility, of the government, the TUC made a 'solemn and binding' promise to use its influence to prevent unofficial strikes. Hence the famous character 'Mr Solomon Binding' invented by Peter Jenkins of *The Guardian*. In fact, the TUC made a serious effort at conciliation, which ended shortly after the Conservative government came to power in 1970.

The unions won a major victory in 1969 but it was brought about by the Labour party and the Cabinet as much as by the unions themselves. Parliamentary sovereignty and responsibility was reasserted, not breached (though it would be possible to argue that the Labour party acted as an instrument of the trade unions; also the government was aware of the power of the unions to resist the Act).

The incident was critical for the Labour party and for the government. The tensions and confusions have been recorded in the books by Crossman, Castle and Wilson, and the whole is brilliantly recounted in Peter Jenkins, *The Battle of Downing Street*.

The Industrial Relations Act, 1971

Spurred on rather than deterred by Labour's failure, the Conservatives undertook, in their 1970 manifesto, to introduce a comprehensive Bill on industrial relations, an unusual example for the Conservatives of policy-making by manifesto. The TUC opposed the Bill from the beginning, using refusal to register as its constitutional weapon. The Labour party fought the Bill inch by inch, establishing a number of parliamentary records in the process. The Industrial Relations Act 1971 included the following provisions.

   (i) A National Industrial Relations Court (NIRC) which might enforce CIR recommendations, authorize ballots and impose conciliation pauses.

  (ii) A register of unions, which must conform to the principles of the Act, for example, in relation to membership and 'unfair' and 'irregular' action. Unregistered unions would no longer be immune from liability for inducing breaches of contract – in effect strikes by such unions would be illegal.

 (iii) Collective agreements would be legally enforceable unless they were specifically declared not to be.

 (iv) A 'conciliation pause' of up to sixty days.

  (v) Compulsory ballots on strike action.

 (vi) Outlawing of 'unfair' industrial practices including sympathetic strikes, action against non-unionists, the pre-entry 'closed shop'. (Offending unions to be fined.)

The collapse of the Act 1972

   (i) The miners' strike of 1972 was settled by resort to an independent commission (Wilberforce). The miners' pay award breached the government's pay policy, and the government turned instead to tri-partite talks with the CBI and TUC to secure agreement on controlling inflation. This was not incompatible with the Act itself, but it marked a departure from the Conservatives' no-appeasement philosophy of 1970. The government, after all, would consult with the unions. In fact Heath spent a great deal of his time thereafter in talking with the unions, and Stage 3 of the incomes policy was designed to meet their demands. But a gulf of distrust separated the unions from the government. The Act collapsed into this gulf.

(ii) Attempts to apply the new law failed in a public and humiliating way. The TGWU was told by the new NIRC to stop the 'blacking' of containers on Merseyside by some of its members (albeit acting unofficially). The union was fined first £5000 and then, since the blacking continued and the first fine was not paid, £50,000. The union paid the fine but appealed on the grounds that it could not be held responsible for the unofficial actions of its members and shop-stewards. The union won in the Court of Appeal but lost, on further appeal, in the House of Lords.

(iii) The rail unions, engaged on a 'go-slow', were taken through a conciliation pause and a strike ballot without any effect. They continued the 'go-slow' and won their wage rise.

(iv) Three London dockers were imprisoned for refusing to give up the picketing of a container depot (they objected to the shifting of jobs from the docks to such inland depots, not manned by dockers). They were released by the unexpected intervention of the Official Solicitor, who asked the Appeal Court to overrule the judgement of NIRC and thus contrived to save the government from the embarrassment of imprisoning workers.

Another group of dockers was imprisoned in a similar case. Strikes in protest broke out all over the country. At this point the House of Lords ruled, in case (ii) above, that unions could be held responsible for their members. So the dockers were released and the TGWU paid its fines.

These somewhat comical capers demonstrated that this particular Act could not work at this particular time. It was condemned by industrialists as well as by the trade unions, and its repeal by the new Labour government in 1974 was not opposed by the Conservatives. However, its failure was not fundamental and inevitable, but, in part, circumstantial – 'the fortuitous outcome of power politics and particular circumstances' (Moran, 1977, p. 2).

The miners and the government, 1972–4

The miners organized two national strikes, in 1972 and 1974 – the first since 1926. (There are some special explanations of this – see chapter 2). The second of these strikes led to the election in which the Heath government was defeated. Both strikes were about pay, not directly the Industrial Relations Act.

(i) The strike of January–February 1972 had a dramatic effect on the life of the country, with regular power cuts, rising unemployment and short-time working in industry.

  The impact of the strike was partly due to its scope and the dependence of industry on electricity produced by coal-fired power stations. But its effect was made more rapid and complete by the 'picketing' of power stations and coal supply depots. The picketing amounted in fact to blockading by large numbers of trade unionists and supporters, moving around the country on the new motorways, and co-ordinated by the Yorkshire miners' President, Arthur Scargill. He became a formidable champion of trade union militancy – a militancy marked by ruthless determination, skilful organization, and articulate justification. 'King Arthur' was a phenomenon of the 1970s; and by 1980 the newspapers frequently speculated whether the 1980s would witness his coronation.

  In 1972 his great victory on the field was at Saltley coke works in the Midlands. At the height of the battle 3000 pickets faced as many police. By then the depot could not be worked nor could the law, which allowed picketing only for the purpose of peaceful persuasion.

(ii) The strike of February 1974 had even more dramatic effects. It began with an overtime ban in the previous November, which was reinforced by a similar ban by power engineers and a work-to-rule by locomotive drivers. At the same time, Britain, like other Western countries, faced a massive cut in oil supplies from the Middle East, and a quadrupling of its price. The government had reason to be alarmed, and introduced a compulsory three-day week and the closing down of television broadcasts at 10.30 p.m. each night (the latter at least being in part an intentional dramatization of the crisis).

In the following weeks three things went wrong for the government, and indeed for the nation.

(a) The situation moved rapidly towards 'confrontation' (a word, indeed a condition, of the 1970s). Each side took up positions from which negotiation was difficult, if not impossible. The Labour party appeared to back the miners without qualification. Some of the miners' leaders spoke openly of 'bringing down the government'. The government was perhaps too sensitive to this rhetoric, but not unreasonably, if a little inflexibly, stood by its incomes policy.

(b) Opportunities for negotiation were passed over. An offer by the TUC to treat the miners as exceptional, thus reducing the costs, both in principles and money, of concessions, was rejected. This was 'a political mistake of the first magnitude' (Stewart, 1978, p. 183), but one which was understandable in the circumstances. A consideration of 'relativities' (another word of the 1970s) by a new Relativities Board was not pursued. Gormley's control of his executive was overrated. In particular it appears that the government had an informal agreement with the NUM President to give the miners extra pay for 'unsocial hours'. But Gormley, concerned with the tactics of appeasing his less moderate colleagues, wanted this conceded after negotiation, not offered straightaway. There is here evident a failure of two men, indeed of two worlds, to communicate.

(c) Heath refused at first to hold a general election on the issue 'who governs Britain?' It would be divisive, would not settle the miners' strike, nor do anything towards a general settlement which could not be done by a government with a working majority. Then Heath reversed his position and called a general election for the end of February. But he was now at a serious political disadvantage, apparently humiliated by the miners, moving unsteadily towards making concessions which he had struggled to avoid; in a new world energy condition which enhanced the miners' claim to reward; and now advocating policies which were the opposite of those he had fought for in 1970. The election proved his undoing. Harold Wilson returned as Prime Minister, though without a majority in Parliament. The miners were soon back at work – on their terms, not the government's.

Plainly it is not quite true that the miners brought all this about themselves. But the sequence of events shows that they played a substantial part in the fall both of the government and of incomes policy.

The Social Contract: Labour and the unions, 1972–9

In 1971 the unions, led by Jack Jones of TGWU, began to mend their relations with the Labour party after the breakdown of 1969. After all, each side needed the other. The Labour party agreed, in effect, to restore and strengthen the legal position of the unions, and to follow other policies of interest to them. It was accepted that incomes policy of any kind was finished. The unions promised nothing in return, so the 'Social Contract' was a contract by Labour to render services without payment. A Labour party–TUC Liaison Committee was set up in 1972 to develop the relationship, and was a significant element in government during most of Labour's subsequent period of office 1974–9.

Indeed the circumstances of the 1974 elections gave a special significance to the relations of trade unions with government, and the Labour party made much of its experience and advantages in this respect. The Labour government certainly delivered generously on its promises of legislation. The Industrial Relations Act was repealed, and the former privileged legal position of the unions restored. New legislation (the Trade Union and Labour Relation Act, 1975) was largely drafted by the TUC, and a union leader claimed they were 'consulted about the dots and commas'. An Employment Protection Act gave further privileges for unfair dismissal, the requirement of notice for substantial redundancies, and an arbitration service (ACAS) based on the promotion of good industrial relations through collective bargaining. The Act, according to a not unsympathetic commentator, made trade unionists 'a kind of privileged caste among the working population' (Eric Jacobs, *The Sunday Times*, 23 April 1978). Other economic policies included further nationalization and state intervention, higher taxation of the rich, and an attempt to extend the docks labour scheme to give unions control over non-unionized ports and container depots (the latter was defeated in the House of Commons).

These massive concessions to the trade unions did not secure any moderation in pay claims. In 1974–5 wage increases rose rapidly towards 30 per cent and government and TUC hastily established a new and draconian pay policy. It was in fact designed by Jack Jones, and provided for a flat rate increase and no increase for the better paid. It was thus of advantage to lower wage earners, including many of Jack Jones's members, who received under the pay policy the largest increases ever. The policy was voluntary not statutory, a distinction valued by the trade unions, but it was backed by the TUC and a Statutory Price Code. The policy was extended in 1976 (Phase II) as Britain headed towards the economic crisis which sent the government to the IMF for help. In Phase III the policy was much relaxed, and had virtually no backing from the TUC.

In the autumn of 1978 both the Labour Party Conference and the TUC rejected any kind of incomes policy. Nevertheless, Callaghan called bravely but unrealistically for a 5 per cent limit. The sanctions used against private firms who broke pay policy were rejected in the House of Commons in December (with the help of the Liberal party which had been the most consistent defender of incomes policies). There followed a series of strikes, notably among lorry drivers, hospital workers and other public employees, in which the least attractive features of trade union activity were demonstrated nightly on television – aggressive picketing, trade union officials giving or withholding permission for lorries to pick up supplies, or even for patients to be admitted to hospital; a strike of grave-diggers. In this 'winter of discontent' it was plain that much trade union activity injured other workers as much as employers.

The Social Contract had come to an end. In the election of May 1979 the Labour government fell. The trade unions, the most unpopular institution in Britain, had played no mean part in that downfall. In the eyes of the critics the Social Contract had been little more than the payment of protection money to wreckers – who had still persisted with their wrecking (see p. 230 above). A more generous view was that it was an experiment in the adjustment and legitimation of trade union power in the state, which was worth trying; but it was an experiment which had clearly failed.

The Conservative government, 1979–80

The Conservatives returned to power in 1979, pledged as in 1970 to restrict the power of the trade unions. Prolonged and damaging strikes in engineering and steel in the winter of 1979–80 reinforced their convictions. The steel strike in particular had emphasized again the power of picketing as a strike weapon, when extended to suppliers and customers of the strikers' employer.

The Employment Act 1980 dealt particularly with this kind of secondary action, with the closed shop and with the encouragement of ballots to replace the intimidation of the mass meeting. At the same time, the government ended the eligibility of strikers' dependents for social security benefits – a trivial but telling illustration of the government's unwillingness to recognize strikes as legitimate behaviour. Again, the trade unions protested, men of good will perceived difficulties in regulating behaviour by law; and right-wing Conservatives demanded stronger measures, the restriction of picketing and the abolition of the closed shop.

But the Conservatives had learned a lesson from the fiasco of 1971–2. There were limits to the effectiveness of legislation. Mrs Thatcher's government expected to influence union behaviour more fundamentally by their general economic policies which involved high unemployment and increased bankruptcies.

Assessment

(i) The relations of unions and government deteriorated in the 1960s and 1970s. In the 1950s governments left wage levels to the unions, and the unions, dominated by right-wing leaders, did not press their claims too hard. Crosland, writing in the mid-1950s, based his revision of socialism on the assumptions of continued growth and moderate inflation, of the order of 2–3 per cent. Governments, he thought, could rely on the good sense of the unions. In the 1970s inflation passed 20 per cent and the pound of 1977 was worth about one-quarter of its 1960 value. The decline of the economy and of governments seemed to be marked by major strikes – a rail strike in 1965, the seamen's strike in 1966, dock strikes in 1967 and so on. The 'union question' moved on to the agenda of British politics, though there was disagreement not only about the answer, but also about the question.

(ii) The trade unions had power – power to disrupt vital industries and services; power within the Labour party (see pp. 217–8 above); power as an acknowledged 'estate of the realm', influencing policy as well as working conditions. But that power was narrow in scope and limited in application. The economy was still largely in the hands of the government, and the great financial and industrial interests. Strikes were disruptive but not always successful, and financial loss for strikers was often involved. Moreover, trade union power was highly visible and strikes aroused hostility, unlike the quiet, effortless and discreet moves of the City, the banks, industry, the legal profession etc. Nor could the unions act with much unity or coherence. The TUC could do very little without the consent of its member unions, and they were unable to control the local activity of the shop stewards. Unfortunately for governments, this did not mean that the trade unions lacked power, only that the trade union national leaders lacked the power to be moderate.

(iii) The three views of the trade unions:

(a) The Conservative view. The trade unions pursued revolutionary aims, exploiting monopoly power to wreck industry, provoke unrest and destroy government. For the majority of trade union members this was not true. But it must be admitted that Communists, being assiduous attenders of meetings and branch workers, were over-represented among trade union officials. Good Communists had little reason to preserve the system they disliked so much. By the 1970s the aims of the Labour left were as radical as the Communists'. Some trade union leaders spoke in the 1970s in terms which suggested revolutionary or at least unconstitutional objectives.

(b) The Union view. The trade unions, while not seeking revolution, reasonably sold their labour as dearly as they could in a free market based on self interest. They aimed to maximize their wealth, just as share holders and managers did. This is a rationalization of the deeply embedded union tradition of sectional solidarity. By that tradition 'scab' and 'black leg' were terms of bitter condemnation, and crossing a picket line an act of betrayal; striking was legitimate and hence properly and simply the severest form of what came to be called in the 1970s, 'industrial action'.

(c) A middle view accepted the logic and economic and social values both of (a) and (b) but held that the old balance of power, which was once plainly tipped against the unions (as in 1926) had moved the other way; that the union emphasis on the pursuit of sectional self-interest by free collective bargaining was a Victorian anachronism in a properly planned and equitable society; and that the modernization of industrial relations required the intervention of government, which had a legitimate role in this field.

In this view there was a place for law in the regulation of industrial relations. Plainly law of some kind is a necessary means for the control of anti-social behaviour, but there are limits to its reach, and complexities and expense in its application. Curiously, while Conservatives opposed laws on race, Labour opposed laws on industrial relations, on the same grounds: the difficulty of regulating individual behaviour. In practice, the strength of the unions was largely based on law, and the Labour government had further strengthened the law in their favour. The collapse of the 1971 Act indicated the difficulties and limitations but not the impossibility of legislative regulation. (Schonfield's argument quoted above is relevant here.)

(iv) Governments reacted to the trade union problem with perplexed anxiety. The diaries and other accounts of the period display senior politicians and civil servants under stress, sometimes bad-tempered, vain, irrational (hence some of the tedium and triviality of the painstaking records of personal relationships). On this issue, and in particular on incomes policy, governments played 'Jekyll and Hyde', forced to do in office what they had foresworn in opposition. They also abandoned the consensual tendencies of government; both parties were impelled by frustration to the 'big bang' of confrontation.

Exercise 1

1.1 Is democracy necessarily hyper-inflationary?
1.2 Did the trade unions bring down three governments?
1.3 If trade unions must be subject to some form of social control and both consent and coercion have failed, what then?
1.4 Was anything gained by these years of conflict?

2 Immigration and race in post-war Britain

Britain had been little troubled by racial problems, apart from occasional, local outbursts of anti-semitism. Historically the British prejudice has been against Catholics, and this had almost disappeared except in Northern Ireland and parts of Scotland. In the post-war period race (meaning distinctions of colour, white or non-white) came to disturb the social harmony of some areas of England, and lurked as a divisive and potentially explosive issue beneath the surface of British politics. This was a quite unexpected development. The Royal Commission on Population of 1949 had declared, with what seemed later to be complacent superiority, that immigration 'could only be welcomed without reserve if the migrants were of good human stock and were not prevented by their religion or race from intermarrying with the host population and becoming merged in it' (quoted in Lapping, 1970, p. 110). In 1950 the Cabinet discussed West Indian immigration and hoped for dispersal and assimilation. In the mid 1950s the Conservatives were opposed to any kind of control over immigration, and for Labour it was a normal feature of British life. Thereafter political reactions changed sharply in response to a rising flow of immigrants.

Immigration to Britain was an aftermath of empire. Like the Australians and Canadians (though lacking their family connections) the people of the former colonies, in Africa, the West Indies, India and Pakistan (which became the 'New Commonwealth') looked to Britain as the 'mother country'. Some had been in Britain during the war. Travel lines were well organized. As the USA in the early 1950s put up barriers against immigration, so Britain beckoned. By the peculiar laws of British nationality all commonwealth citizens had a right to reside in Britain and to become British citizens.

The number of immigrants from the West Indies, India and Pakistan rose unsteadily through the late 1950s, 30–40,000 in 1956 and 1957, about 60,000 in 1960 and over 100,000 in 1961. By then alarm bells were ringing. There had been small scale 'race riots' in 1958, notably in Notting Hill in London which drew attention to the newcomers. In 1961 there were forty resolutions at the Conservative Party Conference, generally expressing misgivings and calling for control.

There followed a series of laws aimed to restrict immigration and to improve race relations. The first of these, the Commonwealth Immigration Act of 1962, introduced a voucher system for immigrants. The Labour party was divided on the issue. In particular, Gaitskell, the Labour leader, was passionately opposed to any legislation which even indirectly recognized colour as a basis for discrimination. The Act had the effect, unintended of course, of encouraging immigration in advance of expected further restriction. Thereafter both parties pursued regulation, but joined with measures to help areas with high immigration, and generally improve race relations and secure equality. Enoch Powell and some fringe groups on the right, notably the National Front, campaigned for stopping immigration completely and arranging repatriation.

The major parties, nationally and formally, avoided open disputation over immigration and race; Heath was soon to dissociate himself from Enoch Powell. But candidates in some constituencies chose to stand on the race issue, notably in Smethwick 1964, when a Labour front bench spokesman was defeated. The bi-partisan approach weakened in the 1970s as it became clear that coloured voters supported Labour (by eight or nine to one in 1979); and white voters near immigrant concentrations were strongly inclined to the Conservatives.

The first years of the 1964–70 Labour government under the Home Secretary Roy Jenkins marked a liberal period in race relations. The Race Relations Act of 1965 endeavoured to prohibit racial discrimination in public places, and made incitement to racial hatred a criminal offence. The Act established a Race Relations Board to engage in local conciliation. More important, these years saw the development of the race relations lobby. The lobby was typical of the small, mainly reformist, pressure groups of this period – there were others active in the fields of housing, poverty, health, education, roads. Such groups were usually small, middle-class, well-organized and well-connected, and able to draw on professional expertise – academics, lawyers, public relations consultants. By comparison, the London dockers, who marched to the Houses of Parliament in support of Enoch Powell in 1968, had little influence

> The small group – the race relations lobby – was like a stage army; popping up at the airport to fight a case; popping up on a specialist panel of the National Committee for Commonwealth Immigrants, to help draft an advisory document on policy; popping up in CARD (Campaign Against Racial Discrimination); popping up in a local liaison committee; popping up at the Labour Party Conference, in a magazine article, in a Society of Labour Lawyers' committee, in a delegation to a minister, in meetings at the Institute of Race Relations. The group centred on a couple of dozen people, mostly under thirty. They won older converts, they provided information and ideas for speeches delivered by more prominent men; their campaigns enjoyed a substantial public impact. But what turned a campaign of mostly white middle class intellectuals into a politically important pressure group was the support of Roy Jenkins. (Lapping, 1970, p. 117)

The race relations lobby drew some force from the evidence of racial tension in America in the 1960s.

This liberal period in the history of race relations ended suddenly in 1968. The Kenyan government began to drive out the Asians who had traditionally dominated commercial life there.They fled in growing numbers to Britain (where they were to employ their commercial skills to the benefit of themselves and the community). Fearful of a great rush of immigrants the new Home Secretary, James Callaghan, hastily added a new section to a Commonwealth Immigration Bill. In effect, 150,000 Kenyan Asians were made stateless, deprived of the protection of the British passports to which they were entitled. The Bill was passionately condemned by Iain Macleod who had been associated as a minister with the original promise of British citizenship to the Asians; and opposed in the House of Commons by thirty-five Labour and fifteen Conservative members, as well as the Liberals and Nationalists. But with the support of the bulk of the Labour and Conservative parties it passed within a few days. At the same time, and in furtherance of the more liberal approach, a Race Relations Act enlarged the Race Relations Board and established the Community Relations Commission. During the enactment of that Bill Enoch Powell made his notorious 'river of blood' speech, predicting racial violence. Heath promptly dismissed him from the Shadow Cabinet.

Immigration was further restricted by the Conservative Immigration Act of 1971, and by new regulations the following year which favoured immigrants with (at least) British-born grandparents. Historically this was a large step towards the definition and restriction of British citizenship, which had once been open theoretically to about a quarter of the world's population. In the 1970s immigration fell slightly (apart from a bulge of expelled Ugandan Asians in 1972) and mainly consisted of dependants of people already settled in Britain. The restrictive policy was by then established, though not without problems of implementation. A Race Relations Act of 1976 extended legal prohibitions on discrimination, and set up a single new Commission on Racial Equality.

Britain had not gone through the experience of substantial immigration unscathed by the tensions and passions which have accompanied similar movements and mixtures of population elsewhere. Three questions hovered uneasily over this theme in post-war British history.

(i) How many immigrants were there? and could the number be controlled? Enoch Powell claimed, correctly, that the government at first did not have accurate figures, and predicted less accurately that there would be 3–4 million people from the 'New Commonwealth' in Britain by 1985. In fact there were about 2 million in 1980, and the number by the year 2000 was thought likely to be 3.3 million (about half of these would be British-born). By the 1970s immigration was tightly controlled, and mainly limited to the dependants of people settled in Britain – a substantial but finite number. Illegal immigration certainly continued but did not add substantially to the overall figures. Birth rates among coloured people were declining. On the other hand, immigrants were concentrated in only a few areas, especially Inner London, the West Midlands and some cities in Yorkshire and Leicestershire. In some of these areas, coloured people made up over one fifth of the population, and concentration was even more intense in some neighbourhoods. When Mrs Thatcher said, during a television interview in 1978, that 'people felt rather swamped' by immigration, she exaggerated by her choice of words a sentiment which undoubtedly existed in these few areas. When about the same time the *Daily Mail* ran a feature headlined: 'One in five babies in Britain are coloured', it was simply wrong. The true figure was one in fourteen.

(ii) Did colour prejudice and discrimination exist? There was ample evidence of both from sample surveys and other investigations. The badge of colour added an edge and immediacy, and some irrational hostility, to the common reactions to strangers based on differences of social background, education, culture, speech. Evidence accumulated of discrimination in employment, and housing, and to a very limited extent in general social behaviour; but there was virtually no segregation as in South Africa or the old American South.

(iii) Could the coloured minorities ever fit in harmoniously in British society? On one side, tending to be Conservative in politics and working class, the answers inclined to be no, so let us keep down the numbers of immigrants. There was, after the 1960s, a shortage of jobs, houses, schools (and the working class mainly suffered from the fiercer competition for these goods). The distrust of strangers, so it was argued, was 'a fact of life', which could not be modified by legislation. Enoch Powell based stronger arguments on the idea of an historic national community. The violence Powell had predicted occurred for the most part, sporadically, but was widespread and ferocious in some areas, notably in London and Liverpool, in the summer of 1981. This confirmed the fears of the fearful.

The more liberally minded simply detested 'racism', and believed that immigration from the 'New Commonwealth' was no different from the long established and substantial influx from the 'Old (white) Commonwealth'. In any case, there were still more people leaving Britain than arriving. The new coloured immigrants were good workers and citizens. Historically, Britain had a debt to the peoples of the old empire. In the contemporary world, the development of good relations with 'the people of the Third World' was essential.

There was much more of a problem than the Liberals allowed for especially in a society in which economic competition between groups and individuals grew fiercer in the 1970s, and in which there was little experience of the toleration of diverse cultures. While West Indians could be assimilated culturally, they were in danger of being excluded economically. Asians often made their own way economically, but were culturally unassimilable. Enoch Powell, drawing an analogy with Northern Ireland spoke of the problems of 'a divided community', and of the way in which the divisions tend to be exploited:

The disruption of the homogeneous 'we' which forms the essential basis of parliamentary democracy and therefore of our liberties, is now approaching the point at which the political mechanics of a 'divided community' (if I may borrow terminology from jargon devised to describe the Ulster scene) take charge and begin to operate autonomously . . . . The two active ingredients are grievance and violence. Where a community is divided, grievance is for practical purposes inexhaustible. When violence is injected – and quite a little will suffice for a start – there begins an escalating competition to discover grievance and to remove it. The materials lie ready to hand in a multiplicity of agencies with a vested interest, more or less benevolent, in the process of discovering grievances and demanding their removal. The spiral is easily maintained in upward movement by the repetition and escalation of violence. At each stage alienation between the various elements of society is increased, and the constant disappointment that the imagined remedies yield a reverse result leads to growing bitterness and despair.

Hand in hand with the exploitation of grievance goes the equally counter-productive process which will no doubt, as usual, be called the 'search for a political solution'.

(From a speech by Enoch Powell, 19 April 1976, printed in Ritchie, 1978, p. 165).

Powell's fierce pessimism was here grounded not just on romantic British nationalism, but on a reasonable if not widely accepted interpretation of how modern political communities work. There were still grounds for other more optimistic views, looking to a pluralist, multi-racial society, drawing on the tolerance that surely exists in the British political tradition. But the optimists, who were the liberals, needed to understand and combat – not simply denounce – the analysis of the pessimists. Race was not the most substantial problem of post-war Britain, but it posed an acute moral and political challenge which was far from fully met by 1980.

Exercise 2

2.1 Was it wise of governments in the 1960s and 1970s to try to use the law in race matters?

2.2 Do the indigenous inhabitants of a territory have special rights in that territory? In particular, do they have the right to keep other people out?

3 Northern Ireland

Northern Ireland figured hardly at all in British history between 1945 and the late 1960s. Attlee's government formally recognized the independence of Eire in 1949, though legally it was not treated as a foreign country in certain respects (notably, Irish citizens could settle in Britain without restriction, and they could vote in British elections). At the same time, the Ireland Act affirmed Northern Ireland's position: '. . . in no event will Northern Ireland or any part there of cease to be part of His Majesty's dominions and of the United Kingdom without the consent of the Parliament of Northern Ireland' (Ireland Act, 1949).

A campaign of violence by the IRA (Irish Republican Army) in the late 1950s mainly directed against the Border petered out. The 'troubles' began again in 1968, British troops were committed in 1969, and Britain took over the province in 1972. Energetic efforts to establish a new form of government based on 'power-sharing' collapsed in 1974–6.

By the end of the period the troubles of Northern Ireland had cost 2000 lives, proportionately to population about six times the casualties of the USA in Vietnam. While it was easy for people in Britain to regard Northern Ireland as a far away country, these figures show that Britain had a civil war on its hands.

The origins of the civil war

To say that Ireland was a British colony (as many Irishmen do) is to read modern imperial relationships into the baronial politics of the Middle Ages. Still, Irish government, from its inception, had been government dominated by the English and Anglo-Irish, with Dublin subordinated to London. By contrast with Scotland (entering the Union partly on its own terms) and Wales (acquiesing in semi-integration) Ireland was a country apart and ruled by aliens, but never fully conquered and integrated. The colonial nature of its history was complicated and intensified by the 'plantation' of Ulster mainly by Scottish Presbyterians in the seventeenth century; and embittered by brutal and bloody military episodes (notably the 'massacres' of 1641 avenged by Cromwell in the 1650s; and the Battle of the Boyne 1690, which marks the beginning of the Protestant ascendancy) and economic exploitation, culminating in the great famine of the 1840s and mass emigration. Such a history was not easy to forget; and even when its consequences were not evident, the traditions and myths were potent, and perpetuated by the annual marches of the Orange Lodges and Republican Clubs.

In the twentieth century there were two major attempts to establish a form of independence for Ireland, by Home Rule as proposed first by Gladstone, or as a Republic (the aim of the rebels of 1916). Home Rule was frustrated by the irresolution of the British government, and the intransigent opposition of Ulster Protestants to separation from Britain and inclusion with their Irish Catholic neighbours. Lloyd George's settlement of the Irish civil war of 1920–2 established the six North-Eastern counties (a substantial part of Ulster) as Northern Ireland, a part of the United Kingdom but with its own Parliament and Prime Minister. The rest of Ireland took a status which soon amounted to independence. Thus, Lloyd George established the form of the modern problem of Ulster; it would be unfair to say that he created the problem. Protestants were in a majority of two to one in Ulster, and a minority of one to three in the whole of Ireland. Lloyd George's Ulster was about the largest area that could be dominated by the Protestants, and it included some areas where Catholics were in a majority.

Ulster's constitutional status was peculiar. It had its own Parliament at Stormont, but representation at Westminster, too. The House of Commons chose not to debate matters in Northern Ireland falling within the province's reserved powers; these included religious discrimination. Stormont accepted its legislative independence. In financial matters it was dependent on the UK government, and drew on UK resources to bolster its economy and provide welfare services of UK standard. (This was known as the 'step-by-step' formula). Altogether the constitutional settlement of 1920 seemed not without promise, but that promise was destroyed by the conflict inherent in the politics of the new Northern Ireland.

The elements of conflict were clearly present in Irish history and its simplified interpretations, in the religious differences of the peoples of Northern Ireland, and in the Republican Nationalism of the Catholics and of the Southern Irish. History was remembered because it seemed to be relevant to the present. These elements of conflict were intensified after 1920.

(i) Religion, specifically the extraordinary 'religiosity' of the province, with very high numbers attending church, almost all marriages in church, almost no 'intermarriage', and separate schools, housing and social life. But the quarrel was not about theology. Religion was the form in which the conflict went on; the substance of the conflict was religion, nationality, discrimination.

(ii) A government permanently dominated by Protestant Unionists, determined to preserve a state in which they were the majority, and using that power to promote their own interests. The Unionist majority at Stormont was secure (PR was dropped in 1929). In local government, the unfair drawing of boundaries ('gerrymandering') provided Protestant majorities even in places like Londonderry which was 60 per cent Catholic.

There was flagrant discrimination against Catholics in the allocation of housing and jobs, including the public service e.g. nine-tenths of the judges were Protestant; in Derry, in 1966, 80 per cent of the salaried employees of the City Council were Protestant, including all the heads of departments. It is fair to add that the ten or eleven local councils which were under permanent Catholic and Nationalist domination were equally sectarian and intolerant.

The Cameron Report (1969) on the disturbances commented on the defects of single-party government (and thus confirmed the virtues of the traditional two-party form of British government): '. . . in Northern Ireland the possibility of any organized Opposition becoming the alternative Government has not so far been one which was in any sense a reality. An Opposition which can never become a government tends to lose a sense of responsibility, and a party in power which can never (in foreseeable circumstances) be turned out tends to be complacent and insensitive to criticism or acceptance of any need for change or reform'. (Cameron Report, Disturbances in Northern Ireland, 1969, Belfast, HMSO. NI Cmnd 532)

(iii) Security forces, the RUC and the 'B specials', who acted as the guardians of the Protestant interest, using the Special Powers Act of 1922 (which would have been unconstitutional under a constitution including modern civil rights).

(iv) A Catholic population which held to its own Irish nationalism. That nationalist tradition included a long historical memory, an admiration for martyrdom and no strong distaste for blood; and the technical, financial, and organizational capability to engage in sophisticated forms of violence. Surveys showed that between a fifth and a half of the Catholic population preferred reunification with the South. Few loved Stormont. But between these two positions, power-sharing was welcomed and direct rule came to be accepted.

(v) The government in the South did little to conciliate the Protestant Unionists of the North. It established its formal independence, built into its constitution a special place for the Catholic church, yielded to Catholic influences in its family and medical policies, remained neutral in the war of 1939–45, and did less than it might have done to suppress the IRA and guard the border.

Civil war in Northern Ireland, 1969–72

The long-standing causes of conflict did not in fact give rise to serious violence until 1969. What then were the immediate causes of the outbreak of what amounted to civil war in 1969?

(i) A moderate government under Terence O'Neill, 1963–9, inclined to reform. (In 1965 O'Neill exchanged visits with the Irish Prime Minister.) Reform encouraged expectations on one side, insecurity on the other – better, almost, to have left bad alone.

(ii) A new civil rights movement opposed to discrimination in elections, local government and the security forces. The movement took some of its inspiration from civil rights struggles of the 1960s in the USA. One part of this was People's Democracy (PD) which drew on the radicalization of the young, and especially students, again in parallel with movements elsewhere in the Year of Revolutions, 1968. In that context the young PD leader, Bernadette Devlin, was characteristic of the movement and of the times: '. . . the first representative to be elected to Parliament, perhaps the first to the national legislature in any of the major democracies, of the younger generation's protest and revolt against conditions which they found materially adequate but spiritually impoverished' (Levin, 1970, p. 262).

Bernadette Devlin hoped to unite the working class across the boundaries of religion. This proved to be naive. The divide was never crossed, and the IRA was certainly active in both movements; but they also reflected the new politics arising from the emergence of a new educated middle class among the Catholics of Northern Ireland, articulate, radical, and resentful of what they saw as injustice – but mostly not seeking the reunification of Ireland. They were demonstrators and disrupters rather than gunmen. The civil rights movement was sparked by particular injustices, and in that sense its ultimate cause can be traced back to a case of housing discrimination in Dungannon.

(iii) Related to this, the emergence of the 'Provisional' wing of the IRA, a reborn revolutionary movement, impatient for action, and ready for violence.

(iv) Violence, once it began, was self-generating. It began in October 1968 with a CRA march on Londonderry, planned deliberately to pass through a Protestant part of the city, and along a traditional Protestant route, in defiance of a government ban. There followed a chaotic battle, in which the police used batons and eventually water cannons at close range, while the marchers threw placards, banners and stones. It was all shown on television. An incident which might have been contained burst into civil war. In January 1969 a march organized by PD was ambushed, and later the police, overreacting to provocation, mounted an assault on the Catholic area of Londonderry, the Bogside. In August, there were even bigger riots in Londonderry and Belfast. The weapons now included petrol bombs (made from milk bottles) and, for the police, CS gas. British troops moved in to restore order. But they faced not just a civil rights movement in conflict with the police, but an increasing civil war between four private armies, the Official and Provisional IRA, and the Protestant Ulster Defence Association and Ulster Volunteer Force.

Each side could with justice accuse the other of brutality, each had its martyrs, and each its complaint of prejudice justified. Altogether, it was a classic illustration of the law of history, equally applicable in the Middle East or in a picket line in the Midlands, that violence begets violence.

The fighting came to a peak in 1971–2, with a tragic climax in Londonderry in January 1972 – 'Bloody Sunday' – when thirteen civilians were shot dead during a massive civil rights march. Subsequently the British Embassy in Dublin was burned, Bernadette Devlin assaulted the Home Secretary on the floor of the House of Commons, six people were killed at Aldershot in England; and the Northern Ireland Home Affairs Minister just survived a machine gunning. The British government, appalled and desperate, suspended the Northern Ireland government, and instituted 'direct rule' from London. The immediate concern was to control security, a power Stormont would not voluntarily cede. The settlement of 1920 had finally collapsed.

Northern Ireland under direct rule

The British government spent four years trying to rebuild Northern Ireland in a form which would secure civil rights from Catholics. A referendum was held to establish whether the people of Northern Ireland wished to remain within the United Kingdom. Just over 57 per cent of the total electorate said yes; but the Catholic parties all boycotted the poll. A new constitution (1973) established an assembly elected by a form of proportional representation, led by a power-sharing executive, i.e. based on the representation of all sections of the Assembly. In the autumn a conference on the future of Northern Ireland between the parties accepted a constitutional settlement on these lines. At the Sunningdale talks (December 1973) the Dublin government accepted that change in the status of Northern Ireland depended on the support of a majority in the province, and there was further agreement on the setting up of a Council of Ireland (as originally envisaged in Lloyd George's settlement). On the first day of 1974 power was returned to a Northern Ireland government, the power-sharing executive.

However, these arrangements did not fit the harsh facts of Irish history. The unfortunately timed general election of February 1974 gave an opportunity for popular opinion to show itself. Eleven of the twelve Northern Ireland seats were taken by Loyalists (a harder line of Unionists), all opposed to the Sunningdale agreement. The Assembly survived until May 1974. When it ratified the Sunningdale agreement, a massive strike was organized by the Ulster Workers' Council; the Northern Ireland government collapsed and direct rule was resumed.

The new Labour government, undeterred, set up a Constitutional Convention which met in 1975. It was dominated by the Loyalists and refused to accept power-sharing in a future Cabinet. The Convention was finally dissolved in March 1976.

During these attempts at constitutional reconstruction, violence had continued at a level a little lower than the 1972 peak. British opinion was particularly horrified by bombings in two public houses in the centre of Birmingham in November 1974 which killed 21 people and injured 161. This was carried out by Irishmen who had been living peacefully in the area for years.

There followed a period of comparative peace, based on direct rule, but with moves towards the restoration of a form of government for Northern Ireland; reassurance to both sides in the North, and some ambivalence to the government of Eire. The level of violence, as measured by deaths, fell by the end of the decade to about 100 deaths each year. But the peace was, to say the least, uneasy, and, just before the election of 1979, the Conservative spokesman on Northern Ireland, Airey Neave, MP, was murdered by a sophisticated explosive device, as he drove out of the Houses of Parliament.

Analysis

(i) The history of Northern Ireland from 1968 demonstrated the difficulties of opposing force by force within a policy aimed at pacification rather than conquest and unconditional surrender. A dozen colonial wars around the world had shown too that it is not possible to fight a civilised and moderate war against armed irregular forces. The 'guerilla' or 'terrorist' is unlikely to lose a war fought on his own terms.

In Northern Ireland the security operation was particularly difficult. The British Army inherited the illegitimacy of the Northern Ireland security forces. Attempts to tighten security, especially by internment, aroused hostility and were not effective. Imprisonment for crimes claimed to be political was resented and exploited (as in the so-called 'dirty protest' and in hunger strikes). Detention without trial was not used after 1975.

(ii) Unionist politicians were squeezed between their loyalist right and the pressures for reform (including the pressures of the British government). Prime Ministers rose and fell and parties fragmented. One new leader, the Rev. Ian Paisley, emerged, as a pillar of Protestant Unionism; and Enoch Powell, one of the few people to love the United Kingdom, won a seat in Ulster.

(iii) British governments stayed out of Ulster as long as they could. Both major parties regarded the province as an anomaly significant mainly as a source of up to twelve safe Conservative seats. As late as 1968 there was no senior civil servant with a full-time responsibility for Northern Ireland.

But the events of the late 1960s forced them to intervene to restore some civility to the security operations. Three major inquiries revealed the grounds for concern. The British government had to endure the obloquy, the loss of international standing (especially in America, with its Irish population), the high cost of security forces, the overall weakening of the British forces and the burden in difficult times, notably 1969 and 1972–4, of an insoluble problem, about which 'something had to be done'. British governments might reasonably think that they had quite enough 'ungovernability' to cope with at home.

(iv) The Dublin government, pressed from all sides, shifted uneasily, but was less vigorous and co-operative in pursuing IRA murderers than the British and Northern Ireland governments and impartial observers (if there are such) would have wished.

(v) The IRA was remarkably successful in sustaining a campaign which brought down the Ulster government, and opened the whole question of its future status. The IRA's success depended partly on the easy advantages of guerila terrorism and hostile reactions to the operations of the security forces. But their success also lay in their resources of sympathy and support. The Catholic people of Northern Ireland felt threatened by the Unionists. The British Army was seen as the prop of the Union; it was not intended so, but it was after all there to sustain the civil power. Like many subversive movements the IRA had been skilful in provoking a response which they could denounce to sympathizers as tyrannical.

(vi) The fundamental nature of the conflict was made clear. It was a communal conflict based on religion, two nationalities, rival claims to the government of the territory, and differing interpretations of history; a recent history of discrimination and abuse, and a tradition of violence and bloodshed. The gunman-martyr faced the Protestant bigot. This was a deadly version of the irrational loyalties of the sports field.

(vii) The Ulster problem had no solution. In that it was not so different from many other political problems. Coercion failed. Compromise was not acceptable. 'Government without consensus' (i.e. agreement on that particular form of government) was impossible. Or was it just difficult? In Northern Ireland the optimists and the pessimists have often been wrong. A significant feature of Northern Ireland history over the last sixty years is the development of 'apartness'. It is a kind of small state, with more autonomy and integrity than its constitution or Irish history should allow it. It may turn out to be one more demonstration of the looser definition of the modern state, in which boundaries are obscure, sovereign power unattainable, and interdependence the characteristic relationship. Thus, paradoxically, the future of Ulster Unionism may lie in the loosening of Ulster's links with the Union.

Exercise 3

3.1 It is sometimes argued that economic conflicts are much easier to resolve than conflicts related to religion and ethnicity. Does the history of Northern Ireland show this to be true? and why?

3.2 Why have the conflicts in Northern Ireland erupted into sustained armed violence?

3.3 How would you have solved the problems of Northern Ireland?

3.4 Should Britain 'get out' of Northern Ireland, withdrawing troops and handing over government to the people?

4 Nationalization

In 1945 for the first time a Labour government commanded a clear majority in Parliament (or, more accurately, in the House of Commons). It operated, as we have seen, in an atmosphere of acute austerity and economic constraint, both internally and externally. None the less, despite an unavoidable – and sometimes desperate – absorption in short-run

issues the government embarked upon a wide-ranging legislative programme which in at least two respects had major long-term repercussions
on the society and economy of Britain. The first can be summarized by
saying that it created what came to be called the Welfare State – especially
by the provision of a comprehensive system of national insurance (offering
on a near-universal basis social security benefits covering maternity,
sickness, unemployment, retirement and death), and by the setting up of a
national health service. Although there were changes, some of them
significant, the essential framework and philosophy was not seriously and
effectively challenged until the end of the 1970s.

The second way in which the 1945 government effected a major
institutional and structural change was by significantly extending the public
ownership of industry through a series of nationalization Acts. Unlike the
welfare provisions, the whole principle of public ownership was persistently opposed although, paradoxically, the changes actually made were
perhaps less substantial than those made to the welfare legislation. Once
again, however, the late 1970s produced a more fundamental challenge to
the existing pattern of public ownership.

The pattern had essentially been established between 1945 and 1951.
This is not to say that public ownership was a novelty in 1945. The BBC,
the Central Electricity Board, the London Passenger Transport Board and
the British Overseas Airways Corporation were all examples of pre-war
creations, whilst the Post Office had long been operated as a government
department. But it was only as a result of the series of Nationalization Acts
introduced by the Labour government of 1945–50 that a significant sector
of industry passed into public ownership. Coal, gas, electricity, the
railways, long-distance road haulage, much of the steel industry and – as
the only excursion into finance and commerce – the Bank of England were
all nationalized. Despite much public sound and fury, the nationalized
sector was relatively little changed – either by addition or subtraction – in
the three decades after 1950. In 1953 the Conservatives gave some
substance to their rhetoric by Acts aiming to return to the private sector
the road haulage industry, and those steel companies which had been taken
into public ownership under the 1949 Act. In each case the private sector
was less enthusiastic to embrace this opportunity than had been expected.
In 1956 the unsold portions of road transport were converted into British
Road Services and remained in public ownership, and when the Labour
government renationalized the largest of the steel companies in 1967 there
was still one major company, Richard Thomas and Baldwins, which was
already in public ownership since it had still not been sold off under the
1953 Act. On the other hand, Labour governments from 1964 onward have
not extended the range of nationalization. In part this reflects the deep
doubts within the party about the desirability – electorally if not in
principle – of nationalization. As a result the most significant post-1950

extensions of public ownership came as pragmatic (and, in intention, temporary) government responses to major individual private firms which were in difficulty. The most prominent of these 'lame ducks' to pass into effective public ownership were Rolls-Royce, British Leyland and Alfred Herbert, the machine tool producers. This form of 'nationalization' was as likely to be effected by a Conservative as by a Labour government.

At all events, a substantial proportion of British industry has been publicly owned throughout almost the entire post-war period. It needs to be noted, however, that this was not a process confined to Britain. Indeed, public ownership was more widespread in some countries, such as France which also extended the principle to embrace several of the basic financial institutions. In Britain the process was mostly confined to public utility industries, like gas and electricity, and to some of the heavy, staple industries like coal and steel. This seems to suggest that the motivation governing the nationalization programme was largely influenced by the desire for the state to control the 'commanding heights' of the economy as a way of ensuring that central planning for the economy as a whole was made effective. Such a conclusion, suggesting as it does a commitment to positive socialist principles by the 1945 Labour government, is difficult to sustain. It is belied by at least three broad considerations. First there was no clear, coherent and consistent exposition by the government of the reasons for public ownership. Second, whatever may have been true of intentions there was no serious actual attempt to plan the economy. Thirdly – and most decisively – the method of organization that was adopted for the nationalized industries was one which would have positively frustrated any such attempts at integrated planning. The device used was that of the public corporation. Compared to state departments this meant that the management of each nationalized industry had a high degree of autonomy: the governing boards were meant to have considerable freedom from Treasury control over finance; they did not have to follow civil service procedures over such matters as staffing; and, although ultimately controlled by a minister, they were intended to exercise their own day-to-day management. It was a system with many virtues, it may even have been the best possible choice: but it was clearly not the system that would have been chosen if the overriding aim was to use the core of nationalized industries as a control centre from which to enforce direct planning on the economy at large.

The experience of post-war years has borne this out. Governments have used the control arising from nationalization of important sectors of industry, but the use has not been for any coherent economic planning. It has simply been found useful from time to time to restrain price rises in nationalized industries as a way of limiting price increases or wage demands in the private sector. Again the level of investment in nationalized industries has been manipulated as an additional means of managing the economy (see chapter 2). Such *ad hoc* interventions undoubtedly contributed to the difficulties of managing the nationalized industries and added to their financial losses (or reduced their profits).

For example, during the first decade under nationalization coal was desperately short. In these circumstances the NCB might have made large financial surpluses if the only aim had been to maximise profits. In fact, successive governments exerted pressure to constrain the price of coal (both to keep down the general level of industrial costs – coal was a major raw material; and to secure political popularity – coal was the major source of domestic heating). Thus the NCB had no accumulation of financial fat to act as a cushion when the overall demand situation changed, as it did dramatically after 1957. Up to 1958 domestic coal was still rationed, at the end of 1959 there were 36 million tons of unsold coal. Up to 1957 the coal industry was being urged 'in the national interest' to maximize output almost at any cost; in the 1960s, on the expectation that cheap oil would, like the poor, always be with us, successive governments were insisting 'in the national interest' that the coal industry should be rapidly reduced. It may be that one of the major successes of nationaliza-tion was the part it contributed to the relatively smooth way in which the coal industry was run down during this period (from 710,000 miners on the colliery books in 1957 to 287,000 in 1970) – in contrast to the bitterness which accompanied the proportionately less severe inter-war decline (from 1,248,000 in 1920 to 791,000 in 1938).

These aspects from the experience of one nationalized industry have been mentioned as background for the establishment of one basic point: the important debates about nationalization in this period have been mainly concerned with technical issues – how should existing nationalized industries be conducted? – rather than with the political issues – should more industries be nationalized (or denationalized)? The latter question does still act as a political touchstone, for Labour activists if not voters are favourably disposed towards public ownership whilst Conservatives are opposed. But since this apparently fundamental difference has – since 1950 – had so little direct effect on the size of the nationalized sector, much of the debate has been ritualistic.

The essential difference between the two major parties in overall attitudes is illustrated by the statements made on industrial policy in their early post-war manifestos. It is indicative of the less central position given to the role of nationalization that it would be more difficult to provide extended illustrations from the manifestos for later elections.

(a) From Labour party manifesto, general election 1945

Each industry must have applied to it the test of national service. If it serves the nation, well and good; if it is inefficient and falls down on its job, the nation must see that things are put right.

These propositions seems indisputable, but for years before the war anti-Labour Governments set them aside, so that British industry over a large field fell into a state of depression, muddle and decay. Millions of working and middle-class people went through the horrors of unemployment and insecurity. It is not enough to sympathise with these victims: we must develop an acute feeling of national shame—and act.

The Labour Party is a Socialist Party, and proud of it . . .

. . . But Socialism cannot come overnight, as the product of a week-end revolution. The members of the Labour Party, like the British people, are practical-minded men and women.

There are basic industries ripe and over-ripe for public ownership and management in the direct service of the nation. There are many smaller businesses rendering good service which can be left to go on with their useful work.

There are big industries not yet ripe for public ownership which must nevertheless be required by constructive supervision to further the nation's needs and not to prejudice national interests by restrictive anti-social monopoly or cartel agreements – caring for their own capital structures and profits at the cost of a lower standard of living for all.

In the light of these considerations, the Labour Party submits to the nation the following industrial programme:

1. Public ownership of the fuel and power industries. For a quarter of a century the coal industry, producing Britain's most precious national raw material, has been floundering chaotically under the ownership of many hundreds of independent companies. Amalgamation under public ownership will bring great economies in operation and make it possible to modernise production methods and to raise safety standards in every colliery in the country. Public ownership of gas and electricity undertakings will lower charges, prevent competitive waste, open the way for co-ordinated research and development, and lead to the reforming of uneconomic areas of distribution. Other industries will benefit.

2. Public ownership of inland transport – Co-ordination of transport services, by rail, road, air and canal cannot be achieved without unification. And unification without public ownership means a steady struggle with sectional interests or the enthronement of a private monopoly, which would be a menace to the rest of industry.

3. Public ownership of iron and steel – Private monopoly has maintained high prices and kept inefficient high-cost plants in existence. Only if public ownership replaces private monopoly can the industry become efficient.

These socialised industries, taken over on a basis of fair compensation, to be conducted efficiently in the interests of consumers, coupled with proper status and conditions for the workers employed in them.

(b) From Conservative party manifesto, general election 1950

The Conservative party will encourage in industry the highest level of efficient production and the most effective partnership between owners, executives and operatives. Today all forms of production and distribution are hampered in a Socialist atmosphere which denies enterprise its reward while making life too easy for the laggards. Monopoly and bureaucracy should give place to competition and enterprise. All enterprises, large and small, should have a fair field . . .

. . . Britain already knows to her cost that the state monopolies created by nationalisation are rigid, awkward, wasteful and inefficient. Large losses have been made. Monopoly powers are being used to force higher prices on the consumers, who have no effective redress. Responsible initiative is crushed by centralised authority. Frustration and cynicism prevail among the staffs. The power of trade unions to protect their members is being undermined and the freedom of choice of consumer and worker alike is being narrowed. If nationalisation is extended, the creeping paralysis of state monopoly will spread over ever wider sections of industry until the Socialists have carried out their declared aim to nationalise all the means of production, distribution and exchange.

Nationalisation

We shall bring Nationalisation to a full stop here and now. Thereby we shall save all those industries, such as cement, sugar, meat distribution, chemicals, water and insurance which are now under threat by the Socialists.

We shall repeal the Iron and Steel Act before it can come into force. Steel will remain under free enterprise, but its policy on prices and development will be supervised as in recent years by a Board representative of Government, management, labour and consumers.

The political rhetoric on nationalization was, then, colourful but ineffective. At a more mundane level, however, all governments found it increasingly difficult to evade such problems as determining what considerations should govern the pricing policies of nationalized industries and what the level of investment should be in such industries. The asking of such questions raises complicated and difficult aspects of economic theory. But although these cannot be profitably pursued here it would be equally wrong to evade their existence and significance. The hope is that the essential nature and flavour of the issues can be indicated by a brief suggestion of the progression of thought in this area. An attempt is made to convey this by giving extracts from two White Papers on the economic and financial obligations of nationalized industries. The first of these reports was issued by a Conservative government in 1961; the second in 1967 by a Labour government.

(a) From the Financial and Economic Obligations of Nationalized Industries, Cmnd 1337, April 1961

[The 1961 White Paper indicates that the financial criteria included in the original nationalization Acts were generally vague.]

5. The undertakings have, in common parlance, been expected to pay their way and most of the nationalizing statutes contain a requirement to this effect. Their statutory obligations prescribe that their revenues should, on an average of good and bad years (or similar phrase) be not less than sufficient to meet all items properly chargeable to revenue, including interest, depreciation, the redemption of capital and the provision of reserves. Thus the Acts prescribe a minimum performance and not a maximum. Moreover, this performance is defined in terms of a surplus or deficit, which differs from the ordinary definition of profit or loss inasmuch as provision is required to be made from revenue for all the items mentioned above before a surplus in the statutory sense arises. The undertakings were thus expected to make some profits in the ordinary sense of that term in order to accumulate reserves from them . . .

17. In the government's view there would be no advantage in altering the basic financial and economic principles which the nationalized undertakings are by their statutes required to observe. If, however, these principles are to provide a satisfactory basis for their operation in the public interest they need to be interpreted more precisely in the form of financial objectives for the nationalized undertakings generally . . . [The document then sets out more detail on these objectives. On the revenue side the main point, apart from definitions, is that surpluses should be at least enough to cover deficits over a five-year period. On the capital side the government would, after annual discussions, set out investment plans for each industry for five years ahead and would be informed of any proposals for investment in projects expected to yield 'a relatively low return.']

25. These requirements flow from the government's responsibiity to keep public sector investment generally within the nation's resources, as well as from the government's role as provider of public capital. It would be the government's task to satisfy themselves that the procedure within each organization for scrutinizing and approving capital expenditure was effective . . .

29. A clear definition of each Board's financial obligations inevitably raises the question of the extent to which the Boards should have freedom in their pricing policies. Although the government possesses no formal power to fix prices in the nationalized industries, nationalized undertakings have, in fixing their prices, given great weight to considerations of the national interest brought to their attention . . .

31. While recognizing the case for greater freedom and flexibility in the pricing policies of nationalized industries the government must interest themselves in the prices of these goods and services which are basic to the life of the community and some of which contain a monopolistic element . . .

(b) From Nationalized Industries: a review of economic and financial objectives, Cmnd 3437, Nov. 1967

[The preamble to the White Paper of 1967 set out the original position.]

2. The statutory duties of nationalized industries are set out in the nationalization Acts. Broadly they are to meet the demand for their products and services in the most efficient way and to conduct their finances so that over time they at least break even, after making a contribution to reserves. The statutes however gave no guidance on what was meant by efficiency in economic terms, and prescribed only a minimum standard of financial performance . . .

[It then summarized the 1961 attempt to make these provisions more specific and indicated why it was necessary to carry this process further.]

5. The government's objectives for industry are to increase the productivity of both labour and capital employed; to raise the rate of new capital formation; to ensure that new equipment is as technologically advanced as possible and is effectively deployed; to increase the profitability of new investment; and to obtain the maximum return in terms of the production of goods and services. The nationalized industries have a vital role to play in the attainment of these objectives as well as in the development of the government's wider social and economic policies. . . the efficiency with which so large a sector operates will have a significant impact on the evolution and rate of growth of the whole economy. In their case the objectives outlined above cannot be achieved merely by maximizing the financial returns of each industry: significant costs and benefits can occur which are outside the financial concern of the industry and it is the special responsibility of the government to ensure that these 'social' factors are reflected in the industries' planning . . .

7. Investment projects must normally show a satisfactory return in commercial terms unless they are justifiable on wider criteria involving an assessment of the social costs and benefits involved, or are provided to meet a statutory obligation. Subject to these considerations, the government's policy is to treat the industries as commercial bodies and the underlying concept behind the control of nationalized industries' investment by rate of return is that the most efficient distribution of goods and services in the economy as a whole can be secured only if investments are made where the return to the economy is greatest . . .

10. The government have decided that 8 per cent is a reasonable figure to use for this purpose in present circumstances . . .

13. The use of this test rate of discount in investment calculations does not of course imply that nationalized industries should never invest new capital in the supply of goods and services which do not show a return of at least 8 per cent in real terms on the capital employed. There are circumstances in which it is desirable for social or wider economic reasons to provide such services; and it is desirable in a few cases to provide services at some direct financial loss. But all projects need to be assessed in a systematic way allowing for uncertainties in the forecasts of demand and of technological developments so that their direct return can be estimated before any other considerations are taken into account.

14. The economic value of investments cannot always be measured by reference to the financial return to the industry concerned. Many investments also produce social costs and benefits which can in principle be valued in financial terms and which, when taken into account, will provide a good economic justification for them. Examples of these are extensions to the underground network in London which take account of congestion costs. Equally so there are cases like the railway branch lines where the government may take social and regional considerations into account . . .

17. The use of correct methods of investment appraisal will only be effective if the nationalized industries also adopt, within the context of national prices and incomes policy, pricing policies relevant to their economic circumstances . . .

The government's policy here starts from the principle that national-ized industries' revenues should normally cover their accounting costs in full – including the service of capital and appropriate provision for its replacement . . .

18. . . . The aim of pricing policy should be that the consumer should pay the true costs of providing the goods and services he consumes, in every case where these can be sensibly indentified. There are of course exceptions to the general rule. . . .

24. . . . In so far as the industries observe the principles set out in the White Paper, the government does not intend to interfere in the day-to-day responsibility of management to propose increases, and will endeavour to leave management the maximum discretion in adjusting their price structure to meet competition and to take advan-tage of commercial opportunities . . .

27. To make the best use of resources, it is not enough merely to ensure that prices properly reflect costs, important though this is. Continuous and critical attention has to be paid to costs themselves in order that an industry must play a full part in bringing about a more efficient and

faster-growing economy. It would obviously be wrong if any industry, public or private, were allowed to exploit a degree of monopoly power so as to attain satisfactory financial results by covering unnecessarily high costs by equally unnecessary price increases . . .

30. . . . All this requires considerable flexibility of approach by both sides of industry to manning questions, and there can be no room for inefficient, out-dated or restrictive practices, particularly in the operation of costly and technologically advanced equipment . . .

37. . . . Nationalized industries, which command much greater resources than all but the very largest private undertakings, should expect to be numbered among the most progressive and efficient concerns in the country. Where there are significant social or wider economic costs and benefits which ought to be taken into account in their investment and pricing these will be reflected in the government's policy for the industry: and if this means that the industry has to act against its own commercial interests, the government will accept responsibility. . .

Documents like these indicate the elaborate attempts that have been made to lay down guidelines for the operation of nationalized industries. The reasoned clauses, however, cannot disguise the persistent tension between the pursuit of profit and the furtherance of social goals. Still, reasonable resolutions of this tension would be possible: but it is unlikely that governments could be, or even should be, induced to play the game according to the rules even though those rules have been devised and laid down by successive governments. There are always overriding reasons which tempt governments to use their control over nationalized industries to further policies that seem more immediately pressing. Thus in the decade before 1975, despite the guidelines, governments of different kinds made eight separate attempts to restrain gas and electricity prices, six to hold down rail prices and five attempts to curtail increases in steel and postal charges which the managements considered necessary. Even a government, like the Thatcher administration, which was supposed to be heavily committed to non-interference sharply curtailed long-run investment – even where profitability could be demonstrated – in order to satisfy the government's short-term concern with the level of public borrowing.

   For much of the post-war period, but especially in the 1960s, it was these technical aspects of nationalization which were most prominent; and the concern with technicalities tended, as it often does, to neutralize the philosophical differences between the parties and led to a more or less bi-partisan party approach to the problems of nationalization. Ideology seemed to slip into the background. It must not be forgotten, however, the concept of public ownership does raise fundamental ideological issues. On the one hand, there is the belief that it is essential to resist any tendency towards public ownership in order to maintain the rights of the individual against those of the state. It is asserted that the private owernship of the means of production keeps the process of decision-making widely scattered in society. Private wealth is then seen as being essential to maintain choice, independence and freedom. Of course, as critics of private ownership point out, only a relatively small group in society directly enjoys these advantages of choice and freedom. Indeed, and this is the other broad ideological position, public ownership is seen by many as necessary and desirable because private ownership gives to these small groups not merely wealth but power. Public ownership is thus mainly seen as a means of effecting a transfer of such power to the representatives of the people. In this broader context issues such as efficiency are, whatever their passing prominence, of secondary significance.

Apart from ideological considerations, the issue of the public ownership of, and public involvement in, industry is much wider than the particular problem of nationalization. Governments, Conservative as well as Labour, have been involved in a number of other expedients. The ill-fated flirtations with planning in the 1960s would be an obvious example. In addition, individual firms which have fallen into financial difficulties have occasionally been assisted or taken over by the government in the belief that such firms were, in one way or another, too important to the economy to be allowed to fail. British Leyland and Rolls-Royce would be the outstanding examples of such so-called 'lame duck' enterprises. More generally throughout the post-war period, industry had been offered a shifting variety of investment incentives (cash grants, favourable loans, tax concessions, etc.) mostly to induce investment in specific regions or industries which governments have wished to foster. Moreover, governments – particularly Labour governments – have attempted to facilitate the 'rationalization' of particular sectors of industry. The main agency was the Industrial Reorganization Corporation (IRC) set up in 1966 as part of Labour's programme to promote a technological revolution. Its method was mostly that of encouraging mergers between firms in sectors where it was considered that a large size of unit was desirable and rational: for example, British Leyland and the vastly-enlarged General Electric Company (swallowing Associated Electrical Industries and English Electric). The IRC was abandoned by the 1970 Conservative government which soon found, in its dealings with Upper Clyde Shipbuilders and Rolls-Royce, that it was easier to jettison the machinery than the policies. Much the same could be said about the next Labour government's National Enterprise Board, designed in part to channel state funds into manufacturing industry. In this case the Thatcher government found it difficult instantly to discard NEB's functions.

The catalogue is far from complete. The point is not to offer a comprehensive coverage but to emphasize that the issue of public ownership and control is much broader than that of nationalization. Indeed, the debate has to a considerable degree passed by nationalization as the central feature. The questions, however, are still of fundamental importance: how far should the level and pattern of industrial activity be left simply to the market? to what degree, and in what ways, is government intervention necessary? feasible? desirable?

Exercise 4

4.1 Why have successive governments been so concerned about the pricing and investment policies of nationalized industries?

4.2 What are the main differences between the 1961 and the 1967 guidelines?

4.3 Should the rate of profit be the only guide for nationalized industries? Suggest other factors which should be taken into consideration.

4.4 Why is nationalization frequently seen as a touchstone of the differences between the main political parties?

5 Incomes policy

An incomes policy is an attempt by the government to influence or control the rate at which incomes change in the economy. In practice this has mostly meant policies to restrain wages and salaries. Various governments have also incorporated controls for interests, dividends and rents. It is, however, at once more difficult to control these and less important that they should be controlled (they account for only some 10 per cent of personal incomes). Thus, despite the application of much political cosmetic, force remains in the contention that incomes policy is really only a euphemism for wages policy.

Attempts to operate incomes policies have been a recurring feature of post-war experience. This is no accident. These recurrences reflect the fact that incomes policies have been seen as offering answers to some fundamental economic problems, problems which have been a persistent feature of the British economy since 1945. There have, however, also been recurrent periods in which there has been no explicit incomes policy in operation. These gaps, too, reflect some basic realities: mostly the very formidable practical difficulties in operating any policy of wage restraint over any substantial period of time and the considerable body of opinion that any incomes policy is both undesirable and unnecessary.

What problems have incomes policies been aimed at?

It could be said that incomes policy has evolved from attempts to deal with three basic interrelated issues. The first is the tendency for the general level of wages to grow more rapidly than the general level of productivity. This problem was recognized in the first report of the Council on Prices. Productivity and Incomes in 1958 which roundly asserted that:

> It is clear that the relationship between the rise in real production and the rise in money incomes – wages, salaries and profit income – is central to the problem of rising prices. If these incomes had risen in line with the rise in the nation's production, instead of very much faster, the rise in prices would have been a minor one – limited to the rise brought about by higher import prices.

From the standpoint of the national economy, the central problem of wage settlement is to keep wages and productivity in step (or, more realistically, to prevent them from drifting too far apart). When total wages rise faster than productivity, wage earners (in their capacity as consumers) find that their money to spend has risen more rapidly than the amount of goods for them to buy. Prices will tend to rise, and to curb this inflationary pressure governments look for means to keep down the pace of wage increases. An incomes policy seems a suitable lid to put on this pot.

The second problem is related to the first because it offers an explanation of why the tendency for wages to outstrip productivity emerged only from 1945 onwards. This source of persistent inflationary pressure simply did not exist before the Second World War. The change was brought about by the government commitment to a policy of full employment; or rather, by the way in which a succession of governments for a whole generation after 1945 accepted and implemented this commitment. Only in the mid-1970s did the concern with inflation over-topple that of unemployment. The effect of the successful pursuit of full employment was simple and dramatic; it vastly increased the bargaining power of labour. The lower the level of unemployment, other things being equal, the greater will be the shortage of labour. In such circumstances the resistance of employers to demands for wage increases is weakened. Employers can in any case easily pass on the higher wage costs because high incomes bring a buoyant level of consumer demand. All this applies independently of the ways in which labour is organized. In addition, however, full employment also strengthens the unions. Because of the general atmosphere of labour shortage unions are more successful in bargaining for wage increases for their members; and because they are more successful they attract more members.

Closely linked to this is the third problem, the problem of the trade balance. Rising incomes and costs react on the trade balance in two ways. Part of the extra income will be spent, not on British goods, but on imports from abroad. At the same time higher costs in British industry mean that British exports are less attractive to foreign buyers. There may be a tendency, then, for a relative rise in imports and a relative fall in exports producing an unfavourable trade balance. It has certainly been the case that the periods in which the most stringent use has been made of incomes policy have generally been periods of acute balance of payments crisis. In order to emphasize the general drift of the argument a great deal has been left out of this exposition. Even so one obvious qualification must be made and met. The process implies that British wages, costs and prices rise faster than those of her main foreign competitors. This does seem to have happened and amongst the many explanations is the fact that trade unions in Britain have generally been stronger than in most other countries.

A great deal of theoretical thin ice has been skated over in the above account. In particular some monetarists would claim that the problems could not have emerged in the way depicted if the money supply had not been allowed to increase to accommodate the higher wages and so on. We can put this aside for the moment. There is no doubt that throughout much of the post-war period many in government and elsewhere have perceived the problems of the economy in something like the way suggested. There is no doubt, too, that many perceived that a solution (or a partial solution) to these problems could be obtained by an incomes policy to restrain the level of wage increases.

Problems of applying incomes policies

A government decision to use incomes policy is by no means the end of the matter. In many respects it is simply the beginning since the application of such policies is beset with difficulties.

(i) What kind of policy?

The kind of policy has to be determined. Thus, for example, incomes policies are either *statutory* or *voluntary*. The former are laid down by Parliament and have behind them the force of law: the latter rely for their implementation upon the voluntary acceptance by the interested parties. The difference, however, is not as clear-cut as such bare statements might suggest. It is not at all clear how a government could impose even statutory limits if large bodies of wage earners and employers chose to ignore them. Pressure of public opinion might be a stronger deterrent against such action than the direct threat of the law. A substantial measure of general acceptance is thus a prerequisite for both approaches. It is partly for this reason that governments have frequently attempted to link an incomes policy with some quasi-independent body in the hope of giving an additional degree of impartial authority to the policy. This is well-illustrated in a comment on the setting up of the first Council on Prices, Productivity and Incomes in 1958 (the 'Three Wise Men') where

. . . the Government was no doubt moved by the hope that these people would achieve a quasi-judical standing and that their recommendations on economic policy, even if unpopular, would have a compelling moral force, like those of judges handing down the law. This idea of bringing in a species of economic judiciary, to supplement the efforts of an executive in need of wider support for its policies . . . lay behind the establishment of the 'Council on Prices, Productivity and Incomes' . . . which was supposed to provide the country with *ex cathedra* judgements on the permissible increase in wages . . . and so on. (Shonfield, 1965, p. 154.)

In the early 1960s Harold Macmillan came to the view that a continuing commitment to a high level of employment would need a permanent incomes policy if inflation was to be contained. But in advocating this he stressed the inherent dangers and difficulties:

> In a free society an incomes policy cannot . . . be imposed. It can come about only by general acceptance, and if this is to be a permanent feature and not a temporary thing in a difficult crisis . . . then it must be regarded both as necessary and as fair . . . It must not, as a permanent feature, be rigid. It must be, perhaps, at the beginning but it must take account of all the varying situations. A temporary measure must necessarily be somewhat rigid and sometimes unfair.
>
> A permanent policy, however, must be flexible so that it can take account of the different conditions and needs of different services and industries and of the intervals that may have elapsed between the last increase and a new claim. (Hansard, 26 July 1962)

(ii) How to win friends and influence people.

The need for acceptance carries with it some form of formal or informal discussion and negotiation with the employers (CBI) and the unions (TUC); mostly, since the whole basis is to limit wage increases, this means with the TUC. The unions naturally tend to press for concessions in return for their support. Thus the TUC might ask for closer consultation with the government on other aspects of economic policy or for a commitment by the government to some particular measures wanted by the unions. The nature of such exchanges can be indicated by the opening paragraph of the Treasury's monthly *Economic Progress Report* for May 1976:

> Agreement between the Govenment and TUC leaders on a new limit for the next pay round . . . was announced on 5 May. As the new agreement satisfies the Government's requirements for reducing inflation the conditional tax reliefs offered by the Chancellor at the time of the Budget will be granted in full.

Such considerations clearly spill over into major political issues. But, as these are separately explored in the section on government and the unions they need not be further pursued here.

(iii) A percentage or a flat-rate?

In addition, the nature of the policy has to be set out. Here – to simplify – there are two basic models. The one lays down a *percentage* wage increase which is to be considered as the norm (for example, between April 1962 and October 1964 the Conservative government laid down a voluntary wage norm first of 2–2½ per cent p.a. and later raised to 3½ per cent). The other sets out a given *flat-rate* increase which is to be permitted (for example, the Labour government between August 1975 and July 1976 placed a compulsory limit of £6 a week on wage increases). Broadly, percentage increases have the advantage of maintaining the differentials between the earnings of the different groups, but have the drawback of allowing the largest absolute increases to those who already enjoy the highest incomes. Flat-rate increases seem 'fairer' because they give proportionately more to lower-paid workers, but 'distort' (or, at least, alter) the differentials between different groups of workers. The third approach is the simple imposition of a freeze which nominally prevents any increase in wage rates (this was the form taken by the first post-war incomes policy conducted by Sir Stafford Cripps from 1948 to 1950; it was also followed by Selwyn Lloyd's voluntary policy between July 1961 and March 1962: and by the statutory Labour policy of the second half of 1966 and the statutory Conservative policy of November 1972). Wage freezes are, of course, by their nature temporary.

(iv) How high is a norm?

The *level* of the norm has also to be settled. If it is to be consistent with a removal of inflation it should be fixed at a level equal to the overall expected increase in productivity for the economy. This was still plausible until the 1960s when the norms ranged between 2 per cent in 1962 and 4½ per cent at the end of 1969. In the 1970s, however, the accelerated inflation rate made it politically impossible to fix wage norms at or near the productivity rate (which in several years was zero or negative). The higher wage norms would thus only be consistent with attempting to slow down, and not to remove, inflation.

(v) A norm for whom?

Should everyone be subject to the norm? It might seem more sensible given the stress placed on productivity, to allow those in industries where productivity is greater than the norm to have more, and those where productivity is below the norm to have less. But for many people – especially in service sectors like teachers, nurses and soldiers – the possibilities of either measuring or increasing productivity may be limited. Should they thus be barred from wage increases? One way of meeting this problem is to link incomes in those sectors where measurement is difficult to 'comparable' sectors where measurement is more feasible. In the 1960s the National Board for Prices and Incomes, established in February 1965, was frequently faced with this problem and – despite its distrust of the whole concept of comparability – was forced to give the idea more precision:

> There are fields from which the concept of 'comparability' cannot be excluded. One clear case is that of the armed forces. We have suggested here the use of job evaluation with a dual purpose. Internally its use should help a structure to be devised in which pay is related more logically to the job servicemen are required to do, with the result that differences in pay should be more acceptable. This is the normal use of job evaluation. But we also went further and suggested an external use. The skills and qualities required of certain military jobs might be matched against those of certain civilian jobs, the ranges of pay obtaining for the latter would be identified, and in this way pay levels and changes in those levels could be settled for servicemen in the light of directly relevant information rather than of averages based on general movements in pay throughout the economy. 'Comparability' would thus be used with greater precision and selectivity than has hitherto been the case. (NBPI 4th Report, 1969)

An alternative possibility is to aim to make all settlements at or near the norm but keep the productivity link by allowing prices to rise by the full amount of the increase in labour cost where productivity has lagged, and to reduce prices in high productivity sectors. But whatever the strategy substantial difficulties are clearly involved.

(vi) Keeping a check on the policy.

A policy necessarily requires some form of institutional embodiment. British incomes policies, partly because they have been so discontinuous, have spawned a variety of institutions. At the end of the 1950s, although the government were not formally running an incomes policy, an institution was set up to offer guidance on pay settlements, guidance which it was hoped would seem to be objective. The institution was the Council on Prices, Productivity and Incomes, the so-called 'Three Wise Men', and it issued four reports between 1958 and 1961. When the Conservative government did turn to an explicit policy – Selwyn Lloyd's 'pay pause' of July 1961 – different machinery was used. The 'Three Wise Men' slipped quietly away and left pay, like other economic issues, to be settled through the National Economic Development Council ('Neddy'). This was the era when planning acquired a right-wing respectability and journals as economically orthodox as *The Economist* held out French-style 'indicative' planning as the desirable model for Britain to follow. It was widely – but misleadingly – thought that successful economic growth in France had been secured by a system in which government 'indicated' a plan which ensured overall consistency and coherence, and then individual industries and firms used the results as essential and feasible guidelines for their own decisions. Amongst the guidelines was included from April 1962, a 'guiding light' for wage settlements, which the National Incomes Commission ('Nicky') was set up to vet. In the event, 'Nicky' was made inoperative because the TUC refused to take part.

The Labour governments of 1964–70 also started with a surge of interest in planning. A National Plan was produced in September 1965, but no serious attempt was made to put it into effect – although George Brown's considerable energies were wasted and frustrated in the attempt. The Plan was formally abandoned in the crisis of July 1966, but one of its institutions – the National Board of Prices and Incomes – lived on to overlook the variety of incomes policies which were used by the first two Wilson governments. In 1970 this body was wound up by a new Conservative government committed to the virtues of the free market as the regulator of the price(s) of labour along with all other goods and services. In 1973, however, the Conservatives introduced two institutions – the Pay Board and the Price Commission – to adminster a fresh burst of incomes policies. The succeeding Labour government of 1974 to 1979 (under first Wilson and then Callaghan) mostly relied on high-level co-operation with the TUC embodied in the so-called 'Social Contract'.

The point here is not to give an exhaustive list of the institutional arrangements which have been used, nor to assess their relative values. It is to emphasize that any pursuit of an incomes policy will raise the problem of devising an institutional framework to put it into effect. One of the many aspects that has to be accommodated is, for example, the very large number of different wage agreements which are made each year. It is not easy, therefore, for any institution to monitor, with any precision, the course of wage negotiations; and, even if it could, the assessment of the information is far from straightforward. Wage settlements are normally complex documents dealing with a wide range of issues; they are not easily reduced to a single percentage figure.

(vii) Relativities and differentials

Most public attention is directed towards the difficulties involved in the relationship between government and unions. But it is probable that a more intractable, but less publicized issue arises from the existence of a large number of different rates of pay. These relativities are of two broad kinds: differentials between industries (the rates of pay are generally higher, for example, in oil production than they are in retail trade); and the differentials within an industry (a skilled worker expects to be paid at a higher rate than an unskilled person).

These relativities are one of the aspects of pay of which people, in their role as individual wage and salary earners, are most acutely aware. And whilst most people are happy enough to see the differential eroded between themselves and those above them, they are passionately keen – at the least – to maintain the difference between themselves and those immediately below them in the pay pecking-order. An incomes policy is likely to disturb some of these relativities. Indeed it may be essential that it should create such upsets (for example, to secure acceptance on the grounds of 'fairness' it may be necessary to protect the lower paid). But any such changes, intended or otherwise, are likely to provoke fierce reactions at the grass-roots level. This, certainly was the considered verdict of the National Board for Prices and Incomes:

> It can be concluded from the evidence that pay differentials have a great capacity to reassert themselves. There appears to have been remarkable stability in the overall distribution of earnings and considerable, if lesser, stability in inter-industry, sex, occupational and regional earnings differentials. (NBPI General Report on Low Pay, 1971)

The problem, as an earlier government pronouncement had pointed out in 1969, was that feelings about the 'proper' level of differentials seemed to be deeply embedded in human nature and industrial tradition:

> Recent wage claims by dustmen and firemen aroused a good deal of public sympathy in the belief that the pay of these groups of essential workers had fallen behind those of workers in manufacturing industry. Yet once substantial increases had been granted, others – many of whom are on higher levels of pay – promptly began to argue that these settlements entitled them to similar increases. (White Paper on Prices and Incomes Policy, 1969)

An outline of post-war British incomes policy

It needs to be stressed that it is not always clear when a policy is being operated. The line between a government having and not having such a policy can be quite thin. There is a wide and continuous spectrum between mere expression of government opinion and compulsory decree; between gentle exhortation or ear-stroking and fines or imprisonment. It is generally accepted, however, that post-war incomes policy in Britain starts with Sir Stafford Cripps's call for wage restraint in 1948. There is no such agreement about when incomes policy was next attempted once the TUC in 1950, had voted to free itself from Sir Stafford's moral pressures. Some commentators consider that the government calls for wage restraint in 1956 were sufficiently explicit to constitute a policy commitment. Others consider its lack of effectiveness was too marked for it to be seen as a policy – wage restraint broke upon its rejection by the TUC congress and on post-Suez price increases. There would be a more general agreement that the reports of the Council on Prices, Productivity and Incomes (the 'Three Wise Men') in the late 1950s were insufficient to be counted as a wage policy.

These doubts disappear early in the 1960s: from mid-1961 to mid-1979 it is abundantly evident for most of the time that the various governments were intent on pursuing some sort of incomes policy as an explicit and integral part of the general economic strategy. Indeed, this shift acts as one of the signals indicating the sharp change around 1960 in the way the performance of the economy was perceived: from reasonable satisfaction in the 1950s to increasing unease thereafter.

Rather than attempting to give a detailed catalogue of the dozen or more significant variations in incomes policy which were made between 1961 and 1979, two broad points will be made about these years. Firstly, even under a single government the nature of the policy pursued could shift quite dramatically. For example, the Wilson government of 1964–70 began with a voluntary policy under which the acceptance of wage restraint by the trade unions was linked to the government's proposals for an overall national plan. The strategy was enshrined in a formal document – the 'Joint Statement of Intent on Productivity, Prices and Incomes' – signed after much feverish persuasion by George Brown, by the TUC, the government and the employers. In the acute balance of payments crisis of 1966, however, this gave way to a statutory wage freeze from July to December, followed in the first half of 1967 (leading up to the devaluation crisis) by a period of severe constraint. Devaluation eased the pressure and the rules were eased from June 1967 to April 1968. From then, to the fall of the Wilson government in 1970, there was a further tightening of control as Roy Jenkins struggled to ensure that the export price advantages of devaluation (making British goods relatively cheaper to foreigners) were not dissipated in higher wages again forcing up British prices. Even apart from political differences, therefore, policy tended to accommodate itself to changes in the general economic climate. In particular, the severest policies (wage freezes or severe restraint) have tended to be associated with balance of payments crises. The second point to notice is that the only period during these years when there was clearly no government incomes policy was from mid-1970 to November 1972. The Conservative government under Edward Heath was initially explicitly committed to abolishing any dependence on an incomes policy. After two years the government reversed its stance and incomes policies then prevailed under both

Conservative and Labour governments until Margaret Thatcher's government of 1979 reaffirmed a determination not to intervene over wage and salary levels.

Have incomes policies been successful?

The conclusion that arises most clearly from a number of careful studies of the operation of incomes policy is that it is generally ineffective. (See, for example, M. Parkin and M. Sumner (eds), *Incomes Policy and Inflation*, 1972, especially chapter 1). The basis for this finding is that whilst such policies slow down wage increases when they are enforced, the level of wages simply catches up when the policy is relaxed or removed. Thus it is suggested that an incomes policy makes no real difference to the determination of wage levels in the economy and hence has no effect on the rate of inflation.

Why did such findings fail to bury the whole idea of an incomes policy? Amongst the many reasons was the consideration that, despite great care, the findings were not entirely securely based. It is very difficult to specify a model which can test what the situation would be if the only change in a given situation was the addition (or removal) of an incomes policy. So many other things are changing at the same time. The lagging of wage increases, which the studies acknowledge, could in any event be quite useful: to avert or soften a particular crisis, for example, or to give breathing-space to launch other policies (like raising the level of investment).

The critics also argue that incomes policies 'distort' market prices and that the results of this distortion – that the mix of output will be changed for the worse – is part of the 'cost' of running an incomes policy. There is some force in this argument, but it needs to be treated with care. The implication is that without the interference of an incomes policy, wages would settle at some obviously 'correct' level; and that the demand and supply of all the different kinds of labour would be brought easily and smoothly into balance. The implicit assumption of a 'perfect' market for labour would require all workers and employers to have full knowledge of wages and opportunities elsewhere; there would be no costs or other barriers to movement; and there would be no institutional obstacles (monopolies or trade unions) etc. Thus some part of the disadvantages which are attributed to incomes policy arises simply because the labour market is, in any event, highly imperfect. Many would thus claim that economic theory offers no tenable explanation of the relative level of wages. Such points add force to the fundamental fact that any decision about incomes policy derives from political as well as economic considerations. Even the decision not to pursue an incomes policy is rooted in political conviction.

Perhaps this can be emphasized if we remind ourselves of the basic problem that incomes policy was meant to resolve. The commitment to full employment (made in the 1944 White Paper on post-war Employment Policy) necessarily greatly increased the bargaining power of labour under conditions of free collective bargaining. So wages would rise and employers, guaranteed high demand, would have their resistance to such increases weakened and prices would rise. And once expectations of price increases became established this would further increase wage demands, so both wages and prices would rise by an increasing rate. The reasonable conclusion – pointed out by many economists of various political persuasions even in the 1940s – was that full employment, free collective bargaining and price stability could not all be had simultaneously. This seemed the lesson driven home by the attempt of the Heath government to secure all three between 1970 and 1972. Incomes policy was an attempt to resolve the problem by modifying free collective bargaining in ways which would preserve generally full employment and reasonably stable prices. The adoption of monetary policies (since an accepted effect of restricting the money supply is that – at least for some indeterminate time – unemployment will increase) chooses instead to secure more stable prices and free collective bargaining (the market) at the expense of abandoning full employment. For the economy as a whole, of course, part of the cost of such an approach is the output lost because of the existence of unemployed resources. Whatever the approach, however, it is a political as well as an economic problem to decide whether the benefits outweigh the costs.

Exercise 5

5.1 'A commitment to full employment must lead to inflation unless there is an effective incomes policy.' Explain and comment.
5.2 What difficulties are involved in using an incomes policy?
5.3 Why does any incomes policy require some method of checking on its operation? What problems arise over such checking?
5.4 What success have incomes policies had in post-war Britain?
5.5 Why have successive governments attempted to impose a policy of income restraint from time to time? Why have they not done so continuously?

6 The Suez affair, 1956

Britain's prestige and interests were at stake in the Middle East, or at least, the Conservative government thought this to be the case, and believed Britain had the power to protect them. But the relations of Britain and Egypt had deteriorated sharply in the early 1950s (see chapter 5) and further continuing trouble with President Nassser was clearly unavoidable even after the agreements of 1954. The crisis finally arose from a number of apparently unconnected events, culminating in a decision that ironically was primarily the work of the United States. The events that soured Ango-Egyptian relations included Nasser's outrage at the conclusion of the Baghdad Pact; the Egyptian arms deal with the Czechs in September 1955 (which made nonsense of Anglo-American attempts to maintain an arms balance between the Arabs and the Israelis); the dismissal by the Jordanian government of its British adviser, General Glubb, early in 1956 (which the British wrongly attributed to Nasser's intrigues); and the regular broadcasting by Cairo Radio of anti-British propaganda in Arabic and Swahili to the Persian Gulf and East Africa. Eden appears to have been particularly outraged by the sacking of Glubb, and his anger with Nasser was heightened by criticism from the right-wing Suez group in the Conservative party that he had 'backed the wrong horse'.

The decision that precipitated the crisis was that of the United States government in July 1956 to refuse Egypt a loan for the Aswan Dam. The British government was involved and certainly concurred, but responsibility for the decision and for the very abrupt and humiliating way it was announced must rest with the United States government and in particular with the Secretary of State, John Foster Dulles. Nasser's immediate response was to announce the nationalization of the Suez Canal, and to take over all the installations of the Suez Canal Company with great speed and success, more or less overnight. The next three months saw prolonged negotiations, indecision, threats, plans for military measures, secret diplomacy of a very old-fashioned kind, and major rifts within the Commonwealth and in Anglo-American relations. The affair reached a climax at the end of October with an Israeli attack – for good reasons of their own – on Egypt, in which the British and the French participated. Complicating the later stages of the affair was the Hungarian revolt on 23 October, and the American presidential election in early November.

The response of the British Cabinet to Nasser's action in July was confused and indecisive and therein perhaps lies much of the explanation of the eventual failure of British policy. The Cabinet very properly was concerned about British interests and property, the security of Britain's and Europe's oil supplies, and the long term interests of users of the canal. About one sixth of the world's sea cargoes passed through the canal, much of it oil and most of it going to or from Europe. The Cabinet had two real choices: action or negotiation. The first, if taken immediately, might have carried with it British public opinion, but the Chiefs of Staff advised that immediate military action was impossible. Consequently, negotiations were attempted, while at the same time preparations were set in train for action should the negotiations fail. The story of the negotiations is a complicated one involving the United Nations, the United States, the main users of the canal, and of course, Egypt, France and Britain. Success was never likely, given Nasser's intransigence, backed by an aroused Arab nationalism on the one hand, and confusion, disagreement and indecision among the major canal users on the other. Moreover, it is clear that on the British side there was not a great deal of enthusiasm for a negotiated settlement, unless of course it involved the complete restoration of the position before July, a most unlikely outcome.

The opinion of the hawks in the Cabinet, like Eden and Macmillan, was that Suez was a test which could be met only by the use of force; Nasser must be overthrown and this could not be brought about without force. Eden put it mildly in a cable to President Eisenhower soon after the nationalization: 'My colleagues and I are convinced that we must be ready in the last resort to use force to bring Nasser to his senses.' Eden was also thinking historically, and it can be argued that he tried to do over Suez what he felt he should have done as Foreign Secretary twenty years earlier over the German remilitarization of the Rhineland in 1936. He developed a fixation about Nassser, comparing him to Hitler. Eden's Public Relations Adviser at the time, William Clark, put it many years later in a broadcast discussion, reprinted in *The Listener* (22 Nov. 1979, p. 691):

> . . . I think it is true that Eden judged the Suez Canal episode as being more or less the exact equivalent of the Rhineland occupation by Hitler, which was exactly 20 years before. Twenty years is not very long. Eden in fact did not act very decisively over the Rhineland matter and he regretted it personally, but above all he felt that that was the moment at which the Second World War could have been stopped if there had been determination on the part of the governments of France and Britain, and there was not.

Eden made his general attitude clear in a prime ministerial broadcast early in the crisis on 8 August:

> The pattern is familiar to many of us, my friends. We all know this is how fascist governments behave and we all remember, only too well, what the cost can be in giving in to fascism . . . with dictators you always have to pay a higher price later on, for their appetite grows with feeding.

The accounts of British policy during the Suez affair, whether sympathetic or critical, tend to concentrate on a number of issues: the political divisions in the country and how far these affected the decision makers, the rift in the Commonwealth, disagreements with the United States – how far the British Government misled the Americans, how far Britain was let down by the Americans – and the issue of 'collusion', the secret agreement between Britain, France and Israel about Anglo-French intervention. All these are important but above all confusion and indecision among the policy-makers help to explain the essential failure of British policy.

The record is a pretty damning one. At a Cabinet meeting held on 27

July the decision to use force in the last resort was taken and the Chiefs of Staff were instructed to prepare plans. On 3rd August the Chiefs of Staff submitted four alternative plans which were considered by the Egypt Committee of the Cabinet on 10 August. The Committee agreed on a full-scale assault on Alexandria, seizing port and airfield, followed by an advance to the Suez Canal via the Cairo area. This plan was as much intended to take care of Nasser as to recover the canal. Eden apparently had misgivings about the plan, but it was approved and landings were scheduled to take place on 15 September. On 22 August these were postponed to 19 September to await the outcome of various diplomatic initiatives. On 28 August there was a further postponement to 26 September. In early September the Chiefs of Staff were told to prepare a new plan, and this was approved by the Cabinet on 11 September. The new plan switched the focus of attack to Port Said to secure the canal. Apart from the stop-go, on-off, nature of the planning, there was also a fatal indecision in the plans finally adopted, for what has been described as an invasion in slow motion, with three ponderous parts to it. The military chiefs were responsible for this, but the soldiers may be forgiven for thus responding to the divided counsels and hesitations of their political masters.

To complicate matters the actual plans and the timing of the operation had to be co-ordinated with the French, whose objectives were not the same as those of Britain. To add to the confusion, from early October onwards there was the question of collusion. While all this was taking place, diplomacy was continuing in a feverish but pointless way, and of course political opinion in Britain was fluctuating in some confusion. It was to be expected that the official Labour opposition would criticize the government both on grounds of principle and of parliamentary tactics. The attitude of the Labour leader, Gaitskell, in the early stages of the affair was ambivalent. But the party soon united in fierce opposition to the military intervention. On the government benches a small number of members – fifteen is a figure often quoted – apparently protested to the Chief Whip about the government's policy, and two junior ministers resigned in protest.

The actual operations were something of an anti-climax. The Israeli attack on Egypt began on 29 October, the contrived Anglo-French ultimatum to both combatants (the product of collusion) was delivered on 30 October, ordering them to 'withdraw' to lines ten miles each side of the canal so that British and French troops could occupy and protect the canal zone. As the Israelis at this stage were nowhere near the canal they could accept the ultimatum and continue to advance. Nasser rejected the ultimatum. On the same day in New York Britain and France vetoed two resolutions at the Security Council calling on all United Nations members to refrain from using force or the threat of force in Egypt. Allied bombing attacks on Egyptian airfields began on 31 October, and finally on 5 November British and French forces began to land. As Elizabeth Monroe summarizes it:

> Deeds that stood a chance of taking the world's breath away if done quickly stood none by Day Six . . . Inevitably five days bombing of Egyptian targets caused all Arabs to deduce that the British had sided with Israel, and gave all other critics time in which to compose and coordinate their strictures. (1963, p. 200)

The military operation, once it began, went well, but on the 6 November, with only half the blocked Canal occupied, there was a cease fire and it was all over. It is still not clear what was the main cause of the decision to stop: American pressure, a run on the pound, Russian sabre-rattling, trouble with the commonwealth, rising opposition at home.

Suez affords a splendid example of how not to conduct foreign policy, particularly if the use of military force is contemplated with the further complication of the co-ordination of effort with an ally. Much has been written on the affair, and as Elizabeth Monroe puts it, 'Detective works of good quality (about Suez) have been published in both Britain and France.' Many questions however remain to be answered, and some probably never will be, for an article in *The Times* (20 June 1978) suggests that much of the sensitive documentary material in the public records was destroyed soon after the affair, and therefore will not be available after the normal thirty-year interval in 1987. The questions which have attracted most attention have already been indicated: the extent of collusion with Israel, the date it began – September or October – and how far the Cabinet as a whole was involved; and what was the main element in determining the eventual ceasefire. Other questions which continue to intrigue historians are the role of Labour and particularly of Hugh Gaitskell; the role of the Prime Minister, Anthony Eden, who dominated British policy-making, and whose career collapsed in a chaos of recrimination and bad health following Suez; and, above all, a judgement on British policy throughout the affair – good or bad, justifiable or not, in character or an aberration. The previous discussion has suggested some arguments and lines of enquiry; it is hoped that the following documents will throw further light on these questions.

Document 6.3

(a) Extract from a discussion between Michael Charlton and William Clark, broadcast on Radio 3 and reprinted in *The Listener* on 22 November 1979.

Clark, as mentioned previously, was Eden's Public Relations Adviser at the time of Suez.

Q. I asked you earlier about bipartisanship at home as a necessary foundation for the conduct of an effective foreign policy, and surely Eden must have been aware of the significance of that. Gaitskell was later to claim that he was misled by Eden. Was he?

A. It's difficult to say. The fact is that Gaitskell's speech on 2 August in the House of Commons was the first to compare Nasser to Hitler; he made a very strong speech against Nasser, and about the necessity of stopping him. Eden made a further speech in which it was perfectly clear that he was going to go ahead and stop Nasser somehow.

Q. What Gaitskell said he didn't know was that the Cabinet had met that very day and agreed to the use of armed force.

A. He didn't know that, and it was true. The fact was that Gaitskell also did put in the item that it should not be used except with the permission of the United Nations. But Gaitskell felt his speech had been misinterpreted and he rang me up (he was a very good friend of mine) and said, 'Is it any good my sending a letter to the Prime Minister?' I suggested to Gaitskell that if he had some difficulty with how the debate had gone he should write a letter to Eden. He did write. I seem to remember a long manuscript letter and one of the Private Secretaries saying 'Gaitskell, unsaying everything he said on Thursday'.

(b) **Extract from an appreciation of Eden 'At empire's end' in** *The Economist*, **on 22 January 1977, the week after his death**

. . . That Eden too, blew up was a natural disappointment. It was something that an increasingly sceptical country put at the back of its mind, and thereafter was content to live with men who had themselves settled for a lesser Britain . . . He simply did not seem to be the man to put it all to the touch in a military operation. He was not even the enemy of the Arabs: one of his ideas had been to impose on Israel a corridor joining Egypt and Jordan. Eden knew how the world was changing . . . So why did he invade Suez? It is said he had been impatient for power too long – and he had been. It is said he could not abide Dulles – and he could not. It is said he was nagged into it by the Conservative party – and they (including Macmillan and columnists like Randolph Churchill) had been getting at him. He did not have the power of contempt of the party which Winston Churchill had had.

It is said that ill-health dogged him at the critical moment. He did have his first liver failure in September 1956; plans for a possible invasion of Suez had been laid before that, but the worst decisions (the secrecy from the Americans, the collusion with the Israelis) were made in the weeks when he could not get rid of much of the toxic matter from his body. Before that illness, he had frequently lost his temper with those around him; after it, for the critical weeks, he bottled his resentments inside him, and became a worse decision-maker in consequence.

His most nagging resentment was that he, the famous anti-appeaser, was being accused of appeasement. In the end, Eden went in, as he said he did, because he really identified in Nasser the successor to Hitler and Mussolini against whom he had directed the best of his mind and energy. 'But Nasser, if a Hitler, is much littler', said an article in The Economist at the time. A colleague pointed this sentence out to Eden. It was not approved.

The main weakness in Eden was not his foibles nor his ill-health nor excessive post-imperial grandeur. It was his conventionality. He did not just master the hard-won lessons of the 1930s; the lessons mastered him – even when it was a different crisis and a different Labour party and a different Britain that he still expected to respond.

(c) Extract from a Review article 'The entanglements of Suez' by Elie Kedourie in *The Times Literary Supplement*, 30 November 1979, pp. 67–70

. . . The policy, Gore-Booth (Lord Gore-Booth, later Head of the Diplomatic Service) felt, was imprudent: if one single Arab were killed in the preliminary bombing of the airfields 'there would be hell to pay'. Furthermore, 'the action we were taking seemed so utterly out of the character of post-war, United Nations Britain' . . . Manifest in this ideal of a 'United Nations Britain' is an intellectual weakness, a wan sentimentality which fails to get a grip on reality. There is here unwillingness to grasp what survival requires in a world from which civility has almost gone, peopled by predators who laugh at the rule of law, and take pride and pleasure in brutal flouting of custom and convention. But if Lord Gore-Booth cannot be right in thinking that Suez was out of character for Britain – how could it be given Britain's martial past? – he is justified in adding that it was out of character for Eden. This was perhaps the reason for the widespread anger which Eden's action aroused among the intellectual and official classes: that this British Nehru had outraged the pieties which he was believed – on the whole rightly – to share . . .

The clerisy at large, then, have succeeded in endowing Suez with a halo of evil which still clings to it. Their tender conscience has made the so-called collusion with France and Israel – a strategem of a kind to which states have immemorially resorted, albeit here clumsy and transparent – an act of especial wickedness. How the pieties which Suez outraged came to strike root, to flourish and luxuriate, how beautiful souls came to set the tone in a public life distinguished not so long ago by some robustness and realism, how scruple decayed into scrupulosity – this remains the central mystery of modern British politics.

Exercise 6

6.1 What British interests were at stake in Suez? Are you sure?

6.2 What briefly was the case for the use of force? and the case against?

6.3 It is difficult to argue that British policy achieved its objectives. It is still possible to give some credit to the policy-makers. How?

6.4 What were the 'lessons' (do's and don'ts) of Suez for British foreign policy?

Guide to exercises

1.1 'Necessarily' is a hard word to justify, but plainly there are pressures on wages which it is difficult to control in a system based on consent and election. The history of Poland in the early 1980s suggests that this may be the case even in less consensual regimes.

1.2 Briefly, in 1969–70 they demonstrated the weakness of the Labour government; in 1974 the government was pushed towards suicide, but it was the electorate which despatched them in the end; in 1979, the answer could well be yes the trade unions destroyed Labour's chief claim to govern; but Labour might have had difficulty in winning the election even without a 'winter of discontent'.

1.3 Try again, is one answer. The answer of old political theory was some kind of social contract, an agreement to keep to the rules, in return for some advantage. A newer political theory suggested some form of incorporation, that is, the incorporation of the unions into the state, or the machinery of government.

1.4 On balance, no; industrial relations were more conflictual and unproductive in 1980 than in 1960 or 1950. There was profit in the demonstration of the limits of the legal regulation of trade unions. But if you take the view that in the end trade unions must be subject to social control then that cause was set back by years.

2.1 The law can be used to control particular abuses; and it can set standards and expectations, provide a framework for social behaviour. While some part of race relations is private and beyond the reach of the law, some part is public and subject to legal restraints. There are practical difficulties about making these effective, but that does not make the attempt futile. (You may think that these arguments apply to the use of the law in industrial relations too; or that the comparison shows the weakness of the arguments.)

2.2 Here, as elsewhere, 'right' is a difficult term. There are practical and historical arguments, that indigenous peoples have a stronger right than others, and might set limitations and conditions. But historically Britain is not in a good position to refuse entry to her former colonial peoples.

Generally it may be argued that modern economies depend on mobility; that the mixing of peoples is valuable in itself; and that the only limits should be the practical ones of a sufficiency of jobs and social facilities.

Note that the problem arises in many ways: the Irish in England, the English in Wales, Manchester businessmen in the Lake District, Puerto Ricans in Florida.

3.1 Yes, this appears to be true for Northern Ireland, though it should be added that there are economic and social grievances involved in the conflict. That conflict was described as 'communal' and includes identities and loyalties (and mutual hostility) based on religious and ethnic background. Broadly, economic conflict may be assuaged if not resolved by available economic measures, jobs, houses, schools and so on. Ethnic conflict tends to be absolute, non-negotiable, based on deeply felt sentiment. Religion too, tends in that direction. Rationally, this need not be so; but if these matters were viewed rationally, there would be altogether less conflict.

3.2 It is not a satisfactory explanation to say that the conflicts were of such profundity and bitterness that violence was inevitable. The violence arose because in the context of bitter conflict a history of violence led to a tradition of violence and the availability of the means of violence. There is now a corps of gunmen in Northern Ireland.

3.3 The best answer perhaps is the 'Irish' one, you would not start from here. You could not solve the problems by conceding to one side or the other. A middling compromise solution seemed impossible. You would be left with holding on, managing from day to day, working to improve relations and so on – playing for time, the percentage game (i.e. don't hope to improve matters by more than 1 or 2 per cent each year.) The direction of this minimal movement would be towards tolerance, civil rights, power sharing and the involvement of the Irish government in pacification.

3.4 It is usually argued that this would lead to more violence as the Protestant majority asserted its power. But it might help to remove a presence regarded as imperialist and convert the conflict plainly to one of Irishmen against Irishmen. Note, though, that Irish nationalists would not accept this implied version of history: for them the Protestant Ulstermen are imperialists too. Nor would the Ulster Protestants accept without protest the loss of the British protection.

4.1 Some part of the concern must reflect the relative importance of the nationalized industries to the economy as a whole. Having looked at this then you need to imagine the general economic effects of different pricing policies (what would happen, for example, if the price of coal was kept deliberately low? or high?), and investment policies. If the government is following a particular economic policy (say, anti-inflation) what is the basis of the temptation of the government to control prices and investment in nationalized industries to further this policy? Should the government resist such temptation.

4.2 Study the excerpts from the two documents and list and assess the differences you detect.

4.3 Requires thinking about the *implications* of using only the rate of profit as the guideline. Essentially the whole issue involves assessment about whether, and in what ways, nationalized industries are (or should be) different from privately-owned industries.

4.4 The need is to determine (or judge) whether a) there are basic philosophical differences between the main parties, and b) if so, where the public ownership of the means of production fits into these different approaches.

5.1 Full employment means a) that the demand for labour is high and b) that the resultant wages make for a high demand for goods. But a) will tend to mean that wages are increased and this means that the costs of manufacturers will increase, and so push up prices. And b) means that a high demand for goods will also push up prices. It is argued that this spiralling effect can be cut off – or, at least, moderated by limiting the effects of a) i.e. although the market for labour suggests increasing wages, an incomes policy prevents these increases (or attempts to keep them in line with the general increase in productivity). You need to comment on this mechanism and also to suggest other possible ways out – for example, if technical change (productivity) was rapid enough perhaps the wage pressure could be tolerated.

5.2 All that is required is a rehearsal of the points made in the text, with such further additions as can be made to this selective treatment.

5.3 Any incomes policy, since it involves imposing restraints on people, requires that these restraints are being applied generally and even-handedly. But actual incomes are determined by a very wide variety of particular agreements and decisions. There is a need to check that these conform to the general guidelines. The problems arise from the nature of the operation: the difficulty of getting, and assessing, the right information on all incomes; and the difficulty of knowing what the information means (consider, for example, the way in which – in most strikes – the two sides can plausibly differ widely over their interpretation of what apparently hard information on wage rates – earnings? – can mean).

5.4 Develop the broad themes suggested in the text. What are the objectives that will have to be tackled before any very useful assessment can be made about degree of success?

5.5 The discussion must consider whether policies have been discontinuous because governments only want to use them to solve particular short-run situations, or because they are inherently unstable. The latter aspect then raises the nature of such instability: the need to placate important interest groups (trade unions, employers); the need in the absence of coercion to carry a consensus; and the need to allow for changes in the economic structure (to accommodate, for example, the apparent need for declining industries and/or skills to suffer a relative lag in wages so labour will shift towards advancing industries).

6.1 There was specific interest in oil and access to oil, and a general interest in political stability in the Middle East. It turned out that Europe could still transport its oil via the Cape in the new giant tankers; and later oil problems were not related to Egypt. The 'general interest' was less than totally convincing, and arguably was a hangover from empire. Whether Britain should concern itself with the stability of the Middle East or not, she no longer had the capacity to do so.

6.2 The case for is that this was the only effective way to achieve political objectives; that it was economical; and moral. The case against is the opposite. The moral argument is ultimately a matter for a personal assertion of values; the other arguments could be regarded as settled by the actual outcome of the intervention (but it might still have been worth trying).

6.3 The British government emerged from Suez with its reputation tarnished. Conservative critics claimed (and few people denied) that the policy had failed, radical critics claimed (with rather more opposition) that the intervention was wrong in principle, as well as disastrous in execution. But there is a case to be made for the government – as the last document suggests. Such a case would rest on the reality and severity of the threat to British interests, and the potential of the military intervention (and of that alone) to rescue those interests. Eden's personal 'fixation' with Hitler would be discounted and the 'collusion' would be interpreted as normal and prudent secret arrangements with allies. In this way, it may be argued, Eden's record in the Suez affair was creditable. In any case, it is well to keep in mind that policies which often proved to be unwise, can rarely be shown to be immoral, according to the standards of the times.

6.4 Many possible answers: don't move too far without US support; if you intend to use force, get on with it; secrecy is fine only as long as your policy succeeds.

But in a broader perspective the lessons were to do with the general limitations on British power after 1945, and the specific limits of the former great powers in dealing with nationalist movements. Egypt was, after all, only one of many small nations to defy the larger powers with impunity; and Britain was only one of the larger powers to be so defied.

Reading list

This is not a bibliography but a list of about fifty books for a working library to accompany this book. The divisions are in some cases arbitrary.

General

ADDISON, P., *The Road to 1945*, Quartet Books, 1977

BARTLETT, C. J., *A History of Post-war Britain*, Longman, 1977

BOGDANOR, V., and SKIDELSKY, R., *The Age of Affluence, 1951–64*, Macmillan, 1970

BUTLER, D., and SLOMAN, A., *British Political Facts, 1900–1979*, 5th edn., Macmillan, 1980

CALVOCORESSI, P., *The British Experience, 1945–75*, Bodley Head, 1978

EATWELL, R., *The 1945—1951 Labour Governments*, Batsford, 1979

HEY, J. D., *Britain in Context*, Blackwell, 1979

MCKIE, D., and COOK, C., *The Decade of Disillusion: British politics in the 1960s*, Macmillan, 1972

NOBLE, T., *Modern Britain, Structure and Change*, Batsford, 1975

PROUDFOOT, M., *British Politics and Government, 1951–70*, Faber, 1974

SISSONS, M., and FRENCH, P. (ed.), *The Age of Austerity 1945–51*, Penguin, 1964

SKED, A., and COOK, C., *Post-war Britain, a political history*, Penguin, 1979

Politics

BIRCH, A. H., *Political Integration and Disintegration in the British Isles*, Allen and Unwin, 1977

BRITTAN, S., *The Treasury under the Tories, 1951–64*, Secker and Warburg/ Penguin, 1964

BRUCE-GARDYNE, J., and LAWSON, N., *The Power Game*, Macmillan, 1976

BUTLER, D., and STOKES, D., *Political change in Britain*, Macmillan, 1977

BUTLER, D., et al, *Nuffield Studies of The British General Election*, from 1951, Macmillan. The volumes for 1945 by MCCALLUM, R. B., and READMAN, A., OUP, and for 1950 by NICHOLAS, H. G., Macmillan

COOK, C., and RAMSDEN, J. (eds.), *Trends in British Politics*, Macmillan, 1978

CROSSMAN, R., *The Crossman Diaries: selections from the diaries of a Cabinet Minister, 1964–70* (ed. A. Howard), Cape, 1979

CROUCH, C., *The Politics of Industrial Relations,* Fontana/Collins, 1979

JENKINS, P., *The Battle of Downing Street,* Charles Knight, 1970

MACFARLANE, L. J., *Issues in British Politics since 1945*, Longman, 1975

MORAN, M., *The Politics of Industrial Relations*, Macmillan, 1977

TAYLOR, R., *The Fifth Estate, Britain's unions in the modern world*, Pan Books, 1980

Economics

BACON, R., and ELTIS, W., *Britain's Economic Problem: too few producers,* 2nd edn., Macmillan, 1978

BECKERMAN, W., *Slow Growth in Britain: causes and consequences*, OUP, 1979

BECKERMAN, W., (ed.), *The Labour Government's Economic Record, 1964–70*, Duckworth, 1972

BLACKABY, F. T. (ed.), *British Economic Policy, 1960–74*, CUP, 1978

BLACKABY, F. T. (ed.), *De-Industrialisation*, Heinemann, 1978

CAVES, R. E., *Britain's Economic Prospects*, Allen and Unwin, 1968

CAVES, R. E., and KRAUSE, L., *Britain's Economic Performance*, Brookings, 1980

DOW, J. C. R., *The Management of the British Economy, 1945–60*, CUP, 1970

NIESR, *The United Kingdom Economy*, Heinemann, 1979

POLLARD, S., *The Development of the British Economy, 1914–67*, Arnold, 1969

STEWART, M., *The Jekyll and Hyde Years: politics and economic policy since 1964*, Dent, 1977

STEWART, M., *Keynes and After*, Penguin, 1967

TIVEY, L. (ed.), *The Nationalised Industries since 1960*, Jonathan Cape, 1973

WRIGHT, J. F., *Britain in the Age of Economic Management*, OUP, 1979

Foreign policy

BARKER, E., *Britain in a Divided Europe, 1945–1970*, Weidenfeld and Nicolson, 1971

BARTLETT, C. J., *The Long Retreat: a short history of British defence policy, 1945–1970*, Macmillan, 1972

CROSS, C., *The Fall of the British Empire 1918–1968*, Hodder and Stoughton, 1968

DILKS, D. (ed.), *Retreat from Power: studies in Britain's foreign policy of the twentieth century, vol. 2: After 1939*, Macmillan, 1981

FRANKEL, J., *British Foreign Policy, 1945–1973*, OUP for the Royal Institute of International Affairs, 1975

KITZINGER, U., *Diplomacy and Persuasion: how Britain joined the Common Market,* Thames and Hudson, 1973

MEDLICOTT, W. N., *British foreign policy since Versailles, 1919–1963*, Methuen, 2nd edn, 1968

MONROE, E., *Britain's Moment in the Middle East, 1914–1956*, Chatto and Windus, 1963

NORTHEDGE, F. S., *Descent from Power: British foreign policy, 1945–1973*, Allen and Unwin, 1974

SHLAIM, A., JONES, P., and SAINSBURY, K., *British Foreign Secretaries since 1945*, David and Charles, 1977

VITAL, D., *The Making of British Foreign Policy*, Allen and Unwin, 1968

WILLIAMS, A., *Britain and France in the Middle East and North Africa*, Macmillan, 1968

WOODCOCK, G., *Who Killed the British Empire? An Inquest*, Jonathan Cape, 1974

References in the text

ABRAMS, M. and ROSE, R., 1960. *Must Labour Lose?*, Penguin

AMERY, L. S., 1947. *Thoughts on the Constitution*, Oxford University Press

AMIS, K., 1977. *Harold's Years 1964–1976*, Quartet

BACON, R. and ELTIS, W., 1976. *Britain's Economic Problem*, Macmillan

BAGEHOT, W., 1963. *The English Constitution*, Fontana

BECKERMAN, W., (ed.), 1972. *The Labour Government's Record, 1964–70*, Duckworth

BEER, S., 1965. *Modern British Politics*, Faber

BEVAN, A., 1978. *In Place of Fear*, Quartet

British Economy: Key Statistics 1900–66, 1967. Times Newspapers Ltd for London and Cambridge Economic Service

BRUCE-GARDYNE, J. and LAWSON, N., 1976. *The Power Game*, Macmillan

BUTLER, D. E., 1952. *The British General Election of 1951*, Macmillan

BUTLER, D. E. and KAVANAGH, D., 1980. *The British General Election of 1979*, Macmillan

BUTLER, D. E. and STOKES, D., 1974. *Political Change in Britain*, Macmillan

CAIRNCROSS, SIR ALEC, 1975. *Inflation, Growth and International Finance*, Allen and Unwin

CARLYLE, M., (ed.), 1952. *Documents on International Affairs, 1947–1948*, Oxford University Press for Royal Institute of International Affairs

CARTER, A., 1973. *Direct Action and Liberal Democracy*, Routledge and Kegan Paul

CAVES, R. E., 1968. *Britain's Economic Prospects*, Allen and Unwin

CLARKE, SIR RICHARD, 1972. *New Trends in Government*, HMSO

COOK, C. and RAMSDEN, J., (edn.), 1978. *Trends in British Politics*, Macmillan

CROSLAND, A., 1975. *Social Democracy in Europe*, Fabian Society

DILKS, D., 1981 *Retreat from Power*, Macmillan

DOW, J. C. R., 1964. *The Management of the British Economy, 1945–60*, Cambridge University Press

FEINSTEIN, C. H., 1976. *Statistical Tables of National Income, Expenditure and Output of the UK, 1855–1965*, Cambridge University Press

FINER, S., 1963. *Anonymous Empire*, Pall Mall

FOOT, M., 1973. *Aneurin Bevan: a biography*, Davis Poynter

GAMBLE, A., 1974. *The Conservative Nation*, Routledge and Kegan Paul

GILMOUR, I., 1978. *Inside Right*, Quartet

GOWING, M., 1974. *Independence and Deterrence*, Macmillan

GOYDER, M., 1979, *Socialism Tomorrow*, Fabian Society

HALSEY, A., 1972. *Trends in British Society Since 1900*, Macmillan

HARROD, R. F., 1963. *The British Economy*, McGraw Hill

HENDERSON, P. D., (ed.), 1966. *Economic Growth in Britain*, Weidenfeld and Nicolson

HOGG, Q., 1947. *The Case for Conservatism*, Penguin

HUTCHINSON, G., 1980. *The Last Edwardian at No. 10*, Quartet

HUTCHISON, T. W., 1968. *Economics and Economic Policy in Britain, 1944–66*, Allen and Unwin

IONESCU, G., 1975. *Centripetal Politics*, Hart-Davis Macgibbon

JAMES, R. R., 1972. *Ambitions and Realities: British Politics 1964–1970*, Weidenfeld and Nicolson

JENNINGS, W. I., 1942. *The British Constitution*, Cambridge University Press

JENNINGS, W. I., 1954. *The Queen's Government*, Penguin

KEEGAN, W. and PENNANT-REA, R., 1979. *Who Runs the Economy?*, Temple Smith

KEYNES, J. M., 1951. *The General Theory of Employment, Interest and Money*, Macmillan

LAPPING, B., 1970. *The Labour Government 1964–70*, Penguin

LEVIN, B., 1970. *The Pendulum Years*, Jonathan Cape

LEWIS, R. and MAUDE, A., 1949. *The English Middle Classes*, Phoenix House

MACKINTOSH, J. P., 1970. *The Government and Politics of Britain*, Hutchinson

MACMILLAN, SIR HAROLD, 1972. *Pointing the Way, 1959–61*, Macmillan

MADGWICK, P. J., 1976. *Introduction to British Politics*, 2nd edn, Hutchinson

MARGACH, J., 1978. *The Abuse of Power*, W. H. Allen

MARQUAND, D, 1980. *Taming Leviathan*, Socialist Commentary Publications

MEDLICOTT, F., 2nd ed. 1968. *British Foreign Policy since Versailles*, Methuen

MONROE, E., 1963. *Britain's Moment in the Middle East and North Africa*, Macmillan

MORAN, M., 1977. *The Politics of Industrial Relations*, Macmillan

MORRISON, H., 3rd ed. 1964. *Government and Parliament*, Oxford University Press

MOSLEY, O., 1968. *My Life*, Nelson

NAGAI, Y. and IRIYE, A., (eds.), 1977. *The Origins of the Cold War in Asia*, Columbia University Press

NORTHCOTT, J., 1964. *Why Labour?*, Penguin

POLLARD, S., 1969. *The Development of the British Economy, 1914–17*, Arnold

PROUDFOOT, M., 1974. *British Politics and Government 1951–70*, Faber

RAISON, T., 1964. *Why Conservative?*, Penguin

RITCHIE, R., (ed.), 1978. Enoch Powell: *A Nation or No Nation*, Batsford

ROSE, R., 1976. *The Problem of Party Government*, Penguin

SHONFELD, A., 1968. Note of Reservation in 'Donovan Report': Report of Royal Commission on Trade Unions and Employers' Associations, Cmnd 3623, HMSO

SINGER, P., 1973. *Democracy and Disobedience*, Oxford University Press

SISSONS, M. and FRENCH, P., 1964. *The Age of Austerity, 1945–51*, Penguin

STEWART, M., 1977. *The Jekyll and Hyde Years*, Dent

TAYLOR, A. J. P., 1965. *English History 1914–45*, Oxford University Press

TITMUSS, R. M. 1950. *Problems of Social Policy (History of Second World War)*, HMSO and Longmans Green

WATT, D. C., (ed.), 1971. *Documents on International Affairs, 1962*, Oxford University Press for Royal Institute of International Affairs.

WHEELER-BENNETT, J. W., 1958. *King George VI*, Macmillan

WILLIAMS, P. M., 1979. *Hugh Gaitskell*, Jonathan Cape

WILSON, H., 1979. *Final Term: the Labour Government 1974–1976*, Weidenfeld and Nicolson

WILSON, H., 1971. *The Labour Government 1964–70*, Weidenfeld and Nicolson

WOODCOCK, G., 1974. *Who Killed the British Empire?*, Jonathan Cape

Index

Acknowledgements

Thanks are due to the following publishers and authors for permission kindly granted to reproduce extracts from copyright works:

Allen & Unwin Ltd: R. E. Caves, *Britain's Economic Prospects* (1968); T. W. Hutchison, *Economics and Economic Policy in Britain 1944–66* (1968). B. T. Batsford Ltd: R. Ritchie (ed.), *A Nation or No Nation?* (1978). BBC Publications: A. King, *Why is Britain Becoming Harder to Govern?* (1976); A. Sloman & H. Young, *No Minister* (1982). Cambridge University Press: J. C. R. Dow, *The Management of the British Economy, 1945–60* (1964); W. I. Jennings, *The British Constitution* (1942). Jonathan Cape Ltd: P. M. Williams, *Hugh Gaitskell, A Political Biography* (1979); G. Woodcock, *Who Killed the British Empire?* (1974); B. Levin, *The Pendulum Years* (1970). J. M. Dent & Sons Ltd: M. Stewart, *The Jekyll and Hyde Years, Politics and Economic Policy since 1964* (1977). Duckworth & Co Ltd: W. Beckerman (ed.), *The Labour Government's Record, 1964–70* (1972). Edward Arnold Ltd: S. Pollard, *The Development of the British Economy 1914–67* (1969). Faber & Faber Ltd: S. Beer, *Modern British Politics* (1965). Hutchinson and Co. Ltd: I. Gilmour, *Inside Right* (1978); J. P. Mackintosh, *The Government and Politics of Britain* (1970). Macmillan and Co. Ltd: M. Gowing, *Independence and Deterrence, vol. 1, Policy Making* (1974); D. E. Butler and D. Stokes, *Political Change in Britain* (2nd ed., 1974); Sir Harold Macmillan, *Pointing the Way, 1959–61* (1972); J. W. Wheeler-Bennett, *King George VI, His Life and Reign* (1958). Methuen and Company Ltd: W. N. Medlicott, *British Foreign Policy since Versailles* (2nd ed., 1968). Oxford University Press: A. J. P. Taylor, *English History 1914–45* (1965); P. Singer, *Democracy and Disobedience* (1973). Oxford University Press for The Royal Institute of International Affairs: M. Carlyle (ed.), *Documents on International Affairs 1947–48* (1952); D. C. Wall (ed.), *Documents on International Affairs 1962* (1971); A. Shonfield, *Modern Capitalism* (1965). Penguin Books Ltd: Q. Hogg, *The Case for Conservatism* (1947); W. I. Jennings, *The Queen's Government* (1954); T. Raison, *Why Conservative?* (1964); J. Northcott, *Why Labour?* (1964); M. Abrams and R. Rose, *Must Labour Lose?* (1960); B. Lapping, *The Labour Government 1964–70* (1970). Quartet Books Limited: G. Hutchinson, *The Last Edwardian at No. 10* (1980). Routledge &

Kegan Paul Ltd: A. Carter, *Direct Action and Liberal Democracy* (1973); A. Gamble, *The Conservative Nation* (1974). Sanctuary Press and Lady Mosley: O. Mosley, *My Life* (1975). Socialist Commentary Publications: D. Marquand, *Taming Leviathan, Social Democracy and Centralisation* (1980). Temple Smith Ltd: W. Keegan and R. Pennant-Rea, *Who Runs the Economy?* (1979). George Weidenfeld & Nicolson Ltd: P. D. Henderson (ed.), *Economic Growth in Britain* (1966); Sir Harold Wilson, *Final Term, the Labour Government 1974–76* (1979), and *The Labour Government 1964–70* (1971). Policy Studies Institute: G. R. Denton, *The National Plan* (1965). Fabian Society: A. Crosland, *Social Democracy in Europe* (1975); M. Goyder, *Socialism Tomorrow* (1979). Anthony Sheil Associates Ltd: L. S. Amery, *Thoughts on the Constitution* (OUP, 1957); G. Woodcock, *Who Killed the British Empire?* (J. Cape, 1974). David Higham Associates Ltd: A. Bevan, *In Place of Fear* (Quartet, 1978). Curtis Brown Ltd: H. Morrison, *Government and Parliament* (3rd ed., OUP, 1964). The Labour Party: extracts from General Election manifestos of 1945, 1964 and 1974, and the constitution of 1918. The Conservative Party: extracts from General Election manifestos of 1950, 1964 and 1970. The Royal Institute of International Affairs: extracts from articles published in *International Affairs* vol. 26, no. 4 and vol. 54, no. 2. The Controller of Her Majesty's Stationery Office: Parliamentary Debates, Commons and Lords; extracts from various Government Papers and Reports, as detailed in text (pages 146–8, 150–2, 171–6, 184, 311–13, 339–42, 347, 349, 351). Michael Charlton and William Clark for extracts from a broadcast discussion published in *The Listener*, 22 November 1979; David Marquand for extracts from an article published in *The Listener*, 8 March 1979. *The Guardian* and Tony Benn for an article published in *The Guardian*, 4 February 1980. *The Economist* for extracts from articles published 22 October 1949, 28 April 1951, 25 November 1967, 28 April 1973 and 22 January 1977. *The Times* for extracts from articles published 14 June 1947 and 27 January 1981. *The Sunday Times* for extracts from an article published 28 May 1978. *The Times Literary Supplement* for extracts from articles published 30 November 1979 and 20 March 1981.

Every effort has been made to trace the owners of copyright material. The author apologises for any omissions, and would be grateful to know of them so that acknowledgement may be made in future editions.